CAPITAL OF THE WORLD

PRAISE FOR *CAPITAL OF THE WORLD*

Charlene Mires provides a fascinating account of the enthusiastic effort to establish a home for the fledgling United Nations at the end of World War II. She creates a powerful sense of suspense as she describes the intense competition among boosters from New York, Boston, Philadelphia, and even the Black Hills of South Dakota. In lively and elegant prose, from the first sentence to the last, she captures the contradictory visions of the "Capital of the World" that persisted from beginning to end.

ALLAN M. WINKLER
Distinguished Professor of History,
Miami University

Capital of the World is an exceptionally imaginative book that warrants an exceptionally diverse readership. Charlene Mires, a former journalist who recognizes the extraordinary in the ordinary, leverages her skill as a public historian and expertise in material culture to tell the complicated and surprising story of the competition to select the site of the UN headquarters. By ascribing meaning to this competition rooted in the defining historical moment in which it took place, Mires offers us an innovative transnational history that provides an unexpected twist to understandings of glocalization.

RICHARD H. IMMERMAN
Edward J. Buthusiem Family Distinguished Faculty Fellow in History, Temple University

With meticulous research and journalistic verve, Charlene Mires tells an overlooked story about American engagement with the world. Writing in a decade when many Americans worry about their nation's place in the world, Mires reminds us about the excitement that the newly created United Nations generated not only in big eastern cities but also in the heartland of the Middle West and Great Plains. Her fast-moving and always entertaining narrative captures the optimistic spirit of the "Greatest Generation."

CARL ABBOTT
author of *How Cities Won the West: Four Centuries of Urban Change in Western North America*

CAPITAL OF THE WORLD

THE RACE TO HOST THE UNITED NATIONS

CHARLENE MIRES

NEW YORK UNIVERSITY PRESS *New York and London*

NEW YORK UNIVERSITY PRESS
New York and London   www.nyupress.org

References to Internet websites (URLs) were accurate at the time of writing. Neither the author nor New York University Press is responsible for URLs that may have expired or changed since the manuscript was prepared.

Library of Congress Cataloging-in-Publication Data
Mires, Charlene.
Capital of the world : the race to host the United Nations / Charlene Mires.
pages cm
Includes bibliographical references and index.
ISBN 978-0-8147-0794-4 (cl : alk. paper)
ISBN 978-0-8147-0835-4 (e)
ISBN 978-0-8147-2386-9 (e)
1. United Nations—Headquarters. 2. New York (N.Y.)—Buildings, structures, etc. I. Title.
JZ4986.M57   2013
341.2309—dc23   2012035350

New York University Press books are printed on acid-free paper, and their binding materials are chosen for strength and durability. We strive to use environmentally responsible suppliers and materials to the greatest extent possible in publishing our books.

Manufactured in the United States of America

10 9 8 7 6 5 4 3 2 1

CONTENTS

INTRODUCTION 1

PART I FROM WAR TO PEACE

   1 INSPIRATION 9

   2 HOPE 29

   3 SCHEMES 52

PART II THE NEW WORLD

   4 BLITZ 81

   5 SHOWTIME! 107

   6 SURPRISE 123

PART III AMERICAN DREAMS

   7 STUMBLE 145

   8 SCRAMBLE 170

   9 DEAL 194

   EPILOGUE 219

   ABBREVIATIONS IN APPENDIX AND NOTES 229

   APPENDIX: CAPITALS OF THE WORLD 231

   NOTES 257

   ACKNOWLEDGMENTS 297

   INDEX 299

   ABOUT THE AUTHOR 319

The United Nations Secretariat building under construction in 1949, when thousands gathered for the ceremony dedicating the cornerstone of the "world capital." (William Eckenberg/*The New York Times*/Redux)

INTRODUCTION

OCTOBER 24, 1949, in New York City was a day of symbolism and silences.

At East Forty-Second Street facing the East River, a sleek slab of a building reached toward the sky, its upper floors still under construction. Seventeen acres, previously a district of stinking slaughterhouses, had been cleared of all traces of earlier times. Where livestock once lumbered through the streets, ten thousand people now sat in wooden folding chairs facing the flags of fifty-nine nations and a platform draped in blue. Onstage, President Harry S. Truman and New York governor Thomas E. Dewey appeared to chat amiably despite their rivalry in the 1948 presidential election. Diplomats from both sides of the Iron Curtain shook hands while a municipal band played a jaunty rendition of *The Sidewalks of New York* ("east side, west side, all around the town . . ."). They gathered on this construction site to celebrate the fourth anniversary of the United Nations and an event that many considered to be a milestone in the history of the world—the laying of the granite cornerstone for the UN's permanent headquarters in New York. The dignitaries spoke of hopes for lasting peace. The *New York Times* wrote of the ghostly presence of thousands of wartime dead whose sacrifices led to this day.[1]

Occasionally, speakers on this occasion also described the UN's headquarters as the "world capitol" and New York, by extension, as "the capital of the world." From 1944 through 1946, as the world pivoted from the Second World War to an unsteady peace, the birth of the United Nations sparked a much more ambitious idea: that a new Capital of the World should be created to serve as a permanent center of international diplomacy. It was imagined as something like a perpetual world's fair, or perhaps a cluster of fashionable embassy buildings, or even an entirely new city where the UN's staff could live and work in modern buildings symbolizing a bright, unencumbered future. How this idea took root, gained momentum in a rush of postwar civic boosterism, but ultimately lost its luster is

1

the subject of this book. This is in part a history of the earliest days of the United Nations, but it is also a story of individuals and communities, their aspirations, and how they imagined their place in the world at a time of local, national, and international change.[2]

The idea of a world capital runs deep in history, dating to at least 27 BCE, when the historian Titus Livy described Rome as *caput orbis terrarum*. Later centers of commerce and culture, such as London and Paris, also became widely regarded as Capitals of the World. By the nineteenth and twentieth centuries, the world capital idea evolved in ways both trivial and grand. While civic boosters deployed the phrase to promote claims to distinction (thus Chicago, "chewing gum capital of the world"), journalists used "capital of the world" as shorthand for any location where international diplomats gathered. The Hague and Washington, D.C., each became "capital of the world," when they hosted diplomatic conferences, and the phrase also was applied to Geneva when it became home to the League of Nations.[3]

The world capital idea also began to take shape physically during the late nineteenth and early twentieth centuries. World's fairs, which began with the Crystal Palace exhibition in London in 1851, and the Olympic games, which were revived in their modern form in 1896, temporarily transformed host cities into places for international exchange and competition, often creating landscapes or structures that remained as lasting monuments to shining moments on the world stage.[4] Meanwhile, diplomatic conferences and the international peace movement inspired proposals for buildings or even cities to promote global understanding. The international conference held in The Hague in 1899 spurred discussion of a "World Centre of Peace" on the scale of a city, although an architectural competition led instead to a Renaissance-inspired Peace Palace. Another idea came forward early in the twentieth century from Hendrik C. Andersen, an American sculptor living in Rome, who waged a campaign to create a "world centre for communication." He tried to interest the League of Nations in the elaborate drawings he commissioned for this permanent gathering place for international organizations, but in Geneva the league opted instead for the Palais des Nations, a headquarters complex rather than a new city.[5]

Although these precedents existed, the birth of the United Nations at the end of World War II inspired fresh public interest in the world capital idea and an outburst of civic boosterism that was spontaneous, widespread, and extraordinary. As might be expected, the competitors included big cities such as New York and Chicago, which by the 1940s already were considered "world cities" by virtue of their size and concentrations of political, cultural, and economic power.[6] But the UN prospect also sparked remarkably widespread campaigning by smaller cities and towns. With bold ideas — but with no invitation whatsoever from the United Nations — public officials, business leaders, and everyday citizens composed letters and telegrams, formed committees, and created promotional campaigns. Architects and other visionaries imagined literal sites, spaces, and symbols to house and inspire the work of world peace. Ultimately, Americans in more than two hundred cities and towns seized upon this transitional moment in history to suggest — quite seriously — that their own hometowns or regions would be the best possible choice as the future Capital of the World.[7]

The Black Hills of South Dakota, perhaps? Tuskahoma or Stillwater, Oklahoma? Philadelphia, Boston, St. Louis, Denver, or San Francisco? Why did postwar civic leaders devise detailed promotional campaigns, which the United Nations had not requested? What motivated them to engage architects to plan the world capital, when the idea was no more than speculation? What possessed them to travel to war-ravaged London to force their ideas on the UN, against the advice of the United States government? Why did they insist that every diplomatic response they received ("your inquiry will be directed to the proper authorities") meant that they were still in the running to become the Capital of the World?

And how, after all this, did the United Nations at first choose a site including part of Greenwich, Connecticut — one of the few locations in the United States where it was not wanted — and then finally end up in New York City, a place where many of the world's diplomats adamantly did not want to be? Was it really as simple as it seemed, that an $8.5 million gift from John D. Rockefeller Jr. diverted the United Nations at the last minute to New York from Philadelphia?

Such questions had no place at the laying of the UN headquarters cornerstone in 1949. The event's printed program recounted a sequence of decisions that seemed to lead inevitably to the headquarters complex in midtown Manhattan.[8] Deposited into the cornerstone for posterity along with copies of the United Nations Charter and the Universal Declaration of Human Rights, the program's account left out the long and treacherous journey that led the United Nations to New York. In fact, finding a meeting place had been a difficult, frustrating, and sometimes comic struggle that had threatened to undermine the effectiveness of the organization in its earliest days. For world leaders and diplomats, the choice was a high-stakes question of whether Europe or the United States would dominate international affairs in the postwar era.[9] For Americans feeling their nation's rise to world prominence, the prospect of a new world capital proved impossible to resist. At a time when most Americans embraced the United Nations as not only desirable but essential for the survival of the world, providing the organization with a suitable home followed naturally from years of sacrifice and patriotic duty. Such a world capital might bring lasting peace, and if the honor also conveyed worldwide attention, prestige, and an economic boost besides, who was to argue?[10]

With so much of the world struggling to recover from wartime destruction, it was a predominantly American crusade. Discussion and speculation about the traditional European centers of diplomacy continued, and some letters to the United Nations suggested sites outside the United States, but these did not spring from organized promotional campaigns. Among several invitations from Canada, the most active campaigns, in Sault Ste. Marie and Niagara Falls, Ontario, were partnerships initiated by the adjacent U.S. towns of the same name. In contrast to Canada, where regulations discouraged competitive boosterism by local governments, a deep history of unrestricted self-promotion in the United States fed popular interest in the new prospect of becoming the Capital of the World. In the century prior to World War II, railroad companies and land speculators had promoted new towns in the American West; corporations had created public relations departments; and chambers of commerce had become involved in recruiting new businesses, conventions, and tourists. By the 1920s, college courses and handbooks provided training for aspiring public relations professionals. Advertising became a function of the federal government, from the propaganda generated by the Office of War Information during the First World War to promotion of public works programs during the Great Depression. The promotion ethic was so integral to American life by the 1940s that it infused popular culture in tunes such as "Anything You Can Do, I Can Do Better" and "Accentuate the Positive." On the crest of these developments, Americans at the end of World War II did not shy from competing with each other for such as prize as becoming the United Nations' home.[11]

Civic boosters, often with the support of hometown newspapers, reached outward from American cities and towns and forged connections among local, national, and international concerns.[12] In the process, they escalated the United Nations' need for a meeting place into a more dramatic search for the Capital of the World, but they also set in motion a sequence of events that revealed the limits of American internationalism. When the abstract notion of a Capital of the World approached reality for some communities, the potential threat to tradition, self-government, and private property—real or imagined—triggered strong resistance. As this unfolded in the suburbs of New York City, the defense of home played a pivotal and underappreciated role in driving the United Nations to Manhattan and demolishing the dream of creating a Capital of the World.[13]

At the heart of this story are individuals who had lived through times of great change and believed that they, in turn, could create change in the world. The civic leaders who leapt into the world capital competition were the parent generation of World War II, who tended the home front while sending sons and daughters off to war with pride and apprehension. Born during the last decades of the nineteenth century or around the turn of the twentieth, they were enmeshed in processes that later became understood as globalization. Their experiences of time and space had been transformed by mass transportation systems, automobiles, home telephones, mail-order catalogs, radio, newsreels, and highly competitive daily newspapers. As a result, they inhabited not only a confined local place (their hometowns) but an expanded, more global space extending as far as technology, migration, and mass culture could go.[14] More than their own parents, this generation traveled to seek jobs, to attend college, for business, or for vacation. Even without leaving the United States, they could glimpse the wider world at one of the era's enormously popular world's fairs. The outside world also came closer to home with the immigrants who surged into the United States until Congress imposed quotas in 1924. Perhaps most importantly, many in this generation had served in the Spanish-American War or the Great War of 1914–18—supposedly the war to end all wars—only to see their sons and daughters engaged in a world war once again in the 1940s. Victory in 1945 did not erase the memory of violence and frustration that many of them carried into the postwar years. The atomic bomb created new urgency to take action to secure a peaceful world.

Civic leaders among this generation—the parent generation of World War II—seized upon the dream of creating a Capital of the World. They chased it beyond reason, although it seemed perfectly reasonable to them at the time. At the end of the Second World War, when so much had been risked, so much lost, and so much achieved, it seemed to be possible, even imperative, to dream.

PART I

FROM WAR TO PEACE

1

INSPIRATION

DURING THE SECOND WEEK of September 1944, the United States Army Air Force delivered a telegram with tragic news to Paul and Lucy Bellamy of Rapid City, South Dakota. Just a few days short of their fortieth wedding anniversary, the Bellamys learned that their younger son, Lieutenant Paul Herbert Bellamy, had died on August 26 in a midair collision seventeen thousand feet over England. Herb, twenty-two years old, had been the lead pilot of two groups of B-17 Flying Fortresses. In flight, Bellamy's crew observed a plane above them getting close — closer — *too close!* — to their own ship. The first engineer shouted a warning, but apparently Bellamy did not hear. The engineer and bombardier both raced toward the cockpit, intending to grab the controls and dive the plane. But it was too late. The planes collided and exploded, and Herb and his copilot went down with the ship.[1]

Half a world away from the physical remains of his son, Paul Bellamy searched for channels for his grief. His thoughts raced over his son's short life — the baby, the playful boy, the teenager, the groom, the volunteer pilot in training at the air base on the outskirts of Rapid City, perhaps a future father, perhaps a future partner in business. Bellamy felt compelled to document this moment, to try to make sense of it, to do *something*. Immediately, he sat down and composed a tribute to his son. In the space of a few minutes of dictation, Bellamy found his way toward explaining his son's death as one among many heroic casualties of war — "the thousands of other American boys of the best blood and breeding, the most precocious and persistent, the most ambitious, were beside him in training and in combat." Bellamy, himself a veteran of the Spanish-American War in the Philippines, struggled to justify this terrible loss. Why did it take the tragedies of war to make those left behind stop and examine their priorities? How could the survivors be worthy of the sacrifices of their sons and daughters? As he began the work necessary to return his son's remains to the United States, Bellamy also thought about new business ventures that would carry out the young man's hopes and ambitions.[2]

Then, on November 3, 1944, after nearly two months of restless pride, grief, and determination, Paul Bellamy rose to offer a resolution to the Rapid City Chamber of Commerce. He was a fixture at these monthly meetings at the Alex Johnson Hotel. At sixty-five years of age, as the long-time proprietor of the Bellamy Transportation Company, he was known for lending a helping hand to any venture that would boost the fortunes of Rapid City and the Black Hills. He had been involved in the planning for the highways that snaked through the hills, for Mount Rushmore, and for the Badlands National Park. With his fleet of automobiles, trucks, and tourist buses, he catered to everyday travelers and celebrities. He had driven the architect Frank Lloyd Wright through the scenic Badlands, Calvin Coolidge to his lakeside "summer White House" in the Black Hills, and Franklin Roosevelt to Mount Rushmore to dedicate the carving of Thomas Jefferson.[3]

As Bellamy joined his friends at the November meeting of the chamber of commerce, the war had not yet ended but diplomats had gathered at Dumbarton Oaks, in Washington, D.C., to create the foundation for a postwar security organization — soon to become known as the United Nations Organization, and then simply the United Nations. These were international events, but for Bellamy they entwined with the fresh memory of loss and prospects for local opportunity. He spoke to his neighbors about the importance of the UN for "conciliation, arbitration, demonstration and action of united armed forces in future international disputes," and he reasoned that the United States would play a leading role. Therefore, the United Nations should have its headquarters in the United States — and, he proposed, what better place than the Black Hills of South Dakota? For generations, boosters had attracted settlers to the American West with claims that even the most remote places could become accessible hubs of economic prosperity. Bellamy launched a similar argument for the world security organization. "It would seem appropriate that such headquarters should be located reasonably close to the center of the United States," he reasoned. The Black Hills, conveniently positioned near this idealized center, would offer a suitable year-round climate, quality of life, recreation facilities, and water supply needed for such a headquarters and its staff. "Therefore, be it resolved," he declared, "that the advantages of Rapid City, the Black Hills and western South Dakota be submitted and offered to the proper authorities as a location for the proposed headquarters of the United Nations."[4]

Paul Bellamy, in the driver's seat, escorts Franklin Roosevelt to Mount Rushmore in 1936, culminating one of the many booster projects that drew attention and tourism to the Black Hills in South Dakota prior to the Second World War. (Paul E. Bellamy Papers, Richardson Collection, University Libraries, University of South Dakota)

Perhaps the most remarkable thing about Bellamy's proposal was that his neighbors did not consider it the least bit remarkable. The boosters of the Black Hills had cultivated a tourism industry in this remote southwest corner of South Dakota, they had attracted international publicity with Mount Rushmore and Calvin Coolidge's summer in residence, and they had lured an army air force base to the outskirts of Rapid City. In November 1944, the "United Nations" still referred to the Allies battling the Axis powers; the Dumbarton Oaks conference had just finished its work for a UN organization after the war. To invite these world leaders to the Black Hills seemed to be not much more than another gracious extension of hospitality—indeed, one that might generate more publicity and help revive tourism after the war.

The Rapid City Chamber of Commerce readily approved the resolution offered by their bereaved friend. The local newspapers duly reported the action, and South Dakota congressman Karl Mundt promised to steer the idea into the proper channels. For the moment, Bellamy trusted the elected representatives of South Dakota to follow through. But he had taken the first step on a journey that would lead him halfway around the world and into the realms of presidents, diplomats, celebrities, and millionaires.[5]

DETROIT

During the same week that Paul Bellamy learned of his son's death, interest in the future home of the United Nations also was gaining traction more than a thousand miles away in Detroit, one of the Second World War's "arsenals of democracy." The notion first occurred to J. Lee Barrett, a former president of the Detroit Automobile Club who had built a career in professional civic boosterism, one of the twentieth century's expanding fields of employment. Working for the Detroit Convention and Tourist Bureau in 1944, he was the first among many in this professional booster class to sniff out the potential benefits of the "World Peace Organization," then under discussion at Dumbarton Oaks. He was only doing his job, albeit at a new height of ambition, when he proposed his city as an ideal location for the postwar headquarters for peace. On September 12, 1944, members of the Detroit City Council took up the idea and endorsed it unanimously. Their reasoning began with Detroit's international location on the peaceful boundary between the United States and Canada, an ideal location for "a living monument to World Peace." Aided by Barrett's public relations skills, the council's resolution sang with the enhanced status that came with

Detroit's role in helping to win the Second World War: "Detroit, with its manufacturing genius of skilled workmen and engineers in mass production, has turned the tide of war into victory for the Allied Nations." Along with civic pride, this statement implied a concern for economic stability after the war, a challenge soon to be confronted throughout the nation in the conversion to a peacetime economy. Perhaps in addition to securing the peace, the United Nations would convey economic benefits as well as prestige.[6]

In the time-honored tradition of boosterism, Detroit's invitation stressed the city's many advantages while leaving out some inconvenient details. Detroit's promoters envisioned the United Nations on Belle Isle, an island park in the Detroit River that they described as a property of one thousand acres "located on the International Boundary" between the United States and Canada and offering "an ideal location for the permanent home of the new World Peace Organization." The proposal stressed the U.S.-Canadian border as an inspirational symbol of peaceful coexistence between two nations. A building on Belle Isle would be "a living monument to World Peace which has been so ably demonstrated here."[7]

This idyllic vision left out another well-known association of Belle Isle, the race riot that had started there and spread into other areas of the city in June 1943. Fighting between blacks and whites lasted thirty-six hours and resulted in the deaths of forty-three people. Fueled by inequalities in the city, with its growing wartime population and limited housing, such racial tensions pointed to the greatest challenges that lay ahead for preventing Detroit's postwar decline.[8] By averting their gaze from local problems to international possibilities, Detroit's boosters chose to imagine Belle Isle as a symbol of the peaceful border between the United States and Canada rather than a reminder of issues needing resolution at home. As a meeting place for the United Nations, this physical reminder of conflict might be converted into a place of peace.[9] The city of Detroit sent its invitation to the diplomats at Dumbarton Oaks and to the U.S. secretary of state and then, like Paul Bellamy in South Dakota, simply waited.

YALTA

On the night of February 8, 1945, in a former tsarist palace overlooking the Black Sea, President Roosevelt's secretary of state awoke at 3:00 a.m. with a vision of San Francisco. He recalled the city as he had known it before the war: grand hotels with views over glittering hillsides, fine restaurants, nightclubs, cable cars, and Pacific breezes, all infused by the international flavors of Chinatown, Fisherman's Wharf, and ships carrying goods and people through the Golden Gate. Such a soothing memory slid into the consciousness of Edward Reilly Stettinius Jr. just in time to solve a pressing need. Stettinius, at age forty-four, a former public relations man for General Motors and chairman of U.S. Steel, was one of the nation's most improbable secretaries of state. Although not a seasoned statesman, here he was, in Livadia Palace near Yalta in the Soviet Union, for the Crimean Conference among the Big Three—the United States, Great Britain, and the Soviet Union. Through the winter of 1944–45, Allied armies had closed in on Germany, and now their commanders gathered to map a strategy for ending war and securing the peace. This presented Stettinius with a problem to solve: Where would the Allies' diplomats be able to gather to begin to create a postwar security organization? And in the midst of war, how in the world would they get there?

The president of the United States, the increasingly frail Franklin Roosevelt, slept down the hall, in the former bedroom of Tsar Nicholas II. Getting FDR to Yalta had required an eight-day voyage across the Atlantic on the cruiser USS *Quincy*, a layover in Malta in the Mediterranean, a seven-hour overnight flight by military DC-3, and, finally, five hours of driving across plains and mountains to the once-fashionable "Russian Riviera." Although the nations of the world were locked together in a global war, physical distances between them remained great. The British team had joined the Americans for preliminary talks in Malta and then for carefully charted flights to the East. From the start, Prime Minister Winston Churchill had despised the idea of this remote location three thousand miles from London; en route, one plane carrying British advisers crashed into the Mediterranean, killing five members of the prime minister's staff and casting a pall of personal loss over the urgency of world events. Even for Soviet Premier Joseph Stalin, who had insisted that Roosevelt and Churchill come to him so that he could simultaneously direct the Soviets' military offensive, the conference required a 900-mile trip from Moscow on an armored train.[10]

On Thursday, February 8, Stettinius went to bed with many unresolved issues on his mind. This conference, taking place as American and British armies closed in on Germany from the west and the Soviets advanced from the east, wrestled with vital issues that would shape the postwar world. The war's imminent conclusion in Europe demanded that decisions be made about the final, coordinated assault on Germany and about that nation's future occupation by the Allies. Agreements needed to be reached on borders and a future government for Poland, which had been liberated by the Soviets from Nazi control. Roosevelt had risked this journey with two great desires: a pledge from the Soviets to enter the war against Japan and a foundation for future cooperation among the world's powers. Already, five days of talks had elapsed, only three lay ahead, and much remained to be done. The foreign ministers—Stettinius and his more experienced counterparts, British foreign minister Anthony Eden and Soviet foreign minister Vyacheslav Molotov—grappled with the issues by day, then reported to the Big Three leaders.[11]

Details remained to be settled for creating the new United Nations organization, which Roosevelt had been nurturing toward existence throughout the war.[12] It was to be the successor to the League of Nations, which the United States had never joined. The basic framework had been hammered out the previous autumn at Dumbarton Oaks, but difficult issues had been deferred. Now, at Yalta, the Soviets finally agreed to a voting procedure for the organization's Security Council, where the major powers of 1945 would wield authority over matters that threatened world peace. Stalin and Molotov also gave up their insistence that all sixteen of the Soviet Union's republics should be represented in the organization's Assembly. Instead, they pressed for three seats—for the Soviet Union, Ukraine, and Byelorussia (White Russia).[13]

The questions of when, how, and where to gather the Allied nations to launch such an organization were technical matters, but critical. The foreign ministers decided that the meeting should include all the nations that had agreed to the 1942 "United Nations Declaration" of commitment to the war against the Axis powers. They selected a starting date—April 25, 1945—and accepted Stettinius's invitation to hold the event in the United States. But where? FDR had once confided to his previous secretary of state, Cordell Hull, that he imagined the permanent home of the United Nations on an island in the Azores or possibly in Hawaii. Through the evening, Stettinius pondered the possibilities that had come forward through the channels of the State Department, where the question had been considered for months without a conclusion. Should he recommend New York or Philadelphia, or a resort like Atlantic City, Hot Springs in Virginia, or Pinehurst in North Carolina? Only partly in jest, Stettinius had suggested the resort at French Lick, Indiana, so that the heartland of American isolationism would be drawn into the orbit of international diplomacy. That night, after a lengthy ceremonial dinner, Stettinius conferred with

Roosevelt at the president's bedside. "Go back to work, Ed," the president said, "and come up with a better suggestion."[14]

At Yalta, the view of azure sky, sea, and hemlock trees reminded Stettinius of the Pacific Coast and prompted the idea that came to him in the middle of the night: San Francisco. The northern California city, with its many fine hotels, its accommodating Opera House, and its government conveniently in the hands of his friend, Mayor Roger Lapham, would be such a gracious, impressive setting.

Stettinius awoke the next morning with the confidence of a public relations man who had hit upon a brilliant idea. He imagined statesmen from Europe traveling across the United States and gaining new appreciation for the nation's beauty, size, and strength. Gathered in San Francisco, the leaders of the world would shift their attentions toward the continuing war in the Pacific. If the Nazis had collapsed in Europe by then, which seemed likely, the Allies would need new resolve to finish the job against Japan. They would find it in the city by the bay, where naval vessels shipped out to meet the enemy and returned in victory or as battered hulks bearing the wounded and the dead. Logistics would be crucial, especially in a city already serving a critical role as a port for the Pacific war. On Friday, amid the continuing discussions of Poland and the postwar fate of Germany, Stettinius sought out the military commanders on hand at Yalta and won their support.[15]

The Americans kept the idea to themselves until Saturday evening. Then, over vodka and caviar before a final conference dinner, Molotov approached Stettinius to ask, "Can you not tell us where the conference is to be held?" Stettinius hesitated. Unsure of his authority to reveal the choice, he crossed the room and leaned down to confer with Roosevelt, seated in a portable wheelchair. "Go ahead, Ed," the president said. "San Francisco it is." By the time the Big Three departed Yalta on Sunday, February 11, the invitation was complete: on April 25, 1945, the nations that had united against the Axis powers would gather in San Francisco to draft a charter for a lasting organization to secure the peace. Soon this organization would draw the interest of civic boosters in many American cities and towns, but for now, San Francisco would have the first opportunity to prove that it could be the Capital of the World.[16]

From Moscow on Monday, Stettinius sent a telegram to his friend, the mayor of San Francisco: "California here we come."

SAN FRANCISCO

News from Yalta traveled around the globe to San Francisco even before the secretary of state's telegram could be delivered. By lunchtime on February 12, as Mayor Roger Dearborn Lapham tried to enjoy his customary meal at the exclusive Pacific Union Club on Nob Hill, waiters began to deliver telephone messages to his table. The first came from a newspaper reporter. What did he know about the United Nations coming to San Francisco? (Nothing.) Next, an anxious State Department man insisted on a meeting and would not wait even fifteen minutes for the mayor to return to city hall. He showed up at the club to personally deliver the Yalta dispatch, which only confirmed what the newspaper reporter had said. The cryptic telegram from Stettinius, when it arrived, said little more. "California here we come," Stettinius had wired. "Counting upon you to make arrangements for good weather during May. Asking [Undersecretary of State] Joe Grew to get in touch with you to start the ball rolling regarding all other arrangements. Affectionate regards, Ed."[17]

Like Stettinius, whom he had known while serving on the National War Labor Board in Washington earlier in the war, Roger Lapham had experienced a life of unexpected turns. Born in New York City into the affluence of an old New England shipping family in 1883, Lapham followed the cargo business down the eastern seaboard to South America, around Cape Horn, up to California, out to the Hawaiian Islands, and finally to San Francisco. He witnessed the waning days of the square-rigged sailing ship, but by the time he rose to president and chairman of his family's American Hawaiian Steamship Company, steamers had taken over the work of carrying sugar from Hawaii, lumber from Alaska, and people through the newly constructed Panama Canal. As a captain in the U.S. Army during the Great War, Lapham survived shelling in the trenches of France and the sting of mustard gas, the new chemical weapon unleashed by the Germans.[18] Now his younger son, Roger Jr., served in the navy somewhere beyond the Pacific horizon.

Since the bombing of Pearl Harbor on December 7, 1941, San Francisco had been consumed by the war to the west. The city's population swelled during the war from 634,000 to 800,000 people, despite the U.S. government's forced evacuation of five thousand residents of Japanese ancestry and the loss of perhaps one hundred thousand others who went into the military or moved for other reasons. The city bulged and bristled with arriving and departing soldiers, sailors, and war production workers, so much so that local boosters were urging tourists to stay away and plan for "Victory Vacations" after the war. Around San Francisco Bay, shipyards worked overtime to fulfill $3.9 billion in government contracts. The war permeated leisure time as well as the work day. On the radio, Japanese propagandist Tokyo Rose could be heard broadcasting her program, *The Zero Hour*, from across the sea. San Francisco's War Memorial Opera House, constructed in memory of lives lost in the last global conflict, swung into service for war-relief events. San Franciscans gathered there to raise money for British war relief and for soldiers' recreation activities, for a Russian-American goodwill concert, and for the closing performances of the musical revue "This Is the Army," featuring a personal appearance by Irving Berlin.[19]

Lapham, who became mayor of this war-dominated city in 1944, embodied the strong ties that bound the interests of business, politics, and international affairs in San Francisco. Civic leaders frequently crossed between the power centers of the chamber of commerce and city hall. In the first four decades of the twentieth century, they rebuilt the city after the great earthquake and fire of 1906, and they gave San Francisco a new, gleaming civic center that echoed the style of a grand European capital. The civic leaders who rebuilt San Francisco in these years also created new visions of the world at two international expositions—the Panama Pacific International Exposition, held in 1915 to celebrate completion of the Panama Canal, and the Golden Gate Exposition in 1939. For this most recent world's fair, a West Coast bookend to the New York World's Fair of the same year, San Francisco built an entire island in San Francisco Bay—Treasure Island, which now served as a military base for the war in the Pacific.[20]

Skilled in the minuet of business and politics that had accompanied San Francisco into the war years, the mayor and leaders of the San Francisco Chamber of Commerce were well positioned to take on the challenge of the United Nations. While Lapham, a businessman with a bit of federal public service, led the city's government, the chamber of commerce elected as its president an expert in international trade who had served in the State Department. Henry F. Grady had joined the faculty of the University of California at Berkeley after his federal service and then leapt to the highest ranks of the shipping business as president of the American President Lines. He was, according to a press release issued by the chamber of commerce at the end of 1944, a "citizen of the world." His association with San Francisco would secure its reputation as a "world city." Little did the chamber of commerce suspect, in 1944, how literal this prospect would become.[21]

Within two days after the news broke about the United Nations conference coming to San Francisco, an even grander goal began to take shape. A columnist for the *San Francisco News*, Arthur Caylor, credited Captain E. H. Pagenhart of the U.S. Coast and Geodetic Survey for being "the first to suggest that the town instantly start thinking of itself as the world headquarters for peace — perhaps permanently." And why not? Caylor asked, elaborating in language that might be found in any number of guidebooks that San Franciscans had been producing for tourists since the late nineteenth century. "We're a world-conscious, cosmopolitan city — long devoted to friendly relations. For San Francisco, peace could be bigger than the Gold Rush." In other words, peace could also mean profit, a new place on the world stage and in the increasingly global economy.[22]

By the first week of March, San Francisco was a city with two new missions. One, dictated from Yalta, had government officials, hotel operators, and citizens scrambling to accommodate the imminent conference of the United Nations. The other mission, suggested by Caylor in February but also echoed in the paneled conference rooms of private clubs and the chamber of commerce, looked to the future. On March 8, Henry Grady called together the directors of the chamber of commerce and appointed a committee to plan quietly for the possibility that San Francisco might become the United Nations' permanent home. As a start, San Franciscans would do their utmost to charm the diplomats soon to arrive from around the world. Another business association, the Down Town Club, the next day called for a survey to locate a suitable headquarters site.[23]

Before the new United Nations organization even existed, aggressive big-city newspapers helped to escalate the UN's needs into grander ambitions. When the *San Francisco Call Bulletin* reported on the actions of the local business community, it raised the volume with its headline "S.F. Proposed as World Capital," one of the first headlines to elevate the UN site to the status of "capital." Meanwhile, across the country, a challenge to San Francisco's claim on the United Nations already was taking shape, pushed by a publisher with a different idea and an intense determination to see his dream become a reality.[24]

PHILADELPHIA

On March 3, 1945 — the Saturday before the San Francisco Chamber of Commerce mobilized to pursue the United Nations — J. David Stern composed a letter in his office at the *Philadelphia Record*, the newspaper he

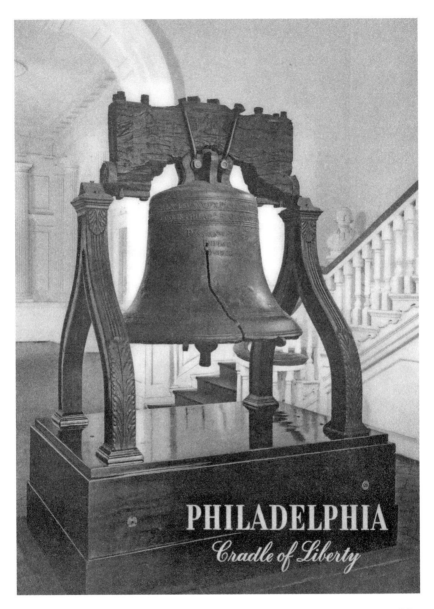

Philadelphia promoted its invitation with a booklet covered by a glossy photograph of the Liberty Bell inside Independence Hall, an image reflecting boosters' expectations that the city's reputation as the "Cradle of Liberty" would persuade the United Nations to anoint Philadelphia as the Capital of the World. (Library of Congress)

owned and published in the City of Brotherly Love. "Dear Mr. President," he wrote. "'We have a rendezvous with destiny.'" He placed the phrase in quotation marks, emphasizing that they were the words of Franklin Roosevelt himself, spoken in 1936 as FDR accepted his second presidential nomination during the Democratic National Convention in Philadelphia. "No truer prophecy was ever made," Stern continued, flattering Roosevelt before moving on to his point. "Now that we have about caught up with destiny, we must decide on the place for that rendezvous." Destiny — victory in the Second World War — seemed imminent. The rendezvous would occur with the convening of the United Nations. The place, it seemed obvious to Stern, should be Philadelphia.

The publisher already had written the editorial for the front page of his newspaper on Monday, March 5. When it appeared in the paper, the headline proposed "Philadelphia — Home of the United Nations," and it ran next to a picture of the steeple of Independence Hall, the Philadelphia birthplace of the Declaration of Independence and the Constitution. Stern's crisp argument linked these local and national symbols of American freedom to hope for the future of the world, just as Roosevelt had done in his acceptance speech in 1936. When Philadelphians picked up their newspapers, Stern's proposal could not be missed: "The City of Brotherly Love should be the permanent home of the United Nations. Independence Hall, recognized throughout the world as the birthplace of political liberty and democracy, is the shrine around which the United Nations buildings should be grouped." Sharing in the surge of American patriotism that had been intensified by war, Stern had no doubt that the birthplace of the United States would inspire the postwar world.[25]

Stern, fifty-eight years old, thrived on editorial crusades. Since buying the *Philadelphia Record* in 1928, he had battled tax increases, sent reporters to investigate conditions at the public mental hospital, helped to bring down the legendary contractor-bosses of the city's Republican machine, and built the strength of the local Democratic Party as he boosted Franklin Roosevelt for president. Five feet, six inches tall, nervous, and nail-biting, Stern had an intensity inherited from his Bavarian-immigrant grandmother and a habit of chain-smoking cigars that began in his twenties, when he was trying to look old enough to be a newspaper publisher. With the *Philadelphia Record*, the little man had a big voice, and he used it frequently. He was a Democrat in a city long controlled by Republicans and a grandson of Jewish immigrants in a city where Quaker heritage remained a valued pedigree. But he also had a degree from the University of Pennsylvania

School of Law, where he made friends who rose to the pinnacles of the Philadelphia establishment, and he had a bit of inherited wealth that he had parlayed into newspaper ownership in Illinois, Rhode Island, New Jersey, New York, and Pennsylvania. Like so many of his peers, David Stern had a personal stake in the war — a son serving in Hawaii as an editor of the military newspaper *Stars and Stripes*. In all, 217 of his employees had gone to war; three were missing in action, and six had been killed.[26]

A Roosevelt supporter since 1930, Stern felt fully entitled and qualified to advise and criticize the president of the United States. Not only did he write to the president frequently; he also requested and received personal meetings at the White House. FDR called him "Dave," and sometimes they mused about publishing a national newspaper together after Roosevelt retired from office. The president's staff called Stern the "hair shirt" — frequently irritating but nevertheless valuable for his loyalty to FDR.[27]

Personally and professionally, Stern surely would have been attentive when his president addressed Congress after returning from Yalta. In a speech broadcast by radio from the Capitol on March 1, Roosevelt called upon the legislators to support the envisioned United Nations organization. Pointedly, he reminded them that the Congress had blocked U.S. membership in the League of Nations a generation before. "Twenty-five years ago, American fighting men looked to the statesmen of the world to finish the work of peace for which they fought and suffered," he said. "We failed them then. We cannot fail them again, and expect the world again to survive."

Roosevelt also appealed to a deeper history by emphasizing that the United States would enter into a world organization within the framework of its own Constitution, which had served the nation for more than 150 years. By including this in his speech, FDR bolstered the State Department's strategy of using references to the Constitution to help sell the UN to the American people. The United Nations charter "has to be — and should be — approved by the Senate of the United States, under the Constitution," the president stressed. In San Francisco, the world's leaders would take a first step, but surely not the last, to forge a lasting organization. "Whatever is adopted at San Francisco will doubtless have to be amended time and again over the years, just as our own Constitution has been," Roosevelt said.[28]

In focusing on the Constitution, the president and the State Department could count on a high level of recognition and pride among the American public. The Constitution had been celebrated vigorously in 1937, the year of its 150th anniversary, and it had been a battleground for proposals such as FDR's court-packing plan to gain additional appointments to the Supreme

Court. In Philadelphia, the Constitution had especially strong resonance because it was also embodied by a place — a landmark brick building with a distinctive steeple, standing on Chestnut Street between Fifth and Sixth streets, in one of the oldest sections of the city. Although the structure was known as Independence Hall, named for the famous declaration of 1776, it was also the meeting place for the Constitutional Convention of 1787. Even people who found little else to love about Philadelphia's mix of brick houses and aging manufacturing blocks looked with pride upon this surviving gem from the eighteenth century.[29]

With Franklin Roosevelt and Independence Hall as inspirations, David Stern aimed his front-page editorial about the future United Nations home at readers in Philadelphia and beyond. He delved deeply into the city's historic heart and reached outward to the landscape of world affairs. For the locals, Stern invoked not only the Declaration of Independence and the Constitution but also the ideals of the city's founder, William Penn, and the memory of Benjamin Franklin, whom he called the nation's first "citizen of the world." With such powerful historic associations, Stern argued, "Philadelphia, more than any other city in the world, embodies those spiritual values which would inspire and strengthen the United Nations Council." On a more practical plane, he described the civic improvements that would emanate from new buildings around Independence Hall for the UN. "Just as when distinguished company is coming for dinner, the home is spruced up, so Philadelphia would be awakened from its lethargy to clean up its rivers, remove the Chinese Wall [a viaduct carrying rail lines into the city], beautify the approaches to the city and improve other areas which we have allowed to deteriorate." The idea also fit neatly with local proposals to replace the aging commercial district around Independence Hall with a pristine, green mall reminiscent of Colonial Williamsburg.[30]

Stern anticipated objections and questions that later consumed enormous amounts of time and energy within the UN. One of the questions that lay ahead involved travel time. Stern argued that diplomats should not be concerned about traveling to the United States because modern aviation was rapidly transforming ideas of time and distance. "Since all parts of the world are within 60 hours of each other," he wrote, "we need no longer choose a location because of travel convenience." Instead, the UN should look for a site to inspire world peace. Stern also foresaw the power struggle that would ensue over whether this place should be in Europe, the traditional center of diplomacy, or in the United States. Geneva, the home of the languishing League of Nations, would be a poor choice, he argued, reasoning that "Europe, storm center of the world, is not the logical place for the peace center of a new world." The postwar world required a fresh start in a new location—the United States and, preferably, Philadelphia.[31]

Stern knew how to run a crusade. During the same week in March 1945 when San Francisco's civic leaders began to work quietly toward securing the United Nations' favor, Stern directed his newspaper's full resources at gaining the prize for Philadelphia. Every day for two weeks, and frequently thereafter, the *Record* carried front-page stories announcing new and powerful supporters for the idea that Philadelphia should be the "Peace Capital of the World." A *Record* reporter solicited the favorable opinions of the governor of Pennsylvania, members of Congress, and civic leaders. Business and labor groups voiced support, and the state legislature passed a resolution saying that "Philadelphia, the first capital of the United States, is ideologically and historically suited to become the World Capital of Peace."[32]

Stern had thrown a spark into a tinderbox of pent-up desire. Philadelphia, like other American cities, had been storing up hopes for the future throughout the challenges of the Great Depression and the Second World War. Across the country, while armies fought, city governments had stockpiled plans for rejuvenating decayed downtowns, for converting industries from war to peacetime production, and for finding jobs and homes for returning veterans. In Philadelphia, the business and professional classes, weary of Philadelphia's reputation as "corrupt and contented," looked forward to a postwar era of reform and renewal. Stern's proposal seemed to offer a path toward global prestige and economic prosperity. The United Nations might be the perfect bridge between the city's Revolutionary-era heritage and a potentially bright future as a hub of commerce, diplomacy, and commercial aviation.[33]

With so many apparent benefits, political support came easily. Philadelphia's Republican mayor, Bernard Samuel, had been talking about hosting peace talks at Independence Hall since 1943. He quickly embraced the UN proposal as an extension of his own idea and summoned several hundred of Philadelphia's most prominent citizens to City Hall to endorse the plan. The wise course, they agreed, would be to send a committee to San Francisco to deliver Philadelphia's invitation to the United Nations.[34]

Even within the choreographed assembly in the Mayor's Reception Room, glints of skepticism appeared. As the meeting ended, three protesters who identified themselves as Blue Star Mothers—mothers of soldiers—shouted their disapproval, apparently associating any project of the "United Nations" with warfare. In the *Record*'s own letters column, Philadelphians punctured illusions of the city's readiness. Some pointed out that the aging industrial city had few advantages, aside from Independence Hall. "Had you thought of the drawbacks?" one writer asked. "We have bad water, a smelly river, dirty streets, no airport, badly run liquor stores, a wage tax, no snow clearance, inadequate police and a very poor climate. What have you against world peace?" Another asked, "How do you reconcile your audacious bid for 'World Capital, Pa.' with the hundreds of pictures the *Record* has run of the unbelievably filthy slums in Philadelphia, pictures of broken water mains, broken fire hydrants and trash piled high?"[35]

On the radio, programs carried the news of Philadelphians' hopes but also some hints of hesitation. By the end of March, Mayor Samuel was on the CBS radio network to promote "the Philadelphia plan." During a fifteen-minute feature about preparations for the United Nations conference in San Francisco, Samuel made the case that "Philadelphia is the spiritual world capital of liberty and freedom." His words emanated from the network's New York headquarters to pickups in Washington, Philadelphia, and San Francisco. But criticisms also echoed nationally as another radio program featured local author Struthers Burt, who called attention to disparities between the city and its suburbs as challenges that lay ahead for Philadelphia as well as its world capital ambitions. "You can't have a city that has been described as a dog's dinner surrounded by beautiful suburbs as an example of what liberty and freedom have done for America," he said, but acknowledged, "The glory of the city can be recaptured if Philadelphians are willing to spend a little money."[36]

Prior to the radio broadcasts, Philadelphia and San Francisco had shown no signs of being aware of their parallel pursuits of the world capital dream. Now, the radio and newswires bridged the distance across the continent and brought each to the attention of the other. In San Francisco, newspapers began to report the growing ambitions of Philadelphia. The Washington correspondent of the *San Francisco News* warned that Philadelphians intended to "invade" San Francisco and "sell" their proposal to the United Nations delegates. Two days after that, on the last day of March, the *Philadelphia Record* reported that San Francisco had organized a committee, but stressed the West Coast city's inferior strategy of moving slowly and cautiously. The *Record*'s reporter also detected stirrings of interest in Los Angeles, Seattle, and Contra Costa County, California. It was clear that the United States had at least two significant competitors to become the Capital of the World, San Francisco and Philadelphia, not to mention more obscure hopefuls beginning to press their case.[37]

WASHINGTON

Cities and towns with ambitions to become the Capital of the World faced an immediate challenge: How could they communicate their interests to an organization that did not yet exist? Fundamentally, the dilemma called for inventing the role of citizen on a global scale so that the voices of individuals and communities could be heard on matters of international concern. At first, the world capital hopefuls turned to familiar channels of power and governance—their elected officials serving in Washington, D.C.

On Capitol Hill one day in March, U.S. senator Francis Case of South Dakota button-holed Nelson Rockefeller, then an assistant secretary of state, to try to impress the urbane New Yorker with the idea that the United Nations should move to the Black Hills. Senator Case also mailed a letter to President Roosevelt to relay the invitation instigated in Rapid City by Paul Bellamy, and like a tourism or business promoter the senator pointed out the congenial climate, scenic beauty, and transportation facilities available in the Black Hills. "This suggestion is offered in the hope that we may be of service," the senator concluded. On April 7, FDR signed a noncommittal reply. Thanking the senator for his "interesting suggestion," FDR's letter assured Case that "it will receive full consideration whenever the question of the location of the permanent seat of the proposed organization is under discussion."[38]

Or, as the *Rapid City Daily Journal* optimistically reported, "FDR Interested in Hills as Peace Capital." Through the last weeks of April and the beginning of May, the Black Hills campaign shifted into high gear with a citizens' committee and support from the governors of South Dakota, Wyoming, and Nebraska. The region's congressional representatives began writing letters to Secretary of State Stettinius and other American delegates to the conference in San Francisco. Paul Bellamy made plans to travel to San Francisco to chat up the diplomats. Meanwhile, in Detroit, attention diverted temporarily to ideas for holding a world's fair or recruiting the Olympics, but in Philadelphia the city council approved ten thousand dollars to print an elaborate invitation and to dispatch a delegation of prominent citizens to the West Coast. Philadelphia civic leaders lobbied cabinet members and members of Congress in Washington, and the governor of Pennsylvania wrote to his counterparts across the country to ask their support. The Philadelphia group engaged a public relations agent in San Francisco and sent an official hostess across the country to plan receptions. David Stern's reporters documented every step.[39]

The first stirrings of the competition to create a Capital of the World showed individuals in San Francisco, Philadelphia, Detroit, and even Rapid City, South Dakota, strongly engaged with international affairs and eager to build additional bridges between their communities and the world. Their interests were local as well as global, and the outlines of a contest were becoming clear. With so much of the rest of the world lying in ruins, the quest to become the Capital of the World would captivate primarily American cities and towns. The competitors would include large cities tied to the wider world by commerce, immigrant populations, or their role in the war, many of them already rivals from earlier battles to host political conventions or world's fairs. But this also would be a contest of smaller towns with civic pride and historic places celebrating American ideals. In some places, campaigns would be waged as memorials to favorite sons or lost heroes. However absurd some of the possibilities might have appeared from afar, a competition to become the Capital of the World — never anticipated, much less announced by the UN — awaited the international delegates who were boarding ships, trains, and airplanes bound for San Francisco.

From floral arrangements in Golden Gate Park to signs of welcome on Market Street store fronts, San Francisco boosters counted on warm hospitality to plant the idea that the United Nations should select the city by the bay as its permanent home. (San Francisco History Center, San Francisco Public Library)

2

HOPE

SAN FRANCISCO HAD SEEN many prospectors in its history, from missionaries seeking souls to eager pursuers of land, fortune, and gold. Now, as diplomats from around the world arrived for the United Nations Conference on International Organization, a new wave of prospectors followed. Like the Gold Rush pioneers of 1849, they struck out for the West without waiting for an invitation. Instead of picks, pans, and shovels, they came with the tools of modern public relations — handshakes, press agents, brochures, and persistence. The new prospectors came from Philadelphia and from another gold region, the Black Hills of South Dakota, with no qualms whatsoever about encroaching on the host city, which also coveted the chance to become the Capital of the World.

Throughout March and April 1945, hope for the future of the world poured into San Francisco. Delegates from the Allied nations came to draft the charter for the new United Nations organization, and dignitaries arrived to bestow official blessings on the project. Hotels filled with men and women who worked for the State Department. People who envisioned a postwar world without discrimination, oppression, or imperialism came to raise their voices. In a city bursting with anticipation, it was perhaps fitting that the arrivals included a man named Hope — the comedian Bob Hope, who entertained servicemen and women at the Alameda Naval Air Station and produced a flourish of jokes about the United Nations for his syndicated humor column.[1]

For San Francisco, it felt like destiny. The city had long prided itself on being "cosmopolitan" and promoted itself as such — a place of many histories and cultures, dating from its earliest years under the flags of Spain, Mexico, and the United States. This did not mean that San Francisco always welcomed newcomers, as its residents of Chinese and Japanese ancestry surely could attest. But with a history of tourism that dated from the nineteenth century, the city had come to appreciate the marketability of an exotic Chinatown, Russian Hill, and the Italian-village flavor of

Fisherman's Wharf. Although international trade had been interrupted during the war, the waterfront had long been a port for sailors and stevedores from around the world. Now, it seemed, San Francisco was being recognized as the world city it had always been.[2]

The question of where the United Nations might find a permanent home was not on the agenda as the Allied nations gathered in San Francisco, but this did not stop newspapers from speculating that the UN might settle in one of the capital cities in Europe, in Washington, D.C., or perhaps somewhere in Canada. Those familiar with the League of Nations knew that diplomats had selected Geneva at the same meetings that produced the League Covenant, so it was not beyond reason that the new United Nations organization might take a similar step. Boosters began to mobilize. Quebec City, where Franklin Roosevelt and Winston Churchill held two wartime conferences, issued a formal invitation. Philadelphia had scored enough publicity to secure a place in many press accounts, and sometimes the Black Hills idea surfaced as well. Attention turned foremost to San Francisco, which became the temporary Capital of the World in the sense of earlier international conferences that accorded the honor to Geneva, The Hague, and Washington, D.C.[3]

Even long-time San Francisco residents, accustomed to living at the crossroads of many cultures and seasoned by the experiences of hosting two world's fairs, marveled at the growing spectacle of the United Nations Conference on International Organization (UNCIO). State Department staff arrived early in March to do the advance work of finding a meeting hall, notifying hotels, arranging for security, and cutting through the red tape of wartime food restrictions so that the great assembly could be fed. In April, a Library of Congress specialist arrived to set up a collection of two thousand volumes in five languages. When San Franciscans clamored to help, Mayor Roger Lapham channeled their enthusiasm into an array of committees for finance, entertainment, press, and decorations. Socialites planned parties, and merchants filled their windows with luxury goods and specially designed United Nations neckties. Twelve military bands began to practice forty-six national anthems.[4]

And then, the world stopped.

On April 12, 1945, at 3:35 in the afternoon, Franklin Delano Roosevelt died from a cerebral hemorrhage while vacationing in Warm Springs, Georgia. The president's health had been failing visibly for months, even when he was nominated for his fourth term in office. But still, his death was stunning. American flags came down to half-staff at the White House, at the Capitol, and then all across the country. The news flashed over telegraph wires, crackled on the radio, and splashed across the front pages of special editions. Businesses closed, churches filled, and silence fell on city sidewalks. The nation united in mourning. Over the next two days, along with the funeral in the East Room in the White House and burial in Hyde Park, N.Y., memorial services occurred across the country. In Philadelphia, the bell in Independence Hall tolled sixty-three times, once for each year of the president's life. In South Dakota, the people of the Black Hills remembered how Roosevelt had come to Mount Rushmore in 1936 to dedicate the carving of Thomas Jefferson. In San Francisco, Mayor Lapham called his citizens together in the rotunda of City Hall. The sounds of taps drifted over the silent mourners, and the mayor paid tribute: "His influence and his name will live, not only for today or tomorrow, but forever." Preparations for the United Nations paused, but only long enough for the new president of the United States, Harry S. Truman, to confirm that the conference would go on.[5]

On the very day that Roosevelt died, the first of the foreign delegations began to arrive in San Francisco. Thirteen staff members for the Soviet Union flew from Moscow "over the top of the world," as the *San Francisco Chronicle* put it, touched down at Great Falls, Montana, and then proceeded to San Francisco Municipal Airport. The pace quickened as the official opening day of the conference approached. The Haitian delegation arrived and expressed determination to fight racial discrimination on a global scale. The royal family of Saudi Arabia, described by the local press as "the most colorful delegation yet," spoke of seeking solutions for the problems of the Middle East. Fifteen ambassadors and other officials from South and Central America landed in a specially arranged American Airlines plane, escorted by Assistant Secretary of State Nelson A. Rockefeller of New York and welcomed by a navy band playing "Ruffles and Flourishes."[6]

As promised at the Yalta conference in February, the federal government also cleared a railway path to San Francisco. At lunchtime on Saturday, April 21, in Denver, Colorado, the city's Union Station suddenly sounded very much like a Capital of the World. Voices in Chinese, Polish, French, and English chattered excitedly as the doors of a nine-car special train flew open to allow an unusual group of passengers a brief break from riding the rails. The 138 passengers from eight nations — mostly young adults, some in uniform — seized the opportunity. They laughed and shouted to each other as they emerged from the train. For most, it was another new adventure on a journey that already had taken them by ship from England to Halifax, Nova Scotia, where they had boarded this train—the "European Delegation Express." They were the stenographers, messengers, security officers, staff advisers, and some of the news correspondents who would work behind the scenes of the conference.[7]

A similar, if more sedate, scene occurred later that Saturday at Union Station in St. Louis, Missouri. Another transcontinental train pulled in around 8:00 p.m. to allow another unusual collection of passengers a one-hour break. There on the platform were Lord Halifax, British ambassador to the United States, with Lady Halifax and the foreign minister from Australia, Herbert Evatt. Out of the train came fifty-five officials from China, a group of high-ranking Soviets, and several diplomats from Norway. On another train moving west, U.S. State Department staff drafted documents to guide the work in the days ahead. Many high-ranking delegates to the San Francisco meeting flew to the West Coast, and the Soviet Union anchored its own well-appointed ship in San Francisco Bay. But these journeys by rail, arranged by the U.S. State Department for diplomats, staff members, and journalists, were exactly what Secretary of State Edward Stettinius had in mind when he imagined San Francisco as the first meeting place for the United Nations organization.[8]

On nine trains, through the back yards of small towns and rail yards of big cities, across the western plains and the great Rocky Mountains, the State Department's transcontinental travelers gained the first-hand view of the United States of America that the secretary of state had imagined. As they admired the scenery, however, diplomats also were gaining indelible memories of how long it could take to get to the West Coast. By train, crossing the continent required four days from Washington or New York to San Francisco. By commercial airline, flights from San Francisco to Washington took sixteen hours, even on TWA's speedy new four-engine Stratoliner, which stopped along the way in Los Angeles, Albuquerque, Kansas City, Chicago, and Dayton, Ohio. Whatever the diplomats' enthusiasm for this first conference in San Francisco, would they want to repeat these journeys?[9]

WORLD STAGE

In and around hotel lobbies, San Franciscans watched for diplomats, journalists, and other celebrities. The diplomats from forty-six nations came in rapid succession—Prime Minister Jan Christiaan Smuts of South Africa,

Brigadier General Carlos Romulo of the Philippines, and lesser-known delegates and staff members from the United Kingdom, the Dominican Republic, Honduras, Ethiopia, Liberia, and Colombia. The biggest diplomatic stars—U.S. Secretary of State Stettinius, British foreign minister Anthony Eden, and Soviet foreign minister Vyacheslav Molotov—were among the last to appear, flying to the West Coast after preliminary meetings in Washington. Media celebrities like Walter Winchell and the Hollywood gossip columnist Hedda Hopper became part of the show. Movie stars James Cagney and Sylvia Sidney were expected for a premier of their new film, *Blood on the Sun*, which featured Cagney as a newspaper reporter discovering the evil intentions of prewar Japan.[10]

The swelling population in San Francisco also reflected the tremendous public interest in world affairs that had grown in the first half of the twentieth century. Times of war, struggles for peace, and issues transcending national boundaries had inspired people and organizations to devote increasing energy to international causes. Forty-two organizations came to San Francisco as official "consultants" appointed by the State Department, a role not clearly defined but eagerly embraced. The consultants spanned a spectrum of service organizations, business and labor associations, religious federations, and groups dedicated to causes of world peace and security. The NAACP, recognizing the connection between African American civil rights and global human rights, sent Walter White, Mary McLeod Bethune, and the renowned W. E. B. Du Bois. They joined the call for UN attention to the colonized people of the world, especially in Africa.[11]

Individual citizens also made their way to San Francisco without official status. Richard Robert Wright Sr., ninety-two years old, an African American educator and banker who had been born in slavery, came as a correspondent for the *Philadelphia Tribune*. Mohawk chief Jimmy Square Hill arrived from Grand River, Ontario, to urge the UN to protect his people's rights to land in Canada. Members of the Jewish Agency for Palestine came to advocate creating a Jewish state. The leading critic of world organization also arrived—Gerald L. K. Smith, leader of "America First," who was determined to educate the delegates about American nationalism.[12]

Fulfilling two of the major requirements for a Capital of the World, San Francisco had the transportation needed to bring these people together and the hotel rooms to accommodate them. Grand hotels, a legacy created by the wealth of mining and banking barons in the late nineteenth century, included the Fairmont and the Mark Hopkins on fashionable Nob Hill, overlooking the rest of the city. Down the steep slope of Powell

Street from the Fairmont, cable cars clambered past the elegant, newer Sir Francis Drake Hotel and then to the stylish and popular St. Francis, which faced Union Square and its monument celebrating Admiral George Dewey and the United States' victory in the Spanish-American War. The flags of twenty-six national delegations fluttered in front of the St. Francis during the conference, signaling the nationalities of the guests within. Closer to the city's business district, the famous Palace Hotel became headquarters for the press corps. The hundreds of journalists moving into the Palace included a 28-year-old navy veteran named John F. Kennedy, on assignment for the *Chicago Herald-American*.[13]

Playing host to such a global assembly also required conference rooms and a meeting hall. No hotel—not even two adjacent hotels as massive as the Fairmont and the Mark Hopkins—had enough meeting rooms for the task of drafting a United Nations charter. Instead, the State Department looked to the Civic Center, the European-style plaza and public buildings constructed after the earthquake and fire of 1906. The Civic Center represented the best of American city planning in the early twentieth century—a dedication to beauty, order, and public spirit exemplified by the "White City" buildings at the World's Columbian Exposition in Chicago in 1893. San Francisco's Civic Center, with its grand domed City Hall, civic auditorium, public library, and other monumental office buildings, stood as a prime example of "City Beautiful" style. Fittingly, the United Nations could convene in the War Memorial Opera House and Veterans Building, two adjacent structures that honored the sacrifices of the First World War. A memorial plaque placed in the Opera House foyer in 1932 seemed to mark its future as well as its past:

> *War Memorial Opera House*
> *A Living Monument*
> *Eloquent of Hopes Realized*
> *And Dreams Come True*
> *Dedicated to the citizens of San Francisco who gave their lives*
> *in the service of their country.*

Veterans' organizations gave up their spaces, and the art galleries in the Veterans Building were emptied so that temporary offices could be built in their place. The Pacific Telephone and Telegraph Company installed a massive new switchboard in the basement. The State Department mapped seating in the Opera House floor, boxes, and balconies for thirty-three

hundred people, including more than eighteen hundred accredited journalists and members of the public.[14]

On the afternoon of April 25, the delegates emerged from limousines
and military vehicles to take their places in the red velvet seats on the Opera House floor. Mingling informally in the aisles, they were accompanied
by a constant clicking, whirring, and flashing of newsreel cameras and still
photography. At the front of the hall, the stage was set simply but symbolically, with a semicircle of the flags of forty-six nations and gold columns
representing the Four Freedoms, articulated by Franklin Roosevelt in 1941
as freedom of speech, freedom to worship, freedom from want, and freedom from fear. The first people to appear on stage were seventeen young
men and women in uniform, representing every branch of the armed services of the United States. They stood at attention, then at ease, solemnly,
eyes forward.[15]

Two friends took the stage — Secretary of State Edward Stettinius and
San Francisco mayor Roger Lapham, along with the governor of California, Earl Warren, and the State Department man who had been designated
secretary-general of the conference, Alger Hiss. At the podium, Stettinius
picked up a gavel made from California redwood, a gift from the San Francisco Sons of the American Revolution, and rapped the meeting to order.
He called for a moment of silence, and sixty seconds passed while this assembly of many faiths drew strength and contemplated the days ahead.
Stettinius, restless by nature, found it difficult to wait. He glanced over
bowed heads and up into the balconies, anxious to continue. The minute
passed. And then, on schedule, surmounting all barriers of time and space,
the voice of the president of the United States, Harry S. Truman, came into
the auditorium, broadcast by radio from Washington, D.C.[16]

Truman, who had been president for less than two weeks, could not
make the trip to the conference but honored its purpose. "At no time in
history has there been a more important conference, nor a more necessary meeting, than this one in San Francisco," he said clearly, warmly,
from across the continent. He called on the conference to fulfill Franklin
Roosevelt's vision and to repay the sacrifices of lives lost in the war. The
experiences of two global conflicts made the work imperative. "With ever
increasing brutality and destruction, modern warfare, if unchecked, would
ultimately crush all civilization," said the president, himself a combat veteran of the First World War. "We still have a choice between the alternatives: the continuation of international chaos — or the establishment of
a world organization for the enforcement of peace." Unbeknownst to his

listeners in San Francisco, a new urgency informed his warning. Earlier that very afternoon, Truman had received his first detailed briefing about the United States' impending secret weapon, the atomic bomb.[17]

Stettinius spoke next. San Francisco, such a hopeful symbol, should inspire the work ahead, he said. He recalled the pioneers who moved westward across the continent until they reached the Pacific Ocean. "Since then Americans have always thought of California, of San Francisco, as a place where hopes come true, where all purposes can be accomplished," said the secretary of state. How fitting that this meeting convened at a city on the Pacific Ocean, "this great ocean named for peace." Governor Warren and Mayor Lapham added their affection for San Francisco and its new role on the world stage. How appropriate, Lapham noted, that the United Nations had gathered in "cosmopolitan San Francisco," the city whose history had unfolded under many flags. How appropriate that this event took place in the boom city of the Gold Rush. "Almost one hundred years ago our port was thronged with vessels and with men of all nations, seeking gold," the mayor said. "Today we are still seeking, but we seek a different treasure." His next words revealed the intensity of a veteran who had served in the First World War, only to see violence return. "Here in this War Memorial Opera House, raised to those who died in the first World War — and to all intents and purposes died in vain," he said, "we look to you thinking men and women for the foundation of a just and lasting peace."[18]

If the mayor felt tempted to invite the United Nations to stay permanently in his city, he resisted. "If we can help, we stand ready to serve," he said, "but we have no intention of making demands on your time and energy while you face this solemn and all-important task." In fact, Lapham did not need to broadcast San Francisco's ambitions from the stage. Already, his guests had received State Department briefings about the city's history, climate, and cultural advantages. The local UNCIO committee had provided them with a booklet titled *San Francisco, World City*, published before the war but reprinted in a special edition for the conference. The *San Francisco News* was publishing essays by schoolchildren laying out the reasons why San Francisco should be the "permanent peace capital of the world," and local newspapers were full of advertisements celebrating the United Nations' temporary home.[19]

If the residents and distinguished guests of San Francisco tuned their radios to the CBS network that evening, they heard an inkling of another idea. The program — a half-hour musical salute to the conference performed by the Philadelphia Orchestra, conducted by Eugene

Ormandy—seemed to be fully in keeping with the day. But along with the music, listeners also heard Robert L. Johnson, the president of Temple University, speak of Philadelphia's historical association with peace and liberty. Not coincidentally, Johnson had recently taken on an additional duty as chairman of the Philadelphia campaign to lure the United Nations to the City of Brotherly Love.[20]

Soon, the delegates began receiving mail from Philadelphia. First came an invitation in the form of a proclamation illustrated by a drawing of Independence Hall and extolling the city's heritage as the "City of Brotherly Love" and the "Cradle of Liberty." Philadelphia's press agent in San Francisco, Ray Krimm, made sure this invitation reached the journalists in the city and the bulletin boards of all the conference hotels. Next came a formal engraved invitation and a promotional booklet featuring a glossy photograph of the Liberty Bell on its cover and photographs inside of colonial buildings, cultural institutions, and recreational attractions. Repeatedly, the booklet built on the phrase "We the People," extending it from the U.S. Constitution to encompass not just Philadelphia and not just the United States but all the citizens of the world. Twenty-one pages in the back of the booklet displayed endorsements of Philadelphia from prominent citizens around the country, including governors of other states. By the end of the conference, more than nine hundred of these booklets circulated in San Francisco.[21]

The diplomats and advisers who now burrowed into their business, who filled San Francisco's hotels, sought out its nightlife, patronized its merchants, and fielded invitations from eager hosts and hostesses, had more urgent things to think about. Stettinius, for one, arrived with the knowledge that he was not Truman's choice to continue as secretary of state. He retained the position so long as the conference lasted, but speculation swirled about when he would be replaced, and by whom. Meanwhile, tensions seethed—especially between the United States and the Soviet Union—over who should preside and whether the Soviet Union should have more than one vote to represent its multiple republics. These issues tangled with the question of whether to seat Poland, where the claims of two rival governments (one backed by the Soviets) had yet to be settled. And what of Argentina, which had given aid to the Axis and declared war only a month before? These questions consumed the greatest energy during the first week of the conference. Finally, the major powers agreed to seat Byelorus, Ukraine, and Argentina, but left Poland in limbo. As for control over the San Francisco meetings, the official conveners—the United

States, the Soviet Union, Great Britain, and China—reached a compromise. They would take turns chairing public sessions, as the Soviet Union had advocated, but in their private meetings, Stettinius would preside.[22]

The delegates went to work on transforming the outline for the new organization, which they inherited from the Dumbarton Oaks conference the previous fall, into a charter for the UN's member nations to ratify. But this, too, was treacherous. Forty-six nations had arrived with hundreds of pages of ideas for amendments. The four major powers found common ground in three days of talks, as might be expected since they had drafted the proposals at Dumbarton Oaks. But smaller nations searched for ways to achieve influence in the new organization, and each proposal needed to be heard. Commissions and committees began the meticulous process of examining each part of the Dumbarton Oaks plan, considering alternatives, and fine-tuning the language that they hoped would guide the world into the future.[23]

On Tuesday, May 8, Stettinius opened the day's meetings with a long-anticipated but still dramatic announcement. On the other side of the world, Allied forces had rolled into Berlin. "The President of the United States has announced the end of hostilities in Europe. Nazi Germany has been defeated," Stettinius announced. Once again he called for a moment of silence, this time in tribute to the armies of the United Nations. It was victory, but only in part. "This hour of victory is not a moment for exaltation," Stettinius told the delegates. "It is time for renewed dedication to the cause of peace." President Truman, speaking to the nation by radio from Washington, called on "every American to stick to his post until the last battle is won." The message moved across the United States to war production workers, service men and women, civil defense volunteers, and civic leaders: finish the job. Look to the Pacific. Finish the war against Japan.[24]

Who had time to think about creating a Capital of the World?

PROSPECTORS

On May 17, a party of Philadelphians appeared in the office of the mayor of San Francisco, presenting themselves as if they were an official delegation to the UNCIO. Roger Lapham, amused, did the only thing he could do as gracious host, and extended his hand in welcome. Collectively, these visitors represented Philadelphia's idea of respectability in 1945—social standing, expertise, wealth, connections, and a deep dash of history. Their leader was Robert L. Johnson, fifty-one years old, the president of

Temple University, a former executive of *Time* magazine, and a descendant of a cousin of William Penn. With Johnson stood John G. Herndon, fifty-seven, a professor of government at Haverford College and expert on the League of Nations, and Common Pleas Court judge L. Stauffer Oliver, sixty-five, a descendant of Mayflower colonists, a founder of the United Nations Council of Philadelphia, and former law school classmate of *Philadelphia Record* publisher David Stern. A reporter from the *Record* came along, of course, as did a Philadelphia advertising executive named Benjamin Eshleman, press agent Ray Krimm, and Sophia Yarnall Jacobs, a Pennsylvania coal heiress who had been designated Philadelphia's official hostess in San Francisco.[25]

Diplomatically, Johnson told Lapham that the most important goal was to have the UN Secretariat in the United States, no matter where its precise location. But the Philadelphians had arrived with a sales pitch, and Lapham had no choice but to listen. "Naturally," Johnson continued, "if it is decided to locate the peace capital in this country, I think its headquarters should be in Philadelphia, birthplace of the Declaration of Independence, and home of the American Constitution." Judge Oliver stressed spiritual qualities. "Those factors are so preponderantly present in Philadelphia's history and background that they should be of great help in firmly establishing an international peace organization," he said. Professor Herndon added that the Pennsylvania General Assembly had just voted to give the UN jurisdiction over any land it might need to place its headquarters in Philadelphia.[26]

Lapham betrayed none of the activity already underway by the San Francisco Chamber of Commerce. "So far as San Francisco is concerned, we have not started any official drive to have the United Nations headquarters located permanently here," he said. "But we would certainly welcome all of the delegates if they would want to come back here."[27]

For the Philadelphians, the stop at the mayor's office was simply a courtesy call. They moved quickly to pursue people who seemed to have the most potential to influence the headquarters decision. Ignoring the fact that no one had come to San Francisco intending to make such a decision—indeed, until the charter could be finished, no organization yet existed—the Philadelphians made appointments to see any delegate who would open his or her door, up to and including the secretary of state. While they waited for these meetings, they went on the radio, beginning with a roundtable discussion broadcast nationally on the Mutual network. In this city packed with news reporters in search of good stories, the Philadelphians found ready listeners.[28]

Approaching his mission like a businessman wooing a new client, Paul E. Bellamy from South Dakota shares a cigar with a delegate from Saudi Arabia. (Paul E. Bellamy Papers, Richardson Collection, University Libraries, University of South Dakota, reproduced with permission of Bell Studios, Rapid City, S.D.)

If the United Nations was to be the mother lode for some fortunate city or town, the Philadelphians were not going to have it to themselves for long. From South Dakota, Paul Bellamy slipped into San Francisco on May 18 with less fanfare and an entourage consisting only of his friend Fred Christopherson, the editor of the *Sioux Falls Argus-Leader*. As the chief prospector for the Black Hills, Bellamy approached this expedition like any other business trip. He would deal with the foreign ministers "man to man," as he saw it. A handshake here, a cigar there, a little friendly conversation about the beautiful Black Hills would be enough to plant the idea for the future. Bellamy learned quickly that he could not just pick up the telephone and ask for appointments, but he could seek out a delegation's hotel, leave his engraved business card, and await a reply. With remarkable frequency, in the spirit of diplomacy, the replies often came.[29]

Bellamy filled his calendar with lunch dates, afternoon appointments, and dinner meetings. In the space of just one day, he met with diplomats from the Philippines, the United States, Czechoslovakia, and Norway, and found that their interest in Mount Rushmore and Black Hills scenery helped to make his case. On other days, he mingled with delegates at the famous Bohemian Grove, shared cigars with royalty from Saudi Arabia, and had breakfast with Alger Hiss, the secretary-general for the entire conference. He did not make it into the inner sanctum of the secretary of state, but he did have a conversation with Adlai E. Stevenson, special assistant to Stettinius and the U.S. delegation. Were his listeners genuinely enthusiastic about his proposal, merely polite, or simply amused? At this moment in the UN's history, all options seemed to be open. Christopherson, the Sioux Falls editor who shadowed Bellamy as he circulated through San Francisco, observed, "Always, there was a bit of a smile as the project was mentioned—somewhat as if the sponsor was thinking about reaching for the moon." But Bellamy did seem to have an effect. "As they reflected on it, they began to wonder, if not the Black Hills, why not? What, for example, has Philadelphia got that the Black Hills haven't? And, beyond that, what do the Black Hills have that Philadelphia does not?"[30]

One thing that the Philadelphians had was a more sophisticated strategy for infiltrating the rituals of diplomacy. On Sunday, May 20, they made a social splash with an afternoon reception at the Mark Hopkins Hotel. Sophia Jacobs made sure that invitations went to all heads of delegations and other officials of the conference. Lord Halifax accepted, and so did Governor and Mrs. Earl Warren of California. In all, two hundred people, including the heads of fifteen delegations, attended. "So far as could be observed," the *Philadelphia Record* reported, "not a single guest present had not heard the Philadelphia story and expressed warm sympathy for the idea of making historic Philadelphia the future peace capital."[31]

The Philadelphians also scored the ultimate audience—a meeting on Monday, May 21, with the secretary of state himself, at the U.S. delegation headquarters in the Fairmont Hotel. The civic go-getters from the East secured a half-hour with Stettinius despite the fact that the conference had just survived a serious crisis, and others loomed. The first problem had concerned Latin America, whose delegates had come to San Francisco with worries that the new UN might overrule their own regional security agreement, just reached in Mexico City. Weeks of negotiation—brokered by Nelson Rockefeller, who had irritated Stettinius by coming to San Francisco without official appointment—had finally produced new charter language that averted a possible breakdown over the issue of regional agreements. Meanwhile, however, smaller nations were mobilizing to challenge the proposed veto that the major powers would have in the UN Security

Council. Furthermore, the Soviet Union and the United States were at odds over the circumstances in which such a veto would be allowed, an issue that the Americans thought had been settled at Yalta. On Monday morning, Stettinius had been on the phone with Truman about this, and they had decided that the secretary would fly back to Washington to confer with the president in person.[32]

In the midst of all this, the Philadelphians presented themselves promptly at 11:30 a.m. at the Fairmont's Room 514. As with the mayor of San Francisco a few days before, Robert Johnson took the lead in this unusual summit and self-importantly congratulated Stettinius on the progress of the conference so far. The Philadelphians presented the secretary of state with the city's original formal invitation to the UN, bound in blue leather and embossed with the great seal of Philadelphia. Stettinius, a perfectionist when it came to the State Department's own official invitations, admired the typography.

But enough ceremony. Stettinius knew their purpose, and he had two things to say. Officially, diplomatically, he promised that he "would present these documents to the proper committee of the conference at the proper time." Unofficially, he offered a private assessment of the headquarters question. He did not reveal his own preference for San Francisco, but he tried to convey to these eager solicitors that many factors were in play, and none of them pointed toward Philadelphia. The organization—when it existed—might want a fixed headquarters for its Secretariat, but rotating locations for the Assembly. FDR had favored this arrangement. The UN probably would not move into the buildings of the failed League of Nations in Geneva, Stettinius said, but Switzerland and France were prepared to offer an international zone for a headquarters in Europe. In any case, no decision would be made in San Francisco. Still, the Philadelphians pressed their case and told Stettinius they were taking steps to convey property in Philadelphia to the United States government, which could then give it to the United Nations. Johnson informed the secretary of state that placing the UN in the United States would help assure Americans' continuing interest in world affairs—as if Stettinius himself had not thought of this, as if he had not heard it before.[33]

For public consumption, the best the Philadelphians could garner from this half-hour meeting was a news release stating Stettinius's official position. He dictated it in their presence, to assure their satisfaction. The secretary of state informed the press that he "would see that the Philadelphia invitation would receive due consideration by the appropriate Conference authorities." The Philadelphians put their own positive spin on things. "It was our definite impression that Mr. Stettinius thought the city of Philadelphia had a good case, and that it would be entitled to very careful consideration when the time comes to select a permanent site," Johnson told the always-nearby reporter for the *Philadelphia Record*. It was enough to allow the *Record* to conclude that whenever the UN took up the site question, "Stettinius himself will present . . . the official invitation of the city of Philadelphia."[34]

The Philadelphians departed San Francisco on May 22, but left Jacobs and Krimm behind to keep stoking the Philadelphia story. Paul Bellamy also lingered in San Francisco, and the diplomats began to receive more unusual mail—a four-page brochure with a statement on the front from the governors of South Dakota, Nebraska, and Wyoming. "UNITED NATIONS OF THE WORLD," the headline beseeched in capital letters. "Where Will Your Headquarters Be?" Answering the question, the brochure stated that the headquarters should be in the United States, specifically in the Black Hills country in the southwest corner of South Dakota and adjacent to Wyoming and Nebraska, "one of the most beautiful and interesting areas to be found anywhere on earth." The brochure presented the location not as remote but rather, in keeping with a long tradition of map manipulation by boosters of the American West, at the center of the nation and therefore at the center of the world. Far from being an isolationist backwater, the Black Hills represented an international crossroads—"The original inhabitants of this continent, the American Indians came here from the Orient, the modern settler and developer came here from the Occident." Government could function in the Black Hills, as Calvin Coolidge had proven with his "White House" in the hills during one summer of his presidency. Peacemakers could be inspired there, especially because the faces on Mount Rushmore, the Shrine of Democracy, were "gradually extending their beneficent influences throughout the world."[35]

On the back of the Black Hills brochure, a map displayed the continents of the world as they might be seen from a point over the North Pole, a practice in cartography that had become common in the new age of aviation, especially during the war. A similar view of the world appeared in the new official emblem for the UN. Over this map, the boosters of the Black Hills overlaid radiating concentric circles, like the rings of a target. Lines leading from little airplanes on each continent pointed toward the center.[36]

In the bull's eye, of course, stood Paul Bellamy's beloved Black Hills.

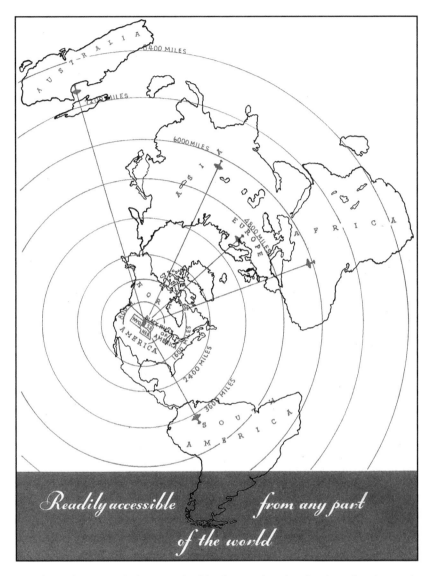

Readily accessible from any part of the world

Extending a booster technique practiced in the American interior since the nineteenth century, this map delivered to the United Nations delegates uses concentric circles to create an impression of centrality for the Black Hills. At the ends of the lines extending to each continent, tiny airplanes suggest a swift line of travel to the midsection of the United States. (Paul E. Bellamy Papers, Richardson Collection, University Libraries, University of South Dakota)

PROSPECTS

Through the rest of May and into June, the United Nations managed to carry on without the advice of civic boosters from Philadelphia and South Dakota. With diligence, and often with struggle, the diplomats in San Francisco turned the blueprint from the Dumbarton Oaks conference of 1944 into the United Nations Charter. They settled on "The United Nations" as the name for the new world organization, despite some reservations that this name came from the wartime alliance against the Axis. They added to the charter a lyrical preamble, modeled on the preamble to the U.S. Constitution: "We the peoples of the United Nations, determined to save succeeding generations from the scourge of war, which twice in our lifetime has brought untold sorrow to mankind. . . . " To prevent future wars, the UN would strive to settle disputes and it would put down acts of aggression, by force when necessary. To promote peace, UN agencies would work toward meeting economic, social, cultural, and humanitarian needs. A Trusteeship Council would oversee new nations emerging from colonial empires, although it stopped short of the sweeping end to imperialism that many of the smaller nations and other human rights advocates desired. A World Court would administer justice on a global scale. In all of this, the charter pledged, the UN would not interfere with the sovereignty of any nation—a provision the San Francisco delegates insisted upon.[37]

This world organization would have an Assembly of all member nations, but the greatest authority would lie with the major powers of 1945—the United States, the Soviet Union, the United Kingdom, and France, as well as China, which FDR had championed as a power in Asia to supersede Japan. These nations would hold permanent seats on the UN Security Council, which had the power to take action against threats to peace, including military action if necessary. Although the council also would have six nonpermanent members selected by the UN Assembly, each of the major five would have veto power, except in disputes involving their own nations. The veto had limits, however. It could not be used to prevent discussion, a power the Soviet Union had long advocated and did not give up until a personal emissary from President Truman appealed to Joseph Stalin in Moscow. The major powers also withstood the movement among smaller nations, led by Australia, to gain a greater role on the Security Council. As defined in the UN Charter, the Security Council locked in place the power structures of World War II for years to come.[38]

While diplomats created a governing structure, American architects began to visualize buildings and environments for a world organization. The first speculative designs gave tangible expression to public enthusiasm for the new organization, but at the same time they suggested that deciding where to place the headquarters would be more complex than simply choosing among competing cities and moving into existing hotels and auditoriums.[39]

Despite the conference location in San Francisco, the first two headquarters renderings to become public ranged from ambivalence to outright resistance to placing the UN in a city. A plan created by Vincent G. Raney for the San Francisco Planning Commission depicted a UN complex atop the city's Twin Peaks, within the city's boundaries but elevated from its business districts. His rendering showed no hint of a surrounding city. Imagined for a slope overlooking San Francisco Bay and described by a newspaper as "crowning a beautiful Market Boulevard," Raney's UN complex included a skyscraper and an illuminated globe, forms reminiscent of the Trylon and Perisphere symbols of the New York World's Fair of 1939–40.[40]

A second plan for a San Francisco–area capital, created by William Wurster of the Massachusetts Institute of Technology (a former San Francisco resident) with colleagues Ernest Born and Theodore C. Bernardi, separated the United Nations from the city entirely. Their renderings, displayed in a downtown shop window during the UN conference, envisioned the UN on a peninsula of Marin County called Strawberry Point. The architects explained that they selected this location "because of the climate and infinite expansibility, as well as for its beauty and accessibility," a rationale that placed a priority on ambiance as well as function, emphasizing the appeal of a location accessible from a city yet standing apart. Their world capital would be, in essence, a suburb with potential for unlimited growth. With modern structures in a parklike setting, anticipating the style of postwar office parks and apartment complexes, the Wurster plan also reflected recent world's fair designs. The complex featured a ground-level dome to enclose an auditorium for ten thousand people, separate midrise office buildings, and a revolving globe in the "library court." The architects noted the international purpose of the buildings with a court of flags, one of the signature features of the UN's eventual complex in New York.[41]

By the close of the conference, San Francisco had become accustomed to being the Capital of the World. The early gawking at celebrities had given way to a comfortable embrace of the intrigue of international affairs. As a reporter for the San Francisco Chronicle put it, during the nine weeks

A plan for a San Francisco–area capital created by William Wurster of the Massachusetts Institute of Technology with colleagues Ernest Born and Theodore C. Bernardi separated the UN from the city and placed it on a peninsula of Marin County called Strawberry Point, extending into Richardson Bay. Modern structures in a parklike setting resembled site plans for world's fairs or for the office parks that proliferated in the postwar era. (William W. Wurster/Wurster, Bernardi, Emmons Collection, Environmental Design Archives, University of California, Berkeley)

of the conference the UN had become "as much a part of San Francisco as the red bricks on Pine Street or the eucalyptus trees in Sutro Street." As the conference reached its last two ceremonial days, the city teemed with restless excitement, like a school about to be let out for the summer. On Monday, June 25, Stettinius, Mayor Lapham, and Governor Warren met again as they rode together in an automobile to welcome the president of the United States. Stettinius, in a reflective mood, took advantage of the moment. "You know, Roger," he said to the mayor, "this would be an ideal spot for the United Nations and you ought to go to work on it." The governor nodded.[42]

The secretary, the mayor, and the governor rode through the mist over the Golden Gate Bridge and twenty-five miles to the Hamilton Army Airfield in Novato, California. Crowds were gathering along the roadways for a glimpse of Harry S. Truman. Soldiers carrying rifles with bayonets already were guarding the route. At the airbase, the president's four-motored Air Transport Command C-54 appeared from the north, then touched down on the concrete landing strip. Into the doorway of the plane stepped Truman, wearing a gray Stetson hat. As he descended, a 21-gun salute sounded from somewhere beyond the tail of the plane, and a band played "The Star-Spangled Banner" and then the "Missouri Waltz." Truman shook hands with Stettinius, Warren, and Lapham, and then the secretary of state presented the members of the United States delegation and each delegation chairman of the conference, in alphabetical order from Argentina to Yugoslavia. Then Truman reviewed the troops standing next to his airplane—a double line of soldiers recently wounded in the Pacific.[43]

The motorcade of seventy-five vehicles, with the flags of nations fluttering, began its journey back to San Francisco, where people waited five and six deep along a six-mile route to cheer the United Nations and their new president. Stettinius, now riding with the president, the governor, and the mayor in an open-topped car, noticed that the airmen of Hamilton Field had marked their place in the world with signs pointing in two directions: "Tokyo 6,282. Berlin 7,800." The detail lodged in his memory together with the sight of wounded soldiers wearing pajamas, sitting in wheelchairs, outside the base hospital. "These mileages seemed considerably less distant when we stopped in front of the hospital for the President to visit briefly with the wounded soldiers," Stettinius observed. The men Truman greeted had been fighting in Okinawa just a few weeks before.[44]

Later that evening, the San Francisco conference unanimously approved the United Nations Charter, sending it forward to be ratified by each member nation. That night, in his penthouse atop the Fairmont Hotel, Edward Stettinius took a long last look over San Francisco. After two months of challenges and accomplishments, knowing that Truman would be replacing him as secretary of state as soon as the conference concluded, he wanted to remember. He made notes of the details, "realizing that this was the last night that I would be looking out over the Bay from the penthouse, the last of many days so full of trials and worries as well as great hopes and success, and that in less than 24 hours I would be flying East well on the way to Washington." He scanned the horizon. On the Ferry Building at the foot of Market Street below, the decorative colored lights were "more than any such display I have ever seen. It was like a diadem glowing white with diamonds and pearls and with flashing rubies and emeralds just touching its white radiance. There were lines of lights like bracelets around the piers of the great long Oakland Bay Bridge." It was a glorious sight, an appropriate mirror for this unlikely secretary of state's satisfaction with work well done.[45]

The next day, the Veterans Building provided the setting for ceremony. Now there were fifty flags in a semicircle—the forty-six from the start, plus Byelorus, Ukraine, Argentina, and Denmark, which had joined the conference after its liberation from the Nazis in May. Upstage from the flags stood a large round table and a small armchair once used in the U.S. Senate by Daniel Webster and borrowed for this occasion from the M. H. de Young Museum in Golden Gate Park. The scene swam in blue, symbolizing peace—a blue backdrop, blue table, blue upholstered chair, and a circular blue rug, surrounded by a cordon of red, white, and blue silk rope to keep back reporters and photographers. One by one, delegations appeared on stage and approached the table, where the delegation chairmen sat down and then solemnly signed the Charter of the United Nations. They also signed a document creating a United Nations Preparatory Commission, which would convene in the fall to launch the organization.[46]

When it came time for the United States delegation, the ceremony paused. Nearly half an hour passed. Reporters stood on their chairs to see what might be happening. A one-minute alert was issued to the press photographers.

Then two men walked onto the stage: Secretary of State Stettinius and the president of the United States. To Stettinius, it seemed that "a shiver of excitement went through the audience." He moved swiftly to the table, sat down, and with Truman standing to his right and looking on, signed his name in blue ink. All of the U.S. delegates, a mix of Democrats and

Republicans appointed by Franklin Roosevelt to help assure bipartisan support for the UN, added their signatures and each shook the president's hand. As a delegation, they marched off stage to enthusiastic applause.[47]

The UN would next convene in London. But after that, permanently, where? Despite the many pressing issues at San Francisco, the headquarters question had run like an undercurrent to the official agenda, helped along by the dabbling visitors from Philadelphia and South Dakota. The charter pointed toward some factors that might come into play. For example, the new document spoke of the importance of freedom and equality for individuals and for nations. With such language as its foundation, the UN would avoid places that might subject any of its members to discrimination. The delegates also had struggled mightily over how to distribute power within the new organization, especially within the Security Council. The location of the UN headquarters could be a further indication of where power would lie in the postwar world. Whether the honor would go to Europe or the United States, or to a great power or a smaller one, were questions for a later day.[48]

As the San Francisco conference came to a close, State Department staff members tried to discern where the delegates stood on the headquarters question. For most of the diplomats at this stage in the gestation of the UN, the choice had to do with continents, not urban or rural settings or particular cities or towns. It appeared that at least three of the other major powers—China, France, and the Soviet Union—leaned toward a location in the United States, or perhaps in Canada if the great powers were to be excluded. They believed that Europe, the traditional center of diplomacy, had been too consumed by conflict and damaged by combat to accommodate the new world organization. For the Soviet Union, a UN headquarters in Europe might also be a roadblock to expansion. The United States, with its cities intact, could offer a fresh start for nations in search of a lasting peace. Some delegates—notably the Latin Americans and Australians—expressed support for a Pacific Coast location. Nevertheless, Europe could not be discounted. Some delegates thought it might be best to place this peace-keeping organization in the part of the world that had generated so much conflict. The League of Nations buildings would be available in Geneva, even if they were symbols of failure.[49]

Philadelphia? The diplomats did not bring it up. So far as the State Department men were concerned, the major cities to consider in the United States were New York, because of its office buildings and communications facilities, and San Francisco, because of its climate and proven hospitality.

The city by the bay had drawbacks, however. To the State Department staff, it was "more of an outpost than a center," and racial antagonism toward the Chinese and Japanese might quickly undermine an otherwise congenial setting. Still, if the UN wanted to break from the past and to place the Pacific at the center of world affairs, then San Francisco could be a contender.[50]

South Dakota? An internal State Department memo stated bluntly that the suggestion of the Black Hills "may be dismissed because of its remoteness from any important center." Paul Bellamy and his friends would never know it, but by the middle of July 1945, their campaign had no chance of success whatsoever.[51]

3

SCHEMES

ON THE LAST DAY OF JUNE IN 1945, four days after the San Francisco conference adjourned, the excursion steamship *Western States* cruised northward on Lake Huron, the second largest of the Great Lakes that straddle the U.S.-Canadian border. In a world of waterways plied by battle-ships and submarines, the *Western States* steamed along its 300-mile route from Detroit in a leisurely twenty hours—time enough to deliver its pas-sengers, thirty-seven governors of the United States, to Mackinac Island for their annual Governors' Conference. The Second World War, now en-tering its last violent weeks in the Pacific, seemed far removed from this secluded resort island near the junction of Lake Huron and Lake Michi-gan, but in reality the Great Lakes region held vital strategic importance. From the upper Midwest, iron ore shipped over the lakes to the nation's steel mills, which rolled out the essential material for the machinery of war. Around the perimeter of the lakes, Americans and Canadians built subma-rines, minesweepers, landing craft, and other small-scale warships. Pilots practiced aircraft-carrier landings on converted passenger liners anchored on Lake Michigan near Chicago. The Great Lakes region had long been linked to the world through exploration, settlement, shipping, and trade, but the activities of war added new dimensions of urgency, responsibility, and sacrifice.[1]

Far from the battlefronts and halls of diplomacy, Mackinac Island was about to become the next arena in the competition to create a Capital of the World. What else would Paul Bellamy and Fred Christopherson, the stealthy South Dakota prospectors from San Francisco, be doing there? They arrived with credentials as "aides" to the governor of South Dakota, and they were not the only unusual guests that the governors would en-counter over the next several days. With statesmen not yet ready to set the terms for selecting a UN headquarters site, civic boosters were eager to do it for them. Looking ahead to the expansion of commercial aviation after the war, the UN's suitors imagined a world of possibilities unlimited by distance and travel time. Leaders of business and government formed coalitions to promote their hometowns, and in doing so they became activists in international affairs. During the summer of 1945, the outburst of boosterism expanded, especially in the Great Lakes region, and raised new expectations about a future Capital of the World.

Aboard the *Western States*, Governor Merrell Quentin Sharpe of South Dakota laid the foundation for the next incremental step to lure the United Nations to the Black Hills. The South Dakotans had no clue that within the U.S. State Department, at least, their cause already was doomed. Even if they had known, it might not have mattered. In the months since Paul Bellamy first unveiled his idea, the campaign had gathered momentum and powerful allies. Sharpe, a 57-year-old World War I veteran and former attorney general, was one of them. A United Nations headquarters in South Dakota would bestow prestige on his state, and the resulting publicity would bolster Sharpe's interest in attracting postwar tourism. An international spotlight might also direct attention to other issues he cared about, such as conservation.[2]

Quietly, Sharpe convened a meeting. From the elite group of American politicians aboard the *Western States*, he pulled together just a few who shared a new common interest in attracting the United Nations to the United States—Earl Warren of California, John Dempsey of New Mexico, Edward Martin of Pennsylvania, Dwight Griswold of Nebraska, and Lester Hunt of Wyoming. Nebraska and Wyoming had joined their neighbor South Dakota in the Black Hills cause; Pennsylvania was promoting Philadelphia; California, of course, hoped for San Francisco. Adding to this roster of known contenders, New Mexico's Dempsey wanted the UN to convene at the Grand Canyon. Together, Sharpe's huddle of governors drafted a resolution calling on President Truman, the U.S. Congress, and the United Nations to place the UN headquarters in the United States. It might turn out to be good for South Dakota. It might turn out to be good for Pennsylvania, California, or New Mexico. But no one would win if the United Nations turned its back on the United States altogether.[3]

Arriving on Mackinac Island, the governors rode in surreys to the gleaming white Grand Hotel, which flew American flags from its broad veranda and looked out over Lake Huron much as it had since the 1880s. Despite the air of nostalgia, over the next four days, it became clear that the approaching end of the Second World War weighed on them heavily, notwithstanding the relief it would bring to the nation and the world. Each of the governors stood at a crossroads of local, state, national, and global concerns, with opportunities and obstacles in every direction. They hoped that the end of the war would shift executive decision making back to the states from the federal government. They worried about how to convert the economy from the work of war to the long-term needs of peace, but they also looked forward to implementing plans for growth that had stalled fitfully through the Great Depression and then the war.[4]

To be a governor in the postwar era would transcend state boundaries, it seemed. At this 1945 conference, the governors gave special attention to the future of commercial aviation, which had the spectacular potential to transform any spot in the nation into a global gateway. If this were the case, then perhaps any location *could* reasonably promote itself as a future Capital of the World, whether for the United Nations or for some other commercial purpose. The governor of Illinois, Dwight H. Green, confidently predicted that "the luxurious transoceanic airliners and the gigantic airports which we envision will surely come into being. Airlines already in existence or definitely planned will link closely the political and commercial capitals of the earth." Ocean liners might still carry freight, but passengers would surely take to the air. Barriers of time and space would fall away. "The inland cities of America will come into their own as ports of entry in world commerce," Green declared. Such a destiny held immense prospects as well as challenging transitions for cities like Chicago, a great crossroads for railroads, which might soon be eclipsed.[5]

As if to reinforce the governors' changing place in the postwar world, directly from San Francisco came one of their own—naval commander Harold E. Stassen, the former governor of Minnesota who had served in the U.S. delegation in San Francisco. Stassen called on the governors to stake out a vital place in international affairs. As leaders in peace as well as war, they would demonstrate that states could cooperate, just as the United Nations called upon the nations of the world to cooperate. They could show how well-conceived plans could address economic, social, and political problems. "We can no longer play the isolationist role of sitting back and waiting to see what other nations wish to do before we begin to study and form a viewpoint and a program on vital worldwide problems," Stassen said in a dinner speech at the Grand Hotel on July 2. The next day, the governors affirmed their commitment to international affairs by drafting a resolution supporting U.S. ratification of the UN Charter. In a flourish of patriotism, they approved it unanimously on the Fourth of July.[6]

It was time for the next step in the South Dakota strategy.

Under the radar of official conference business, Paul Bellamy and Fred Christopherson, the temporary "aides" to the governor of South Dakota, circulated among the select and captive audience. At cocktail receptions, they talked up the advantages of patriotic inspiration, hometown hospitality, and scenic beauty, all to be found in South Dakota. Had the governors seen Mount Rushmore? Would they like to visit, as guests of the good people of South Dakota? And by the way—perhaps they had heard that the United Nations already had been invited to make its headquarters in the beautiful Black Hills? Between speeches and press conferences, the operatives from South Dakota paved the way for Governor Sharpe's resolution urging the United Nations to place its capital in the United States.[7]

As the South Dakota crew spread the word about the Black Hills, it became clear that a much wider competition was taking shape. Two months of headlines about the United Nations meeting in San Francisco had primed a combustion of interest among chamber of commerce officers, government officials, and private citizens across the country. The governors of Pennsylvania and South Dakota had fueled states' desires by mailing letters to their counterparts seeking endorsements for Philadelphia and the Black Hills. At the Governors' Conference, the South Dakota prospectors encountered the governor of North Dakota, Fred Aandahl, who was suggesting that a lovely site could be found in the International Peace Garden on his state's northern border with Canada. The governor of Colorado, John Vivian, said that no fewer than fourteen communities in his state would be suitable, although he did not name them. Governor Thomas E. Dewey of New York, the Republican Party's presidential nominee in 1944, reported that he had been approached by boosters from around Niagara Falls and in New York City. It would be months before any official steps were taken on behalf of New York City, but Niagara Falls promoters already had embarked on a full-fledged campaign together with the adjacent Canadian town of Niagara Falls, Ontario.[8]

The Great Lakes region, so interconnected by the movement of goods and people through and across the lakes, so inherently international in its position overlaying the United States and Canada, seemed to its civic leaders during these summer months to be especially ideal for a new Capital of the World. Because of press speculation that the UN might favor a site in Canada, which could offer a North American location apart from the major powers, the notion did not seem at all far-fetched. Detroit already had issued its invitation, and now a promoter from Chicago circulated among the governors, stirring the same pot that Bellamy and Christopherson were tending for South Dakota. The South Dakota boosters also met a newspaper publisher from Sault Ste. Marie, Michigan, who had begun his own quixotic campaign to attract the UN to the Upper Peninsula.[9]

It was no wonder, then, that the governors unanimously approved Sharpe's resolution calling for the UN headquarters to be placed in the United States. In that sense, the South Dakota strategy succeeded. But in the peaceful confines of Mackinac Island, the South Dakotans and their newfound colleagues had unfurled the idea of the UN headquarters in the midst of the nation's most ambitious and successful politicians, each of them focused on his state's place in the postwar world. Any governor who harbored hopes for a United Nations headquarters in his state could now see that vigorous action would be needed to combat the competition. The territorial governor of Hawaii, Ingram M. Stainback, succeeded in amending Sharpe's resolution so that it did not limit the UN possibilities to the "continental" United States. "I think Hawaii would be a good place for the headquarters," he said. Add one more contender to the contest to become the Capital of the World.[10]

For the folks back in South Dakota, Sharpe put the best possible face on the situation. "The more the merrier," he said. "We've got something in the Black Hills that none of the others can duplicate and we aren't worried about competition. We knew we'd have a lot of it before we started our campaign." Indeed, the South Dakota strategy had primed an expanding competition among world capital hopefuls large and small.[11]

SAULT STE. MARIE

Whatever made George A. Osborn, the 61-year-old publisher of the *Evening News* of Sault Ste. Marie, Michigan, think that his little town should be the Capital of the World?

During April and May, reports from San Francisco had clattered into the *Evening News* office by Teletype, including speculation that the UN might favor a U.S.-Canadian border location. The wire services also reported on the unusual lobbying in San Francisco on behalf of the Black Hills, complete with a photograph of Paul Bellamy puffing on cigars with Saudi Arabian royalty. If the UN could consider such an interior location as Rapid City, South Dakota, then why not the two Sault St. Maries, adjacent border towns in Michigan and Ontario?[12]

The UN and its potential also were matters of concern and conversation among members of George Osborn's extended family. At the end of March

1945, Osborn's nephew, U.S. Army corporal Chase S. Osborn III, had written home from a hospital bed in Europe as he looked forward to rejoining the Seventh Army in its final advance through Germany. Aware that politicians and diplomats were laying the groundwork for peace, the soldier reflected on harrowing experiences and the tragedy of war. He could not shake the memory of Anzio, the Allies' surprise landing behind enemy lines in Italy more than a year before. He had tried to save the life of a friend there, but the soldier had died in his arms. "I wondered what his mother would think if she really knew what an unnecessary thing—what a useless thing it was for her son to die, and all the other sons," Osborn wrote home to his wife. He had stayed with the body in a dugout for three days, in hiding from the Germans and determined to keep the remains out of the rain. "The tragic waste of it is appalling and I know we can't afford another—we can never afford one," Osborn lamented. "Soldiers know that better than anyone and it is up to us or some of us to see that our government or any other government does not forget that—and the time to avoid another war is now and in the next few years—not twenty years from now." George Osborn's newspaper published the soldier's call to action a few weeks later, just prior to the UN's first gathering in San Francisco.[13]

For the people of the "Soo," the Second World War left no doubt about their region's significance in the world. The war had revived shipping in the Great Lakes, especially at this point where freighters carried iron ore out of the northern ranges, through the massive locks, toward the steel mills of the industrial Midwest. As much as the people of San Francisco and Philadelphia, the residents of the two Sault Ste. Maries considered themselves to be potential targets for the enemy. Many adults could remember that during the Great War in 1915, Canadian authorities had arrested a German citizen for drawing and mailing to Germany detailed plans of bridges, railroads, and other strategic sites in the Upper Peninsula. Now, the neighbors of the locks feared that German warplanes might fly over the polar route from Europe and try to take out this vital gateway for the iron ore so essential to the Allied war effort. The U.S. War Department thought the Nazis capable of dropping paratroopers to capture control of the locks, and the arrival of U.S. military police and army troops seemed to prove the danger. The importance of the passageway increased during the war with construction of the new MacArthur lock, joining the three "Soo Locks" already in service. More than 522 million tons of iron ore shipped through the Great Lakes during the war, 90 percent of it moving between the two towns named Sault Ste. Marie.[14]

Midway through the UN conference in San Francisco—around the same time that the prospectors for Philadelphia and the Black Hills were circulating among the diplomats—Osborn published his first editorials promoting Sault Ste. Marie as the site for what he called the "Peace Temple." From the perspective of the Upper Peninsula, the United Nations seemed on one hand to be a logical extension of an internationalism inspired by the U.S.-Canadian border, "where good will and a better understanding among nations has not only been preached but practiced." But the argument for Sault Ste. Marie, similar to the case being advanced by the Black Hills, also showed how expectations for postwar air travel were reshaping ideas about location and distance. The prospect allowed Osborn to imagine his town "at the crossroads of future world air travel, over the pole to Russia, over the north Pacific to China and Japan; over the North Atlantic to Europe"—a claim that might be made by any locality in the northern United States. In fact, unbeknownst to Osborn, a similar argument was being floated in upstate New York by the publisher of the *Niagara Falls Gazette*, who also saw his two peaceful border towns, Niagara Falls in New York and in Ontario, as ideal for the UN. There, too, the Niagara Falls publisher noted "every advantage in the way of accessibility, transportation and communication." In Niagara Falls during the summer of 1945, the world capital idea drew its momentum from a cross-border alliance of powerful business leaders and government officials. In smaller and more remote Sault Ste. Marie, the improbable dream gained strength as a highly personal crusade.[15]

Even the most ardent Sault Ste. Marie boosters acknowledged how ridiculous they might appear—the mayor of the Michigan town warned his Canadian neighbors to expect "plenty of horse laughs"—but it seemed that there was nothing to lose and everything to gain. By the first week of June, the city council of Sault Ste. Marie, Michigan, endorsed the UN idea, and the mayor sent an invitation directly to Secretary of State Edward Stettinius in San Francisco. By the middle of June, the Canadian Soo joined in the campaign, and the boosters invited President Truman to visit and consider their invitation if he came to the Governors' Conference on Mackinac Island (he did not). By July, Osborn was mingling among the governors to promote the cause.[16]

As the campaign moved forward, its promoters came to see more and more reasons why the UN should take their invitation seriously. It seemed that they had earned the honor with their contributions to the war effort, and furthermore, their history now seemed to point inevitably to their future as Capital of the World. In keeping with common practices among tourism and business promoters, they explained the region's history as unique and especially well suited for the prize they pursued. The two Sault St. Maries were "the twin Mothers of the Northwest and the Middle West civilizations in America," their mayors wrote in a joint letter to Stettinius and the prime minister of Canada, W. L. Mackenzie King. "They are situated on an undefended frontier 3,000 miles long which has been without war for more than 125 years," since the War of 1812 between the United States and Great Britain. "The atmosphere for peace is supreme here." Like the boosters of the Black Hills, the people of Sault Ste. Marie placed themselves at the center of everything that mattered, in the "central position on the continent at the heart of the Great Lakes country, the bread basket and arsenal of democracy," all of which pointed to "fertile ground where the roots of world peace would thrive everlastingly." Like the promoters of San Francisco, the people of Sault Ste. Marie portrayed themselves with a "cosmopolitan complexion, embracing many of the nationalities of the United Nations." By this, they meant people of European descent, from the original French and English settlers to the more recent immigrants who worked in the region's mines and lumber camps. The mayors did not mention it, but for the first time, the Second World War also had given Sault Ste. Marie a significant population of African Americans, the 168 soldiers in the army's 100th Coast Artillery, which guarded the safe passage of iron ore through the locks.[17]

To promote their strong convictions, the boosters of Sault Ste. Marie looked forward to enlisting the support of their most well-known and well-connected citizen, George Osborn's father, the former governor of Michigan Chase Salmon Osborn. At the age of eighty-five, Chase Osborn—one of the last great pioneers of the Midwest, the newspapers sometimes said—was a legendary, beloved eccentric who divided his time between a log cabin on Duck Island near Sault Ste. Marie and an equally rustic winter camp in Georgia. He had championed numerous causes for the Upper Peninsula over the course of his long life, which began in rural Indiana but led him to wealth and prominence in Michigan as an iron-ore prospector, newspaper publisher, politician, and philanthropist. He had seen such great change in his lifetime, from railroads to automobiles and telegraphs to telephones, that he believed travelers of the future might be whisked by vacuum tubes across the United States in a mere three hours. Such a well-known and forward-looking figure seemed to be the ideal champion for Sault Ste. Marie as Capital of the World, and to all outward appearances in 1945, he seemed to be leading the charge.[18]

There was just one problem: at the same moment that Sault Ste. Marie leapt into the competition, the great and once-powerful Osborn lay near death and could not possibly spearhead a new campaign. He came home to Sault Ste. Marie in July 1945 on a stretcher after a fall at his cabin in Georgia and subsequent complications from a broken hip. Suffering from what he called "creeping paralysis" and failing vision, he showed little interest in correspondence or his weekly column in the newspaper now run by his son George. Oddly, though, high-energy appeals to the United Nations poured from Sault Ste. Marie under the name of Governor Chase Osborn. The illusion resulted from the actions of the governor's caregiver, Stellanova Osborn, who remained out of the spotlight but gave voice to the campaign.

In later life Stellanova Osborn became a leader in the Atlantic Union Movement, which proposed a confederation among western democracies, but she credited the world capital campaign of 1945 as the beginning of her career in world affairs. Even before the United Nations campaign, she had lived a life with international dimensions. Born to English parents in Hamilton, Ontario, in 1894, Stella Lee Brunt felt an early allegiance to Queen Victoria; she spent summers in the United States with family members in New Jersey and as a young woman briefly pursued an acting career in New York. At the University of Michigan, where she studied literature and aspired to become a poet, she formed a lifelong friendship with a Japanese-American student from Seattle.[19]

While still a student in 1921, Stella Brunt first came in contact with Chase Osborn; he was sixty-one years old and she was twenty-eight, older than most students because she had done office work and tried acting before finding her way to college. She was delighted when the former governor donated five thousand dollars to bring the poet Robert Frost to campus for a full academic year, so much so that she wrote Osborn a letter of thanks. He replied, a correspondence between them continued, and eventually they met in person. Brunt became Osborn's full-time secretary and hoped to become his wife. But Osborn, who was separated from his wife, with whom he had seven children, said he did not believe in divorce. Instead, in 1931 he proposed adoption, an unusual arrangement that satisfied "appearances," Stella later explained, and remained their legal relationship until after the original Mrs. Osborn died, in 1948. At Osborn's request,

Stellanova Osborn, pictured in 1949, launched a career as a citizen activist in international affairs with her determination to make Sault Ste. Marie the Capital of the World. (Stellanova Osborn Papers, Bentley Historical Library, University of Michigan)

Stella became "Stellanova," meaning "new star." In 1933, two years after the adoption, she became an American citizen.[20]

By 1945, as long-time secretary, literary collaborator, and daughter, Stellanova Osborn remained the former governor's constant companion. Together they published two massive books about the borderland of the Upper Peninsula. *Conquest of a Continent* (1939) traced the history of the long-peaceful border between the United States and Canada. The internationalist outlook that led to Stellanova's later career as a citizen activist was apparent in descriptions of the border as "one of the wonders of the world, with more of a sentiment and power to stir the imagination than the Great Wall of China." The Osborns predicted that the continuing integration of the world would lead to a United North America, governed in cooperation by English-speaking people in the United States and Canada. While looking outward to the world, however, the Osborns remained vigorous defenders and boosters of local heritage. Their next major work, in 1942, sought to boost the region's reputation by defending the local origins of the legendary tales of Hiawatha.[21]

As the Sault Ste. Marie campaign to lure the United Nations gathered steam during the summer of 1945, Chase Osborn's name appeared on letters and speeches, and his endorsement attracted attention to an idea that otherwise might have been dismissed out of hand. But out of the public eye, his son George and moreover his adopted daughter and literary collaborator propelled the campaign.[22] For Stellanova, the cause stirred ambition and excitement that she had not felt since her college days, and it relieved the stress and tedium of nursing an old man in grave health. The former governor rebounded somewhat, and he lived four years longer. He did not discourage Stella's dedication to the Sault Ste. Marie cause, but neither did he see any hope of success. Earlier in 1945, in fact, he had told a friend in Georgia that he liked the locals' idea of locating the UN in Warm Springs, as a memorial to Franklin Roosevelt. Nevertheless, through the late summer and early fall of 1945, speeches and letters by "Chase Osborn" crafted an elaborate vision of a United Nations home on Sugar Island, situated in the St. Marys River not far from the Osborn summer camp. In one of these emphatic missives, Osborn—more likely Stella than Chase, whose name appeared as author—declared, "Only once in the lifetime of the earth, perhaps, its capital is to be chosen: NOW." The rhetoric escalated to stress international urgency as well as the many benefits to be found in Sault Ste. Marie.[23]

In the Osborn vision, interpreted through drawings by Ed Kreiger of the U.S. Corps of Engineers, the UN would occupy a world-capital compound both modern and rooted in regional history and folklore. Sugar Island would be outfitted with its own airport, sea plane base, and steamer dock. Bridges and tunnels would connect with the mainland United States and Canada. The roads from both countries would meet in a traffic circle, then continue jointly toward a United Nations Center, a modern building with a tall office tower flanked by semicircular wings. Inside that building, the peace keepers would draw strength from *The Song of Hiawatha*, the "world epic of international cooperation" and the subject of the 697-page book the Osborns had published in 1942. The UN delegates would be surrounded by murals of Hiawatha and take inspiration from Longfellow's poem, first published in 1855:

> *All your strength is in your union*
> *All your danger is in discord*
> *Therefore be at peace henceforward*
> *And as brothers live together.*

Like others of their generations, Stella and Chase Osborn shared Longfellow's romantic vision of Native American culture, but around this envisioned "temple of peace," the landscape preserved the names and landmarks of conquerors as well as the indigenous people of the Upper Peninsula. Even if the U.S.-Canadian border symbolized peaceful cooperation, the line negotiated between the Americans and the British also had settled the "conquest of the continent," to borrow the title of the Osborns' book. Place names such as St. Marys River and Sault Ste. Marie, marking the region as Christian and European, were fully in keeping with the Osborns' view of the world but far removed from the Native American cultures that preceded the French and English into the Great Lakes region.[24]

Sault Ste. Marie, together with other world capital hopefuls around the Great Lakes, added to the developing and contradictory vision of what a Capital of the World might be. Like the architects who created speculative plans for San Francisco, boosters in this region emphasized that a secure future required not only fine hotel rooms, spacious meeting halls, and dependable transportation, but also inspiring surroundings. Promoting their natural environment, they stressed the soothing qualities of water and especially the suitability of islands as secluded sanctuaries from the

A plan for Sugar Island near Sault Ste. Marie (created by Ed Kreiger of the U.S. Corps of Engineers) simultaneously looked forward and backward in time by envisioning a modern,

high-rise office building with an interior decorated with inscriptions from Henry Wadsworth Longfellow's poems of the legendary Hiawatha. (United Nations Archives)

Niagara Falls boosters envisioned a "capital" for the world as a stylized adaptation of Washington, D.C., placed on nearby Navy Island. Like the site plan for Sault Ste. Marie, this prospective capital anticipated visitors arriving from both the United States and

Canada and merging symbolically into one united traffic circle with a monument in the center. (Library of Congress)

turmoil of cities and the world. Yet the plans produced in Sault Ste. Marie, as well as a similar scheme developed for an island site near Niagara Falls, also staked out connections with the modern world with transportation facilities for automobiles and airplanes. In pastoral settings, the imagined island capitals featured mid- to high-rise buildings, suggesting that the United Nations would require an urban architecture even if it existed on a remote island. The Niagara Falls plan, by an uncredited architect, introduced additional complications by interpreting the world capital as a stylized version of Washington, D.C., with midrise office buildings flanking a central mall, an obelisk like the Washington Monument, and a circular structure recalling the U.S. Capitol dome. This offered a strongly national, and particularly American, perspective despite booster promises of internationalism along the U.S.-Canadian border. Local, national, and international interests would have to be reconciled if the Capital of the World idea were to be transformed from abstraction to reality.[25]

CHICAGO

The largest of the Great Lakes cities, Chicago had long established its place as a crossroads of the United States and the world. On the southwest shore of Lake Michigan, Chicago grew to importance in the era of the steam locomotive, then stood proudly and firmly as the nation's second-largest city in the age of diesel. Railroad lines from the east terminated in Chicago; lines headed west began there. Because of the railroads, Chicago became a destination for immigrants from Europe, for lumber from the north woods, and for cattle shipped from the west to the Union Stock Yard. The railroads brought millions of visitors to the World's Columbian Exposition in 1893, dazzling not only for the exhibit halls, the midway, and the introduction of the Ferris wheel but also for the city itself, impressively rebuilt since the disastrous Chicago Fire of 1871. At this hub of the railroads, Montgomery Ward and the Sears Roebuck Company pioneered mail-order merchandising, which changed habits of life and spending across the country. During the First World War, the railroads brought African American migrants who fled racial oppression in the South to fill factory jobs left behind by men who had gone to war. During the Great Depression, the rails brought job seekers and the desperately indigent, who built shantytowns beyond the skyscrapers of the famous business district, the Loop. Visitors came also for the Century of Progress Exposition of 1933–34, a lakefront escape from troubled times. And now, during the Second World War, the railroads placed Chicago at the center of the constant movement of soldiers, war production workers, and manufactured goods for the troops.[26]

With its strong tradition of self-promotion, integral role in the war effort, and a Democratic mayor closely tied to FDR, this Midwest metropolis was in many ways poised to join the pursuit of the United Nations. Yet there were obstacles. Chicago boosters struggled constantly against the darker aspects of their city's reputation, which seemed permanently stained by memories of disastrous fires, violent strikes, and notorious gangsters. By the 1930s, these images gained an extended life in pulp fiction and in movies featuring Al Capone–like characters shooting it out in the streets of Chicago.[27] The notion of Chicago as an international capital also flew in the face of the city's strong tradition of isolationism, which was reinforced every day in the pages of the powerful *Chicago Tribune*. Chicago was the birthplace of the America First Committee, which worked to keep the United States out of the Second World War. The city did have some internationalists—notably Adlai Stevenson and others who formed a local chapter of the Committee to Defend America by Aiding the Allies—but any question of foreign affairs raised in Chicago prompted strong arguments in favor of national interest over global cooperation. Furthermore, the city's many ethnic communities held allegiances to their homelands as well as the United States. Irish Americans in Chicago supported Franklin Roosevelt, but the nationalists among them balked at his pro-British policies. The unsettled status of Poland at the end of World War II made Chicago, the home of the largest Polish-American population in the United States, a potentially tense environment for the United Nations. Fear that the Soviet Union would dominate postwar Poland was an intense and loudly debated local issue, not just a matter of distant diplomacy.[28]

None of this stopped the international ambitions of Mayor Edward J. Kelly, who rose through the ranks of the city parks and sanitation departments to become Chicago's ambassador to the world.

Kelly, sixty-nine years old, the son of Irish and German immigrants, had taken office in 1933, the same year that Franklin Delano Roosevelt became president of the United States. (His predecessor, Anton Cermak, was killed by a bullet intended for FDR in an assassination attempt in Miami, Florida.) Kelly came to prominence through the ranks of the Democratic Party machine. In Chicago at the turn of the century, his patronage positions in parks and sanitation were far from mundane assignments. The World's Columbian Exposition inspired a nationwide enthusiasm for creating parks, plazas, and boulevards as antidotes to urban life. Kelly rose to the challenge by transforming a lakeside dump near the Loop into Grant Park, a landscaped lakeside front lawn for the city, with the ornate Buckingham Memorial Fountain as its centerpiece. His reputation as the "Father of the Lakefront" carried forward into his first term as mayor, when he presided over the Century of Progress Exposition on Northerly Isle, a peninsula created from landfill adjacent to Grant Park.[29]

Kelly worked hard for Chicago. During the Depression, he pulled in New Deal funds from the federal government, and he delivered votes to keep Franklin Roosevelt in office. The mayor loved his president—"Roosevelt is my religion," he said in campaign speeches during the 1930s—and FDR welcomed Kelly into his inner circle in return. Three times out of four, Roosevelt accepted his nominations for the presidency in Chicago. The close connections between Chicago and the federal government carried over into wartime. Along with Chicago manufacturers, Kelly lobbied for government contracts, and he succeeded. Like Detroit and other industrial centers across the United States, Chicago became one of the nation's "arsenals of democracy" and embarked on a record-setting barrage of factory construction to meet the needs of the military. Kelly, meanwhile, personally took charge of the city's civil defense, organizing Chicagoans into disciplined units of fire wardens, air raid wardens, and scrap collectors.[30]

On June 29, 1945, three days after the UN adjourned, the day before the nation's governors began their cruise up Lake Huron toward their annual meeting, Mayor Kelly called a press conference to unveil his new ambition for Chicago. Even the isolationist *Tribune* could not overlook the enormity of the mayor's proposal—that Chicago should become the permanent headquarters city for the diplomats of the world. The mayor outlined criteria for the future world capital in terms of geography, population, and politics. As paraphrased by the *Tribune*, Kelly argued that "from a geographical standpoint, Chicago is the most conveniently located of all cities equipped to serve as an international headquarters. . . . It is the western hemisphere's greatest rail and highway center, and is destined to become the world's greatest air transportation terminal after the war." The city's population also marked it as a suitable world capital because "Chicago, more than any other city in the world, is a human melting pot," the mayor argued. The city's masses of immigrants, which had seemed quite dangerous to native Chicagoans in earlier times, now became an asset. The world could come to Chicago, because the world was already there. "Here," Kelly said, "representatives of the United Nations would find the children and grandchildren of their own nationals, proving by their living example that peace and understanding can replace war and hate."[31]

Without a trace of irony, the mayor praised his city as "a vivid example of the actual working of the democratic process, which the united nations are banded to foster." In fact Kelly, according to the historian who has studied him most, stood at the head of "the most powerful—and probably the most infamous—political machine in the nation." In promoting his UN idea, Kelly boasted that political conventions in Chicago had nominated Abraham Lincoln as well as Franklin Delano Roosevelt for the presidency. Just as naturally, the mayor omitted the story of Roosevelt's precedent-breaking third nomination in 1940, which had been helped along artificially by chants of "We want Roosevelt! Everyone wants Roosevelt!" led by the Chicago superintendent of sewers, who was stationed in the basement of the convention hall with a microphone.[32]

By the middle of July, Kelly put together an elaborated invitation to the United Nations for the approval of the Chicago City Council, which obliged by voting unanimously on July 17 to invite the diplomats of the world to the shores of Lake Michigan.[33]

The UN headquarters that Kelly imagined would be on the lakefront—specifically, on Northerly Isle, which had already served as a world capital of sorts during the Century of Progress Exposition of 1933–34. The "Isle" was not an island, strictly speaking, but a man-made peninsula linked to the mainland by a short causeway. The national pavilions, the midway, and the international villages had been dismantled, leaving a site offering the best possible view of Lake Michigan. One of the architects of the fair's buildings—Charles Morgan, an associate of Frank Lloyd Wright—produced drawings to envision a lakefront Capital of the World. His plan retained some elements of a world's fair, such as an "Avenue of Nations" for buildings from each of the member nations, a museum, and a building devoted to science and research. The proposal also left in place landmarks and cultural amenities such as Soldier Field, the Chicago Museum of Natural History, and the Shedd Aquarium, which had been developed prior to the Century of Progress and therefore constituted part of the landscape of the fair.

Like other early visions for the UN's headquarters, Morgan's plan displayed an ambivalence about cities as it stressed both closeness and separation from the urban core. His renderings depicted the UN buildings in the foreground, with the background fading into a hazy suggestion of the

Like earlier plans for a San Francisco headquarters, Charles Morgan's plan for a UN complex on Northerly Isle displayed ambivalence about cities as it displayed the UN buildings in the foreground with the buildings of the Loop appearing as a hazy suggestion in the background. Key to numbers on plan: (1) Administration Building; (2) Auditorium and commission meeting halls;

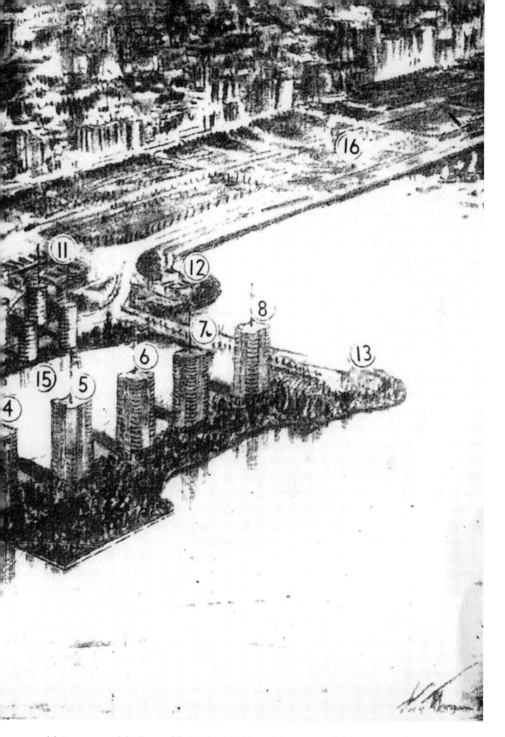

(3) Restaurant; (4) Library; (5) Archives Building; (6) Museum; (7) Press and Information Building; (8) Research and Scientific Building; (9) Avenue of Nations, with a building for each of the member nations; (10) Soldier Field; (11) Chicago Natural History Museum; (12) Shedd Aquarium; (13) Adler Planetarium; (14) Seaplane landing base; (15) Small craft harbor; (16) Buckingham Fountain. (*Chicago Herald-American*)

buildings of the Loop and beyond. Yet to a large degree, Morgan's plan transplanted the city to Northerly Isle as it envisioned a dense complex of modern skyscrapers. As imagined in Chicago, diplomats would have a scenic waterfront view, but they would work in a small city created specially for them.[34]

NEW HORIZONS

The United Nations Charter, bound in blue with a gold seal, traveled from San Francisco to Washington by plane in a 75-pound safe accompanied by the conference secretary-general, Alger Hiss. Scarcely more than a week after the closing ceremonies in San Francisco, on July 2, President Truman personally delivered the document to his former colleagues in the Senate. In contrast to the fight over the League of Nations a generation before, ratification of the United Nations Charter appeared certain. The experience of a second, even more deadly war within the lifetimes of most American political leaders had produced a more international outlook that crossed party lines. Franklin Roosevelt had crafted support for the United Nations by appointing leaders of both major political parties to the UN's first meeting, and his State Department had cultivated favorable public opinion by teaching Americans to regard the UN Charter as the equivalent of the United States Constitution on an international scale.[35]

Even committed nationalists who disliked parts of the charter acknowledged the need for a world organization to prevent future war. Republican senator Harlan J. Bushfield of South Dakota—one of the few political leaders in his state who had not been drawn into the Black Hills booster campaign—had reservations about the document but announced he would support it. "I dare not face my soldier son if I fail to do what I can to stop the senseless maniacal slaughter of my fellow man," he said as the Senate hearings began during the second week of July. Opponents came to the hearings to argue that the charter threatened U.S. sovereignty, or that it did not go far enough to establish world government, or that it did not properly acknowledge the hand of God in world events. But support far outweighed dissent. On July 28, 1945, the United States Senate ratified the United Nations Charter by a vote of eighty-nine to two.[36]

San Francisco, meanwhile, felt very, very quiet after its two exciting months on the world stage, and Mayor Roger Lapham grew anxious about his city's future with the UN. Not only were Philadelphia and South Dakota lobbying for the UN, but following the Governors' Conference, contenders emerged around the country. Some of them seemed silly, but others, such as Chicago, posed real competition. President Truman inadvertently inspired two new world capital suggestions when he traveled home to Independence, Missouri, and accepted an honorary law degree from the University of Kansas City. Along with praising Truman, the university's president suggested that the UN should take a look at Kansas City. Then, in Jackson County, where Truman served his political apprenticeship, the locals stirred with the notion that Truman's home county would make an excellent world capital. Truman stopped that idea in its tracks. But other invitations were on their way to the UN's next meeting place, in London, suggesting that the diplomats might like Baltimore, Maryland, or Baguio in the Philippines.[37]

Among the business and political leaders of San Francisco, it was beginning to seem that their subtle strategy of charming the United Nations with gracious hospitality might not be nearly enough. On July 17, the day the Chicago City Council issued its invitation to the UN, Lapham reached out to the friend who had gotten him into this predicament in the first place—Edward Stettinius, the former secretary of state. Although removed from his prestigious cabinet position, Stettinius had been awarded the consolation of representing the United States at the UN when it next convened, in London in the fall. Surely, he would still be in a position to help San Francisco. "Dear Ed," the mayor of San Francisco wrote delicately to the former secretary of state. "I have been asked by various people when, where, and how is the site of the United Nations headquarters going to be determined. . . . If you feel free to furnish me any information, of course I will be glad to have it."[38]

Ironically, and unknown to the mayor, the birthplace of the new world peace organization also was serving as the point of departure for the Allies' newest and most destructive weapon of war. In San Francisco Bay on July 16, 1945, in utmost secrecy, the warship USS *Indianapolis* accepted dangerous and delicate cargo. One large crate and one small metal cylinder held most of the parts required for the first deployment of the atomic bomb—all but the Uranium-235 needed for nuclear fission. Almost immediately, the *Indianapolis* sailed for Hawaii, and then to Tinian in the Mariana Islands, the busy airbase captured from the Japanese in 1944. Since March, American B-29 bombers had been taking off from the Marianas for night firebombing missions over Japan, in one night alone igniting as much as sixteen square miles of Tokyo and killing as many as one hundred thousand Japanese. On Tinian, the secret weapon would be assembled and dispatched to its target, the industrial city of Hiroshima. On July 26, the Allies issued an ultimatum to the Japanese: surrender unconditionally or risk destruction by air, sea, and land.[39]

The first atomic bomb plummeted toward Hiroshima on August 6, 1945, from an American B-29 Superfortress bomber named after the pilot's mother, Enola Gay. With an explosion two thousand feet above the city, a flash, a fireball, and a giant cloud like a mushroom, one hundred thousand people instantly died. American forces exploded a second bomb over Nagasaki three days later. The atomic bombs had their desired effect of forcing the surrender of Japan on August 14, 1945. After seven years of violence (four for the United States) and an estimated fifty-five million military and civilian deaths, peace came to a violent world—except, ironically enough, in San Francisco. More than one hundred thousand soldiers, sailors, and marines were stationed in the Bay Area at the moment that they learned of Emperor Hirohito's capitulation. As they swarmed into San Francisco, their jubilation turned first to mayhem and then to destruction. Drunken young civilians joined in three nights of rampage. The "victory riot," as the newspapers called it, left five people dead, five hundred in the hospital, numerous shattered storefronts, and more broken glass on Market Street than anyone could remember since the Great Earthquake of 1906. Rioters molested women, overturned cars, looted liquor stores, and smashed into the glass door of City Hall with a flagpole. For this city, the final military maneuver of World War II came on the night after the Japanese surrender, when three thousand city and military police dispersed the mob and the navy ordered all of its personnel back to base.[40]

In the aftermath of the atomic bomb, Americans found themselves unexpectedly and unavoidably involved in a new world of exhilarating and frightening prospects. Cities and towns across the United States learned that they had contributed to the war's violent end. Local newspapers reported that the pilot who dropped the first atomic bomb, Paul Tibbets Jr., had attended Southside grammar school in Miami. Two scientists from Tulane University in New Orleans had recruited technicians for the bomb project laboratories and conducted advanced research that made the bomb possible. Faculty and students at Washington University in St. Louis had done bomb-related research using the university's sixty-thousand-dollar cyclotron. Parents in Cincinnati learned that their sons and sons-in-law had worked in the bomb-making plants in Oak Ridge, Tennessee, and Los Alamos, New Mexico. Five hundred boiler makers, sheet metal workers, truck drivers, and clerks had been recruited for the project from Wisconsin. The

Allis-Chalmers Company in Milwaukee and the Hooker Electrochemical Company in Niagara Falls, New York, among other firms, acknowledged major, but still secret, roles.[41]

As the world pivoted from war to peace, Americans were united in victory, stirring with plans for the future, and anxious about the looming threat of nuclear weapons. Mayors and postwar planning groups pulled out their blueprints for new airports, highways, parks, and housing developments. Governors escalated services for returning veterans, and chambers of commerce launched membership drives to shore up the business community's conversion to a peacetime economy. Tourism promoters happily braced for the return of leisure travel following the end of gas rationing. But these bursts of activism and optimism proceeded with the understanding of a new reality, that cities and towns could be obliterated by an atomic bomb dropped from an airplane. Knowing of the targets selected in Japan, major industrial cities in the United States calculated their risks. Newspapers published maps showing the potential loss of life and property if an atomic bomb hit an American city. In the postwar era, few localities would stand separately and safely isolated from the world. All had a stake in the peace—and, therefore, in the success of the United Nations.[42]

All of this created a climate quite suitable for nurturing additional ideas about creating a Capital of the World and inspired new strategies among contenders already in the fray. In Rapid City, South Dakota, Paul Bellamy felt new confidence in his personal postwar mission. During the summer, his neighbors voted him Man of the Year in a contest sponsored by the Rushmore Mutual Life Insurance Company. Accepting the award less than a year after his son's death, he reminded his neighbors, "It is our responsibility as leaders in our community . . . to see that these men did not die in vain." He looked forward to doing his part by continuing the Black Hills booster campaign, and after Hiroshima and Nagasaki, it occurred to him: Who would possibly want to bomb the Black Hills of South Dakota? Wouldn't this make the hills an especially appealing place for the Capital of the World? Local interests and international affairs seemed inseparable as the world emerged from war in the shadow of new threats of destruction.[43]

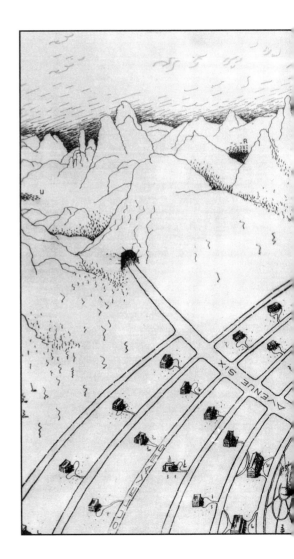

PART II

THE NEW WORLD

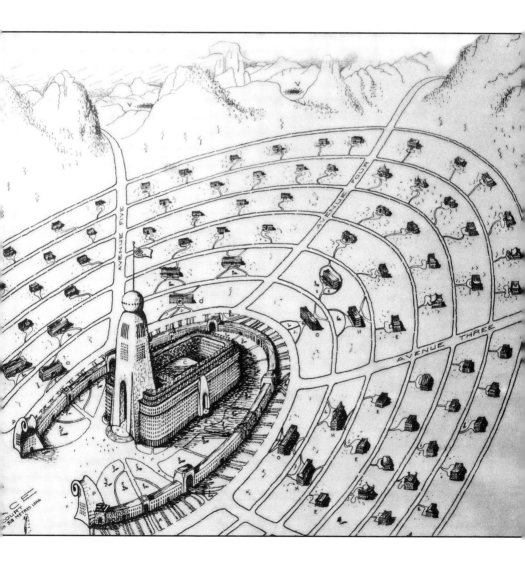

Featuring booster slogans on billboards, a syndicated cartoon depicts the onslaught of interest in the United Nations headquarters decision during the autumn of 1945. (Associated Press)

4

BLITZ

THE COMPETITION TO BECOME the Capital of the World—which no one had announced—reached London in the fall of 1945 with a bombardment of invitations that no one had solicited: a resolution from the town board of Hyde Park, New York! A letter from the chamber of commerce of Beloit, Wisconsin! Promotional brochures from Boston, St. Louis, Miami, and Newport, Rhode Island! Petitions from Claremore, Oklahoma, and suggestions from Saratoga, Valley Forge, Monticello, and Williamsburg. Bizarre communications signed by Chase Osborn of "Possum Poke in Possum Lane," somewhere in Georgia. Site plans from South Dakota and photographs from Philadelphia. Starting with a smattering of five suggested capitals in September, the proposed locations increased by thirteen in October, seventeen more in November, and then a torrent of eighty-five in December. A few suggestions arrived for locations outside the United States, but most of the correspondence came from American public officials, publishers, business leaders, or other individuals promoting their own hometowns.

All of this descended on the desk of Gladwyn Jebb, a career British diplomat overseeing the London meetings of the United Nations Preparatory Commission, the group of delegates designated to take the next steps in launching the UN. Jebb had served alongside Churchill at Yalta and at the more recent Big Three conference at Potsdam in Germany, and he had worked toward the UN's creation at Dumbarton Oaks and San Francisco. As executive secretary for the Preparatory Commission, he was nurturing an already cumbersome bureaucracy toward more stable and permanent operations. Amid such pressing concerns as refugees displaced by the war, the fates of colonies and empires, and the new power of the atomic bomb, the mail kept arriving from the United States. Not only that, but the American civic boosters also were preparing to advance from the west by air and sea, aiming to personally pitch their uninvited proposals to the United Nations, an organization so fundamentally diplomatic that it could neither object nor resist. The boosters would not take "no" for an answer—and conveniently for them, "no" did not seem to be in the diplomatic vocabulary.

Despite their common interests in securing a peaceful future for the world, the perspectives and cultures of boosterism and diplomacy were fundamentally at odds. The boosters were impatient dreamers who worked in the realm of snappy slogans and Main Street parades. The diplomats were striving to create a world organization that was new, yet built upon time-honored and time-consuming rituals of private meetings, meticulous memos, and deliberative debates. The gulf between these cultures became clear as boosters and diplomats wrestled with the question of how to locate the "center" of the world at a time of political power struggles and changing ideas of distance, space, and time.

In contrast with the boosters' visions of a pristine capital symbolizing peace, the scars of war remained visible in the streets, buildings, and people of London. While Americans had worried about imaginary bombs dropping on the Liberty Bell, the locks at Sault Ste. Marie, or the Golden Gate Bridge, the British had experienced thundering destruction. London alone weathered 354 attacks from 1940 through 1945; nearly thirty thousand people died in the capital city, fifty thousand more were seriously wounded, and vast expanses of the urban landscape were pummeled into ruin. While Londoners took cover in home bomb shelters, trenches, and the Underground subway, the Luftwaffe's bombs obliterated thousands of homes and treasured churches that had stood for centuries. Great symbols of British nationhood and empire—even Buckingham Palace—suffered hits, but survived. Westminster Abbey and nearby buildings that the British regarded as "the centre of the political and spiritual life of England" still stood, and now they provided the backdrop for the next step in postwar security. The UN Preparatory Commission moved into offices in Church House, the Church of England's four-story brick office building next to Westminster Abbey.[1]

The first wave of diplomats to arrive in London consisted of members of the Preparatory Commission's Executive Committee—fourteen men, selected in San Francisco so that they represented the geographic reach of the UN and the interests of both large and small nations. The rest of the Preparatory Commission would come later in the fall, after a majority of member nations ratified the UN Charter. Around the conference tables in Church House, the question of where to place the UN headquarters moved for the first time from cocktail-party chatter and secret State Department surveys onto the official agenda. The significance of the issue went beyond simply selecting a site. The organization could not come fully to life until it had a place to do so; choosing the place would be an important early test of the UN's ability to evaluate options, resolve differences, and make effective decisions.[2]

Determining the future center for world affairs was a matter of high stakes for veteran diplomats who, like many of the civic boosters, had experienced a lifetime of war and upheaval. Most of the Executive Committee members were men in their fifties and sixties who had reached adulthood in the midst of the Great War, the Mexican Revolution, or the Russian Revolution, then turned to careers in diplomatic service. They were veterans of Yalta, Dumbarton Oaks, and San Francisco. Andrei Gromyko from the Soviet Union, born in 1909, was considerably younger than the rest, having advanced in government service after more seasoned veterans were vanquished in the Stalinist purges of the 1930s. But he carried the undeniable clout of the Soviets in the emerging arena of superpower politics, which would soon harden into Cold War. The diplomats at Church House included Europeans who were formidable veterans of the League of Nations, including the tenacious British minister of state Philip Noel-Baker, who viewed Europe as the center of international affairs and was determined to keep it that way. The old hands were so rooted in tradition that they spoke of the Americas as the "New World," and their empires faced an uncertain future.[3] Latin Americans at the table, meanwhile, had little role in the league and inclined toward a new start for a new age. The Soviet Union had advised Edward Stettinius in San Francisco that it favored the United States as the UN's location, but the positions of Australia, China, and Iran remained to be seen. Where indeed was the center of the world in the aftermath of war in 1945? With so much of the Second World War fought in the Pacific, had the center shifted from Europe to the United States?[4]

Stettinius, now the United States' chief delegate to the UN, had devised a strategy that the Americans would come to regret. The United States would remain neutral on the headquarters question, not actively pursuing the honor but instead making clear that it would support the UN in any choice. By deferring in this way, the United States would enhance the authority of the new organization, at apparently little risk. Stettinius knew from the State Department's surveys that the delegates were likely to opt for the United States, especially with the Soviet Union wielding its considerable power in that direction. At a White House meeting in August, he persuaded President Truman and the new secretary of state, James F. Byrnes, that public neutrality was the best course of action. The Americans certainly wanted to see the seat of diplomacy cross the Atlantic. President Truman had warmed to the idea of historically symbolic Philadelphia, and Byrnes was mindful of the political influence of the Philadelphians as well as the Chicago campaign led by Mayor Edward Kelly. Stettinius still harbored dreams of San Francisco, but as a matter of public policy in London, he would maintain neutrality. Such a standoffish strategy not only affected the actions of diplomats but also created a vacuum of leadership and information that American civic boosters were eager to fill.[5]

The UN's deliberations about a headquarters location moved forward as a matter of international geopolitics, focused on continents and regions of the world. Still, the diplomats shared collective memories of two recent meeting places. One was San Francisco, where they had been so warmly received, fashionably housed, and comfortably seated in the War Memorial Opera House. The other was Geneva, the home of the League of Nations. Geneva had been selected in 1919 during a stormy discussion among the diplomats who were drafting the League Covenant. While representatives of France and Belgium had argued for Brussels because of its central location, communications facilities, and symbolism as a site of war, their wish was defeated by the Americans, British, and others who preferred to place the league in a neutral nation. Although the location was decided quickly, it had taken until 1936 to complete a fully operational headquarters, the Palais des Nations, a complex of white stone buildings on a five-acre site with a view toward the Alps of Savoy. Fully in use for only a few years before the outbreak of the Second World War, this palace headquarters had become a symbol of failure. The lessons of the past might serve to inspire a new world organization meeting there; but on the other hand, the surroundings of Geneva might hover too dismally over the challenges of the future.[6]

On October 3, 1945, the Executive Committee of the Preparatory Commission convened to make a recommendation on the UN location. The fact that it was a committee (of a commission), poised to make a recommendation (but not a decision), already signaled the difficulties that lay ahead for UN decision making. The multilayered organization, still in the process of inventing itself, left doors open for endless challenges on disputed issues, the headquarters choice among them.

The diplomats' positions were already well rehearsed in private conversations by the time the official debate began. Delegates from the Pacific region and Latin America argued vigorously that the United Nations should have a new start, in a new location. Victor Hoo, a career diplomat representing China on the UN's powerful Security Council, spoke from experience in such diplomatic centers as Paris, Brussels, Berlin, Berne, and Washington. In Geneva, he had been secretary-general of the Chinese delegation at the League of Nations—and he did not want the UN to go back there. "We believe that the memory of the seat where all the attempts to maintain peace have failed would influence the whole atmosphere," Hoo argued. In earlier times, "the spirit of Geneva" might have carried positive implications, but now it seemed as dismal as "the spirit of Munich," where appeasement failed to stop Hitler's armies. "So the Chinese government would favour another seat, and in another part of the world," he said. Specifically, San Francisco, in the United States, "which has done so much . . . to help the United Nations to win this war."[7]

Before Great Britain could counter with its preference for a European headquarters, a member of the British Commonwealth moved swiftly to assert its independence by supporting San Francisco. Herbert V. Evatt, representing Australia, saw his country's future linked more with the Pacific than with distant Britain, and he had championed the rights of smaller nations at the San Francisco conference. More than anyone else in the room, perhaps, Evatt knew how a new world capital might take shape. Australia had its own new capital, Canberra, created after Australia gained commonwealth status in 1901. Like the capital of the United States, it was a city designed to symbolize a new phase in the nation's history. Evatt, a legislator and judge before the war drew him into international affairs, got straight to the point. "I think it is obvious that the peoples of the world expect a fresh start to be made in world organization," he said. Not only did San Francisco have all the necessary facilities, but it promised the best conditions. "San Francisco is a city which breathes the very spirit of freedom," he said. "It is a city of progress, it looks with courage and confidence in the future."[8]

The Soviets, who had broken off diplomatic relations with Switzerland in the aftermath of the Russian Revolution, and who had been expelled from the League of Nations after invading Finland in 1939, stood firmly against Geneva. "The United States is located conveniently between Asia and Europe," Gromyko said. "The old world has had it once, and it is time for the New World to have it." Although Gromyko did not say it, a United Nations presence in Eastern Europe could be a barrier to Soviet influence and expansion. Once the Soviets stated a preference for the United States, Yugoslavia quickly joined the argument that a location in the United States would place the UN "more or less in the center of the world." For many diplomats, the center had shifted as a result of the war fought in Europe and the Pacific, with the United States lying in between.

What of Europe? "There are ruins everywhere, and even where there are no ruins, there are terrible problems," acknowledged René Massigli of France, a League of Nations veteran, who two years before had eluded capture by the Nazis in occupied Vichy. But, he argued, Europe needed to be pulled out of its ruins and nationalist preoccupations. "It is very important that Europe should be set on its feet again and that its morale should be re-established, including its faith in an international order." The UN's presence in Europe could help achieve this, he said. The location also would help to assure participation by the poorer, most damaged nations of Europe, which would find it difficult to maintain delegations in the United States.[9]

As the United Kingdom's chief representative at the Preparatory Commission, the 56-year-old British minister of state, Philip Noel-Baker, brought to the table patience and negotiating skills forged by a lifetime of international peace making and the goal-oriented steadiness of a middle-distance runner in three Olympic games. Born in England, educated in the United States and at Cambridge, Noel-Baker was a committed Quaker pacifist. During the First World War, he had volunteered for the Friends Ambulance Unit, coming away with an Italian Silver Medal for Valour and the Italian Military Cross. He served as an assistant at the Paris Peace Conference and then built his diplomatic career at the League of Nations, rising from a staff position to the status of British delegate. He wanted a ceremonial last meeting for the league, so that it might be remembered for its accomplishments and not only for its failures. If that meeting were held at the end of 1945, he reasoned, the United Nations should simply remain in Geneva to continue the work.[10]

Noel-Baker defined the center of the world in a different way, by pointing out that Geneva would be convenient to far more national capitals than San Francisco. Twenty-eight capital cities lay within two thousand miles of the center of Europe, he pointed out; within two thousand miles of San Francisco, there were none. "Europe is in fact the center of the most heavily populated area of the world," he argued. But Europe also occupied the center of Noel-Baker's world in other, less tangible ways. "Europe has been the mother of the civilizations of the New World," he said, and "the cradle and exporter of democratic government through parliamentary institutions." And so it should remain in the postwar world, Noel-Baker firmly believed.

Some of the discussion fell into contours already present in the world capital dreams of American cities and towns. Once again it became clear that ideas about distance were being reshaped by the prospects for

commercial aviation, but that individual perceptions of these changes varied widely. Some diplomats spoke about distance in terms of miles, while
others viewed proximity as a matter of time—and time could be expected
to be cut drastically as the technology of air travel improved. And as the
representative of Mexico, Luis Padilla Nervo, pointed out, communications technology also would draw distant populations closer together. The
population of Europe, said the poet-turned-diplomat, "could not be said
to be far or near the Organization according to the number of miles that
separates them from the physical place. . . . Regardless of the physical place,
they can be approached through the press and broadcasting, through
newsreels and educational films and through preaching of certain ideals."
Padilla Nervo firmly advocated the United States as "a fresh start in an atmosphere of faith and optimism."[11]

     In other respects, the UN discussion occurred in a wholly different realm from the boosterism of American cities and towns. Since the
spring, with the encouragement of local and national press, American
boosters had been spinning dreams of a Capital of the World, whether
in the shadow of Independence Hall, on the shores of Lake Michigan,
or in the city of San Francisco. Around the conference tables in Church
House in London on October 3, 1945, not a single diplomat uttered that
phrase. The debaters spoke instead of finding a place for a "seat" or a
headquarters, a place of business for world diplomacy. They developed
criteria for this headquarters that leaned toward the practical, such as auditoriums and office space, not the inspirational qualities of historic or
scenic settings.[12]

     When the votes were called, the United Kingdom and France voted
for a European headquarters. So did the delegate of the Netherlands, Jan
Van Roijen, who recalled that it had taken seven days for him to return
home from the first conference in San Francisco. The United States, despite its representative's personal affection for San Francisco, maintained
its neutrality and abstained. So did Canada, another member of the British
Commonwealth, whose delegate demurred that he did not have instructions from his government on how to vote. The rest, from Latin America
(Brazil, Chile, and Mexico), the smaller nations of Europe (Yugoslavia and
Czechoslovakia), the Pacific (Australia and China), the Soviet Union, and
Iran voted for a new start for the new organization, in the United States.[13]

     Europe's supporters were not about to give up. Noel-Baker intended to
press the question again, when the full Preparatory Commission arrived in
London in November. But to the American public reading the headlines

about the decision on October 3, it seemed that the UN had settled on the United States as the location for its headquarters—and surely that place would be the Capital of the World.

More mail headed toward the office of Gladwyn Jebb. During September, the United Nations had received invitations from Hyde Park, New York, the home of Franklin Roosevelt; Jacksonville, Florida; Saratoga Springs, New York; Beloit, Wisconsin; and Vancouver, Canada. Now, with the vote favoring the United States, the mail showed that the United Nations was becoming a high-stakes contest for American cities. Invitations arrived from New York, Denver, Miami, Salt Lake City, Honolulu, and Atlantic City. Interest on the West Coast spilled outward from San Francisco to the Moraga Valley and Monterey Peninsula. From the nation's midsection came invitations from the governor of Indiana and a state legislator recommending Tuskahoma, Oklahoma. In the East, Philadelphia's continuing campaign did not discourage an invitation from nearby Media, Pennsylvania; nor did the patriotic appeal of Independence Hall prevent the similarly symbolic Monticello, home of Thomas Jefferson, from being offered by boosters in Charlottesville, Virginia. In response to concerns about travel time, interest now stirred most of all in New England, the region of the United States geographically closest to Europe.

Promotions became increasingly elaborate. San Francisco, for example, extolled its virtues in a leather-bound book thirteen inches by eighteen inches in dimension and embossed with the seal of the city and county.[14] Hawaii sent a wood-bound "brochure" touting Honolulu. Often produced by chamber of commerce committees, these richly illustrated publications combined tourist-promotion hype about beautiful surroundings and recreational opportunities with odes to internationalism and nuts-and-bolts civic information. The boosters were trying to impress, but their salesmanship smacked of years of experience in luring tourists, conventions, or factories into their local economies.[15]

Along with the sales pitches, every missive from the United States carried an American dream—a vision for how one locality's attributes and traditions, firmly united with American ideals, warranted prominence as the center of the postwar world. While reaching toward a common goal, the world capital invitations captured the essence of many Americas, from old New England to western frontiers, from Native Americans and Puritans to more recent immigrants and strivers for commercial success. The world capital campaigns showed that the connections among local, national, and global concerns were being created in many ways, based upon histories,

Promotional "brochures" as large as this creation from San Francisco arrived by the crate load in London. Stewardess Momi Harrison is shown posing with one of the sixty albums heading to the UN by United Air Lines air express. (San Francisco History Center, San Francisco Public Library)

landmarks, or prominent citizens, by the spirit embodied in cherished ide-als, in literature, or even through Broadway musicals and the open road.

AUTUMN IN NEW ENGLAND

A belief ran deep in the northeastern states that liberty, democracy, and the essence of America had sprung from New England, a region graced with stunning scenery, mountains, lakes, and seashores. This distinctive regional identity persisted in the early twentieth century in the work of historians, decades of tourism promotion, the pages of *Yankee Magazine*, and the po-etry of Robert Frost. Town meetings continued traditions older than the nation. In Massachusetts, especially, New Englanders had reveled through the 1930s with a series of three-hundredth anniversary celebrations mark-ing the founding of the Massachusetts Bay Colony. The Second World War reinforced connections with heritage as New Englanders invoked the spirit of Revolutionary ancestors on Patriot's Day each April, and on Flag Day in June, to inspire new generations to fight for freedom.[16]

At just the right moment, Boston had a salesman in the State House. In fact, Governor Maurice J. Tobin—at age forty-four, considered something of a wonder boy in Massachusetts politics—had once dreamed of being a traveling salesman. Like Mayor Edward Kelly of Chicago, he was a son of Irish immigrants who found his niche in urban politics. After the Great Depression killed his hopes of a career in sales, he went to work for the telephone company, and as a Roosevelt Democrat with roots in the Irish neighborhoods of Boston, he moved quickly into the state legislature, the Boston School Committee, the mayor's office when he was just thirty-six years old, and the governor's office eight years later. As mayor of Boston, Tobin inherited a city in decline. The population was dropping after fifty years of record growth. Industries were leaving. The city's storied history as a seaport had faded as sailing ships gave way to steamers. Shipping in the twentieth century moved in and out of New York and San Francisco, the cities where San Francisco mayor Roger Lapham and his family had taken their business, despite their New England lineage.[17]

For eight years as mayor and continuing as governor, Tobin worked on selling Boston to industry, to potential visitors, and to the state capital's own beleaguered citizens. In a region where outlying communities were fast becoming suburbs of Boston, he promoted this "great metropolitan center" as a place to do business and as the "gateway to the beauties of New England." As mayor, he traveled to Los Angeles in 1938 to secure the

1940 national convention of the American Legion for Boston. As governor, Tobin promoted government's role in economic development and enlisted Ambassador Joseph P. Kennedy to generate support for creating a new state Department of Commerce.[18]

And now, Tobin intended to sell Boston to the United Nations. A foundation for his campaign had been in place for many years. In 1858, the writer Oliver Wendell Holmes bestowed the nickname "Hub of the Solar System" on the Massachusetts State House, but he did not mean it as a compliment. In his story "The Autocrat of the Breakfast-Table," appearing in *Atlantic Monthly*, Holmes called attention to Bostonians' tendency to see themselves at the center of the universe, casting indispensable light on lesser folk in outlying orbits. The story's narrator observed wryly that this attitude was not unique to Boston. It seemed that wherever he traveled, "The axis of the earth sticks out visibly through the centre of each and every town or city" and, "If more than fifty years have passed since its foundation, it is affectionately styled by the inhabitants the 'good old town of'—(whatever its name may happen to be)."[19]

Over time "the Hub" lost Holmes's satirical intent and found its way into booster campaigns for business and tourism. Cut down to its essence, "the Hub" served as a headline-handy abbreviation for the city itself, and the original "Hub of the Solar System" evolved into the more dramatic "Hub of the Universe." So it appeared in 1938, when the *Boston Post* published a cartoon with then-mayor Tobin serving up "Historical Boston—The Convention City" on a promotional silver platter, with a "Hub of the Universe" flag fluttering atop the State House dome.[20]

If Boston could be the Hub of the Universe, then why not—as the *Boston Globe* put it—the Hub of the World?[21]

Tobin began his quest to bring the United Nations to Boston quietly, with a telegram to President Truman on October 3, the same day that the diplomats in London recommended a United States location. Interest in bringing the UN to Boston had been building among city officials since July, and by November Tobin announced a booster coalition including presidents and professors from the city's prestigious universities, bankers with backgrounds in international finance, former diplomats from the Brahmin set, and the editor of the *Christian Science Monitor*, who had once covered the League of Nations. Echoing decades of chamber of commerce promotions, Tobin described his city to the UN as tightly integrated into global networks of communications and transportation, supportive of the new peace-keeping organization, and offering an all-around pleasant place to live and work. He pointed out that as a business center, Boston could supply capable office workers and that local publishing firms could produce documents in thirty languages. While building its own "city," the United Nations could have its pick of existing office buildings and perhaps hold Assembly sessions in Symphony Hall. Delegates and staff members could make temporary homes in hotels.[22]

The Boston boosters also rested their hopes on New England's roots in "old" England, a connection that had been enhanced by the Second World War. There had been a sense of common danger as coastal New England communities looked anxiously out to sea, knowing that they offered the closest mainland targets for German warships and submarines. When the lights went out in Britain during wartime attacks, short-wave radio broadcasts had extended voices of support across the Atlantic from "new" Boston to "old" Boston, from Taunton to Taunton, and from Gloucester to Gloucester. Sometimes the airwaves carried the voice of a child who had been removed from dangerous England to the safety of Massachusetts, to reassure parents an ocean away.[23]

With such emotional ties in recent memory, Tobin's team promoted Boston to the UN as the U.S. city geographically closest to Europe. Furthermore, according to Tobin, the housing stock in Boston included "pleasing town houses, small and large, which are reminiscent of the London squares." He described Boston's suburban railway system as operating "on the European model." Although the Massachusetts group identified the state reserve lands in the Blue Hills and at Middlesex Fells as ideal sites because of their proximity to Boston, they also noted that the headquarters could be placed close to the Longwood Cricket Club.[24]

Many Bostonians and other New Englanders continued to prize and protect British heritage, at least in part in reaction to the influx of other European groups early in the twentieth century. But in reaching out to the United Nations, Tobin and his fellow boosters also called attention to Boston's multiethnic character. As in Chicago, the city's more recent immigrant population became a selling point. The Bostonians pointed with pride to the many languages, religions, and cultural practices alive in the city. They did not, of course, include the suspicion that had been directed at Italian Americans during the war or the anti-Semitic violence that had been carried out by Irish-American youth gangs.[25]

Even as they promoted Boston as a forward-looking, international metropolis, the city's boosters reached back as far as the Mayflower Compact and the Massachusetts Constitution to offer the UN "an atmosphere in which the ideals of freedom and liberalism have long flourished." In a radio address in November, Tobin said, "The very names of Boston and Massachusetts are symbolic of man's quest for liberty based upon law, and for peace based upon justice. These in effect, are the basic ideals of the United Nations Organization." The group's promotional materials called attention to Greater Boston as a region of 152 separate communities, each with historical traditions and political independence. "One of the most truly democratic of all institutions, the New England Town Meeting, is still the basis of town government throughout the area," noted the first paragraph in the promotional booklet that the Boston group sent to the UN. A photograph of a town meeting appeared prominently in the booklet's opening pages.[26]

Within weeks of Governor Tobin's telegram to President Truman, another young politician with Irish roots developed his own dream for another New England state, Rhode Island. While Massachusetts represented Puritan heritage (despite its varied immigrant population), Congressman John E. Fogarty saw his state as a resonant alternative. Rhode Island traced its history to Roger Williams, a dissenter banished from Puritan Massachusetts for his unorthodox views. As Fogarty and other like-minded Rhode Islanders saw it, this made their state "the birthplace in America of true religious liberty." What better place for the United Nations? On October 26, 1945, the congressman wrote to Secretary of State James F. Byrnes, "The State of Rhode Island and Providence Plantations came into being because of one man's protest against the dictatorship of his day. . . . The citizens of this proud state can provide confidence and enthusiasm and inspiration to the delegates who will attend the deliberations of the United Nations Organization."[27]

Fogarty was booked the next day for a speaking engagement in Newport. The island community best known for its enormous Gilded Age mansions and the summer socializing of the very rich was a long reach from Fogarty's experience. He had grown up in grittier Providence and followed his father and older brother into the brick-laying trade. His first elective office, at age twenty-three, was president of the Bricklayers Union Number 1 of Rhode Island; but just four years later, in 1940, the labor vote helped elect him to Congress. For his impending speech to commemorate Navy Day, Fogarty was an especially apt choice. In 1944, he had quit the House temporarily to enlist in the Seabees, the navy's construction corps. Incognito among the laborers on the island of Guam, he studied the problems of enlisted men first-hand as a bricklayer, his former trade.[28]

Like Fogarty, Newport had taken on new duties in recent years. Elite summer "colonists" still migrated to the seaside resort for their social season, but the island's peak years as the undeniable center of high society were beginning to give way under the pressure of taxation, a shortage of servants, and the burdens of maintaining the enormous mansions of earlier days. The Mt. Hope Bridge to the mainland, completed in 1929, opened Newport to automobile vacationers and the convention trade. With the Second World War, Newport's seaside location gave it an increased population devoted to the military and war production work at the Newport Torpedo Station, the Naval Training Center, and the Newport Fleet Post Office, which dispatched mail to all of the Atlantic Fleet. Across the nation, when families of servicemen addressed their letters to "New York FPO," the mail actually flowed from Newport to the ships at sea.[29]

With the war over, Newport's civic leaders shared the concerns of many other public officials and business people in the autumn of 1945. How could they put their community on a firm economic footing? How would they cope with a declining military presence and provide jobs and homes for returning servicemen and their families? Could Newport revive its fishing industry? Could it encourage construction of affordable hotels to lure weekenders back to the island? With issues such as these on the community's agenda, Congressman Fogarty struck a responsive chord when he suggested a new future for Newport—as the permanent home of the United Nations.[30]

Within weeks, Newport developed its own vision of what a United Nations capital might be, fed by its history as a luxurious retreat for diplomats and well-heeled capitalists. While many of the other world capital contenders imagined a newly built, modern home for the UN, Newport's offer suggested an Old World–style compound of fashionable embassies. Robert Goelet, a multimillionaire financier and a decorated veteran of World War I, offered his fifty-room seaside villa, Ochre Court, as a home for the United Nations. The Newport City Council and Chamber of Commerce bundled this generous offer with two other properties—Fort Adams, the site of a nineteenth-century military installation, and another mansion that had fallen into public ownership for lack of a buyer willing to take on its taxes. This second mansion, Seaview Terrace, was a relatively recent addition to the Newport landscape, built in 1925 by the late Edson Bradley, a prominent art collector. Three stories high, modeled after the Chateau of Chenonceaux in Touraine, France, the concrete villa's fifty rooms had once been filled with precious antiques, rare stained glass, and such decorative touches as Elizabethan-period paneling and sixteenth-century Italian ceilings. But after Bradley's death, when no suitable buyer could be found, the house fell into disrepair. The army used it briefly as a barracks during the war, and the city hoped to find a developer to turn it into a hotel or to lease it to the navy to be a convalescent center.[31]

As in Boston, the Newport UN campaign crossed class lines, beginning with the idea of a working-class politician, mobilizing government and business leaders, and attracting the attention of the storied Brown family, whose history dated to Rhode Island's earliest colonial days. Multimillionaire John Nicholas Brown, a naval veteran of World War I, stepped up to lead the Newport campaign. In addition to the magnificent properties they could offer, Newport's promoters argued that the war had changed their community in ways that would benefit the United Nations. Newport's invitation pointed out the office space, barracks, and other buildings available at Fort Adams and the Naval Torpedo Station. Such facilities showed that local labor could build anything that the United Nations required; furthermore, workers no longer needed for the war effort were available for technical, mechanical, and office work. Like Boston, Newport promoted its connections to the values of liberty and democracy, especially the tradition of the New England town meeting. Newport's boosters illustrated their invitation with photographs of estates with stately iron gates opening onto curving drives, leading to massive homes fit for the most discriminating diplomat.[32]

In Boston and Newport, the two longest-running campaigns to attract the UN to New England showed local traditions, American identity, and modern attributes coming together to make a case for each community's status in the postwar world. While asserting their support for international cooperation, their promotional materials celebrated the distinctive qualities of each city—Boston as a cosmopolitan center of business, culture, and education, and Newport as a seaside colony of fashionable estates. Even as they pointed out their ability to serve a postwar world with the latest technologies, both cities reached deeply into local and regional histories to emphasize such values as freedom, liberty, and democracy, especially democracy as exemplified by the New England town meeting. Such foundations, the cities argued, would serve the United Nations well.[33]

OKLAHOMA!

While New Englanders looked to Puritan ancestors for the origins of American strength and character, another powerful strain of the nation's vitality lay on the western frontier. The idea of the American West as a land of promise and progress had resonated through the arguments in favor of

San Francisco as a location for the United Nations. There was more to the story of this mythic West, of course. Not that anyone in the United Nations had inquired, but why not Oklahoma? Suppose this new world organization, concerned with colonized lands and refugee people, could be recruited to a state populated by Native Americans who had been pushed west by expansion rather than pulled by opportunity?

When Ben P. Choate was born in southeastern Oklahoma in 1903, the green rolling hills, forests, and coal deposits north of the Texas border still appeared on U.S. maps as "Indian Territory." At the turn of the twentieth century, some Indian leaders nurtured hope that the Indian Territory might be admitted to the Union as an Indian-governed state. But by 1908, the Indian Territory had been subsumed into the new state of Oklahoma, governed by whites but with a name derived, ironically enough, from the Choctaw words for "red people." Its population included people from more than sixty Native American tribes, including the "Five Civilized Tribes" pushed out of the Southeast in the nineteenth century—the Choctaw, Cherokee, Creek, Chickasaw, and Seminole. Choate was born into the Choctaw Nation, whose people had been pushed westward out of Mississippi more than a century before, and his grandfather had presided over the last Choctaw senate. With statehood, the Choctaw Nation, like other tribes, became a nation within a state within another nation, the United States of America.[34]

Even before statehood, Oklahoma did not sit isolated from the outside world. Railroads had crossed the territory since the 1880s, and the oil, coal, and timber industries linked Oklahoma to the national and world economies. European immigrants were among the white settlers who pushed into Indian lands during the late nineteenth and early twentieth centuries. By the 1920s, radio broadcasting connected Oklahomans with events and entertainment beyond the state's boundaries, and newspaper editors enthusiastically promoted aviation as the key to a prosperous future. The Second World War placed Oklahoma on a world stage as never before. With open spaces and a mild climate, Oklahoma provided the year-round training bases where hundreds of thousands of American soldiers, sailors, and airmen prepared for battle in Europe and the Pacific.[35]

By 1945, Choate held office as an Oklahoma state legislator. He worked in the state capital in Oklahoma City, and he corresponded with the congressmen representing Oklahoma in Washington, D.C. But the "capital" that beckoned to him most was the former capital of the Choctaw Nation, Tuskahoma, where the old Council House remained standing as a historic site. It was this place, rooted in Choate's personal and tribal heritage, that fired his imagination in October 1945 when the news spread that the United Nations wanted to place its headquarters somewhere in the United States.

Gripped by the idea that Tuskahoma might once again serve as a capital, this time for the world, Choate consulted with the Choctaw chief, Will Durant, and he wrote persuasive letters to the governor of Oklahoma, to Oklahoma's representatives in Congress, to the president of the United States, and even to John D. Rockefeller Jr., who had a known interest in American Indian affairs. Like Massachusetts governor Tobin, who was pursuing his campaign for Boston at exactly the same time, Choate extolled the merits of Oklahoma climate and geography, and he imagined that air transportation would make Tuskahoma as accessible as any other place on the planet. But he saw the suitability of his homeland through a fundamentally different lens. While Tobin and the New Englanders celebrated their region as the birthplace of American ideals, Choate called attention to the injustices that might be corrected if the United Nations placed its headquarters in a location that would benefit Native American people.[36]

On October 6, 1945, just three days after the diplomats meeting in London recommended a United States location, Choate sent his first letter straight to the top, to President Harry S. Truman. "Since I am of Choctaw blood," he said, "I wish to offer as a possibility the present site of our old Choctaw Capitol and Council grounds as a future City or International Capitol of the World to come." It would be a tribute for the administration to locate "such a capitol at the present site of the Government of one of our own Minority groups right here in our own land, that of the Choctaw Nation of people." To a fellow Choctaw, Congressman William Stigler, Choate confided, "This might be a brain-storm but a few of them in the past have changed the course of world affairs. And besides us Choctaws should get some recognition before it is too everlastingly late and we are all gone." By the time Choate sent a long-shot plea for support to Rockefeller later in the month, he elaborated on the justice of the idea. "Since the prime motive of the [United Nations] was for the protection and help to the minority nations or races, no more fitting and timely gesture could be made than by placing the World Capital here," in Tuskahoma, "at a place formerly used as the seat of a Government of a minority Nation here in our own country." Choate's promotion of Tuskahoma reflected the growing global consciousness of the common concerns of colonized people, whether Native Americans in Oklahoma or peoples in Asia and Africa seeking freedom from European empires. For many, the United Nations represented hope for a more equitable future.[37]

In Oklahoma, the popular imagination of the United Nations remained fixed on a "world capital" city, not simply a headquarters building. The *McAlester Democrat*, a southeastern Oklahoma newspaper, told its readers, "This new or future city of such world-wide importance will be a continuous world's fair, and the magnitude and importance which it will display and have over world affairs is hardly possible for the mind to conceive at this time." Even the Tulsa *Daily World*, 140 miles north of Tuskahoma with no regional or cultural ties to the Choctaw capital, allowed that the idea of the United Nations at Tuskahoma "isn't nearly as funny as it sounds." The editorial writer imagined that "the converging trails of the old Indian country would be appropriate pathways for the peace sachems of the world to tread."[38]

Choate's idea also fit neatly with Oklahoma's plans for economic development following the war. Governor Robert S. Kerr had come into office in 1943 with promises that government would work to enhance Oklahoma's reputation in the nation and the world, especially to overcome the unfortunate *Grapes of Wrath* image of "Okies" fleeing the dust-bowl conditions of the 1930s. Kerr traveled the nation to promote Oklahoma agriculture and industry and to recruit new businesses. The agency at the forefront of these efforts, the Oklahoma Planning and Resources Board, readily embraced Choate's world capital proposal as an opportunity for economic revival in southeast Oklahoma. By mid-October, the agency was assisting Choate by drawing maps for the United Nations and developing a promotional brochure to send to London.[39]

In many ways, Choate was seizing and inverting a powerful force in Oklahoma history. Earlier boosterism by railroad promoters and politicians had crowded Indian lands and culture with white settlement, but now Choate embarked on a booster campaign of his own to benefit the Choctaw Nation. Like other world capital hopefuls, he could envision Tuskahoma as the best-suited, most central place on the planet for a United Nations home. "Any point of importance on the entire North American continent can be reached within a few short hours' time from Tuskahoma," he wrote to John D. Rockefeller Jr. "This area is beautifully located and the climate is ideal." More than the world capital hopefuls in New England, Choate stressed proximity to Mexico and other Latin American countries.[40]

Despite Choate's leading role, the state of Oklahoma took steps to distance the Tuskahoma proposal from its Indian origins. The promotional brochure that the state prepared—a modest, single-sheet quarter-fold, far less elaborate than others—described the Choctaw people in the past tense, easily and happily absorbed by progress into the American way of life: "This Nation whose councils occupied this site did not fall into decay as have many civilizations in the past, but rather, due to its democratic quality, has been blended into the newer government of our Nation." The brochure included a photograph that portrayed Indian people wearing feathered head-dresses, carrying bows and arrows, with a teepee in the background. The chamber of commerce in McAlester, Oklahoma, supported the Tuskahoma campaign by assuring the United Nations, "The Indians of Oklahoma are fully civilized and mingle with other people so well now that they are scarcely noticeable." For promotional purposes, Indians were simultaneously colorful relics of the past and invisible, notwithstanding the fact that a member of the Choctaw nation was leading the campaign.[41]

Oklahoma had acquired an oddly prominent place in American popular culture during the decades leading into the Second World War. It signaled "the West" to automobile vacationers who followed Route 66 on its diagonal from Chicago to California, a journey marked by a series of hotels shaped like Indian teepees and cafes decorated with faux Mexican sombreros. Oklahoma was the birthplace of Will Rogers, the part-Cherokee humorist who spun trick ropes, cowboy stories, and political satire for millions who watched him on stage or in the movies, read his newspaper columns, or heard him on the radio. When this "ambassador to the world," as he became known, died in a plane crash in 1938, Route 66 was rechristened the Will Rogers Highway, and he was laid to rest at the Will Rogers Memorial museum. Oklahoma struggled against the Depression aura left by John Steinbeck's *Grapes of Wrath*, published in 1939 and made into a movie in 1940, but it also came to life on Broadway in the sprightly 1943 musical *Oklahoma!*[42]

All of this served to build the pride and reputation of one particular small town east of Tulsa, where yet another world capital idea came to life in the autumn of 1945. Claremore, Oklahoma, was the first town that westbound travelers on Route 66 encountered when they crossed the state line. It was, arguably, the hometown of Will Rogers, who had been born on a ranch nearby. While visiting the new Will Rogers Memorial in Claremore, travelers could stay at the Will Rogers Hotel. Claremore was even the setting for *Oklahoma!*—based on the play *Green Grow the Lilacs,* by local writer Lynn Riggs. Along with "Oh What a Beautiful Morning" and "People Will Say We're in Love," the Rodgers and Hammerstein show retained passing references to Claremore as a town where rural folk might catch the train to up-to-date Kansas City, where ranch hands might get drunk, or where a traveling salesman might lure an unsuspecting maiden upstairs in a hotel. This was not Ben Choate's Oklahoma of Native American nations, but the Oklahoma of the pioneers who had pushed them aside.[43]

With the state government already backing the Tuskahoma campaign, Claremore mayor Elmer Tanner took matters into his own hands and wrote to the United Nations on December 1, 1945, to call the UN's attention to the spirit of international goodwill embodied by Claremore's favorite son, Will Rogers. Because Rogers's "life and efforts were dedicated to promoting peace and good will among men, it would be fitting and proper to establish the capitol of the United Nations Council in the home town of a man whose life and deeds exemplified the high aims and purposes of the United Nations Council," Tanner reasoned. Simultaneously, a telegram from N. B. Johnson, president of the National Congress of American Indians of the United States and Alaska, assured the UN of Indians' pride that "Will Rogers was a member of their race, that he was a world citizen, and an ambassador of good will." A United Nations capitol at Claremore would be "a fitting tribute to him and in recognition of his world service."[44]

The next day, Tanner called a meeting of Claremore's civic organizations and soon letters and telegrams flew from the Claremore chapters of the American War Dads, the Farm Women's Clubs, the Business and Professional Women's Club, the American Legion, and more, to the offices of Harry Truman, to members of Congress, and to the United Nations in London. As they wrote their appeals, the Claremore boosters knew they had competition. The very morning of their meeting, the *Tulsa World* carried an Associated Press report from London headlined "27 Areas Bid for UNO Site." Every booster invitation that had reached London by that time appeared in the article, including Tuskahoma (identified as "the Kiamichi Mountains of Oklahoma"). For Claremore and other cities and towns awakening to the world capital prospect, there was no time to lose.[45]

CENTERS OF THE NATION, CENTERS OF THE WORLD

Boosters in the midsection of the United States, far from the East Coast and from Europe, worked mightily to present themselves as logical "centers" of the world. In St. Louis, Missouri, for example, the world capital idea reawakened ambitions that dated to the late nineteenth century, when the city's boosters had waged an aggressive campaign to make St. Louis the capital of the United States. Arguing for their city's centrality, the U.S. capital campaigners had pointed out that the nation had grown far beyond

The St. Louis Chamber of Commerce stressed local and global connections with illustrations such as this St. Louis figure, representing local heritage, literally embracing the globe while pointing out an offered location at nearby Weldon Spring. (Missouri History Museum, St. Louis)

the thirteen original colonies on the eastern seaboard and that the capital should follow the westward migration. Noting that civilization seemed
to be on a continual path toward the west from its origins in Europe, the
campaign's chief promoter in 1870 labeled St. Louis "the future great city
of the world." St. Louis continued to compete for prominence, especially
with Chicago, its rival as a railroad gateway to the West. Chicago prevailed
in winning the world's fair staged in 1893; St. Louis scored by winning the
1904 Olympic Games away from Chicago.[46]

St. Louis presented itself to the United Nations as both local and global.
The city's promotional booklet, produced by the St. Louis Chamber of
Commerce, depicted relationships between the city and the world in a variety of ways. Like other world capital hopefuls in the West and Midwest,
St. Louis emphasized centrality with a globe that showed its position between the European and Pacific theaters of the Second World War. A bold
arrow pointed to nearby Weldon Spring, the site of a former TNT-produc-
tion facility that St. Louis now proposed for the United Nations. Later in
the same booklet, a St. Louis figure representing local heritage literally embraced the globe. Such an image suggested a view of local communities as
significant—even essential—protectors of the world.[47]

Maps, easily manipulated to create perceptions of distance, appeared
frequently in world capital campaign brochures. The promoters of the
Choctaw Nation capital at Tuskahoma included a map showing concentric
circles of distance, labeled with "air miles" to national capitals. The list of
highlighted capitals served to associate Tuskahoma with the most significant powers in the world, as if such a relationship already existed. A drawing of a prospective "Allied World Capitol," prepared by the Oklahoma
Planning and Resources Board, delivered the message that distance could
be easily overcome by including an airliner as a symbol of modern convenience. The artist reinforced the theme of centrality with a modern, circular high-rise building, with a roadway leading toward the structure and
lines in the background suggesting Hollywood premiere–style spotlights
aimed outward toward the sky.[48]

A concentric-circle map had been featured in the first brochure distributed by promoters of the Black Hills of South Dakota at the San Francisco
conference. During the autumn of 1945, they took the symbolism of centrality a step farther with a "spiral and cyclopic" world capital design. Prepared by architect Luvine Berg, a former San Francisco resident employed
during the war at the Black Hills Ordnance Depot, the plan envisioned a
hybrid of modern office structures, postwar residential development, and

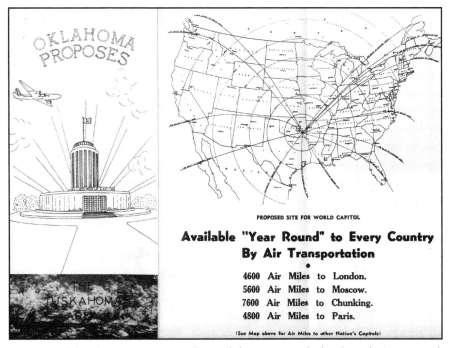

OKLAHOMA PROPOSES

THE TUSKAHOMA

PROPOSED SITE FOR WORLD CAPITOL

Available "Year Round" to Every Country By Air Transportation

—•—

4600 Air Miles to London.
5600 Air Miles to Moscow.
7600 Air Miles to Chunking.
4800 Air Miles to Paris.

(See Map above for Air Miles to other Nation's Capitols)

Promoters of the Choctaw Nation capital at Tuskahoma prepared a brochure depicting a modern, circular high rise and a map that looked toward the future of postwar aviation by adding "air miles" distances to national capitals. (Carl Albert Center Congressional Archives, University of Oklahoma)

permanent world's fair. The "cyclops" at the center consisted of a sphere representing the world at the top of a tower somewhat reminiscent of Coit Tower in San Francisco, with the tower flanked by office buildings.

The surrounding suburbanlike roadways appeared to be concentric circles but actually constituted a spiral, a form that would allow the UN complex to continually grow. The rings also had a space-age quality, noted in the *Rapid City Daily Journal's* description of the plan as "so colossal a place that it may well accommodate the capital of Jupiter." Embassy buildings and hotels were arrayed on cul-de-sacs around these roadways. Connections to the outside world were indicated by the avenues leading from every direction toward the center, most notably "World Highway Place." Here, Berg incorporated the conviction of Black Hills boosters that postwar transportation would include a highway making it possible, with just a few waterway interruptions, to drive around the world. In a final world's

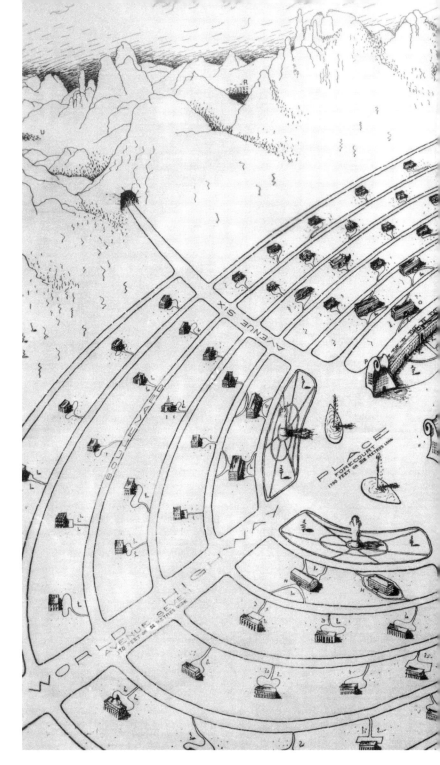

Promoters of the Black Hills of South Dakota emphasized their centrality with a "spiral and cyclopic" site plan envisioning a hybrid of modern office structures, postwar residential development, and permanent world's fair. Key to labels: (A) Areas for parking;

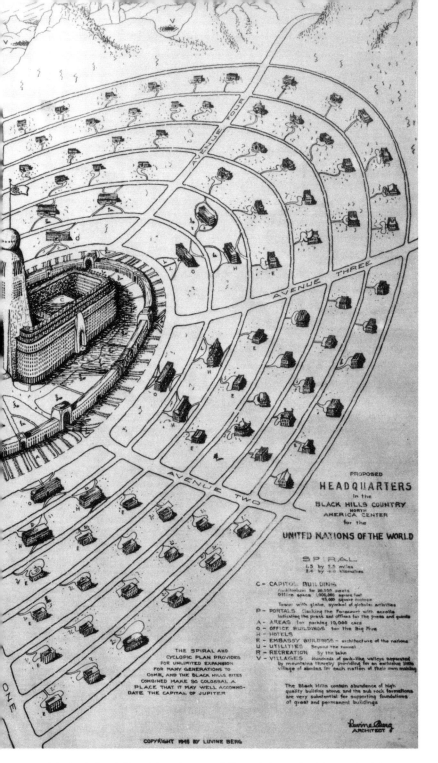

(C) Capitol Building; (E) Embassy Buildings; (H) Hotels; (P) Portals; (R) Recreation; (U) Utilities; (V) Villages. (Paul E. Bellamy Papers, Richardson Collection, University Libraries, University of South Dakota)

fair–like flourish, Berg provided housing in the form of villages in the mountains, each serving as "an exclusive little village of abodes for each nation of their own making."[49]

While diplomats argued about whether the center of the world lay in Europe or the United States, American communities were demonstrating that the "center" was a matter of perspective that could be manipulated to suit many purposes. In global terms, especially in an age of aviation, the center could be imagined anywhere. As world capital hopefuls generated maps, site plans, and brochures seeking to make this point, it seemed that nothing could stop the growing list of competitors and piles of mail reaching the office of Gladwyn Jebb, the busy secretary of the United Nations Preparatory Commission. In London, the United Nations was about to experience the great lengths to which American boosters would go in pursuit of a dream.

5

SHOWTIME!

THE STATE DEPARTMENT told them not to go.

The president of the United States told them not to go.

The secretary of the United Nations Preparatory Commission in war-scarred London suggested—diplomatically, of course—that they really shouldn't go.

But neither cost, time, nor inconvenience could keep determined American civic boosters from racing across the Atlantic during November and December 1945 to offer their services to the United Nations. By the end of the year, sixteen of the most persistent world capital hopefuls from the United States forced their attentions on the UN in person, and more were on the way. For all of their eagerness, the boosters' time-consuming journeys across the Atlantic contradicted their claims that distance did not matter. And their sales pitches, so painstakingly prepared and intensively rehearsed, were merely tolerated by the diplomats, whose attention remained on the struggle over whether to center the organization in Europe or the United States.

The United Nations officially came into existence on October 24, 1945, when a majority of member nations ratified the charter drafted in San Francisco. Soon thereafter, on Sunday, November 11, three of the Philadelphians who had lobbied the UN in San Francisco—advertising man Benjamin Eshleman, Judge L. Stauffer Oliver, and professor John G. Herndon—met at Broad Street Station in Center City Philadelphia to catch a 9:00 a.m. train. In their pursuit of the United Nations since March 1945, the Philadelphia ambassadors had been downplaying one minor detail: the City of Brotherly Love had no transatlantic air service, although they looked forward to its inauguration later in the year. They had a plane to catch, but it was 104 miles away, at LaGuardia Field in New York City, where they also would be joined by the chairman of the Philadelphia campaign, Temple University president Robert L. Johnson.[1]

The trip seemed imperative. In late October, the Philadelphians had gone to see President Truman, who directed them to the State Department. Staff members there advised them to be patient, but they also learned that a UN committee might soon begin to narrow the headquarters choice. Would their chance be lost, without a fair hearing of their proposal? There seemed to be no time to lose, but in New York, weather delayed their flight for two days. Anxious about the delay, they tried but failed to book passage on the *Queen Mary*, betting that the ocean liner would beat the airline over the sea. Finally, they received word of an outgoing flight on Pan-American Airways and boarded the plane, but could be sure of nothing until they were in the air.[2]

Such were the uncertainties of international travel in the autumn of 1945, as American cities and towns were assuring the United Nations that swift air transit would easily transform any location into a potential Capital of the World. Transatlantic flights from the United States to England in the 1940s followed the route of thousands of military transport planes during the war, first heading north to Newfoundland for refueling, then across the North Atlantic to Ireland, and then England. To avoid difficult weather, the pilot for the Philadelphians' flight flew farther north and higher than usual; according to the hostess on board, the outside temperature was seven degrees below zero. In the morning, the sun rose over formidably dark clouds, and the coast of Ireland appeared. Much to the Philadelphians' pleasure, they discovered at the Rineanna Airport at Shannon, County Limerick, a country-club-like setting where they could enjoy breakfast before the next leg of their flight. Pan-American then flew them as far as Hurn, England, where a bus carried them to a train for another journey of more than one hundred miles to Victoria Station in London. They arrived at 8:00 p.m. on November 14, three days after leaving Philadelphia.[3]

During the same week that the Philadelphians landed on Pan-American, Paul Bellamy from the Black Hills of South Dakota and an advance team of boosters from Chicago also showed up in London. Then came Mayor Edward Kelly of Chicago himself, accompanied by his nineteen-year-old son, just discharged from the navy. The Kellys arrived on November 20 with great fanfare on the first promotional flight for American Airlines' service from Chicago to London. With a single flight, it seemed that Chicago had transcended geography, as a reporter for the *Chicago Herald-American* assured his readers: "In this shrinking world, Chicago and London now live one day's flying time apart. No longer land-locked, but a seaboard city to the air-minded, Chicago today became in reality the hub of the international air transport system." The route from Chicago offered the advantage of skipping New York and aiming straight for Newfoundland before crossing the Atlantic. Except for a slight rerouting because of fog, the trip concluded in England according to plan, on schedule.[4]

In true booster fashion, the newspapers' glowing reports about the flight omitted some realities. The mayor traveled in a "handsomely-appointed DC-4," according to the *Herald-American,* but the British consul general to Chicago who accompanied the junket noted that it was a hurriedly converted army transport plane. "There was no sleeping accommodation and we either sat in our chairs or lay on the steel floor," Wilfred Hansford Gallienne groused in a confidential dispatch to the British Foreign Office. "Toilet arrangements were inadequate; the water froze and we could not wash, while the water-closet was merely a tin pail."[5] Despite discomforts, Mayor Kelly made it to London and moved into a suite at the Savoy Hotel, where he summoned European reporters for interviews about the wonders of Chicago. By November 24, San Francisco mayor Roger Lapham also was in London (arriving late and without ceremony because of bad weather). Checking into the Savoy Hotel, he found Mayor Kelly "under the same roof handing out potent literature and cocktails," reported the *San Francisco Chronicle.* The same day, Governor Maurice Tobin began his journey from the airport in Bedford, Massachusetts.[6]

With each passing day of November, it seemed, more world capital hopefuls were showing up at the American embassy in London and expecting help with introductions, accommodations, and arrangements for their eventual return flights to the United States. At embassies and hotels around London, they requested and received meetings with diplomats. The Philadelphians appealed directly to the British minister of state, Philip Noel-Baker, who had been a classmate of Benjamin Eshleman's at Haverford College. American civic boosters became regulars at the Preparatory Commission office of Gladwyn Jebb, the diplomatic recipient of their many telegrams and promotional brochures, who now shooed them toward Benjamin Cohen, an American placed in charge of gathering data about possible headquarters locations. At every opportunity, the boosters granted interviews to American and British journalists, who shared information and suggested that an excellent public relations strategy would be to arrange cocktail parties for London-based reporters. The mayor of Chicago obliged by hosting one hundred reporters in the swank River Room of the Savoy, where they enjoyed drinks in exchange for viewing a promotional film about the Windy City. The Philadelphians planned a similar soiree for early in December.[7]

The Americans were taking up space in crowded hotels and dining in restaurants in a city where food was in limited supply. They sometimes crossed paths, as when Robert Johnson from Philadelphia visited the Houses of Parliament, only to find himself being introduced to their lordships by none other than Paul Bellamy from the Black Hills, who was already there as a guest of Lord Astor. One of the Chicago boosters spotted the *Philadelphia Record* publisher David Stern at the Savoy and taunted, "What are you going to do, internationalize the Liberty Bell?" Stern, who had launched the Philadelphia world capital idea back in March, was in London to lobby for a Jewish state in Palestine. But he thought this sounded like a fine slogan and recommended it to the boosters of Philadelphia's world capital campaign.[8]

By the last week of November, at least five aggressive booster posses from Philadelphia, Chicago, Boston, the Black Hills, and Atlantic City were in London, and more were known to be on the way. Back in the United States, even the most unlikely contenders, including the Sault Ste. Marie partisans led by Stellanova Osborn and the Oklahoma promoters of Tuskahoma, were trying to assemble teams of traveling salesmen. South Dakota congressmen touring Europe to assess the impact of the war were chatting up heads of state about the merits of the Black Hills. As the full United Nations Preparatory Commission came into session for the first time on November 24, 1945, it was clear that in the spirit of diplomacy—and simply to stem the tide—the Americans would have to be allowed to state their cases.[9]

The famed London correspondent Edward R. Murrow, whose voice had captured the harrowing experience of the Nazi blitz and other world-changing events, summed up the situation on the CBS radio network and noted one American booster in particular. Paul Bellamy, with a talent for making friends no matter where he went, now counted one of the world's biggest radio news stars among them. "One of the most impressive things I've heard said about this whole thing was when Paul Bellamy said he had a son who was a flight leader in a B-17 group and was buried up near Cambridge," Murrow said. "He thinks this United Nations is pretty serious business and something ought to be done about it. And maybe people would think straighter and clearer in the Black Hills than anywhere else."[10]

ANYTHING YOU CAN DO, I CAN DO BETTER

On Saturday morning, December 1, the most assertive rivals for the UN's attention assembled together for the first time in Church House next to Westminster Abbey. As a reporter for the *New York Times* saw it, "The oak-paneled room in Church House never housed so strange a group as appeared before the subcommittee." The applicants included delegations from Philadelphia, San Francisco, Boston, Chicago, and the Black Hills of South Dakota. And they had company. A British cousin of the Brown family of Newport, Rhode Island, arrived to describe the enormous seaside mansions that the UN might have, just for the asking. The executive secretary of the New Jersey Invitation Committee to the United Nations came to extol the virtues of Atlantic City. And the president of the University of Colorado, Robert L. Stearns, appeared with a former foreign service officer to make a case for Denver.[11]

Officially, it was the first meeting of the Site Sub-Committee of Committee 8 (General Questions) of the Preparatory Commission of the United Nations. But the composition of the subcommittee signaled just how little importance the UN attached to the performances that were about to begin. The subcommittee represented the regions of the world, but none of the Big Five powers of the Security Council had been appointed. The boosters made their pitches to delegates from less powerful nations—Australia, Colombia, Cuba, Egypt, Ethiopia, Iran, the Netherlands, Uruguay, and Yugoslavia. The gavel rested with the Yugoslavian Stoyan Gavrilovic, a man with a special interest in the United States, where his wife and son had found a safe haven in New York City during the war. Gladwyn Jebb, the executive secretary of the Preparatory Commission who had received the Americans' many communications and endured their persistent visits to his office, sent Benjamin Cohen, the deputy assigned to collect headquarters information.[12]

This was, nonetheless, an important day. The Americans in London were creating a detailed record of how civic leaders in the United States viewed their communities' place in the postwar world. Two world wars within the span of a lifetime had given them a strong generational determination to contribute to assuring peace, and the atomic bomb now made that essential. But becoming the Capital of the World also was a mouthwatering business proposition. On that level, luring the UN was like recruiting a new industry, attracting a big convention, or reeling in tourist dollars, but with a loftier purpose on a much greater scale. Cities and towns already had promotional materials for such purposes that celebrated local attributes such as distinctive histories, cultural institutions, climate, and livability. The additional challenge now was to reconcile this very local perspective with the requirements of an international, forward-looking enterprise in the postwar world.

After several months of guessing what the UN's desires might be, the boosters could now aim squarely at criteria developed by the Executive Committee of the Preparatory Commission. The requirements included a mundane list of essential auditoriums, offices, and meeting rooms—nothing to suggest anything so grand as a Capital of the World, but on the other hand nothing to rule it out. The list emphasized technical matters such as accessibility and communication but also included items such as a healthful climate, a congenial local population, and opportunities for culture and recreation, which fit well with the boosters' existing schemes for luring business and tourism. Instead of making the selection process easier, the UN's criteria presented such an easy target that any self-respecting civic promoter would be foolish not to take a shot.[13]

The hearing proceeded in alphabetical order. First up, Atlantic City. If the United Nations needed a meeting place with hotels and auditoriums, like San Francisco, what better place than this seaside resort, which had been promoting itself as "The Playground of the World" since the 1920s? For this project that so much resembled selling a convention site, the New Jersey group dispatched to London Adrian Phillips, the 47-year-old convention manager for the Hotel Morton, along with restaurateur Charles Harp, forty-one, who had been in the air force in England and therefore would know his way around. The pair distributed a brochure depicting hotels, beaches, and auditoriums, and they talked their way into diplomatic offices with the aid of two welcome novelties: Atlantic City salt-water taffy and Colgate soap products. With the advance work completed, Phillips now took only five minutes to remind the diplomats about the brochure and its accompanying motion picture. In doing so, he also revealed the enormity of the expectations that Americans were attaching to the future UN home. Not only could Atlantic City provide the necessary hotels and convention halls for an immediate meeting place; for a permanent site, Phillips promised that the UN could have any or all of an "international island" consisting of the immense expanse of sixteen hundred square miles in southern New Jersey.[14]

Enter the booster for the Black Hills of South Dakota, Paul E. Bellamy, who in just over a year had traveled from the podium at the Rapid City

Chamber of Commerce into the chambers of international affairs. He had not changed his conviction that world peace would best be nourished in the quiet comfort of an isolated area. Better to be "a big toad in a little puddle and not a little toad in a big puddle," he told the diplomats, "and to be safely distant from any city that might be a target for the new threat of the atomic bomb."[15]

As a man in the transportation business, Bellamy could not resist describing in extensive detail the roads and rails that linked the Black Hills to the rest of the nation and the world, and he assured the diplomats that affordable housing would be available. Bellamy's enthusiasm for the Black Hills had no limits. As he painted the picture of a world capital growing on perhaps one hundred square miles of wooded hills and golden-green valleys in southwestern South Dakota, he saw no peril in mentioning an asset that would surely appeal to anyone subsisting in London at the end of the Second World War: "I do not want to make your mouths water," he said, "but you can get a very good dinner for about a dollar or a dollar and a quarter, which will consist of soup, a small relish or hors d'oeuvres, and if I were there tonight I would probably get a beefsteak about *that* long," he motioned, "about *that* wide and about *that* thick."

Reporters smiled and scribbled. After all of Bellamy's sacrifices, work, and dedication, the beefsteak remark would become the identifying characteristic of the Black Hills effort to become the Capital of the World. It made headlines, attracted ridicule, and became an anecdote frequently repeated in later histories of the United Nations. But it was no joke to Bellamy, who finished describing the typical Black Hills menu ("two or three vegetables, and a cup of coffee, tea or milk, or whatever you wish to drink"). He then outlined the pure and plentiful water supply and communications facilities. He was sure that shortly, Rapid City would broadcast on far more than its single 5,000-watt radio station.[16]

As a businessman, Bellamy had one more idea that he could not resist offering. It seemed obvious to him that the United Nations capital, situated near Mount Rushmore in the Black Hills, would be a spectacular tourist attraction. Suppose that every nation sent its products to this place, making it "the world's trading center," with small items also on sale for those insatiable tourists. The profits from this grand bazaar could underwrite the United Nations. "It is not inconceivable that there will be something like four million or five million tourists each year," he predicted. "Each of them will buy something. I would almost undertake myself to underwrite the entire cost of the operation of the United Nations headquarters and the various delegations from the profits that would be made from tourists in the Black Hills."

As only the second presenter of the day, Bellamy at first felt satisfied that he had opened a friendly conversation that would continue, in the same way that he had been chatting up diplomats since his trip to San Francisco earlier in the year. But as the day progressed, he began to feel that he had made terrible mistakes that had doomed his favorite cause.[17]

Next came the very formal Bostonians, dressed like diplomats in long-tailed morning coats and striped trousers to add a dash of international sophistication. Governor Tobin introduced an all-star cast from Massachusetts: Karl T. Compton, the president of the Massachusetts Institute of Technology; Orson Adams Jr., an international banking expert from the First National Bank of Boston; Erwin Canham, editor of the *Christian Science Monitor*, who had covered the League of Nations; William J. McDonald, the New England manager of *Time* magazine; G. Holmes Perkins, a professor of regional planning from Harvard; and Robert B. Stuart, a former State Department official from Tufts.[18]

Such a formidable lineup gave Bellamy cause for regret and the Philadelphians cause to worry. Not only that, but Boston had an attribute that no other American competitor could claim: "Boston is closer to Europe than any other large American city," the governor emphasized. The men from Massachusetts laid out their case in a series of polished speeches that ran from the details of office space and radio stations to the glories of New England's scenic beauty, illustrated by a movie, *New England Holiday*, and a series of colored slides of Boston. They even unveiled a package of seventy-five scholarships that the region's many colleges, universities, and prep schools would offer to the sons and daughters of United Nations delegates.[19]

The pitches for Chicago, Denver, and Philadelphia were similarly orchestrated and delivered by experts in government, education, or publishing. Chicago's mayor had junketed home, leaving the formal presentation in the hands of his persuasive city attorney, Barton Hodes, and a team consisting of an economics professor from the University of Chicago, a labor leader, and a journalist-turned-advertising man. The Chicago boosters took turns describing their city as central and world-famous in every important way, and only a reporter from the *New York Times* seemed to notice that a Chicago newspaper they displayed carried the banner headline, "Gangland Murder on North Side."[20]

The promotional brochure prepared for the United Nations by Chicago boosters depicted their city as easily accessible from all points of the globe. (Chicago History Museum, reproduced with permission of the Chicagoland Chamber of Commerce)

More than three hours had elapsed, and the diplomats needed an intermission. They adjourned for lunch. Afterward, fewer than half of them returned.

Resuming the performance at 3:00 p.m., Robert Stearns, president of the University of Colorado, presented the case for Denver. He lacked the sizable entourage of Boston or Chicago, but he possessed military experience and academic credentials. A 53-year-old veteran of World War I (disappointed that his duties did not send him overseas), Stearns had served in the Pacific during World War II as a civilian analyst for the army air force's long-range bombing campaigns against Japan. He had long believed that an organization such as the United Nations would be essential in the aftermath of the war and that the United States must lead the way.[21]

Denver had moved more quietly toward the world capital prospect than the aggressive promoters of the Black Hills, Boston, and Chicago, but with no less determination. Throughout the twentieth century, the Colorado capital had competed vigorously with other cities for business and political conventions, and it had offered to host the winter Olympic Games of 1932. With Denver already promoting itself as "The Second Capital of the United States" because of the expansion of federal agencies there during the Roosevelt years, it was a small step for a Democratic national committeeman for Colorado, James A. Marsh, to propose the city as potential Capital of the World.[22]

The president of the University of Colorado—now addressing delegates only from Australia, Cuba, Egypt, and Yugoslavia—promised that Denver could provide all the facilities the UN needed. "It has had for many years the reputation of being one of the host cities of the United States," Stearns explained. Distinguishing Denver from some other disaster-prone cities, he pointed out, "It is accessible either from the Atlantic or Pacific Coast and has had the reputation for never having had a natural disaster of any kind, no earthquakes, floods, tidal waves, tornados, fires other than of local consequence." Setting Denver's interest apart from the contenders from the East and Midwest, Stearns also called attention to the western city's orientation toward Latin America. "Colorado was originally peopled by people that came from the Mexican border," he said, acknowledging Hispanic but not Native American culture. Not only was Denver "the outstanding center of Latin American culture," but it had a heterogeneous population from all over the world. Like the eastern cities touting their European immigrant populations and the Oklahomans describing Native Americans, Stearns assured the UN delegates that the various nationalities represented in Denver were well "assimilated into our community." To conclude, Stearns showed yet another promotional film, this one providing twenty minutes of scenes of Denver and the nearby Rocky Mountains.[23]

Awaiting their turn, the Philadelphians had been impressed most by the dignified presentations for Denver and Boston, although they could not fathom why such fine representatives would show such crass promotional movies. The Massachusetts film struck them as tawdry and inappropriate, with its scenes of girls in bathing suits on New England beaches, and the Denver film was a commercial travelogue. They scorned the Chicago city attorney as too aggressive and prone to hyperbole, and they observed incredulously that his group had run fifteen minutes over its allotted hour of time.[24]

By the time the Philadelphians' turn came, late in the afternoon, they were convinced that they must rise above the spectacle that much of the hearing had become. A reporter for the *Philadelphia Record* tipped them "that the presentation of the American cities, with its accompanying showmanship and brashness, and with a few cracks made by one city as against another, was being derisively and unfavorably commented upon by the newsmen, particularly those representing Great Britain and the European countries." Knowing this, they resolved to avoid a hard sell and dwell especially on "the spiritual background and appeal of our city and the fact that it offers the right kind of fertile soil for the growth and development of the United Nations."[25]

Philadelphia had revised its offer considerably from the original idea of placing the United Nations in the heavily commercial and industrial area around Independence Hall. To persuade the UN that Philadelphia had room for an enormous world capital, the city now offered a spacious plateau in beautiful Fairmount Park, once the setting for the 1876 Centennial world's fair. The Philadelphians did not let go of their pride in the city's historic associations, but in their printed materials they adapted the city's image for the postwar world by emphasizing modern conveniences as well as the Liberty Bell and the Declaration of Independence.[26]

Judge Oliver opened with Philadelphia's impressive history and significance, from William Penn and the Declaration of Independence to its enthusiastic support for the United Nations. He described the beautiful sites available in Fairmount Park along the Schuylkill River and enumerated the city's hotels and meeting halls. Professor Herndon provided a briefing about state government and Philadelphia's many cultural institutions. Eshleman addressed the still somewhat delicate topic of airline transportation: "It is just like any other American city," he said. "Within a comparatively few months we will have what we believe to be the outstanding airport in the country." The Philadelphians finished within their allotted one hour and distributed packets of promotional materials.[27]

With the clock ticking toward 5:00 p.m., it seemed to Roger Lapham, the mayor of San Francisco, that fifty-five minutes of Philadelphia had exhausted the subcommittee's stamina, whatever was left of it. The alphabetical order left him the last speaker of the day, but he had no need to introduce himself or his city. "I believe this is the last Delegation to be heard, and I am sure you are not too sorry," he said. He affirmed the San Francisco Bay area's interest in seeing the UN return and directed the diplomats' attention to the elaborate brochure prepared by the San Francisco Chamber of Commerce. Like a man among old friends, he dispensed with formalities in favor of some good-natured jabs at his opponents, especially claims made for the climate of Boston and Philadelphia. The UN would have its best chance in the friendly atmosphere and congenial climate of California, Lapham said. Joking aside, "I for one want the United Nations to grow up. We feel, in San Francisco, as if we gave it birth there. We know it is going through some difficult times," and San Francisco would be best suited to nurturing the organization toward adulthood.[28]

From 10:00 a.m. until 5:00 p.m., with a two-hour break in the middle, the diplomats had listened politely. They requested no additional information, and they asked no questions, even when the Americans invited them to do so. The chairman profusely thanked every group, extending courtesies that the American boosters heard as encouragement. "I would like to propose a vote of thanks to these American gentlemen," Gavrilovic said at the end of the day. "They have come in a spirit of friendliness and assistance, and I can assure them that the Committee will be delighted to submit to the General Conference of the United Nations . . . all the information which they have placed at our disposal." The meeting adjourned.[29]

With one notable exception, the Americans declared the day a success and reported to their hometown newspapers that their invitations stood at least as much chance as any other. Privately, the Philadelphians reveled in their impression of the boastful Chicagoans ("Obviously Chicago has the greatest Great Lakes to be found anywhere!" they joked). They began to plot ways of undermining their most threatening rivals, perhaps by drawing attention to the undesirable "Irish element" in Boston. Paul Bellamy, meanwhile, returned to his room at Claridge's Hotel to write a tortured letter to the UN's Benjamin Cohen, apologizing for his informality, insisting that he had been serious, and pleading for attention to the Black Hills' many advantages. Please, he said, come to South Dakota and see for yourself.[30]

I CAN DO ANYTHING BETTER THAN YOU

When newspapers informed the rest of the world about the American boosters' hearing on December 1—beefsteaks and all—the reports persuaded more Americans to pass resolutions, send telegrams, and pack their bags for journeys to London. If the UN was receiving proposals, shouldn't they go? How could they miss this opportunity?

By the following Saturday, December 8, enough boosters had arrived in London to require another session of the subcommittee, this time to hear invitations from Miami; Navy Island near Niagara Falls; Hyde Park, New York; and the state of Indiana. Five delegates, barely a quorum, returned to Conference Room 3 in Church House. Hyde Park drew attention as a sentimental favorite because of its association with Franklin Roosevelt, but boosters from Niagara Falls offered support from towns on both sides of the U.S.-Canadian border; Miami offered the climate and hotels of a resort city; and Indiana presented the UN with its choice of several state parks. In the next session on December 20, only four delegates returned to listen to boosters from three river cities of the American midsection: Cincinnati, St. Louis, and New Orleans. Cincinnati mayor James G. Stewart, a trial lawyer known for his oratorical skills, launched into an impassioned, sweeping history of his city, skirting its reputation as "Porkopolis." St. Louis offered surplus military property at Weldon Spring outside the city, and New Orleans built on its long history as an international port of trade (with emphasis on Europeans and Latin Americans, minimizing the city's significant African American culture and population). Finally on this day came an unusual proposal from an individual, Ruth Cutten of Ridgefield, Connecticut, who sent an emissary to offer her personal estate in the countryside north of New York City.[31]

Long-standing civic rivalries were crossing the Atlantic. St. Louis and New Orleans had battled for the honor of hosting conventions and world's fairs, and St. Louis had wrestled with Chicago over supremacy as a railroad hub. For New Orleans, the UN also represented a rematch with San Francisco, which had beaten it for the honor of hosting the 1915 Panama-Pacific International Exposition that had marked the opening of the Panama Canal. New Orleans and Miami both were positioning themselves as gateways to the lucrative trade with Latin America that they expected would increase and thrive in the postwar years.[32]

This was all irrelevant to the ongoing power struggle among the diplomats. While the Americans took their turns trying to impress the little subcommittee appointed to placate them, Great Britain and France maneuvered the United Nations into yet another debate over whether the headquarters should be in the United States or Europe. In the multilayered bureaucracy of the new organization, it remained to be seen whether the full Preparatory Commission would accept its Executive Committee's recommendation of the United States. Seizing upon this uncertainty, the British and the French launched a new offensive on behalf of a European location during the first two weeks of December. With the full Preparatory Commission now in London, they could take the matter to a committee with representatives from all the member nations, not just the fourteen who comprised the Executive Committee. The arena shifted to the blandly labeled Committee 8 (General Questions) of the Preparatory Commission, where in thirteen meetings spanning more than two weeks, diplomats clashed once again over whether the UN would operate best in the midst of Europe's turmoil or in new surroundings in the United States.

The arguments were familiar. Would an American location prevent the United States from backsliding into isolationism? Would it be better to choose Europe so that the headquarters could be placed in a smaller nation instead of one of the great powers? And what about those travel distances? With the Soviet Union and its bloc holding firm for the United States, the champions of Europe, led by Philip Noel-Baker of Great Britain, did everything in their power to prolong the debate and recruit allies. They came to the brink of success, holding onto their bloc of support in Europe and gaining allies elsewhere in the British Commonwealth and in the Middle East. But supporters of an American site succeeded in pushing the issue to a vote before the Europeans could muster a majority. On December 15, 1945, after a final impassioned speech by Noel-Baker, the delegates affirmed the Executive Committee's recommendation that the United Nations headquarters be placed in the United States.[33]

This settled one question but left open another—if in the United States, where? On this question, the American world capital hopefuls were having an effect, but not the one they intended. Each came to London intending to persuade the UN that he represented the best location possible, but instead the boosters were showing that just about any location could fulfill the role. As the delegate from Mexico saw it, the UN faced a situation like "those judges in Atlantic City when they are going to choose Miss America from among 100 or 200 beautiful girls, each of whom could rightly be elected as Miss America." Instead of clarifying the choice, the Americans had overwhelmed the diplomats with details, all of them favorable. And the boosters in London did not even include such likely contenders as New York City, where Mayor Fiorello LaGuardia was certain his city would win the UN's favor without engaging in "a scramble of cheap competition." It was becoming clear that the headquarters site decision could not be made before the Preparatory Commission adjourned on December 24. Before a location could be selected, additional issues remained, such as whether it should be inside or outside a city, whether it should be close to Washington or far removed, or whether it should be in the East or the West. Furthermore, how could the diplomats of the United Nations possibly assess the many available choices?[34]

Day by day, a rising chorus of American cities and towns clamored for the United Nations' attention. For all of the civic leaders' serious intent, the London hearings understandably struck some as a theater of the absurd. The syndicated columnist Fred Othman wrote that the UN was "almost reduced to blindfolding a Goldwyn girl and having her stick a pin in a map of the U.S.A." He spun the merits of St. Louis as a place where delegates could enjoy free beer and pig's knuckles, Philadelphia "where the mayor takes a padded hammer and rings the Liberty Bell on state occasions," and the Black Hills as "surrounded by plenty of nothing except scenery and fresh air." In the *Miami Herald*, a writer playfully suggested Daytona Beach as the place with "the dandiest souvenir stores I have ever seen" and a hot dog stand "where you drive in, blow your horn, and get a hot dog thrust at you before the echo dies away." That all of these columns appeared in cities with active world capital boosters indicated that even the most ardent campaigns carried with them an undercurrent of bemused skepticism.[35]

During the period of the hearings in London, from December 1 through 20, thirty-four additional invitations from local officials and suggestions by private citizens emerged, bringing the total to at least eighty sites in the United States. Most came from points scattered around the country from Lucerne, Maine, and Portsmouth, Virginia, to Los Angeles County, California, and Grand Coulee, Washington. When the UN confirmed on December 15 that the headquarters indeed would be in the United States, "The chambers of commerce and boards of trade seem to have been thrown into fresh frenzies of civic ambition," observed the *Washington Post*. "Such lesser problems as the atom bomb, the management-labor impasse, housing, the consumer goods shortage, and the State Department's China policy and so on, are pushed aside while the boosters shove, gouge, maul and trip each other in their zeal to present the claims of their respective cities to be chosen as the capital of our brave new world." The elaborate performances of cities such as Boston, Philadelphia, and Cincinnati did not guarantee allies among neighboring communities back home—to the contrary, they spawned more competition. From Massachusetts came new offers from Springfield and Lenox, and from Pennsylvania came an invitation from Punxsutawney, the place best known for the tradition of watching for the groundhog's shadow every second day of February. Cincinnati's campaign did not stop a similar effort by nearby Greenville, Ohio.[36]

Mixed in with all of the American mail came a suggestion that would find a place in UN news coverage and histories for years to come. A woman living in Wales, Mabel Morris of Lower Pontnewydd near Newport, wrote on December 2, "Why not have a ship for the headquarters of the United Nations? It could then be moved to any nation." Like all other suggestions, "anywhere on the high seas, a ship" henceforth appeared on the list that Gladwyn Jebb's office dutifully provided to reporters. Like Paul Bellamy's remarks about beefsteaks, Morris's suggestion became an often-repeated (but in her case, never attributed) example of the United Nations headquarters follies of 1945. But in hindsight, the ship at sea was just the right metaphor for the long and storm-tossed journey that lay ahead for the United Nations as it tried to narrow the choices for its permanent home.[37]

6

SURPRISE

THE MAYOR OF San Francisco stayed in London longer than any other American civic booster. Roger Lapham circulated among the diplomats to remind them of the warm welcome they had experienced in his city, and he was gratified to hear San Francisco mentioned frequently during the lengthy debates over whether to place the headquarters in the United States or in Europe. By December 20, when the Preparatory Commission of the United Nations determined that the site question needed further study by yet another committee, Lapham decided he had done all he could for the moment. An interim committee had instructions to select up to six well-qualified locations for the UN's General Assembly to consider, and Lapham felt confident that San Francisco would be among them. He knew that a final decision had been deferred until the first meeting of the General Assembly in January.[1]

And so, on Saturday, December 22, 1945, joining a tide of Americans heading home from war, the weary but hopeful mayor of San Francisco began his long journey back to the United States after nearly a month of courting the United Nations. Waiting at the airport, he heard stunning news:

San Francisco was out of the running.

What?

While Lapham had been on a train from London to the airport one hundred miles away, the long-winded Committee 8 of the Preparatory Commission had moved with highly unusual efficiency to limit the head-quarters search to locations east of the Mississippi River. Lapham was in no mood for diplomacy now. "It's a hell of a note," he declared angrily to a reporter who caught up with him at the airport, "after being in London so many weeks and after believing that we were dealing with the proper out-fit, suddenly to discover that the vote has been taken this way." It smacked of back-room dealing, not careful deliberation. "When it comes down to brass tacks, we can only draw the conclusion that this vote has been taken in the atmosphere of regular ward politics. It's a cheap, dirty trick. I'm sorry, but that's the way I feel. That a great international organization should stoop to such a level staggers me."[2]

How could this have happened? The events that led to Mayor Lapham's surprise, and to the series of rapid and unexpected developments that followed, showed that civic boosters and diplomats were approaching the headquarters site question with fundamentally different priorities and contrasting mental maps of the world. Even though the boosters viewed their interests as both local and global, they ignored, downplayed, or could not perceive international factors that blocked many of them from the prize they so confidently pursued. Meanwhile the diplomats, who saw the world in terms of nations, continents, and the balance of power, had no experience to guide them through the tangle of local factors that complicated finding a location to do business in the United States. There were far more competitors than any previous contest to host the Olympics or a world's fair, and the circumstances of deciding upon a permanent home for diplomacy differed greatly. The diplomats could not separate the task from international intrigue as their nations jockeyed for influence in the postwar world.

"BEAUTIFUL SMALL TOWNS IN THE EAST"

During the four months of meetings in London in the autumn of 1945, the British minister of state, Philip Noel-Baker, had suffered one defeat after another. He had been denied a grand ceremonial last meeting for the League of Nations, where he had spent much of his career, and he had lost two fights to place the United Nations at the league's headquarters in Geneva. Despite his best efforts to change the course of history, Western Europe—the region of the world that he regarded as the cradle of civilization—was giving way to the newly prominent United States. When the vote confirming the United States occurred on December 15, Noel-Baker had been the model of gracious defeat as he offered a motion to declare the choice unanimous.[3]

But this experienced strategist recognized that his moment of defeat also presented new opportunity. While the American government's neutrality left a leadership vacuum on the headquarters question, the decision to place the UN in the United States created a groundswell of sympathy for Europe. Within hours of the December 15 decision, Noel-Baker circulated a memorandum benignly titled "Some Further Considerations in

Choosing the Site in the United States." As events progressed, it became the memo that sank the hopes of many potential capitals of the world but ignited the aspirations of many others. The memo guided the United Nations firmly toward locations on the Atlantic Coast, especially the Northeast region geographically closest to Europe. In one especially evocative sentence, quoted widely in U.S. newspapers, Noel-Baker observed coolly, "There are a number of beautiful small towns in the East of the United States, some with fine historical and cultural associations." He argued that the staff members and diplomats of the United Nations required a location with excellent schools, universities, and a beautiful setting—all of which suggested the Northeast, at least to Noel-Baker, who had attended Haverford College near Philadelphia and had given lectures at Yale University in New Haven, Connecticut. If the United Nations must be snatched from Europe, Noel-Baker resolved, it would go no farther than absolutely necessary.[4]

In some respects, the British diplomat's strategy resembled the civic booster appeals as he challenged his colleagues to reach beyond technical concerns about a "seat" or "headquarters." Offering a broad vision of what the United Nations' home should be, Noel-Baker outlined a new set of criteria that had a powerful effect on the next phase of discussions. Like the speculative world capital plans created by American architects, he called for a distinctive location standing apart from a city, especially apart from the influence of Washington, D.C. The headquarters should be close enough to a city for diplomats to take advantage of urban cultural amenities, but far enough away that the organization would not become simply another city landmark. The UN should move cautiously and not limit the search to the self-nominated world capital boosters who had traipsed in and out of London, he counseled. Important questions remained to be decided, such as what sort of buildings would house the UN and how much land would be needed. These matters should not be decided in haste, based only on the testimony of self-selected American cities and towns.[5]

The British diplomat also injected the powerful issue of race relations into the mix, once again steering the United Nations toward the Northeast indirectly through an issue that would discourage consideration of other regions. The United Nations, he said, should be in a place where "all members of the United Nations should be able to feel quite at home . . . whatever their racial origin or the character of their state." This statement struck at a characteristic of American society that the civic boosters had consistently ignored or denied. The Second World War had produced a heightened awareness of civil rights issues as the Allies waged war against tyranny abroad. However, as the Swedish economist Gunnar Myrdal pointed out in 1944 in his highly influential study, *The American Dilemma,* a sharp contradiction remained between the "American Creed" of equality and persistent discriminatory treatment of African Americans. The ongoing "Negro problem" posed a moral dilemma not only in regions of the United States where many African Americans lived but throughout American society, Myrdal concluded. Racism, anti-Semitism, and other forms of discrimination could be found anywhere in the United States in 1945 as the UN considered where to place its headquarters. By calling the diplomats' attention to this problem, Noel-Baker focused attention especially on the region where racism seemed most prevalent, the American South.[6]

A delegate from India, Sir Ramaswami Mudaliar, soon joined Noel-Baker in asking the UN to consider the factor of racial discrimination. He recalled that during a recent visit to Washington, D.C., his hotel had refused to allow an African American member of the State Department to join him for dinner. "I was shocked to find that sort of discrimination in a national capital," said Mudaliar, who had become a prominent advocate for human rights within the UN. At the San Francisco conference, he chaired the committee addressing economic and social problems and led the movement to strengthen the language on human rights in the United Nations Charter. With its call for "universal respect for, and observance of, human rights and fundamental freedoms for all without distinction as to race, sex, language, or religion," the charter would be undermined by any potential world capital with circumstances like those Mudaliar encountered in Washington.[7]

On December 21 and 22, as the mayor of San Francisco packed and left for the airport, the British pressed and won their case for the eastern United States. Speaking for the British delegation, Charles Kingsley Webster demanded deference to the interests of Europe, which had been so badly battered by the choice of the United States for the headquarters location. "I should think not only sound judgment but chivalry was dead in the world if after the narrowness of the vote on Europe the seat was removed 2,000 miles further away from us," he declared. His position won sympathy not only from Britain's customary allies, such as South Africa, but also from nations that had voted against a European headquarters. "We should try to do our utmost to put the seat as near as possible to Europe, which would mean on the Atlantic Coast," said the delegate for Brazil, Cyro de Freitas-Valle.[8]

For diplomats who harbored hope of returning to San Francisco, limiting the potential sites in the United States without further study seemed rash and arbitrary. "It would be regarded as an insult to all those delegations who have come here and laid down evidence, if we decide and it goes out to the world without even having any tabulation before us," argued William R. Hodgson, representing Australia. "A lot of people said, 'Do not let us make a hasty decision, let us have the facts.' Now they do not want the facts. They simply say: eastern America. What about the north? What about the south? Are they to be ruled out? I say we cannot do it." Others asked how the boundary between the East and the West would be determined. Even France, which favored placing the headquarters as close to Europe as possible, declared it would vote against both East and West because it did not consider the procedure logical. "The vote is evidently aimed at excluding one particular city"—San Francisco—the French delegate, Vincent Boustra, protested. "Well, we must always remember that this city [was] chosen by Marshall Stalin, by the Right Honorable Winston Churchill and by the late President Roosevelt—three names before which we all bow very profoundly." Should the city be so rashly eliminated? "I really believe that the vote taken under such conditions in the haste in which we are going to take it is against logic, sound judgment, and equity," Boustra concluded, just before the voting began.[9]

To reach the ultimate surprise for Roger Lapham, sitting at the airport one hundred miles away, required a series of four votes. First, the delegates voted on whether to even take such a vote. Clearing that hurdle by a margin of twenty-three to nine, with six abstentions, they next voted on whether their first decision should be an up-or-down vote on the West. To this they also agreed. Finally reaching the substance of the matter, the forty delegates present sealed the fate of San Francisco. Reflecting the empathy among diplomats who had long considered Europe the center of world affairs, all but six—Australia, Chile, Ecuador, Honduras, Iran, and Saudi Arabia—voted against a location in the western United States. Twelve nations abstained, some simply to protest the procedure. The committee then took a final vote to determine whether the UN should place its headquarters in the East. The results were similarly decisive. Twenty-five delegates voted in favor of the East, the region of the United States closest to Europe; five voted against; and ten abstained. Notably, four of the five powers of the UN Security Council—the Soviet Union, China, Great Britain, and France—now aligned in favor of the East. The United States, as usual, abstained.[10]

If the diplomats thought their votes would end the ambitions of boosters from Denver, the Black Hills, or San Francisco, they were wrong. With ten nations absent from the vote and such a large number of abstentions, Americans saw clear grounds for appeal (ignoring the fact that the United Nations had no such process). In Denver, the chamber of commerce temporarily reverted to recruiting East Coast industries and the headquarters of Rotary Clubs International, but the boosters kept watch for an opening to resume their United Nations quest. In South Dakota, the promoters of the Black Hills refused to concede that they were out of the race. Paul Bellamy called the vote on December 22 "simply advisory," and Governor M. Q. Sharpe pledged to carry the Black Hills' excellent case to the UN General Assembly in January. While Mayor Lapham fumed about the insult to San Francisco, cooler heads in California considered sending Governor Earl Warren to London to launch a dramatic appeal. Even the governor of Oklahoma began making telephone calls to Washington to try to set up meetings with the UN committee during its expected tour of possible sites in January.[11]

Meanwhile, for world capital hopefuls east of the Mississippi River, hope surged anew. Surely the vote on December 22 meant that their chances had improved. "Indiana Chances as UNO Capital Still Good," read the headline in the Indianapolis Star. "City's Chances Brightened," said the Michigan City News-Dispatch, in the Indiana town closest to the International Friendship Gardens, one of the sites that the state proposed. "Even Chance UNO to Come Here," declared the Niagara Falls Gazette in bold capital letters beneath the slogan always displayed on its front page: "Power City of the World."[12]

In a season of joyful postwar reunions and prayerful holidays, civic leaders in the eastern United States, especially in New England, composed letters inviting the United Nations to consider their particular beautiful small town. Responding to Noel-Baker's memo, invitations arrived in London from Hartford and New London, Connecticut, and from Bar Harbor and four other communities in Maine. Massachusetts citizens offered Auburn, Beverly, Cape Cod, Lexington and Concord, Northampton, Orange, Plymouth, Rockland, Springfield, and Worcester, among others. From New Hampshire, the UN received an invitation from the World Fellowship Inc., a peace organization with headquarters in Conway. Rhode Island invited attention not only to Newport but to the state at large; from Vermont came the suggestion of Burlington. The invitations endorsed the goals of the United Nations and addressed the organization's practical requirements, but especially among the smaller cities and towns, they also highlighted deeply rooted, traditional regional characteristics. The numerous letters pouring into the UN celebrated history, scenic beauty, and elite appeal—exactly the sort of qualities suggested by Noel-Baker's memo describing the "beautiful small towns of the East."[13]

RACE AND ISOLATIONISM

Although United Nations diplomats continued to refer to a "seat" or "headquarters" for the organization, the place they imagined was in some ways coming to resemble the Capital of the World dreams of American civic boosters, but with a very important difference. By the end of December 1945, guided by Philip Noel-Baker's memorandum, the UN delegates did not think of their task as bestowing the title on an existing community but rather as finding a location where they could develop a home of their own. As a result, Australia gained an unusually high degree of influence that further escalated expectations that the United Nations would create a Capital of the World. Building upon their recent experience developing a new national capital at Canberra, on December 27 the Australians added another influential memorandum to the headquarters discussion. This document, for the first time, offered specifics about the acreage that the UN should seek. The Australians advised that an environment of natural beauty consisting of about one square mile would be needed for buildings of "impressive architectural treatment combined with practical convenience." Surrounding this central area should be parkland or a forest two to three miles wide, with a nearby five-mile stretch of property for an airport. Additional building areas would be needed for housing and support staff, with room to grow for the next fifty years. In all, the Australians advised, the UN should seek a minimum of forty to fifty square miles—an expanse fully in keeping with the idea of creating a Capital of the World. If not a city in the traditional sense, the headquarters site would at least be a distinctive kind of suburb. The Australians agreed with the British that people working for the UN should have access to the cultural amenities of a city, but that the organization should be located some distance outside a city's boundaries in order to maintain a separate identity.[14]

As the UN's new eleven-member Interim Committee on Headquarters gathered for the first time on December 27, the Australians also joined Great Britain and India in calling attention to the problem of racial discrimination in the United States. "It is quite impossible for the United Nations to locate itself in any community where persons may be excluded from hotels, trains, or street cars, or even made to feel uncomfortable because of their race or color," the Australian delegation advised. "It would also be undesirable that, in order to reach the site, delegates had to pass through communities where such discrimination was practiced." This issue soon rose to the top of the list of "essential criteria" that the new Headquarters Committee developed to guide the next phase of the headquarters search. The list retained some of the technical matters that had concerned the UN throughout the fall, but it also showed Noel-Baker's continuing influence, now reinforced by the Australians. Any prospective location would, foremost, need to demonstrate "local political conditions and general character of local press and public opinion in harmony with the Preamble and Article 1 of the Charter," which meant "no general racial discrimination" and "fundamental freedoms for all without distinction as to race, sex, language, or religion." Accessibility and worldwide communications also were deemed "essential." Beyond this, "desirable" qualities included a healthful climate; cultural conditions such as educational and recreational facilities; and sufficient land and buildings. A list of "other points" included "beautiful country and setting," which had been an ongoing theme in the American booster campaigns as well as a priority stated in Noel-Baker's memorandum. The "other points" also stated that the UN should be a "sufficient distance" away from Washington, D.C., and other large cities. Just what that distance should be would depend on the city, but the committee agreed that three hours' travel distance from the nation's capital would be an appropriate buffer between the United Nations and American political interference.[15]

In this new committee, in other words, the diplomats were shuffling their priorities and adding new criteria. The civic boosters who had forged ahead on the basis of their own ideas and the UN's earlier list of requirements would see this as a betrayal. But they had forced themselves into the process while the UN's intentions were still evolving, as the committee's next moves demonstrated.

The vote for East over West on December 22 had primed the committee to think of U.S. geography in terms of regions. The committee had a list of all the known invitations from U.S. localities—fifty of them east of the Mississippi River, so far as they were aware—and their documents categorized the contenders into "areas" associated with particular cities, states, or regions. With "no racial discrimination" high on the new list of essential criteria, it seemed to the Headquarters Committee chairman, Roberto

MacEachen of Uruguay, that this provided grounds for making a quick cut in the territory that the UN should consider. The list made it easy to focus on the South, where the lasting legacies of slavery and the Civil War seemed to most clearly contradict the United Nations Charter, despite booster efforts to reposition the region as modern and industrial.[16]

"We might adopt the Mason-Dixon line," MacEachen suggested. This boundary, established by the English surveyors Charles Mason and Jeremiah Dixon in the eighteenth century to settle a long-standing border dispute between Pennsylvania and Maryland, also came to be the well-known line between slave states and free states prior to the Civil War. Now, eighty years after the surrender at Appomattox, the distinction lingered in the minds of these men seeking a discrimination-free location for the United Nations.[17]

But it was not as easy as that. Meeting behind closed doors, unrestrained by the presence of reporters or boosters, the diplomats struggled to imagine how they might find any location in the United States that would live up to the UN's stated goals for human rights. Their candid conversation showed how issues of race were penetrating international affairs in the aftermath of the Second World War, and how perceptions of race relations in the United States could affect its standing with other nations. The Australian delegate on the committee, Paul Hasluck, admitted that his knowledge about conditions in the United States was limited. When the UN delegates discussed racial discrimination, they tended to think only of "the treatment of Negroes or persons of Negro origin in the United States," Hasluck observed, but he had been inquiring about "whether there is any racial discrimination apart from color." He had come to understand that "racial discrimination has a much broader sense. . . . Anti-Semitism is racial discrimination. And if we exclude the southern States for discrimination against persons of color, should we not exclude any other place with actions against other peoples? I think we have to face that." These were practical issues as well as matters of principle. "We have a United Nations which is going to have in its membership at least two pure African delegates—Liberia and Ethiopia—and Haiti," Hasluck noted. "We have delegations which will come from Asiatic countries; we have delegations from India, and I think if any delegate traveling to or from the headquarters is going to be subjected to humiliation or discrimination, we have put the headquarters in an unsuitable place."[18]

The British delegate who five days earlier had steered the UN toward excluding the western states, Charles Webster, pointed out the additional complication that discrimination could be a matter of tradition, not stated in law. So how was the UN to sort this out? "We cannot establish definitely that there is not in any State a certain amount of social discrimination," Webster commented. "As a matter of fact, in all States there is some kind of discrimination." If the western states were still in contention, the UN would find discrimination against "orientals" as much as against "negroes," he pointed out. Indeed, there were many examples of racial and ethnic tension in the United States, including in northern cities offering themselves to be the UN "peace capital." In 1943, smoldering tension between blacks and whites in overcrowded wartime Detroit had erupted into a 36-hour race riot that left thirty-four people dead, and in Philadelphia in 1944, transit workers had gone on strike rather than accept African Americans as streetcar operators. Boston and New York had experienced violent anti-Semitic attacks on Jews carried out during the war years by Irish-Catholic youth gangs. African Americans in New York in 1945 organized pickets at Yankee Stadium to protest "Jim Crowism" in baseball. Two more years would pass before Jackie Robinson broke the color line in the major leagues. In Hartford, Connecticut, during the summer of 1945, a hotel clerk was arrested for refusing accommodations to an African American couple and their grandchild in defiance of the state's recently enacted antidiscrimination law. The child's father was a soldier in the army, stationed in the Philippines.[19]

What were they to do, Webster asked, rule out everywhere? The wisest course, in his view, was to aim for the Northeast, which was of course in keeping with the British preference all along. By the end of the day, with road maps from the American Automobile Association spread on the table, they came back to MacEachen's initial suggestion: the Mason-Dixon Line. They agreed: they would be more likely to find a welcoming home for diplomats from all nations above the Mason-Dixon Line than below it. All locations south of the line would be eliminated.

This decision, reached behind closed doors on December 27, meant the end of the world capital hopes of Miami and New Orleans, at least as far as the Headquarters Committee was concerned. Their orientation toward Latin America, diverse populations, and offers of scenic settings did nothing to overcome the simple fact that they were located in the South. The committee also rejected proposals from the Upper South, where world capital hopefuls had stressed their contributions to American history prior to the Civil War, sounding very much like the boosters of Philadelphia and Boston as they emphasized their ties to colonial settlement and the

American Revolution. The Mason-Dixon Line decision ended the world capital aspirations of Charlottesville, Virginia, where residents had invited the United Nations to inhabit the "peaceful central Virginia countryside" so richly associated with "the great international humanitarian, Thomas Jefferson." The UN's exclusion of the South came as an especially harsh surprise for three civic boosters from Newport News, in navy-dominated southeast Virginia. Unaware of the Mason-Dixon Line decision, they boarded a plane for London on December 28 with their proposal for placing the United Nations at Camp Peary, a navy training site south of Colonial Williamsburg. The world capital they envisioned would have a "picturesque situation on historic York River" with historic resonance "near Jamestown, the first permanent settlement of English families" and "near Yorktown, where the surrender battle was fought between George Washington and the British." By the time they arrived in London, none of this mattered.[20]

The Headquarters Committee, encouraged by its progress in narrowing the field so far, turned next to the Middle West, another region that some considered incompatible with the United Nations. The committee's list of qualifications for a location included "proper political conditions," including "no considerable isolationist movement." Webster saw in this another opportunity to steer the decision toward the Northeast: "It seems to me that would rule out Chicago," he said, thinking especially of the still strongly isolationist *Chicago Tribune*. "The *Chicago Tribune's* influence is so immense in all that area, and its hostility to such things as the United Nations so great that it might be moved out on that ground almost." The delegate for France, Francois Brière, agreed but argued that the Midwest generally had shifted away from its prewar isolationism. As a "fair matter of courtesy" to such an "important intellectual and cultural center," the committee should at least visit Chicago, he argued. A draft itinerary for inspecting potential sites included "Chicago or Cincinnati," although greater time was to be allotted to the East Coast. But Webster, determined to narrow the field, pointed out that Chicago and other midwestern sites could be eliminated on additional grounds, especially the qualification of "accessibility to the world at large, and adequate and satisfactory means of worldwide travel." Surely the Atlantic Coast would fit this criterion better than any location in the Midwest. Webster did not see how Cincinnati could possibly offer the metropolitan amenities of such Northeast cities as Boston, New York, or Philadelphia.[21]

The British delegate's arguments once again prevailed. However, no one wanted to offend the United States or American public opinion. The committee members agreed that they would not publicly report their lengthy private discussions about race relations, the Mason-Dixon Line, or isolationism. Instead, they would announce a decision pointing to the UN's desire to have the headquarters in close proximity to Europe and release a list of eligible states without further elaboration. The list would omit the West, the South, and the Midwest; to the public, it would simply be a list of best-qualified states. The committee's interpreter read them into the record from the AAA road maps spread on the table: Maine, New Hampshire, Vermont, Massachusetts, Connecticut, Rhode Island, New Jersey, Pennsylvania, Delaware, and New York.

Howls of protest came immediately from rejected world capital hopefuls who found this list to be arbitrary and illogical. Stellanova Osborn, who had vigorously promoted Sault Ste. Marie throughout the fall while nursing the ailing former governor of Michigan, wrote to her mother, "It seems shallow thinking, to base the decision on the mere item of distance, in an age in which distance is being so rapidly annihilated. The choice cannot alter the dramatic facts that make the Saults an ideal site." The lieutenant governor of Indiana pronounced himself "amazed" that his state had been eliminated without closer inspection, and the *Indianapolis Star* editorialized that the UN committee's attitude reflected "lack of knowledge of the great Middle West and its designation as the real heart of America." Indiana was proud to be a "typical American state," the *Star* continued. "It merely regrets that the world headquarters may be handicapped by location in the effete East." In Chicago, Mayor Edward Kelly expressed disappointment but took comfort in his belief that the UN would instead choose Hyde Park, honoring his hero Franklin Roosevelt. A stronger reaction came from St. Louis, where Mayor Aloys P. Kaufmann sent a cable to London declaring, "The entire middle west is concerned and incensed over the arbitrary decision" to rule out the site that his city had proposed.[22]

In the Black Hills, boosters saw the December 27 list as yet another challenge to continue the fight. "The decision . . . to rule out all the United States except a small portion in the northeastern section of the country will not be accepted by the Black Hills World Capital Committee as either a final or a logical method of decision," the governors of South Dakota, Nebraska, and Wyoming telegraphed immediately. Dismissing the issue of distance, they once again described all of the attributes the Black Hills could offer to the United Nations—as if this mattered, which from the standpoint of the United Nations, it never had.[23]

ABSOLUTELY NOT NEW YORK

"Are there any objections to Bar Harbor, Maine? Who knows anything about it?" Such startlingly vague, gentle questions from Roberto MacEachen opened the Headquarters Committee meeting on December 28, a day that would end in more jolting news for long-time pursuers of the world capital prize. Working now from the list of acceptable states, the committee began the process of deciding which of the remaining known contenders would merit an on-site inspection. Cutting out the South and Midwest had reduced their original list from fifty to twenty-nine; but overnight, the recent mail from New England caught up with them and they were back up to forty possibilities. Up to this point, the spontaneous outpouring of invitations from the United States had made little difference, except to the boosters who put so much effort into them. The Headquarters Committee had peeled away entire regions of the United States rather than weigh the merits of so many cities and towns, all of whom seemed capable of spinning themselves into acceptable headquarters locations. They had not looked at the invitations and promotional materials that had been pouring in since August. But now, the simplified list of places, organized by region, provided an orderly, alphabetical way to proceed—at first.[24]

Concerning Bar Harbor, "It is not quite what you would call a seaside resort, Mr. Chairman," said the delegate from France. "There are excellent villas there and pleasant scenery, and it is cool in summer, but there are not the educational or press facilities which we require."

"Is there a large city nearby?" MacEachen asked.

A staff member estimated the distance from Bar Harbor to Boston as 125 to 150 miles, with no direct railway or highway. The secretary of the committee, Boston-born Huntington Gilchrist, said no, by road it would be 260 miles. In any case, the committee members wanted the headquarters to be close enough to a major city to allow for access to schools, medical care, and such cultural amenities as music and theater. So far as Charles Webster was concerned, distance alone ruled out Bar Harbor and a number of other communities on the list. As the committee drifted into musings about whether such Massachusetts towns as Worcester or Springfield might be nice, Webster lost patience with a discussion that seemed already to be off point.

"It does not seem to me that we would decide on them because they are nice little towns," he said in the midst of the banter about Worcester and Springfield. "I know them both, but they are not the kind of towns of which we are thinking when we take into consideration the amenities that will be necessary for the Secretariat, including the medical attention, the educational facilities, the facilities of recreation, and so on, and the factor of nearness to a pretty big metropolis." With the committee focusing first on its list of invitations from New England, Webster had another opening to maneuver the process toward Great Britain's desired outcome. The only useful standard now would be proximity to Boston, he argued—close enough to enjoy all of its attributes, but far enough away so that the UN site would not one day become absorbed into the city. Places like Worcester and Springfield could not compare to Boston, so far as he was concerned. He tried to be diplomatic in saying it, but Boston simply had more class. The United Nations Secretariat would of course "be composed of men of the very highest attainments," and "we do want them, if it is possible, to be in touch with a center where they can meet, shall we say, their equivalents, as they would be able to do in the neighborhood of a great university and a great center of culture."

In other words, they needed to be in the vicinity of Boston. Somewhere within sixty to seventy-five miles of Boston would do, Webster thought. As the day wore on, it became clear that the British diplomat had been making a special study of one Massachusetts town in particular—Concord, the small historic town that was all the more alluring because of its proximity to Harvard University. Concord, Lexington, and other nearby towns had been recommended to the UN earlier in December by Massachusetts congresswoman Edith Nourse Rogers, prompted by one of her constituents. Webster, a history professor by profession, had come to the meeting prepared with a tutorial on Concord, and he sounded very much like Philip Noel-Baker's memorandum as he described "a very typical New England town of considerable beauty, with quite nice country round about."[25]

The committee members continued to sift through the individual invitations they had received, but finding a location outside a city—but not too far outside—became their guiding concern. They continued through their list of New England invitations with the aid of guidebooks produced during the 1930s by the Works Progress Administration and, for the first time, the materials submitted by the cities and towns.

Webster's lesson about Concord reminded the French delegate, Francois Brière, of the nearby and very pleasant North Shore of Massachusetts, a frequent summer destination for diplomats seeking to escape the heat of

Washington, D.C. The UN had not yet received an invitation from any of the North Shore towns, but Brière pronounced them *magnifique*—"perfectly lovely; it is beautifully cool, but it is expensive." Webster had his doubts about whether the shore would provide a "suitable atmosphere," but the suggestion of a location not on the list gave him an idea. The committee might simply establish an appropriate radius around Boston, and allow the site inspection team to use its judgment within that area. The ongoing discussion of New England towns that had submitted invitations helped to establish a radius of sixty miles, which would include some attractive areas near Providence, Rhode Island, and allow for a look at the North Shore of Massachusetts.[26]

Such a radius offered the added benefit of providing a diplomatic way of excluding more distant Newport, which the diplomats in this closed-door meeting dismissed from consideration because of the "character of the city." Newport's elaborate offerings of Gilded Age mansions had not impressed Brière, who informed his colleagues, "Newport gives the impression of a dead city, with large houses built by the wealthy of the last century, which are now falling to pieces, and I do not see how a town of this sort could form a convenient centre for the United Nations." Because of its distance of seventy miles from Boston, Newport's contention to become the Capital of the World ended in the committee room on December 28.[27]

The Headquarters Committee turned next to invitations received from New York cities and towns, reserving New York City for last. In order for Niagara Falls to qualify as a site in the United States, its boosters had strategically shifted their offer from Navy Island, which lay in Canadian territory, to nearby Grand Island. The continued involvement of Canadians in the proposal momentarily kept it in contention, but committee members ultimately decided that nearby Buffalo was "not sufficiently a cultural center." Hyde Park, eighty miles up the Hudson from New York City, posed a challenge to their desire for close proximity to a city. Nearby Poughkeepsie might offer some hotels and services, but, well, it was not Manhattan. Still, for "sentimental reasons," as Webster put it, Franklin Roosevelt's home at Hyde Park should remain on the list. Perhaps Vassar College in Poughkeepsie could serve their purposes temporarily. The distance from New York City could actually be an advantage, Webster said. For New York was "a city of magnetic force. I have lived in it for twelve months at a time and I know what it is. It has a tremendous effect on the souls and minds of men. Many people who have once lived in it cannot live anywhere else." Within a year's time, Webster's words would seem like prophecy.

The committee looked favorably on the suburban areas of Westchester County, New York, and around Ridgefield, Connecticut, but when it came to New York City itself—absolutely not. New York officials were offering Flushing Meadows Park in Queens, the site of the 1939 world's fair and an ongoing project of the influential city parks commissioner Robert Moses. They had not dispatched a team to London, characteristically thinking that New York was such a natural choice that such an effort was unnecessary, but they had issued a formal invitation and had begun making plans. "There is no place in the United States that is better located," Mayor Fiorello LaGuardia told reporters in New York. "We are the center of transportation, the center of communications, the cultural center of the world." New York produced preliminary sketches of a headquarters on the site of the U.S. Government Building of the 1939 fair, with additional administrative buildings flanking a landscaped lagoon. None of this mattered to the delegates on the Headquarters Committee, who agreed that any site within a city would be utterly unacceptable.[28]

When MacEachen read "Flushing Meadows" from the list of invitations, only a brief sputter of discussion followed:

Delegate from the Netherlands, Adrian Pelt: "I think that one is impossible."

Secretary Gilchrist: "That is right in New York City, in the Borough of Queens, near the airport."

Chairman MacEachen: "Clearly impossible, so we strike that out."

Agreed. The United Nations would not go to New York City.

The committee members also dismissed an invitation from Riverdale in the Bronx. They were so wary of New York City that they decided to establish a minimum distance away from the city as well as a maximum range, so there would no chance that the organization would be subsumed into the metropolis. The invitations on their list helped to establish those distances. They would direct their inspection team to sites no closer to New York City than twenty-five miles (which would allow them to include suburban Westchester County) and no farther than eighty miles (the distance needed to retain Hyde Park), and they would only consider New York locations close to or east of the Hudson River. South of New York City, these distances also encompassed parts of New Jersey, but the committee members saw only Princeton as a suitable contender there. No one had officially invited the UN to Princeton, but they had a nice telegram from the

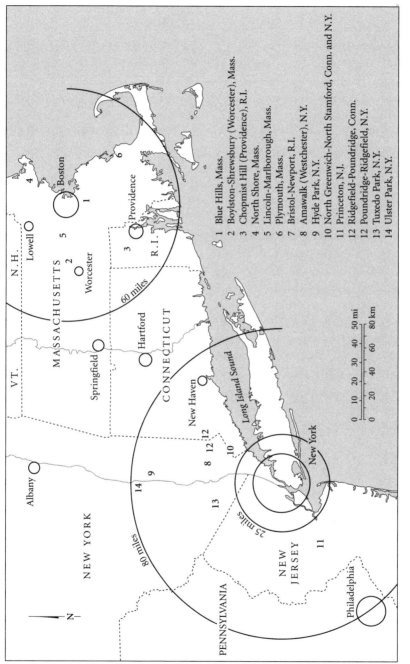

1 Blue Hills, Mass.
2 Boylston-Shrewsbury (Worcester), Mass.
3 Chopmist Hill (Providence), R.I.
4 North Shore, Mass.
5 Lincoln-Marlborough, Mass.
6 Plymouth, Mass.
7 Bristol-Newport, R.I.
8 Amawalk (Westchester), N.Y.
9 Hyde Park, N.Y.
10 North Greenwich-North Stamford, Conn. and N.Y.
11 Princeton, N.J.
12 Ridgefield-Poundridge, Conn.
12 Poundridge-Ridgefield, N.Y.
13 Tuxedo Park, N.Y.
14 Ulster Park, N.Y.

Focusing on suburban areas that would provide access to urban amenities, the United Nations site committee dispatched inspectors to tour sites within designated distances of Boston and New York. The numbered sites on the map were scheduled for inspection during January 1946. (*Geographical Review*, vol. 365, no. 3, reproduced with permission of the American Geographical Society)

president of Princeton University remarking on how closely the university town corresponded with the British memorandum that he had read about in the newspaper.[29]

And what of Philadelphia? Even if the Philadelphians' persistent courting could have set aside the committee's aversion to cities, a single question doomed their nine-month quest to make Philadelphia the Capital of the World. The delegate from the Netherlands asked, "What is the distance from Philadelphia to Washington?" Informed that it was 140 miles, Pelt continued, "Do you not think that the whole area is far too near Washington? I think we ought to cut that out altogether." The conviction had persisted, from Noel-Baker's memo through these two days of site-sifting, that the United Nations needed to avoid the political entanglements that might occur near the nation's capital. Philadelphians had never considered their city especially close to Washington (geographically or otherwise), but this committee viewed anything closer than three hours' travel time to be too close. Without further discussion, the committee agreed to exclude Philadelphia and any nearby contenders, which to that date included adjacent Delaware County and symbolic Valley Forge.[30]

Like the mayor of San Francisco, the Philadelphians had expected the site inspectors to visit six locations, and they fully expected to be one of them. Their hopes had grown during their stay in London. After the actions of the Headquarters Committee became known, L. Stauffer Oliver, one of the Philadelphia boosters, complained to his U.S. senator, "It is of course obvious to anyone who knows America that Philadelphia is not too close to Washington and has never been under Washington influence or domination." The Philadelphians themselves had included mileage to Washington in their promotional materials, thinking that it would appeal to smaller nations who might want to maintain a single ministry to serve both the nation's capital and the UN. If the inspection team did not visit Philadelphia, then the Philadelphians certainly would be paying another visit to the UN, to appeal to the General Assembly to overturn these unfair developments.[31]

At the end of its two days of private discussions, the Interim Committee on Headquarters announced to the press that it would soon send an inspection team to the United States. The rapid narrowing of potential sites for the United Nations showed that at the end of 1945, perceptions of place from the top-down perspective of international affairs differed markedly from the home-grown views of the civic boosters who had flooded the UN with invitations and appeals. But now the diplomats were poised to move into local arenas. Like suburban house hunters, the UN inspectors would look for a headquarters site in only two general areas: within a sixty-mile radius of Boston and in the vicinity of New York, not closer than twenty-five miles and not more than eighty miles away. The swift and seemingly arbitrary nature of their decisions so far had stunned many in the United States. Soon, it would be the diplomats' turn to be surprised.

PART III

AMERICAN DREAMS

7

STUMBLE

PRIMED BY THE eagerness of civic boosters across the United States, an inspection team from the United Nations touched down in New York in January 1946 to find a site for the future Capital of the World. The leader of the group, Stoyan Gavrilovic of Yugoslavia, embraced the dream. He believed that the United Nations would create not merely a headquarters but a world capital that would be a symbol and assurance of peace for perhaps fifty, or one hundred, or even fifteen hundred years. "What the builders of the United Nations have in view is one of the finest things that the world has ever seen," he said in an interview broadcast on the CBS radio network. "The idea is to build a place which will be reserved entirely for the United Nations, a place which will become the Capital of the World."

Gavrilovic believed that a UN capital in the United States, far removed from the power struggles of Europe, would be a place where "every problem concerning every people, big or small, regardless of size, regardless of race, regardless of religion and everything else, will be handled." What a difference such a place would have made for his country, which had been caught in two world wars during his lifetime, and for his own family. In 1941, just two days before the Nazis invaded Yugoslavia, his wife and son had escaped Belgrade in a small boat; they ended up in Palestine while he, transported by British plane and warship, landed in Cairo. They reunited briefly at his next diplomatic post in Cape Town, South Africa, but another harrowing experience lay ahead in 1942, when torpedoes hit a ship carrying Vera and young Ivan Gavrilovic to the United States. They spent two days on a life raft before being rescued by the United States Coast Guard. For the duration of the war, they settled in New York while Gavrilovic continued his work for Yugoslavia, sometimes in New York but often far away in London, Belgrade, Washington, or San Francisco.[1]

The nation that sheltered the Gavrilovic family seemed to offer an unrestrained welcome for the United Nations as well, judging by the numerous eager Americans who had dispatched their elaborate brochures, promotional films, and important representatives to London. Thus encouraged, the diplomats came to the United States to shop for forty to fifty square miles of American real estate—an area roughly twice the size of the island of Manhattan. Gavrilovic explained that such an expansive territory would provide the United Nations with room to establish its own identity, to grow in size and magnificence, and to inspire future generations. The world capital would have "momentous and historic meaning," he said. "A place of this kind attracts world-wide attention. A place of this kind will become a Mecca to which thousands and thousands of people will flock from all over the world." The Capital of the World as Mecca implied a spiritual quality, a place of pilgrimage. Imagining the world capital as Mecca conveyed serious purpose, solemn duty, and connotations that reached beyond Western tradition even though Western powers dominated the UN.[2]

When the diplomats arrived at LaGuardia Field on January 6, 1946, they found an official welcoming committee from New York City, photographers, and reporters who pressed eagerly for any clue about their preferences for a site. At the team's temporary headquarters at the Waldorf-Astoria Hotel, more solicitous letters and telegrams were accumulating. The mayor of Morristown, New Jersey, began an especially vigorous campaign to persuade the UN team to visit his town, "the military crossroads of the Colonies." A man from Hawthorne, New Jersey, sent an invitation complete with drawings of world capital buildings named for Roosevelt, Churchill, and Stalin. An official from Easton, Pennsylvania, pointed out that with just a bit more travel, the UN could have a lovely site in the Poconos. Boosters from New York and Philadelphia sought meetings to try to put their cities back into the scope of the diplomats' search. From greater distances, promoters of Niagara Falls, the Black Hills, and San Francisco continued to believe that they would still, somehow, have a chance.[3]

Nevertheless, in the areas around Boston and New York, the perspectives of diplomats and the interests of the UN's potential neighbors were about to collide in unanticipated ways. The UN's actions in selecting a location, whether for a headquarters building or a grand capital city, tapped into one of the most contentious issues confronting the new international organization—the issue of sovereignty. In a world increasingly connected by networks of politics, economics, culture, and diplomacy, what degree of self-government would survive? Could the United Nations take any site it wanted, regardless of local opinion? How would citizens make their voices heard? And in a nation with layers of local, state, and federal government, how would the United Nations know which way to turn? Such issues

resonated deeply in one of the regions where the United Nations most desired to be—New England, where town meetings remained a cherished
tradition of direct democracy. As soon became clear, Americans were in
favor of creating a Capital of the World, so long as it was their idea in the
first place.

WALDEN POND AND THE WORLD

The people of Concord, Massachusetts, confronted an astonishing prospect at the end of 1945: their town, because of its proximity to Boston,
might actually become the Capital of the World. In this town with deep
literary traditions, the people appreciated the irony that the world might
descend on secluded Walden Pond, but that did not mean they had to like
it. Never mind that cities and towns all over the United States were scrambling to lure the United Nations. In Concord, the world capital idea was
not simply a dream; it seemed to be an impending reality.

Concord could trace its history and tradition back to Puritan colonists
and the American Revolution, but like other towns its size in similar settings, it was not simply a quaint Norman Rockwell image of village life.
Across the United States, within the orbits of larger cities, the advent of
commuter railroads, highways, and especially automobiles had transformed once-rural hamlets. Situated just twenty-five miles from Boston,
Concord had become a suburb as well as a town, and its population grew
rapidly as the automobile made commuting to the city more attractive.
Automobiles also brought more tourists to Concord and nearby Lexington to follow the trail of Paul Revere and the Minutemen and to seek the
haunts of such famous literary figures as Nathaniel Hawthorne, Louisa
May Alcott, Ralph Waldo Emerson, and Henry David Thoreau. The town
retained much of its traditional charm, with a business district of red-brick
and clapboard buildings facing a village green. But signs of modern life
mixed with the colonial ambiance, and by the time Concord emerged from
the Great Depression and the Second World War, the side streets named
Walden, Lowell, and Thoreau were home to automobile showrooms and
mechanics' garages.[4]

The UN's interest in Concord sounded an alarm among people who
were already balancing time-honored traditions with changes beyond their
control. Volleys of letters flew to the town's two newspapers, the *Journal*
and the *Enterprise*. Concord divided into discord. The dispute did not have
much to do with the merits of the United Nations; indeed, some Concord

citizens were activists in the world federalism movement, which sought a much stronger form of world government. The debate focused instead on the character of the town and control of its future. What further changes might occur if a Capital of the World came to occupy the undeveloped two-thirds of the surrounding township? Most of the letter writers overlooked or did not know that the suggestion to bring the UN to Concord had originated with a local citizen in November 1945. By the end of December, prominent local residents were complaining that their rights to self-government had been trampled by Congresswoman Edith Nourse Rogers, who had extended the invitation to the UN without consulting them.[5]

Some Concord citizens embraced the world capital prospect as a fitting tribute to the town's history as an important site of the American Revolution, but others feared that the UN would bring crowding, traffic, and unwanted change to a cherished New England village. Famous figures of the past were drawn into the argument. Some Concord residents claimed that Thoreau would deplore such an encroachment on the town's serenity, while others quoted Emerson: "Whence this worship of the past?" Befitting the local literary tradition, the debate escalated into poetry. "If Jesus came to Concord Town / And told us wars might cease, / We'd turn our backs and walk away; / We'd snub the Prince of Peace," wrote Gertrude H. Rideout in a letter to the *Concord Journal*.[6]

Concord's contemporary writers joined the fray. Allen French, author of books about the American Revolution, wrote that Concord was "a town of quiet homes and simple living, and its inhabitants have long regarded it as pleasantly apart from the world." To graft an international organization into this setting "would not merely change Concord, it would destroy it," he argued, in concert with others who viewed Concord as a historical gem to be safeguarded. Ruth Wheeler, author of local histories and a founder of the Thoreau Society, countered that change could be good for Concord. "In 1840 people were sure Concord would be spoiled by the railroad; in 1890, by the trolley; in 1910 by the automobile; and in 1940 by the airport," she reminded the readers of the *Journal*. "Each time Concord changed physically but remained unique. I believe Concord can be spoiled only by stagnation." Change would come, and perhaps the UN offered a way to control the nature of that change. "Already on the drawing boards . . . are the plans for a hundred houses," Wheeler pointed out. "These houses can be filled by our own sons and daughters, they can be filled by the intellectual cream of the countries of the world, or they can be filled by the unselected overflow from Metropolitan Boston. It is this last alternative we should be worrying about." Facing an uncertain but certainly different future, Concord might find that welcoming the UN would be its best defense against the encroaching suburban expansion of Boston.[7]

In Concord as well as in nearby, much smaller Sudbury, Massachusetts, residents feared that newcomers and the demands of the UN would displace long-standing residents from their homes. Similar concerns were stirring in wealthy Greenwich, Connecticut, which lay within the UN's desired radius of New York City, although the managing editor of the *Greenwich Time* newspaper saw no sense in dwelling on such a remote possibility. The United Nations, he wrote, "has about as much chance of getting into Greenwich's sacrosanct confines as a glue factory." Nevertheless, in these towns, people were beginning to worry that the very virtues that New England's civic boosters had been promoting to the United Nations might be destroyed in the event of success.[8]

The symbolism of the pristine, exemplary New England town had appeared in many of the letters that local boosters had dispatched to the UN during the last weeks of December. As the news spread that the diplomats desired distance from major cities, New Englanders had stressed their separation from the distracting chaos of urban life. Boosters of Burlington, Vermont, argued that the UN would benefit from being "far enough from the teeming metropolitan centers to escape their confusion, noise, congestion, discords and discomforts." Letter writers portrayed the New England town as fundamental to the democratic values of the United States, central in the nation's history, and a fitting inspiration to the world. Plymouth, Massachusetts, with its famous rock, offered the most dramatic example of these connections: "The town of Plymouth is the site upon which a great nation had its beginning," the Plymouth county commissioners wrote to the UN. "We believe the nations of the world might here find the answers which would give birth to a greater and better world of nations." Orange, Massachusetts, created a brochure touting itself as "a sturdy new England Town" with "stable political background" and enthusiasm for the "town meeting type of government—the purest form of self-government." Lenox, Massachusetts, informed the UN that "[h]ere are all the conveniences of a modern, progressive civilization together with the dignity and charm of an old New England village." Notwithstanding the controversy in Concord, between twenty and thirty communities in Massachusetts alone notified Governor Maurice J. Tobin of their eagerness to host the UN.[9]

The outpouring of boosterism made New England towns seem especially appealing and welcoming to the United Nations. But the skirmish in Concord and stirrings in Sudbury and Greenwich were small warnings that in some communities, strongly felt local identity could be a barrier rather than a bridge to the outside world, especially when private property was at stake.

THE SIDEWALKS (AND SUBURBS) OF NEW YORK

New York City was the location that Gavrilovic and the other UN diplomats adamantly did not want, but a contender they could not avoid as they settled into their rooms on the eighth floor of the Waldorf-Astoria, the luxurious art deco hotel on Fifth Avenue in midtown Manhattan. Their very presence in New York and their activities for the next three weeks showed how suitable the city could be as a United Nations home. From Manhattan, they were able to take a train to Washington to pay a courtesy call on President Harry S. Truman. They could motor along landscaped parkways to the Hudson Valley, the Connecticut suburbs, and Long Island, and they could catch a quick flight to Boston. They could find all the engineering consultants, business services, and legal advice they needed, and more press attention than they could ever want. When they were ready to depart, they needed only to make their way back to LaGuardia Field for return flights to Europe.[10]

Joining Gavrilovic in the inspection group were diplomats from four nations on the UN Security Council (France, the United Kingdom, the Soviet Union, and China) and, to broaden the representation, from Uruguay and Iraq. Like Gavrilovic, committee members Shuhsi Hsu of China and François Brière of France had significant experience with diplomatic postings in the United States. But two other members—Kenneth G. Younger of the United Kingdom and Awni el Khalidy of Iraq—had never been in the United States before, and Soviet representative Georgii Saksin's experience in the United States was limited to the United Nations Conference on Food and Agriculture held in Hot Springs, Virginia, in 1943. On a tight schedule to report to the first meeting of the UN General Assembly, soon to begin in London, the committee relied on the guidance of a small staff led by Huntington Gilchrist, an American born in Boston, briefings from the New York Regional Planning Association, and a hastily recruited team of engineers and technical consultants. The United States, maintaining neutrality on the site question, had no representative on the committee, which left a vacuum for local advice that civic boosters were all too eager to fill.[11]

To Robert Moses, the New York City parks commissioner, it seemed like amateur night at the Waldorf. Moses, who had masterminded the parkways and bridges that linked Manhattan Island to the suburbs, had been trying since October to find out exactly what the United Nations diplomats wanted so he could give it to them. But they offered him no specifications for roads and buildings (because they had none). Their preferred distances around New York and Boston seemed maddeningly arbitrary. Extending the search far enough to include Hyde Park, FDR's home eighty miles away from the city, struck Moses as absurd.[12]

Surely now that the UN's representatives had planted themselves squarely in the middle of New York City, they could be persuaded to see the logic of the location the New Yorkers were offering at Flushing Meadows, Queens, the site of the 1939 New York World's Fair. True, the site had a previous life as the Corona Ash Dumps, the "valley of ashes" made memorable in F. Scott Fitzgerald's 1925 novel *The Great Gatsby*, but it had been gloriously reclaimed for the fair dedicated to "Building the World of Tomorrow." To Moses, there could be no better site for the future peacekeepers for the world.

The inspection group, ever mindful of protocol, accepted an invitation to meet with Mayor William O'Dwyer (Fiorello LaGuardia's successor) and other civic leaders at New York City Hall on January 8, a day after visiting President Truman in Washington. The New Yorkers came prepared with a 26-page promotional "brochure"—a publication two feet square, bound in blue leather, with a map folding out ten feet in length and five feet wide. Despite the presence of such persuasive personalities as Robert Moses and Nelson A. Rockefeller, the diplomats resisted the appeal. They stuck firmly to the "terms of reference" approved in London, which meant they would consider no site within twenty-five miles of New York City. Declining to even accept the New Yorkers' brochure, they conceded only that the city might be suitable as a temporary meeting place while the UN built a suburban capital. This did not assuage the New Yorkers, who were equally committed to their own terms. They had no interest in the consolation prize, which would mean expense and inconvenience with no long-term benefit. It should be all or nothing, they insisted. And they wanted it all.[13]

People in Poughkeepsie, New York, also wanted it all, and they had been planning for months for the moment about to arrive. The idea to transform Franklin Roosevelt's ancestral home into the Capital of the World sprang from Poughkeepsie, where Dutchess County Clerk Frederic A. Smith and a former American Legion commander, Harold K. Joseph, came up with the idea around the same time. Poughkeepsie, a county seat city of forty-five thousand people, lay about ten miles south of the Roosevelt estate, close enough to share the honor and benefits of a world capital at Hyde Park. Since August, Smith, Joseph, and other civic leaders had built community support by recruiting allies among local organizations and public officials. Their committee to promote Hyde Park created brochures, gathered intelligence from congresspeople and the State Department, and dispatched a chamber of commerce leader to London to appeal personally to the UN. By the end of December 1945, reporters were listing Hyde Park among the leading choices to become Capital of the World. The selection seemed imminent when the UN's site committee established its desired radius around New York City at eighty miles, exactly the distance needed to include Hyde Park.[14]

The people of the village of Hyde Park (population 4,065 in 1940) were themselves nonchalant about the idea. Some were ardent Roosevelt supporters, but as in the rest of the country, others were equally opposed. More than one thousand Hyde Park residents signed a petition supporting the invitation to the UN, but reporters also found one villager angry enough to sputter, "It's bad enough to have Roosevelt buried here without bringing in a lot of damn foreigners!" In any case, when the Poughkeepsie people promoted Hyde Park for the United Nations, they did not mean the little village with its four churches and a Main Street intersection consisting of a drug store, grocery, barber shop, auto dealership, post office, and Odd Fellows' Hall. They meant the Roosevelt estate nearby, together with the two other Gilded Age estates of the Vanderbilt and Rogers families that might be combined to create a suitable site. During the war, the Roosevelt estate had been a "diplomatic crossroads of the world," the boosters boasted, reminding the UN of visits by heads of state, including the king of England.[15]

The booster campaign omitted any hint of controversy about Roosevelt's policies or legacy, despite intense opposition even in his home county. A Republican state senator pushed for a referendum to see if FDR's neighbors agreed with the invitation to the UN. A letter from a New York banker indicated the trouble that might lie ahead if the UN opted for Hyde Park: "There hasn't been anyone in our lifetime who has been so roundly hated by large sections of the people," Pierre Jay of the Fiduciary Trust Company declared. But whatever controversy lingered about FDR, in the eight months since his death the Hyde Park estate had become a shrine.

Political and business leaders in Poughkeepsie, New York, promoted Franklin Roosevelt's family estate at nearby Hyde Park as the UN's future home. On the cover of their promotional brochure, camera angles create a capitol-like impression by focusing on the Corinthian columns adorning the Roosevelt home. (United Nations Archives)

Roosevelt had bequeathed the estate to the federal government, had established the first presidential library and museum on the property, and now his gravesite gave Hyde Park irresistible appeal. As the Poughkeepsie boosters' brochure proclaimed, "Hyde Park's magic spell has been apparent since Franklin D. Roosevelt was laid to rest in the rose garden between the homestead where he was born and the Roosevelt Library." The photograph of the Roosevelt "homestead" on the brochure's cover emphasized the mansion's Corinthian columns, suggesting not a private home but a capitol building just waiting for the opportunity to serve its natural purpose.[16]

It seemed magical, indeed, on January 10 when the UN site hunters arrived, gathered around the radio in FDR's own study, and listened while their colleagues in London convened the first meeting of the United Nations General Assembly. Intensifying the connection, the delegates on the other side of the Atlantic included Eleanor Roosevelt, the president's widow, beginning her own diplomatic career. A practiced expert in deflecting requests for public endorsements, she had declined to become involved in the campaign to bring the United Nations to Hyde Park. The Poughkeepsie people were on their own and rather disappointed in the site searchers' businesslike approach, which prohibited entertainment or gifts. But the inspection group showed every sign of seriously considering Hyde Park. After their one-day tour they dispatched an engineer to study the terrain and advise on its suitability. Fortunately for the boosters, it did not become known until much later that the engineer's plan for a Capital of the World on the Hudson would have eliminated the village of Hyde Park altogether.[17]

From Hyde Park, the inspection team motored next into Westchester County, New York, and adjacent Fairfield County, Connecticut, the suburban counties closest to New York City. In each, officials and interested citizens had been reaching out for the UN's attention, and like suburban real estate developers they now saw their chance to seal the deal. The scenery created a favorable impression as the motorcade moved south into Westchester County on parkways and gently winding, wooded roads. The southernmost tip of Westchester County, closest to New York, already was solidly developed by 1945, but this northern region of small towns and sprawling estates lay beyond the outcroppings of urban life. The site hunters spent the night of January 10 at the gracious Westchester Country Club, adjacent to an expanse of forty-seven square miles that county officials had identified as a potential headquarters site. Situated twenty-five miles from midtown Manhattan, this was as close as the diplomats could get to New

York and remain true to their desired distance away from the city. The site offered access to Long Island Sound and to the new county airport at Rye Lake. "This place has got everything—name it and we've got it," promised one of their local hosts, Gustavus T. Kirby, the chairman of the Westchester Planning Department.[18]

Not knowing exactly what the UN might need, Westchester County officials were prepared to offer anything that might be desired. At the county government center in White Plains on January 11, they displayed maps showing two sites large enough to accommodate a free-standing Capital of the World. Along with the Westchester Country Club area, they outlined a site farther north near the towns of Somers and Yorktown, which the diplomats had viewed during their drive the previous day. Sharing a common assumption that the UN might gravitate toward embassylike mansions and estates, they described opportunities to occupy Rockwood Hall, the former home of William Rockefeller near North Tarrytown, among others. When reporters pressed Gavrilovic for his opinion, he clearly was impressed. "It is the most beautiful country, this Westchester," he said, and added, "I think your roads in Westchester are particularly beautiful and fine." He showed no concern about the cost of such highly desirable real estate, but he was warned: "It will cost a lot of money," said Kirby, the local host. From the start, Westchester County emphasized that its offer consisted of opportunity, not a donation. The large tracts in Westchester County could cost $25 million or more.[19]

Motoring north into Connecticut, the diplomats found Governor Raymond E. Baldwin and a convoy of state police waiting to escort them through Fairfield County. Close to the state line between Connecticut and New York, near Ridgefield, they joined another local host, Ruth "Sunny" Cutten, who had been so determined to offer her estate to the UN that she had dispatched a personal emissary to London in December. Wearing a mink coat, Cutten accompanied her distinguished visitors on a drive through her estate, situated fifty miles northeast of Manhattan. They toured the sixteen miles of private roads linking her fourteen properties, including the mansion called Sunset Hall. Cutten told the site searchers that she offered her beautiful home and its grounds to help the UN in its vital work—and she would let the property go for a mere $1.5 million, less than the $2 million it had cost to develop.[20]

The diplomats ended their day in Stamford, Connecticut, which had jumped into the competition to attract the UN in December, soon after residents learned of the organization's decision to place its headquarters in the Northeast. Even though this town could trace its history nearly as far back as Concord, Massachusetts, the prospect for a nearby Capital of the World unfolded through a different series of events that built support rather than opposition. As in Concord, the idea began with a local citizen. Reading about the UN proceedings in the newspaper, Arthur I. Crandall, a real estate developer, thought immediately of the undeveloped area of the Mianus River Gorge in southwest Stamford. Crandall, whose projects included the Merritt Parkway through southeastern Connecticut, was well attuned to the potential of this region thirty-five miles from midtown Manhattan, but he did not know exactly what the UN might require. "I only knew that here was a large family seeking a home," he later recalled.

Instead of reaching out to a distant congressional representative, as Concord's first promoter had done, Crandall acted locally. On the evening of December 22, 1945, he visited the home of the publisher of the local newspaper, the *Stamford Advocate,* who thought Crandall was joking when he asked, "Why shouldn't Stamford be a part of the Capital of the World?" But within days, the newspaper began publishing stories about local residents' support for the idea, and the Stamford proposal gathered momentum rather than controversy. By the end of December the Stamford Board of Selectmen issued an official invitation, and a committee of local citizens assembled at the Ferguson Library to discuss the idea. Within less than two weeks' time, the UN diplomats themselves now arrived to survey the landscape.[21]

Unfortunately, they arrived after dark. Approaching the end of another 9:00-to-midnight work day, the convoy of diplomats, staff members, and reporters turned back to New York City. In three days, they had inspected Hyde Park and completed a circuit of the northern suburbs of New York City, from the Westchester Country Club north to Ridgefield and back to Stamford, Connecticut. Thinking back over the whirlwind of FDR's study, views over the Hudson, the mink-coated mansion owner, the country club, the property maps, the boosters, and the police escorts, one of the reporters remarked to his colleagues, "You know, this would make a wonderful movie. Only who would believe it? Nobody would."[22]

WEEKEND IN JERSEY

The diplomats' drive into New Jersey the next day did not match the impression they had gained of suburban New York and Connecticut. One of their rented automobiles suffered a flat tire on the Pulaski Skyway between

Hoboken and Newark, and their New Jersey escorts had to assure them that a planned superhighway would soon bypass the scenery that a reporter described as consisting of "disfiguring signs, deserted houses, garish roadhouses, and rubbish heaps." To their great relief, the inspection team found pleasant surroundings in Princeton, which they had determined in London to be the only site in New Jersey worthy of consideration. They stopped at the New Jersey governor's mansion, toured the university with Allen Dulles of the U.S. State Department, and viewed two large tracts of land nearby. The people of Princeton neither promoted nor resisted the UN's interest in their university town and its countryside, a stance the *Princeton Herald* regarded as good sense rather than apathy. Better to be judged by merit and remain "unblemished by ballyhoo."[23]

The "terms of reference" that the diplomats had agreed upon in London proved to be a convenient shield against the unwanted attentions of still more world capital hopefuls. The mayor of Morristown, New Jersey, was especially persistent, and a town meeting endorsed his idea to place the United Nations near the inspirational campsite of George Washington's army during the American Revolution. While the site inspectors deflected this and other regional contenders, including Philadelphia and sites in the Poconos, they leapt far beyond their predetermined boundaries for their next stop—Atlantic City. The seaside resort was 125 miles away from Manhattan, but its hotels and convention facilities suggested it as a temporary home if the UN opted for Princeton as a permanent location. With New York remaining obstinate about serving as an interim meeting place, the inspection group needed options. And so the diplomats motored one hundred miles southeast from Princeton to spend one night at the Jersey shore.[24]

In contrast to New England communities like Concord, where a Capital of the World would bring radical change, the prospect of hosting the UN in Atlantic City reaffirmed local history and traditions rooted in conventions and tourism. From the standpoint of tourism promoters, the UN was in essence a very special convention, a step beyond the Rotary International, which would be arriving in June. Atlantic City had been marketing its resort facilities to Europeans since 1909 and had hosted diplomats once before, during the organizational meeting of the United Nations Relief and Rehabilitation Association in 1943. Although Atlantic City's boosters had hoped to see a permanent world capital rise on adjacent Brigantine Island, they competed vigorously for the opportunity to make "the Playground of the World" the UN's temporary home.[25]

Welcomed by local and state officials, the site inspectors toured Atlantic City's residential areas and its famed boardwalk on January 13 with an escort of police on motorcycles. The local hosts could not resist embellishing the tour. At the City Auditorium, the site inspectors were impressed by the seating capacity and asked questions about how the space might be divided—all to the tune of international folk music played on the "world's biggest" pipe organ. As men of the world, they were accustomed to respecting local culture, but at their hotel they found themselves subjected to a custom especially strange. At the behest of their hosts, Stoyan Gavrilovic—the diplomat guiding the search for the Capital of the World—removed his shoes, stood on a chair, and watched while a hotel manager emptied an envelope of local sand into his footwear. The *Atlantic City Press* reported approvingly that the Yugoslavian "left with Atlantic City sand in his shoes, thus virtually insuring his return." Indeed, the committee decided on the spot that Atlantic City would be a suitable interim site.[26]

BLIMP OVER BOSTON

After an interlude of two days in New York, the UN team flew to Boston, where flowers, fruit baskets, lobsters, filet mignon, and a private elevator awaited them at the Hotel Statler, their home base for surveying sites surrounding the city. Even though temperatures hovered near zero when the site searchers arrived at Logan International Airport on January 16, Governor Maurice Tobin came out to meet them in his continuing role of chief salesman for Boston and the metropolitan area. Escorted once again by police, the diplomats dined at the Statler, attended an official welcome at the Massachusetts State House on Beacon Hill, and did not decline arrangements for evening entertainment—a Boston Bruins hockey game. Because Boston might serve as a temporary headquarters if the UN selected a site in the surrounding area, work resumed the next day with a city tour that required three buses, two of them for the growing retinue of newspaper and radio reporters. En route, members of Boston's UN booster committee pointed out the Boston Museum of Art, the Gardner Museum, Harvard University, and hotels that soon would be vacated by the armed forces. Through careful orchestration, the convoy arrived at Symphony Hall just in time to hear a rehearsal of the Boston Symphony under the direction of a British conductor, Sir Adrian Boult.[27]

Towns north and south of Boston were taking no chances that the resistance in Concord and Sudbury would harm their prospects. To head off conflict and broaden support, promoters of both the North Shore and South Shore recruited allies among neighboring towns. To the south, a proposal to place the United Nations in the Blue Hills region envisioned the UN cradled between the hills and the shore, with the hills offering a scenic buffer from Boston as well as a supply of available mansions that had fallen on hard times during the Great Depression. This idea originated with the chamber of commerce in Quincy, the ancestral home of the presidential Adams family, but Quincy boosters gave their neighbors a voice in the process by organizing a summit with other towns—Milton, Randolph, Canton, Needham, Norwood, and Dedham. Similarly, along Boston's North Shore, boosters in the town of Beverly—long a summer retreat for diplomats seeking relief from the heat of Washington—recruited support from towns surrounding the centerpiece of their site, the 994-acre Princemere estate, which financier and philanthropist Frederick H. Prince offered to donate. Closer to Boston, communities around Medford also united to promote a site in the Middlesex Fells state reserve lands.[28]

The strategy worked. Warm welcomes greeted the UN inspection group as it toured the Blue Hills and continued south as far as Plymouth, then traveled northward to the area offered by Beverly. Although the UN committee came to see property, boosters used history to tie together local interests, national history, and the world's future. Promoters on the North Shore wisely steered away from celebrating their region's early history, marked as it was by the witch trials of Salem. But the boosters of Beverly celebrated their more recent history as a summer escape for Washington diplomats and dignitaries, including the prince of Wales and Presidents William Howard Taft and Calvin Coolidge. At Plymouth, proud local citizens could not resist placing the diplomats in the position of offering ceremonial praise to humble Plymouth Rock. Stoyan Gavrilovic obliged: "We are deeply impressed by this piece of stone which means so much in your history."[29]

At Plymouth, the diplomats also paused and puzzled over a monument to Massasoit, the Wampanoag Indian chief at the time of the Pilgrims' landing. If Indians were as large and strong as the statue, Gavrilovic wondered, what had happened to them? "Oh," Huntington Gilchrist responded mildly, "they all went out West to reservations." In another conversation between the Soviet and British members of the committee, Kenneth G. Younger of Great Britain explained the fate of the Indians by saying that "the English fed them lots of liquor and the race gradually deteriorated." If the diplomats were reflecting on the nature and breakdown of empire in

the twentieth-century world, their intentions were overlooked by reporters who quoted the conversations as amusing anecdotes of foreigners trying to make sense of American history.[30]

The diplomats also ventured into the sensitive vicinity of Concord and
Sudbury. Mindful of local resistance, Gavrilovic took questions from reporters while seated before the fireplace in the 261-year-old Wayside Inn
in South Sudbury, a building rescued and restored by Henry Ford in 1923.
Gavrilovic pledged that the UN would not harm any "antiquities," but
he acknowledged that town boundaries would have to be altered if the
UN settled into a site in the vicinity of Concord, Sudbury, and Thoreau's
Walden Pond. State officials tried to reassure residents that their property
would not be threatened, and Governor Tobin himself led the tour of the
nearest airport, at Bedford, and to the top of Nobscot Hill for a view that
heightened the committee's interest. Soon in Sudbury, petitions circulated
to ask local officials to protest the UN's focus on their community. Local
officials agreed. Why hadn't they been consulted by either the UN or the
governor? The community already had lost three thousand acres to the
federal government for a munitions dump during the war, and that seemed
like sacrifice enough.[31]

In between their journeys to the western suburbs and the North Shore,
the diplomats took an opportunity for an unparalleled view of their choices
near Boston. From the time of their arrival, the dirigible Victory waited
at anchor at the naval air facility at South Weymouth to provide an aerial
view of the suburbs around Boston. At 10:00 a.m. on January 20, the 310-
foot ship took off with three of the diplomats, their staff, and assorted state
officials for a three-hour tour. Cruising forty to fifty miles an hour at an
altitude of one to two thousand feet, the blimp gave the diplomats a view
that clarified their choices. The aerial perspective eliminated the Middlesex
Fells site north of Boston, which appeared much too hemmed in by existing towns and development. But from the air, the site inspectors still liked
the area that wanted them least, Concord and Sudbury.[32]

Back on the ground, the diplomats' itinerary also carried them west to
Worcester and south to view several more sites in Rhode Island, including
Bristol, Portsmouth, and the Chopmist Hill area west of Providence. Meanwhile, Boston's promoters felt they had successfully culminated their world
capital campaign. They took it as a good sign that the UN committee stayed
in the region until January 24, a visit twice as long as the originally intended
four days (even though the extra time included the day they were snow-
bound in Boston by a blizzard and a full day and night in Rhode Island).

They did have one nagging worry. Just as boosterism could not determine the outcome of the contest, it could not guarantee consensus in Boston. On the night of January 20, with the site searchers still ensconced at the Statler, the Massachusetts Knights of Columbus gathered in Boston for a dinner honoring their supreme knight, Superior Court judge John E. Swift. Before an audience of fifteen hundred people, including Governor Tobin and other members of Boston's UN booster committee, the judge offered a "humble prayer for success" for the UN—which was needed, he said, because the organization had "banished even the name of God from its deliberations." With this, he shared the views of other American Christians who criticized the organization for omitting references to a deity in its proceedings and charter. Judge Swift also blasted the Soviet Union. "All the world knows that godless Russia has torn the Atlantic Charter to tatters and enslaved millions of our fellow-Catholics," Swift declared, "all the way from Finland and Poland to Catholic Austria and Yugoslavia, and almost to the very gates of Rome." If members of the audience disagreed with the judge, they did not show it by leaving the event. Swift, after all, was the guest of honor. The best that the UN boosters could do in the aftermath was to plead that the judge was only one individual, voicing one man's opinion in a nation that guaranteed the right to free speech.[33]

With such anti-Soviet statements resonating as the diplomats headed back to New York, would Boston have any chance at all?

RUMORS, RESISTANCE, AND DEMOCRACY

In Greenwich, Connecticut, a town of thirty-six thousand residents just thirty miles from midtown Manhattan, these were days of mystery and speculation. During the middle weeks of January, it became increasingly clear that the UN inspection group was taking an interest in the rural backcountry of Greenwich, which stretched from the town center near the coast of Long Island Sound inland to the state line between Connecticut and New York. The tract was near Stamford, which had invited the UN's interest, but mostly in Greenwich, which had done nothing of the sort. After the first January night when the site searchers arrived in Stamford in darkness, a subcommittee of two diplomats returned to view not only Stamford's recommended area around the Mianus River, which lay between the town centers of Stamford and Greenwich, but also eight hundred acres for sale within the "Yale Farms." This rural land, bequeathed to Yale University, extended from the northwestern Greenwich backcountry across the state line into North Castle in Westchester County, New York. The university had been offering its 1,400-acre good fortune for development into country estates of five acres or more, stressing its unspoiled rural character, "from high meadows to deep-wooded ravines, from shady wood lots to rolling fields, from ridges with commanding views to sunny valleys with streams"—all within ten to fifteen minutes' drive of rail stations for commuting into Manhattan. Soon the diplomats' hired technical consultants were on site, looking for ways to combine the Mianus River Gorge offer, the Yale Farms property, and more into a site for the UN. The work of consultants dispatched to this and other likely locations constituted a much less publicized, but crucial, step in narrowing the range of sites. During the last week of January, the entire inspection group returned for another tour after concluding its visit to Boston.[34]

Following specifications from the inspection group, a planning consultant outlined an area of forty-two square miles, enough to create an independent city, but went even farther to suggest that in this unusually protected expanse of rural land so close to New York City, the world organization might eventually expand to 172 square miles. The consultant, Ernest P. Goodrich, was a traffic engineer who had worked for cities around the United States. In 1928 he also had been hired for a team to plan the national capital Nanjing, in China, which had been designated to replace Beijing as the seat of government for Sun Yat-sen's Chinese Nationalist Party. Like the "model capital" plan for Nanjing, Goodrich's ideas for the United Nations capital drew inspiration in part from Washington, D.C. With just five days to work on his report for the site inspection group, he described possibilities that included a central headquarters structure in the form of a tower or "pentagon idea" or, alternatively, low-lying buildings spaced apart around the site. He also envisioned a wide avenue and adjacent mall, again like Washington's mall and Constitution Avenue.[35]

While Goodrich's plans remained unknown for the time being, the movements of the diplomats made the front page of the local newspaper. The people of Greenwich, secure in their own disinterest, did not react. But then, on January 30, 1946, early in the evening, the telephone rang in the Greenwich home of John L. Gray, a forty-year-old lawyer specializing in estates and trusts with a New York City firm.

It was an old family friend who had a country home nearby and ties to someone involved with the United Nations site search—a person whose identity Gray never publicly revealed. The site committee, he reported, had just voted to recommend a rural area including parts of Greenwich,

Stamford, and North Castle, New York, as the best site for the future Capital of the World.

Gray, whose home stood in the targeted area, immediately telephoned his senior law partner, Wilkie Bushby, to sound the alarm. Bushby, as Gray later described him, "was a very energetic lawyer, and if he fought in a cause, he fought to the end with great ability. He didn't waste any time, and he didn't fuss with trivialities."[36]

True to form, Bushby swung into action. He reserved the meeting room at the Greenwich Country Day School for the following night, and he directed Gray to begin calling as many people as possible. The next morning, he decided, he and Gray would meet at the office and put materials together to alert the community. By morning, the *Greenwich Time* also had the news, "from a source of unquestionable credibility." The front page also carried a tone of alarm: "This revelation—which will come as a veritable bombshell to the town—may draw denials from official quarters, but it should dispel the skepticism which has met discussions of this possibility up to now."[37]

And so, before the UN site committee had announced any recommendation at all, two hundred Greenwich residents, many of them socially and politically prominent, filled the meeting room at the Country Day School on the evening of January 31. They came to denounce, not to deliberate. They shouted down one neighbor, Holgar Johnson, who counseled restraint. Johnson pointed out that "millions would like to have" the world capital, "but by our action taken tonight we must face the world and say we don't want the United Nations Organization." He asked, "Is this what you want to do?"

"Yes!" came the response.

"You should think twice about it," Johnson cautioned, warning that Greenwich ran the risk of becoming the "laughing stock of the world."

Unmoved, his neighbors approved a petition to the UN stressing that they supported the organization's work, but they did not want the Capital of the World in Greenwich. Because they did not yet know the precise properties the UN had in mind, everyone in the room could imagine the worst possible fate for themselves and their town. A UN headquarters would drastically "change the character of the community, which up to this time has been purely residential," they argued, and "the home environment of many thousands of people will be seriously disturbed." Indeed, the consultant's report they had not yet seen acknowledged that about three thousand people lived within the proposed site. The petitioners explained that they would oppose similar plans by any large institution, not just the United Nations. "We believe that a sacrifice must be made by some community in order that the United Nations Organization capital may have an appropriate location," they acknowledged. "However, we hope and believe that such a location can be found in a less populated region where few people would be disturbed." As in Concord and Sudbury, Massachusetts, the protest reflected a tension for localities in the postwar world, where deep attachments to home coexisted with inescapable connections to international affairs. In towns that voluntarily sought the UN's attention, local and international interests had fused into boosterism. But in towns that resisted, connections between local and global interests broke down when personal property and local sovereignty seemed to be at stake. The UN's intentions were perceived as an imminent threat that called for swift, preemptive action—and Greenwich had wealth and an abundance of resident attorneys to lead the fight.[38]

Although many communities had worked strenuously to have a voice in the process of selecting a site for the Capital of the World, the decisions were made behind the scenes. Technical data gathered by consultants mattered more than history or hospitality, and the field was narrowed by the votes of seven people who were not bound by the will of constituents—the diplomats in the inspection group. They huddled at the Waldorf-Astoria Hotel in Manhattan with staff members and their consultants' studies of sites in the suburbs of New York and Boston.[39] In addition to revisiting the Stamford-Greenwich area, they sent a subcommittee back to Hyde Park and Kingston, New York, for a last look. And on February 2, as they left for London, they announced the recommendations that the people of Greenwich feared and very few others beyond the eighth floor of the Waldorf-Astoria expected. Going beyond their instructions to report on suitable locations, they recommended building a permanent headquarters in a "district" identified only as North Stamford and Greenwich, Connecticut—the site already being protested in Greenwich.[40]

For the interim headquarters, surprisingly, the inspection group recommended New York City. Initially the city's boosters had refused to consider the consolation prize, but they shifted their strategy as it became clear that the diplomats were seriously contemplating Atlantic City, Boston, and other sites as far away as Fort Ethan Allen in Vermont. The New Yorkers temporarily set aside their vision of a world capital at Flushing Meadows and focused on the UN's interim needs as a step toward winning the ultimate prize. Robert Moses and his team pointed the diplomats toward Long

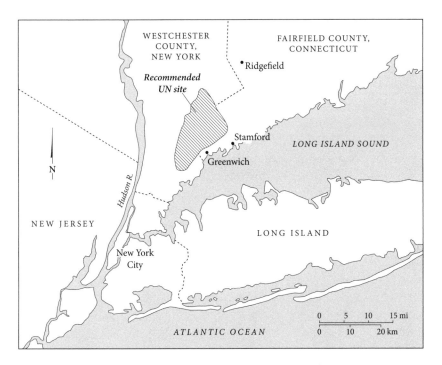

The site inspectors' choice of a vaguely defined area spanning Fairfield County, Connecticut, and Westchester County, New York, grew from an invitation issued by Stamford, Connecticut, but affected the adjacent town of Greenwich most of all.

Island, where the organization could have offices in space being vacated by the Sperry Gyroscope Plant, in a community with a compelling name, Lake Success. Finding housing for the delegates and UN staff would be a challenge, but the New Yorkers also offered meeting places in Manhattan, including the Whitelaw Reid mansion on Madison Avenue for committees and possibly a theater in Rockefeller Center for the General Assembly.[41]

Because the committee had been asked to find up to six suitable locations, its report also described additional sites. As alternatives for the permanent headquarters, the committee members described the Blue Hills and North Shore areas of Boston as well as Hyde Park, N.Y., although they noted the likelihood of political controversy if the UN selected Hyde Park. They made no mention of Concord or Sudbury, Massachusetts, except to note the date of their visit. As alternatives for the interim site, they described Boston and Atlantic City. In Boston, the site searchers were impressed by history and culture, but they viewed the available offices and meeting rooms as too small and inconvenient. The report noted the Soviet delegate's protest of the anti-Soviet remarks in Boston, but emphasized that the other committee members were satisfied with the Bostonians' demonstrations of goodwill. Atlantic City, meanwhile, offered excellent facilities but also the disadvantages of a tourist resort. "The city is dotted with curio shops, souvenir shops, bowling alleys and moving picture houses," the diplomats noted. It was certainly not the cultural ambience they preferred, which could be found in New York or Boston.[42]

As they had shown in the past, world capital hopefuls in the United States could hold onto any shred of hope. Because the final choice would be made by the UN General Assembly in London, boosters in Boston and Hyde Park considered themselves still in contention, especially as opposition exploded in Connecticut. Competitors in other parts of the country still believed that the UN might come to its senses. The governor of South Dakota, who had flown to New York to make yet another pitch for the Black Hills, cabled a new invitation to London. Boosters in San Francisco were encouraged by word that Australian delegates still wanted the organization to be on the West Coast. Niagara Falls promoters considered their proposal still "definitely a possibility."[43]

In the area of the inspection group's favored site—still not publicly defined beyond the label "North Stamford-Greenwich"—anger intensified and spread. By rallying quickly, opponents had the upper hand over other residents who called for more deliberate consideration and negotiation. The region included estates of prominent individuals; some of them, including Congresswoman Clare Booth Luce, said they would be willing to sell to the UN, but others, including the boxer Gene Tunney, joined the resistance. Even in Stamford and in Westchester County, New York, officials who had invited the UN's interest were surprised that the world organization planned to occupy far more territory than they had offered.[44]

The fight in Greenwich escalated into a full-out defense of the very foundations of the American way of life. Critics of the UN's plans began their protest on the basis of preserving the character of community, a position that reflected anxiety about the changing nature of suburbs. They envisioned their countryside caught between the spreading population of New York City to the south and a massive United Nations complex in their back yards. The result, they feared, would be an entirely different type of suburb—not a historic town and country estates, but a place with more people, packed together more closely, and distinctly more urban. As the resistance continued, they argued that even more might be at stake. The

Cartoonists portrayed the UN as a threat to the home—a powerful symbol at a time when families were reuniting at the end of the Second World War. The state capital newspaper of Connecticut, the *Hartford Courant*, published this depiction of a businessman defending his home against a much larger, formidable United Nations figure in diplomatic dress with a pile of baggage indicating intentions to stay. (Associated Press)

UN's actions threatened nothing less than the principle of democracy. Telegrams and letters to Connecticut governor Raymond E. Baldwin criticized the UN's unilateral actions as unfair and un-American. [45]

Stung by the lack of local input, Greenwich turned to democratic processes to address the crisis. On February 5, 1946, the Greenwich Town Meeting gathered at Greenwich High School. More than a thousand people—far more than the 165 elected representatives entitled to vote—filled the seats of the auditorium, stood in the aisles, and sat on the floor. Another thousand or more people wanted seats but were turned away. [46]

The moderator of the meeting, Prescott S. Bush, shared many of the characteristics of the nation's most vigorous world capital competitors. Born in 1895, soon to celebrate his fifty-first birthday, he was a combat veteran of the First World War, and he had a son who recently completed service as a naval aviator in the Pacific—George Herbert Walker Bush, the future president of the United States. Prescott Bush, a partner in a New York banking firm, served on the home front in this second war as chairman of the fund-raising campaigns of the USO and the National War Fund. No less connected to the world or involved in wartime sacrifice than the world capital boosters, he was nevertheless quick to join the Greenwich resistance. He acted not out of opposition to the world organization and its purposes, he said, but in the best interests of the community. In a letter published on the front page of the local newspaper, he carefully enumerated flaws in the site committee's choice. Many people would be displaced. The town had difficulty finding homes for its returning veterans as it was. Traffic would be a problem. The beaches on Long Island Sound were already inadequate. Many other communities wanted the UN, so why Greenwich? And most of all, wrote the town meeting moderator, "It certainly appears that the decision of the Committee was reached without the citizens of our community having had any opportunity whatever to express their sentiments regarding the proposition, which was sprung as a complete surprise to our community." [47]

The Greenwich Town Meeting now asserted the community's rights to self-government. In a town with many lawyers, three hours of debating and parliamentary maneuvering produced two decisions. The elected representatives to the Town Meeting were divided but voted 110–55 to protest the UN's recommendation. They also agreed to call a referendum to gain a broader measure of public opinion. The question would ask, mildly, whether the town's residents wished to protest the UN's intentions. [48]

The next day, and for a month to follow, Greenwich divided into vigorous campaigns for and against the UN's choice of location. As some residents feared, Greenwich drew national and international publicity as an enclave of rich folks unwilling to sacrifice for peace. "Arise, Greenwichers, Ye Prisoners of the UNO," a headline in the *New York Post* sarcastically proclaimed. The *Chicago Daily News* portrayed "one-worlders" who would ban the UN "from their own." In London, where the UN General Assembly waited to make its decision about a future home, readers of the *Daily Mail* learned that Greenwich was a place with "mansions with 30 servants to run them; golf clubs that cost $400 a year to belong to if you are the type that 'belongs'; private beaches, and everything that a man can wish if he is a millionaire." Because of the UN inspection group, "The millionaires of Connecticut are angry," the *Daily Mail* reported. "Yes sir, the temperature in Greenwich is high."[49]

Controversy echoed across the Atlantic, and dreams of creating a Capital of the World began to die.

8

SCRAMBLE

WHILE THE SITE inspection team carried out its mission in the United States, the United Nations General Assembly convened for the first time in London and shouldered the challenge of securing peace for the world. "We realize that, as perhaps never before, a choice is offered to mankind," British prime minister Clement Attlee said, addressing the delegates of fifty-one nations on the Assembly's first day, January 10, 1946. "Twice in my lifetime war has brought untold sorrow to mankind. Should there be a third World War, the long upward progress toward civilization may be halted for generations and the work of myriads of men and women through the centuries be brought to naught." The United Nations seemed not just desirable, but essential. The question of where to place the UN's headquarters, while not the weightiest issue on the agenda, had to be settled for the new world organization to be fully operational.[1]

Focused on dire matters of war and peace, not to mention the problem of raising the money for a United Nations budget, the General Assembly learned that its emissaries were recommending some of the most expensive real estate in the United States for the UN's future home. Not only that, but they had selected one of the few places in the nation that seemed to want nothing to do with becoming the Capital of the World. Instead of simplifying matters, the process of narrowing the site choices detonated into a confusion of difficult problems. The UN's efforts to resolve these multiple dilemmas exposed weaknesses in the young organization as well as the insecurities of suburban homeowners in the changing landscapes at the fringe of American cities. Local and global interests, which had seemed to be in alignment at the end of the Second World War, also were producing conflicts, with no structure in place to mediate disputes or minimize the damage.

"Fabulous and fantastic," declared U.S. senator Arthur H. Vandenberg, a member of the American delegation in London, when he learned of the site committee's recommendations. He did not mean it as a compliment.

During the first weeks of the Assembly, Vandenberg had been toiling on a committee wrestling with the budget for the new world organization. The difficult task pitted small and less wealthy nations who wanted to economize against the large and more prosperous, and the work involved deciding how much each nation would contribute to the UN's operating expenses. Finally, after much struggle, the delegates settled on a provisional budget of $21.5 million for the organization's first year of operation. For the recommended property near Greenwich, Connecticut, the cost of the land alone was being estimated at $51 million—a figure not computed until after the inspection group returned to London.[2]

Vandenberg's presence at the United Nations reflected the remarkable changes that had taken place in the world in recent times and their effects on individual lives. In his earlier days as editor and publisher of the *Grand Rapids Herald,* Vandenberg had written strongly isolationist editorials, and he had opposed U.S. participation in the League of Nations. He carried those views into the Senate in 1928. But gradually, Vandenberg became convinced that the United States could no longer stand apart. By 1942, he became more publicly internationalist as he called for nations to cooperate after the war to preserve peace; by 1944, he was consulting with the State Department to develop plans for the organization that became the United Nations. After representing the United States at the San Francisco conference, he advocated Senate ratification of the UN Charter—which he could have blocked, given his position as the senior Republican on the Foreign Relations Committee.[3]

Vandenberg could not abide the idea that the United Nations needed to build a Capital of the World on forty-two square miles in the suburbs of New York. The organization "must impress itself upon the world through its deeds and through its articulate conscience—not with its physical magnificence and its monumental bricks and mortar," he argued. The United Nations needed no more than the equivalent of a college campus, "which would be far more in keeping with the genius of this precious institution which we serve. Let us not mistake pomp for power." His reasons also were practical, because the price of land and upkeep for a more ambitious capital would make the budget for the UN's first year "look like pin money." The United Nations must "live within our common means," Vandenberg declared, foreseeing the crucial role of finances in the organization's future chances for success.[4]

With Vandenberg's statement, the site question became contested once again, but the ground had shifted. In the fall, the diplomats had waged their battle over whether the headquarters should be in Europe or the United States. Now, as news of resistance in Connecticut reached London, small nations mobilized against the recommended site because of its expected cost, and they had allies. Australia, a leader of smaller nations since the San Francisco conference, still pressed for San Francisco. Delegates from the Middle East opposed the New York area because they believed its large Jewish population would influence matters related to Palestine and the creation of a Jewish state. Other delegates, including the French, were swayed by the news of the protests in Greenwich and argued against a site that would require displacing existing residents. Combined, these forces of opposition created a powerful bloc against the inspection group's recommended site and launched ten days of bitter and repetitious debate within the UN's Permanent Headquarters Committee.[5]

Larger issues were at stake. As some diplomats maneuvered to reopen the site question and overturn earlier decisions, and others needlessly prolonged debate to prevent a vote, the integrity of decision making for the new organization seemed at risk. Sir H. Ramswami Mudalier of India, who had raised the issue of racial discrimination during the previous fall, now reminded his colleagues of the principles that could be undermined. "We represent democracy here," he said. "The first principle of democracy is to accept loyally the decisions of the majority." The UN's developing habit of continually reviewing and possibly overturning earlier decisions could have disastrous consequences.[6]

The Permanent Headquarters Committee stalled in a deadlock over whether to postpone a decision until September. Predictably, new invitations from U.S. cities and towns began to arrive. Schoolchildren in California, rallied into action by the *San Francisco News*, sent hundreds of air-mailed letters pleading for a return to San Francisco. When San Francisco officially renewed its invitation on February 10, the committee defeated the option by only two votes. A new suggestion arrived from U.S. senator Harley M. Kilgore of West Virginia, who advised that the town of Berkeley Springs in his state would be much more affordable than the suburbs of New York. Back in the United States, a senator from North Dakota wrote to President Truman to renew the suggestion of the International Peace Garden on the U.S.-Canadian border, and individual citizens wrote to elected officials to tout Bear Mountain and Harmon-on-Hudson, New York; Palisades State Park in New Jersey; and Glacier National Park in Montana. A lengthy new appeal for the Black Hills, which had been

World capital hopefuls refused to give up. Here, high school students in San Francisco receive instructions for writing letters to the United Nations to try to persuade the UN to
give up on its search for a location on the East Coast of the United States. (San Francisco
History Center, San Francisco Public Library)

submitted to the UN's site inspectors in January but ignored, appeared in the *Congressional Record.*[7]

The solution in London, when it came, reduced the chances that the future home of the United Nations would also be a world capital city. A series of compromises broke the deadlock, but also created new problems. The United Nations would still look for its permanent location in the suburbs north of New York City; but instead of focusing only on the resistant Greenwich-Stamford area, the search would broaden to all of Fairfield County, Connecticut, and Westchester County, New York. In other words, the compromise gave all of the property owners in two populous counties reason to believe their homes might be at risk. Instead of looking only for a large site needed for a Capital of the World, a planning commission would look for suitable locations ranging from two to forty square miles. This would provide more choices, including the option of a far more modest headquarters, but at the same time it would surely embroil more localities in the process. To ensure oversight on cost, the General Assembly would vote on the planning commission's ultimate recommendation in the fall. Finally, in keeping with the UN's commitment to human rights, a resolution declared that the organization would inflict no injustice on its future neighbors.[8]

The compromises proved satisfactory enough for the delegates to narrowly pass them out of the Headquarters Committee and, with the battle over, to support them nearly without dissent in the General Assembly. Late at night on February 14, the last day of the Assembly's session in London, only one delegate rose to speak against the action about to be taken.[9]

"Never in my life had I expected that I would be called upon to vote against a place I like best and love most," began Pedro Lopez of the Philippine Commonwealth, which would soon gain its independence after nearly fifty years as an American territory. During the Second World War, Lopez had led guerilla fighters against the Japanese occupation of his homeland, and in recent days he had paid close attention to news reports about the people in Greenwich who rose to protest UN incursions into their town. Once during the long meetings of the Headquarters Committee, he read aloud from the *New York Times* in order to place the views of the protesters into the record. Now, speaking after 11:00 p.m., reflecting on the past days of debate, he captured the flavor of personal discussions and dilemmas among the delegates making this choice. The suburban area north of New York, he said, "is ideal; its surroundings are idyllic, with beautiful hills, trees galore, serenity that is conducive to meditation and contemplation, helpful for our studies to solve all these problems that are heaped on us by a suffering and miserable world." The area around Stamford and Greenwich, especially, "offers many things that are nearest to my heart as a human being. . . . They say that in Stamford and Greenwich is a beautiful golf course. And, boy, I love to play golf! They say that the prospective site is only about thirty or forty miles from the center of New York; and even if I am a married man, I also like night clubs and theaters."

But the United Nations should not go where it was not wanted, Lopez argued. Yes, the diplomats had assurances of welcome from the governor of Connecticut and some of the county officials, but, Lopez cautioned, "It would be most embarrassing if we should go there and find ourselves one morning faced with pickets and placards saying, 'We do not want the United Nations here.'" It would be better to turn and run than to face such a fight.[10]

And fights there would be. With another vote scheduled in the fall, homeowners in the suburban counties north of New York City had every reason to fight for the rest of the summer. The lawyer leading the resistance in Greenwich made the homeowners' motives and determination clear in a telegram to London: "As [the] committee representing thousands of Greenwich home owners who support [the] UNO [and] whose sons made great sacrifices in war we protest the destruction of our homes for [an] unnecessary and extravagant site," Wilkie Bushby wired across the Atlantic to the United States delegation. "We are organized and will organize [a] campaign among all home owners in America. . . . "[11]

THE BRONX, LONG ISLAND, AND QUEENS

Twenty-two miles but a world away from Greenwich, Connecticut, James Joseph Lyons presided over the Bronx, the populous northern borough of New York City. Lyons, fifty-six years old, had lived in the Bronx since the age of three. During his childhood, the Bronx was the southernmost tip of Westchester County, but in 1898 it was consolidated into the city of New York along with Manhattan, Staten Island, Brooklyn, and Queens. Soon, most of the Bronx transformed from farmland to city with 420 miles of new paved roads, the IRT subway, and a building boom of homes for immigrants and their descendants who migrated north from the dense neighborhoods of lower Manhattan. In this urbanizing borough, Lyons left school after the eighth grade and made his living as a salesman. He was good at it. Even during the Great Depression, he sold enough shoe leather

An invitation to place the UN in the Bronx depicted a high-rise office tower facing the Hudson River, with a nearby multiple-lane highway suggesting easy movement to and from Manhattan. (United Nations Archives)

SITE

NIZATION

UARTERS

JNX, N.Y.

SUGGESTED SITE
FOR
UNITED NATIONS ORGANIZATION
PERMANENT HEADQUARTERS

RIVERDALE   THE BRONX, N.Y.

to make four million pairs of women's shoes. If the leather was defective, he punched holes in it and declared a new style that "allowed the feet to breathe." A good salesman, he believed, could sell electric fans to Eskimos.[12]

As the borough president of the Bronx, first elected in 1933, Lyons simply shifted his product line and worked on selling a new public image of the Bronx. As the *New York Times* later wrote, he aimed to show that "the Bronx was not just a land of six-story tenements, the Bronx Zoo, the Yankee Stadium and chicken fat and chopped liver." He wanted it to have "an aura of splendor—the splendor of Byzantium, of Biarritz at the turn of the century, of Paris in the spring."[13]

He wanted the Bronx to be the Capital of the World.

Characteristically, Lyons embarked on his own singular crusade for the Bronx, and in particular for Riverdale, the fashionable residential district overlooking the Hudson River. As Lyons described Riverdale in a letter to the United Nations in December 1945, "It is practically virgin territory, located on the banks of the Hudson River with the beautiful vista of the fascinating Palisades." It was nothing less than a "Bronx Utopia," he declared. "This Riverdale, Bronx, site preserves all the quiet solitude of the country but is within short range of the very center of our busy city. The high woodland undeveloped area lends itself for an unparalleled home for the important nations who are to deal with our future destiny." Lyons enclosed a photograph that showed what a United Nations headquarters in the Bronx might look like—an office tower and landscaped square overlooking the Hudson River. Like many of the other speculative plans produced for the world capital, the Bronx rendering provided the United Nations with a waterfront view and placed urban architectural forms in a pastoral setting, distinct from the surrounding city.[14]

Lyons did not have to travel to London to make his pitch, as so many American boosters had. Now that the diplomats needed a temporary meeting place in New York, the United Nations came to him. Lyons outmaneuvered his competition by extending his offer to Mayor William O'Dwyer and to Grover Whalen, the "official greeter" for the city of New York who was heading the effort to welcome the UN. As a result, on February 23, 1946, the booster for the Bronx had the opportunity to lead scouts from the UN executive staff to a site that seemed to be just what the customers wanted—the campus of Hunter College, one of the schools that inspired Lyons to boast of the Bronx as the "Borough of Universities." The memory of Senator Vandenberg's call for a campus-sized headquarters was fresh, and the Hunter campus was vacant after its wartime occupation by the navy. The UN scouts also toured sites favored by Robert Moses, including the Sperry Gyroscope Company plant on Long Island, the Empire State Building, and the Whitelaw Reid Mansion on Madison Avenue. But here in the Bronx were four ivy-covered buildings already being reconditioned by the navy and a landscaped campus the size of six city blocks, just north of the tip of Manhattan and convenient to the suburban counties targeted for the UN's permanent home.[15]

Once again, the United Nations personnel were working on deadline, a situation created by the lengthy deliberations in London. Although the General Assembly would not meet again until the fall, the Security Council needed quarters for its next session in the third week of March. The United Nations staff, the Secretariat, needed to settle into the city and get to work. Under these demands of space and time, the UN scouts judged Hunter College to be the only feasible option. Two days after their first visit to the Bronx, they opted for the gymnasium building of Hunter College for the Security Council meetings and negotiated a lease for three of the campus buildings until the middle of May. Lyons had clinched the sale. In the process, he also outraged the college president, whom he had not consulted before offering the campus to the world. Lyons hoped the forthcoming Security Council meeting would be only the beginning. "I am going to pursue the thing further with the idea of turning over all the buildings to the United Nations," he said.[16]

Two thousand craftsmen went to work on the Hunter College gymnasium for fifteen days and transformed it from a basketball court into a carpeted, paneled, draped, and thoroughly modern meeting hall for the eleven members of the Security Council. When the new secretary general of the United Nations, Trygve Lie of Norway, arrived to inspect the transformation on March 23, two days before the Security Council session, he pronounced it "marvelous." Publicly, all seemed well when the council convened its first session in the United States, a meeting described by James B. Reston in the *New York Times* as "the culmination of a dream that has persisted from William Penn through the two Roosevelts and Woodrow Wilson."[17]

Despite appearances, however, the realities of postwar New York were shaking James Lyons's dreams for a world capital in the Bronx. As in the rest of the country, the transition from war to peace created dilemmas as well as opportunities. Returning veterans were beginning to crowd into college classrooms under the G.I. Bill, and as a result neither the Hunter College president nor the higher education authorities of New York State were inclined to give up a campus. The veterans and other young families comprising the first wave of the postwar Baby Boom also were struggling with a housing shortage, which the employees and diplomats of the United Nations only compounded. Trygve Lie's own wife reported that she could not find suitable living space in the Bronx. Office spaces, too, were at a premium. At Hunter, offices for the Secretariat had to be carved out of classrooms, and the rush to create the Security Council chamber had left no time to begin the work. As the first delegations arrived for the Security Council session in March, they claimed offices wherever they could find them, from Wall Street to the Upper East Side, closer to Manhattan's finest hotels than to the Hunter College campus. Trygve Lie worried that the commuting from various locations in Manhattan would make it difficult to assemble quorums and would cause meetings to run behind schedule. The diplomats' inclination to fade away to their hotels already had been a problem in London, where the distances had not been nearly so great.[18]

Compared to San Francisco or even war-ravaged London, it was a nightmare. Before the Security Council meeting even began, disgruntled delegates and staff members were complaining about New York and suggesting that the UN would be better off in San Francisco or Geneva. Privately, Edward Stettinius and his successor as U.S. secretary of state, James F. Byrnes, discussed sending the organization to Atlantic City if things did not improve. In part, the American officials faced problems of their own making. In San Francisco and in London, the host nations had gone to great lengths to assure the delegates' comfort. But now, the United States remained so firmly wedded to its position of neutrality on the site question that the accommodations had been left entirely to the UN and the city of New York. Frustrated by the city's apparent shortcomings, and fearing that the UN might decamp for Europe, Stettinius tried to help by compiling a list of everything that San Francisco had provided for the charter conference. He believed that the organization would have been better off in Boston, which had been so eager to guarantee meeting halls, offices, and hotels.[19]

These were all barriers to James Lyons's world capital dream, but perhaps the greatest hurdle was the New York City parks commissioner, Robert Moses, who thought the choice of Hunter College was ridiculous. Moses, fifty-seven years old, had grown up in Manhattan as James Lyons was growing up a few miles to the north in the Bronx. Moses lived a far more privileged life, including studies at Yale, Oxford, and Columbia universities. But like Lyons, he gained prominence as a promoter. Brilliant, imperious, and charming when he wanted to be, Moses became much more powerful than the title of parks commissioner implied. With highly visible, big-money projects such as parks, bridges, parkways, and highways, he had remade the city and its growing suburbs. He lived on Long Island, and among his many other achievements, he was responsible for transforming the ash heaps in Queens into the site of the 1939 New York World's Fair, the "World of Tomorrow" symbolized by the white Trylon and Perisphere. Now that most of the fair buildings were gone, the reclaimed green space served the city as Flushing Meadows Park, although Lyons continued to deride it as "the Corona dumps."[20]

Robert Moses desperately wanted the United Nations to settle permanently at Flushing Meadows. He knew how to take advantage of the crisis that was developing as diplomats tried to negotiate their way around New York, not to mention the challenges that lay ahead as they tried to quell resistance to a permanent world capital in the northern suburbs. In Greenwich, Connecticut, more than a month of vigorous campaigning by both supporters and critics of a local site for the UN had culminated in a referendum on March 2. Some residents welcomed the United Nations' interest and argued that world peace should prevail over local concerns, but the referendum showed that a majority of those voting favored continuing to protest the UN's interest in their town. While public statements focused on concern about local control and the character of the town, some letters to the governor of Connecticut revealed uglier, racially tinged complaints about "foreigners." Opinion polls among other communities and homeowners' groups in Fairfield and Westchester counties also demonstrated resistance, even as county and state officials prepared to work with the UN to find a suitable site.[21]

In New York, meanwhile, the pursuit of the United Nations proved to be "Moses's most effective use of the power of money," according to biographer Robert Caro. As with other projects, "The money involved was not so much Moses's own as that of other people."[22] Moses and his allies on the United Nations Committee of the city of New York embodied the city's status, wealth, and power, a fact reflected by their usual meeting place, the exclusive Metropolitan Club on East Sixtieth Street and Fifth Avenue, steps away from Central Park. The committee included Nelson A. Rockefeller, the former assistant secretary of state and president of Rockefeller Center; his uncle, Winthrop Aldrich, president of the Chase National Bank; Thomas J. Watson, president of IBM; John W. Davis, a former ambassador and the Democratic Party's candidate for president in 1924; and others of similar wealth and prominence. They had been pushing from the beginning to make New York the United Nations' permanent home. Encouraged by the UN's selection of their city as the interim site, at least, they did not realize the magnitude of their new challenge until less than a week before the Security Council was to convene at Hunter College. Gathering at the Metropolitan Club on March 19, they were stunned by Grover Whalen's report that all was not well in the Bronx, as reports in the newspapers had led them to believe. Whalen revealed to them for the first time that some of the UN people were so unhappy with New York that they might take the organization back to Europe. Something had to be done, and fast.[23]

The next day, Mayor O'Dwyer, until recently a brigadier general in the army, began to reposition his troops to give greater authority to Robert Moses and Nelson Rockefeller, a move that placed Rockefeller in position to greatly influence the events that followed. Rockefeller and Moses were appointed as chairpersons of two subcommittees, but they might as well have been named as Trygve Lie's official new best friends. They welcomed him with a luncheon on March 21, his first day in New York. They were by his side when he proclaimed the renovation of the Hunter College gymnasium "magnificent," which satisfied public interest but masked the fact that Lie had decided that the campus facilities could not possibly meet the organization's long-term needs. In addition to the scattering of delegation offices all over New York, the spaces at Hunter lacked air-conditioning, and he saw nothing that could be converted into a large auditorium. "By no stretch of the imagination or construction could the General Assembly be held there in September," he concluded. In any case, the president of Hunter College firmly opposed long-term occupation of his campus.[24]

The secretary general needed a way out, and the New York boosters made it their business to provide it. They acted swiftly to assert local influence over the international organization's choices and then, one step at a time, to lead Trygve Lie to the solution that they had wanted all along. Robert Moses revealed the goal on March 27, when the New York boosters gathered to review options with UN staff members at the office of Edward Stettinius in the Savoy Plaza Hotel on Fifth Avenue. With so much opposition stirring in Greenwich and other communities in the northern suburbs, Moses asked, might it be possible now for the UN to consider placing its permanent headquarters in New York City? Despite the fact that the Headquarters Planning Commission had not even started its survey of Fairfield and Westchester counties, the UN's representatives at the meeting acknowledged that, yes, when the General Assembly came into session in September, anything might happen.[25]

This was all that Moses needed to hear.

Conveniently for the New Yorkers, the new secretary general harbored similar hopes for the United Nations' eventual home. Lie, forty-nine years old and most recently foreign minister of Norway, spent most of the Second World War in London with other government officials exiled from Europe by the Nazi occupation. Their conversations there turned to musings about the future United Nations organization and how to protect it from being trapped by war on the European continent. It was at that time, Lie later recalled, that he began to think of New York City as the best location for the UN. "The huge metropolis and international crossroads would in many ways offer the best contact with the world at large," he concluded. He was glad to be in New York. "Men and women being what they are, I reasoned that once Headquarters were set up—even though temporarily—considerable effort would be required to move them again," he wrote later in his memoir of the UN's early years.[26]

Knowing Lie's inclinations, the New Yorkers once again offered the Sperry Gyroscope Company plant in Lake Success, Long Island, which they had shown to the inspection group back in January. It was twenty-two miles from midtown Manhattan—farther away than Hunter College—but the buildings were modern, air-conditioned, and could consolidate the Secretariat and delegation offices in one location. The amenities outweighed the uncomfortable irony that the peace-keeping organization would occupy a factory that had manufactured equipment for war.[27]

Still, the General Assembly needed an auditorium capable of seating three thousand people. Such a hall would cost $1 million to construct at either Hunter College or the Sperry Plant. Because Security Council members still hoped that all of the UN's functions might be consolidated in Manhattan, Lie and his staff inspected the limited options on the island. Rockefeller Center had only one floor available, and using its theater would require an expensive labor contract; the Waldorf-Astoria ballroom was booked with conventions and expensive; and the Empire State Building would require spreading the organization over multiple floors, which in any case were occupied by essential federal agencies.[28]

Wouldn't it be better, the New Yorkers suggested, to place the offices in the Sperry Plant and then build or find an auditorium closer to that location? What about, say, the former world's fair grounds in Flushing Meadows Park?

The site that the New Yorkers had been promoting from the beginning stood seven miles from midtown Manhattan—closer than Hunter College—and in the direction of the more distant but appealing office building at Lake Success. On April 5, members of the Security Council toured the former New York City building of the world's fair, which the New Yorkers promised could be renovated from its current use as a skating rink into a large auditorium.[29]

In the space of about two weeks, Robert Moses achieved almost what he had wanted in the first place: the United Nations at Flushing Meadows. By the second week of April, the city of New York agreed to bear most of the expense of renovating the New York City building into a handsome, landscaped hall for the United Nations General Assembly. This apparent act of generosity also would allow them to argue that the UN should not waste this investment by moving away. The organization would stay at Hunter College until the middle of August, but then its offices would move to the Sperry plant, in the community of about seven hundred residents with the promising name of Lake Success. The problem of housing for the UN's expected four thousand employees remained, but the suburban building boom was about to take off. Developers promised that new housing would be constructed by the following January. The United States government pledged "appropriate assistance" for the United Nations to stay in New York for an interim period of three years—enough federal assurance to waylay any hesitation that the New Yorkers might have about investing city funds. The United Nations would stay in place for at least three years, it seemed. And why not longer?[30]

Before the UN could pack up its files at Hunter College, Robert Moses was setting in motion the plans for a United Nations permanent home in Flushing Meadows Park, and his wealthy allies were raising the funds to pay architects and engineers. Up in the Bronx, James Lyons protested that the UN had not fully explored its options in his borough, but it was too late. The borough president could only muse that the United Nations' first location in the United States would be remembered as a sacred place in world history, in the same way that Americans revered Independence Hall in Philadelphia. He was very sure: "History will record that the Bronx was the first capital of the world."[31]

STALEMATE AND CIRCUSES

Time and again during the summer of 1946, negotiators for the United Nations motored from New York City into Westchester County, New York, and Fairfield County, Connecticut, the two suburban counties where they hoped to find a site for a headquarters. But in the meeting rooms of county and municipal authorities, it became clear that even diplomats who had served kings and presidents, who had kept governments afloat in exile during the war, and whose nations had subjected entire populations to colonial rule, were no match for local governments and suburban property owners. Complicating the procedure, the UN continued to seek a location without a clear vision of the size or character of the place the organization would create.

In June, the world-renowned architect known as Le Corbusier (Charles-Édouard Jeanneret-Gris) raised questions that the UN had never explicitly addressed: Did the diplomats want a headquarters, or did they want to create a Capital of the World? Did they understand the difference? The Swiss-born architect had been appointed by France to the United Nations' Headquarters Planning Commission, which was carrying on the work of finding the UN's site, but this was not the first time he had tried to inject his ideas into the world of international affairs. Nearly twenty years earlier, he and his cousin Pierre Jeanneret had submitted one of the winning designs in the architectural competition for the League of Nations headquarters at Geneva. Le Corbusier remained bitter that the diplomats of 1927 had passed over his modern headquarters plan for a more traditional design that he abhorred as "compromise, conformism, and failure."[32]

Now, at age fifty-seven, a recognized pioneer of modern architecture, Le Corbusier insisted that the United Nations must clarify its desires. On June 19, the architect answered his own questions in a report for the Headquarters Planning Commission, which had been easing into its task by meeting quietly with state officials in New York and Connecticut. For Le Corbusier, the specter of a Capital of the World represented much that he despised. "The word 'World Capital' is nothing but ambiguity, equivocalness, uncertain dimensions, emphasis, and artificial acceptance," he wrote with characteristic bluntness and flair. "It is a source of error, bloated with false deductions." He predicted that such a place would begin with a pompous, pretentious palace and that the city growing around it would have to be "at least as magnificent and grandiose" as any national capital in order to be regarded as the Capital of the World. No wonder the potential neighbors of such a place were objecting. In this architect's view of recent history, "Confronting such a menace, the inhabitants of Connecticut, terror stricken, took the bit between their teeth and flatly voted against the invasion of their domain by the people of the United Nations."[33]

In contrast to the ambiguous, ominous Capital of the World, Le Corbusier argued that a "headquarters" suggested precision and suitability to the tasks of the modern world. "Headquarters means an assemblage of persons and instruments at a given spot connected with the zone of operation by the most efficacious means of communication," he wrote. In other words, it meant simply a location for the people and offices of the United Nations that would allow them to communicate efficiently with the world.[34]

As Le Corbusier described and sketched his ideas for the UN Headquarters Commission, he envisioned the United Nations and its people occupying a complex resembling a "vertical garden city," a form that he was advocating for postwar construction. He favored building such a headquarters north of New York City in the general area of White Plains, New York, and Greenwich, Connecticut. He disdained New York City itself, "a thrilling city but so disputable that it cannot take the Headquarters of the United Nations into its lap." In contrast, these suburban areas, because of their wealth, were "polished and policed, endowed with the attractions which men . . . can draw from the harmonious cultivation of nature." Le Corbusier envisioned apartment buildings for the United Nations staff, the best of hotels for transient visitors, and structures for national delegations that might be left to their own design. In addition to the buildings that would house auditoriums, offices, and meeting rooms, he imagined a world museum and library, supposing that two delegates in disagreement might stroll through the exhibits of human history and find common ground. All around, open green space would promote physical fitness and well-being.[35]

Le Corbusier illustrated his report with sketches of high-rise, rectangular slabs faced with glass. They looked a great deal like buildings he had designed for cities in Europe, and they forecast features of the United Nations headquarters building that would one day rise in Manhattan. Elsewhere during the summer of 1946, the writer and critic Lewis Mumford advocated elevating the UN project into a demonstration of international unity by clearing slums and regenerating one or more cities with "world center" communities.[36] But neither of these influential thinkers dislodged the process that the UN had agreed upon in London, which required

Did the United Nations need a world capital or a headquarters? The architect Le Corbusier argued for a high-rise headquarters and provided sketches in a report submitted to the Headquarters Planning Commission during the summer of 1946. (United Nations Archives)

searching for locations of various sizes in the two suburban counties north of New York City.

During July 1946, consultants hired by the United Nations computed the square footage and acreage that the organization would need, and by the end of the month they identified fifteen locations ranging from two to forty square miles in the UN's two targeted counties. By the middle of August, after attempts at diplomacy with residents in each locality that might be affected, the UN gave up entirely on the resistant communities in Connecticut and narrowed the choices to five locations in Westchester County, New York. But in Westchester County as well, dreams of creating a Capital of the World ran squarely into American dreams of freedom, home, and family. After four years of fighting for their country, Americans were instinctively vigilant about protecting their own homes.[37]

In the southern end of Westchester County closest to Manhattan, the UN's consultants pinpointed sites of two and five square miles in the town of Harrison, just east of the White Plains county seat. In the northern and less-populated area of the county, larger sites kept alive the idea that the UN might still develop a world capital city. In that more rural region, the citizens of one village, Croton-on-Hudson, actually seemed to want the attention. Villagers who attended a community meeting in August voted 190–2 to welcome the UN to a nearby site of ten square miles, which overlapped Cortlandt Township (including the village) and Yorktown, New York. The UN's site team also identified locations of twenty and forty square miles spanning Yorktown and Somers, a town that claimed fame as the proud birthplace of the American circus.[38]

From one end of the county to the other, property owners argued about the UN's plans. Some felt honored by the diplomats' intentions and went so far as to offer their property to the organization, but others—like the earlier dissenters in Greenwich, Connecticut—proved to be more vocal and better organized as they predicted disaster. Both sides organized meetings, circulated petitions, and conducted opinion polls. Each side accused the other of manipulating the results. Meanwhile, the diplomats' overtures ran into roadblocks of local interest. When a UN team attempted to negotiate with residents of Harrison, N.Y., local officials arrived with a list of sixty questions about the UN's designs on their town. How would this affect the school district? What about the taxes? Who would provide the police? What would the buildings look like? Would they be in a walled compound? If the diplomats could not answer these questions (which they could not), why should local leaders cooperate? When a legal adviser

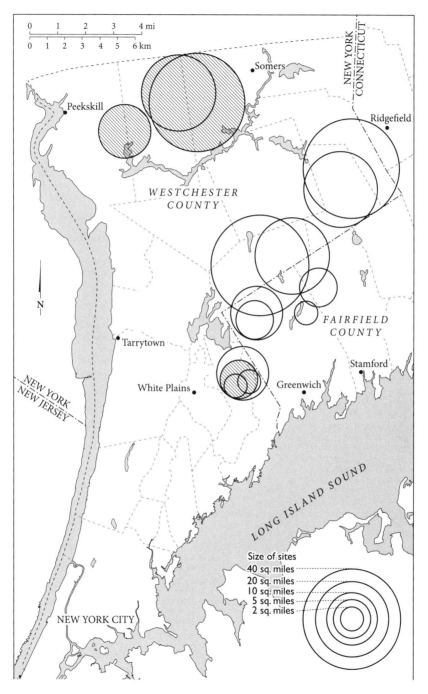

Alarming homeowners throughout the two suburban counties north of New York City, UN planning consultants searched for sites ranging from two to forty square miles, indicated by circles on the map. Strong resistance in Greenwich, Connecticut, led the planners to reduce the options to the shaded areas in Westchester County, New York.

from the United Nations Headquarters Commission arrived at a community meeting in Somers to explain the site choices, he was shouted down by the audience. The adviser had no choice but to give up and retreat to New York.[39]

Disagreements flared within the UN's five targeted areas as each community fought its own battle over its uncertain future. Then, in the first week of September, the protest groups of scattered towns merged the five-ring circus into one organization, the United Westchester Citizens Committee to Save Our Homes. The very name of the group resounded with the convictions of the resistance and reflected the postwar turn toward domestic security. The homeowners were united, like the United States of America. They were citizens, who expected to be heard and heeded. They had mobilized to save—not merely defend—American homes, the bedrock of family, community, and country. The homes were not abstractions on a map or numbers in a census; they were "our" homes. The fight was personal. The new coalition hired a public relations man from Chicago and printed pamphlets, a publication called *The Minuteman*, and bumper stickers proclaiming "SAVE OUR HOMES" in red letters. They invited their opponents to debates on the radio. And in a terrific double back flip of boosterism, they began to promote *other* places for the honor of becoming the Capital of the World. Wouldn't it be lovely for the United Nations to be on the other side of the Hudson River in, say, Sterling Park, New York? Look at all of the space available over there![40]

SPIES VS. SPIES

While homeowners in Westchester organized their resistance, operatives from places that still hoped to become the Capital of the World began to appear at the United Nations' new offices in Lake Success, Long Island. They were a relatively benign presence, compared to the ominous and intensifying beginnings of the Cold War. In February 1946, Soviet leader Joseph Stalin had delivered a speech in Moscow that blamed monopoly capitalism for the Second World War; soon thereafter, an American diplomat in Moscow, George F. Kennan, drafted his "Long Telegram" describing the Soviets as fanatics seeking world domination. In June, Winston Churchill declared in a speech at Fulton, Missouri, that an "iron curtain" had fallen across Europe. Against the backdrop of such history-defining events and the UN's dilemma in Westchester County, hope revived among world-capital boosters from Philadelphia, San Francisco, and other locations across the country.[41]

On multiple levels, finding a suitable location for the United Nations had become a serious problem with international consequences, threatening not only the effectiveness of the new organization but also the United States' stature as a world power. During the summer, *The New Yorker* magazine suggested that the UN should perhaps settle in the Black Hills after all, especially to be inspired by the giant concrete dinosaur figures at Dinosaur Park near Rapid City. "Here let the new halls be built," E. B. White teased, "so that earnest statesmen, glancing up from their secret instructions from the home office, may gaze out upon the prehistoric sovereigns who kept on fighting one another until they perished from the earth."[42]

Contributing to the problem, the United States remained neutral, leaving diplomats from other nations to deal with homeowners and local, county, and state governments. The potential for a more assertive stance by the United States emerged in May 1946, when the architect of the neutrality policy, former secretary of state Edward Stettinius, resigned as chief delegate to the UN. Taking his place would be U.S. senator Warren F. Austin of Vermont, a Republican member of the Senate Foreign Relations Committee. As news of these transitions became public, world capital hopefuls sensed opportunity and took action to introduce their ambitions to Austin and other new players on the world stage.[43]

By the summer of 1946, notwithstanding the resistance to the UN's plans in the New York suburbs, close to 250 American cities and towns had been suggested as potential world capitals, the majority of them nominated by their own residents. Among the most persistent of the agents who remained in circulation at Lake Success was Robert Gray Taylor, a self-appointed champion for towns in eastern Pennsylvania (although not Philadelphia, which he considered unsuitably urbanized and densely populated). For Taylor, a Quaker with Pennsylvania ancestors reaching back for more than two centuries, the legacy of William Penn loomed large as he envisioned a United Nations headquarters that would sustain the Pennsylvania founder's ideals of tolerance and peace. Taylor was eager to meet anyone connected with the United Nations during 1946, even if they were not eager to meet him. He shadowed the UN's inspection teams, once even asking questions during a press conference at the White House. He secured a personal meeting with UN secretary general Trygve Lie, and he invited senior members of the UN executive staff to spend their Fourth of

July weekend in Pennsylvania. The trip never occurred, but Taylor made enough of an impression that "The Delaware Valley Project" appeared on the agenda for discussion at a meeting between Lie and his staff. The secretary general himself suggested that senior staff members should quietly go to Pennsylvania and take a look around. Taylor became so persistent that before the year was over, he was banned from the delegates' lounge of the UN General Assembly.[44]

Meanwhile, the original booster team for Philadelphia also sensed renewed opportunity. More than a year had passed since they had launched their campaign, which had seemed to end in inexplicable defeat. During the summer of 1946, with the transition from Stettinius to Austin as head of the American delegation, their hopes revived. Privately, the Philadelphia boosters wrote to Austin with a simple reminder of Philadelphia's warm attitude toward the United Nations and the city's abiding interest in giving the new world organization a suitable home. They remained certain that dignity would prevail over showmanship.[45]

San Francisco, too, began a quiet reconnaissance mission on the East Coast. In August, Bedford Brown, vice president of the San Francisco Bank and treasurer of the San Francisco Chamber of Commerce, started sleuthing in Washington. At the State Department, he picked up on uncertainty and worry over the UN site situation, especially the fear that the organization's displeasure with New York might send it back to Europe. With the United States' postwar prestige at stake, the State Department wanted to be in a position to offer alternatives. Soon, Brown became a familiar presence at the United Nations' new headquarters on Long Island and in the scattered offices and hotel suites of diplomats already in New York. He learned about the swelling dissent in Westchester County and the work being done by Nelson Rockefeller, Robert Moses, and the team for New York, who intended to make an elaborate pitch to secure the United Nations permanently on the world's fair grounds at Flushing Meadows Park.[46]

San Francisco's boosters seemed to have reason to hope once again, and perhaps a long shot to succeed. Armed with the intelligence gathered by Brown, Mayor Roger Lapham and the chamber of commerce prepared to give the United Nations a California version of everything it had been searching for in the New York suburbs, but without the homeowner dissent. In effect, they duplicated the work of the UN's own Headquarters Commission by surveying the counties around San Francisco and locating sites that ranged in size from two to twenty square miles. Some of these sites had been offered by the surrounding communities during the world capital competition's earlier rounds. The San Franciscans knew that their distance from Europe remained a major obstacle, but they also knew they could eliminate the most persistent problem that the United Nations faced in the New York suburbs. In less densely developed California, they could offer the diplomats land that was not populated—and, therefore, free from homeowner objections. With new proposals in hand, Mayor Lapham and California governor Earl Warren were in New York by the time delegates arrived for the first New York meetings of the United Nations General Assembly, scheduled for October 23, 1946. New York City's boosters, meanwhile, sent an emissary to Paris to mingle with the diplomats gathered there to negotiate the final settlements of World War II.[47]

The UN General Assembly was about to descend on New York. But just how the headquarters struggle would end—and where it would end—had not yet become apparent. About the most optimistic thing that could be said about the United Nations' public relations disaster was spelled out on a plaque in the new office of the secretary general in Lake Success, Long Island: "The difficult is that which can be done immediately, the impossible that which takes a little longer."[48]

Finding the Capital of the World—if there was to be a Capital of the World—would take a little longer.

9

DEAL

IF THE UNITED NATIONS needed further evidence of its increasingly precarious relationship with Westchester County, a single memorable event on a Saturday afternoon in October provided it. One of the UN's staunchest friends, Nelson Rockefeller, invited one thousand delegates and alternates to lunch at his family's estate, Pocantico Hills, near Tarrytown in Westchester County. But more than two hours after the "typical American" luncheon was to begin, more than half of the expected guests were missing. They were not snubbing one of the nation's richest and most influential families—they were lost in the unfamiliar terrain beyond Manhattan. Even the staid *New York Times* delighted in the symbolism as it reported, "United Nations delegates, long accustomed to complications of international politics, were baffled today when confronted with the geographical problems of navigating darkest Westchester in chauffeur-driven cars." The diplomats were hapless wanderers on back country roads. "For all anyone knows," a *Times* reporter noted in the next day's newspaper, "some statesmen may still be floundering around Tarrytown Lake, hoping the gasoline holds out."[1]

Within this incident also lay a clue to the eventual resolution of the United Nations' dilemma. Throughout 1945 and 1946, little public attention had been paid to the recurring role of Nelson Rockefeller, the grandson of the nineteenth-century oil baron John D. Rockefeller. The Rockefeller estate lay in Westchester County, but Nelson Rockefeller was deeply involved with the booster campaign to attract the United Nations to New York City. In fact, the Rockefeller family had been enmeshed in the world capital competition intermittently since it began. In the spring of 1945, when the frenzy was just beginning, Nelson Rockefeller held the position of assistant secretary of state for Latin American affairs. The energetic, charismatic heir to a family fortune was just thirty-seven years old, but he already had been president of Rockefeller Center and the Museum of Modern Art in New York. He had been on Capitol Hill one day in March 1945 when a congressman from South Dakota approached him to make the oddest suggestion—that the United Nations should consider placing its headquarters in the Black Hills. Three months later, at the first United Nations conference in San Francisco, Rockefeller encountered this strange idea once again. Although he was in the thick of negotiations over the regional interests of Latin America, he also came away with the business card of Paul E. Bellamy, the chief booster for the Black Hills.[2]

By the end of 1945, Rockefeller was out of the State Department and pursuing business projects in Latin America. But like other members of his family, he remained intensely involved in the business, cultural, and social whirl of Manhattan, and this included the campaign to bring the United Nations to New York City. With footholds in the realms of local affairs, international diplomacy, and big capital, Nelson Rockefeller knew how to finesse a deal, how to make things happen, and how to have a good time in the process. In January 1946, at the end of the ill-fated site tour that led the UN to Greenwich, Connecticut, Rockefeller made sure that the visiting diplomats had tickets to the Metropolitan Opera. And when the UN ran into difficulties settling into New York, he was the man whom the mayor and the chief American delegate, Edward Stettinius, called. For a time, Rockefeller tried to arrange for the General Assembly to meet in the Rockefeller Center theater. Gradually, mostly out of the public eye, Nelson Rockefeller became the individual at the center of events that would end the search for the Capital of the World.[3]

Nelson Rockefeller's father, John D. Rockefeller Jr., also became drawn into the UN site question, although not by choice. Well known for his interest in international affairs as well as his wealth, John D. Rockefeller Jr. had given the League of Nations $2 million for a library, which still stood in Geneva. With the creation of the United Nations, a remarkable number of people felt entitled to write letters to Rockefeller appealing for his help in securing this or that location, from as near as Manhattan to as far away as Oklahoma. Closest to home, Westchester County's earliest overtures to the UN—from government officials who did not anticipate the outcry that might follow—included the idea that the organization might move into Rockwood Hall, the estate of the late William Rockefeller, Nelson Rockefeller's great-uncle. In all cases, John D. Rockefeller Jr. diplomatically declined to become involved, although he gave five thousand dollars to help his son's campaign for New York City.[4]

By the middle of 1946, various other Rockefeller family members and friends also were caught up in the situation that the United Nations faced in New York and its suburbs. Nelson Rockefeller's uncle Winthrop Aldrich served with him on the New York booster committee. They were joined there by another Rockefeller relation by marriage, Wallace K. Harrison, one of the architects of Rockefeller Center, a close friend who also had followed Nelson Rockefeller into Latin American affairs work during the Roosevelt administration. Even in Westchester County, the top elected official, County Executive Herbert Gerlach, had done legal work for the Rockefeller family. Whatever the outcome of the search for a United Nations home, the Rockefellers and their circle of influential family members, friends, and associates were destined to be involved.

FLUSHING MEADOWS

Each "decision" about the United Nations' future home had opened a new set of questions. The early battles over Europe versus the United States had given way to questions about regions of the United States. Issues of geography became enmeshed in questions about cost. Now, as the General Assembly arrived in New York, the UN's "interim" headquarters, in the fall of 1946, diplomats and their staffs became immersed in questions that had more to do with the local conditions of their workplaces and quality of life. The site question had become a matter of suburb versus city, and more specifically a question of Westchester County versus New York City. Public relations battles raged on both sides. If the homeowners of Westchester County persisted in pushing the United Nations diplomats away, New York City boosters intended to catch them.

The New Yorkers invested in facilities for the United Nations, especially at Flushing Meadows Park in Queens, with the expectation that their efforts would yield a permanent UN headquarters in New York. For the General Assembly, Robert Moses and his team transformed the indoor skating rink at Flushing Meadows into a crossroads and meeting place for the world. When delegates took their seats behind the curved walnut desks in their new auditorium, they gazed forward toward a spectacular map of the world, sixty feet across and thirty-five feet tall, with deep blue oceans and continents of gold. This map displayed no cities, towns, or national boundaries, only unified continents connected by the seas. There were no indications of the hardening lines of the Cold War, conflicts between large and small nations, or the layers of local, state, and federal interests that complicated the United Nations' search for meeting places in the United States.[5]

New Yorkers invested heavily in facilities for the United Nations at Flushing Meadows in Queens. The UN General Assembly found that the former skating rink inside the New York Building of the World's Fair had been transformed into an auditorium featuring a map of the world. (United Nations Photo Library)

THE PROPOSED WORLD CAPITOL

THE PROPOSED SITE DURING THE WORLD'S FAIR 1939-1940

Artists' renderings, like this one depicting a future world capital at Flushing Meadows, enticed diplomats in the "exhibit" room reserved by the New York booster committee at the General Assembly's temporary auditorium. (Art and Architecture Collection, Miriam and Ira D. Wallach Division of Art, Prints and Photographs, New York Public Library, Astor, Lenox and Tilden Foundations)

Lest anyone forget who was responsible for the impressive new auditorium, its designers left a remnant from the building's former incarnation as a pavilion for the world's fair of 1939. The words "City of New York" marked the entry into the building, a silent but inescapable advertisement for the boosters who sought to make these diplomats so comfortable that they would not want to leave.[6]

The New York United Nations Committee also retained control of one room inside the building. The contents were described as an exhibit, but in fact the room served as a full-color, three-dimensional advertisement for Flushing Meadows Park as permanent headquarters for the United Nations. It was a bold, brilliant, and audacious move, simultaneously a hand of friendship and a slap at the United Nations' site-searching efforts. Establishing an advantage that no other world capital competitor could match, the "exhibit" displayed an architectural model of a future United Nations headquarters at Flushing Meadows Park, featuring a domed Assembly Hall, three low-rise office buildings, and fifty-one symbolic pylons representing the founding nations of the UN. Gorgeous color drawings breathed life and ambiance into the architecture and suggested the connection between the headquarters and Manhattan by showing highways with automobiles speeding swiftly toward the city. Maps showed Flushing Meadows' close proximity to Manhattan, obscuring the fact that covering the distance by automobile required a minimum of forty minutes. In publicity arranged in advance by the booster committee, the *New York Times* described the plan as "an idyllic World of Tomorrow on the very ground where that vision took shape during the World's Fair."[7]

If only people, events, and, most of all, traffic could be managed as easily as art and architecture. The General Assembly convened more than a month behind schedule, a delay forced by the need to first complete the postwar peace talks in Paris. To compete with the comforts provided to the diplomats in Paris, New York faced a daunting challenge. The stakes were high. If the United Nations came to New York, but then left, the damage to the city's reputation would be deep and long-lasting. To avoid this fate, New York's boosters had been making every attempt to overcome the debacle of the previous spring's meetings of the Security Council at Hunter College. They persuaded the city's largest hotels to make way for the United Nations by canceling bookings for five major conventions—but they had counted on the diplomats arriving in September. By the time the General Assembly's delayed meetings approached in October, a crisis had developed for hotel space throughout the city. It resulted partly from the continuing housing shortage, which left homeless New Yorkers moving from one hotel to another. This made rooms scarce for the usual flow of visitors for openings on Broadway and buyers making their seasonal pilgrimage to the city's manufacturers and wholesalers. The city also experienced an upswing of tourism as Americans rediscovered vacationing after the years of wartime restrictions on travel.[8]

Even before most of the United Nations people arrived, hotel operators were begging YMCAs to take more guests, and people had been observed sleeping in subway stations or Turkish baths for lack of hotel rooms. Exasperating situations developed as diplomats arrived. Yugoslavian delegates—except for Stoyan Gavrilovic, who shared a cramped apartment with his wife and son—felt slighted by their assigned accommodations in the Hotel Wellington at Fifty-Fifth Street and Seventh Avenue and threatened to stay away. A group of Liberians suspected racial discrimination at work when they were placed at the Lido Hotel out on Long Island. Office space also remained scarce, as delegations sought to remain in Manhattan rather than work in distant Lake Success. Once again, Nelson Rockefeller intervened to secure offices recently vacated by the federal government in the Empire State Building. Failure to resolve such practical matters could doom New York's chances, he knew. The difficult conditions confronted by the chairman of the UN Headquarters Committee, Eduardo Zuleta Angel of Colombia, especially signaled danger. As Rockefeller wrote to Robert Moses, "His assistant told me that to talk about staying in New York at the present time when the whole delegation was operating from Zuleta Angel's apartment was really laughable. Frankly, the delegates are all so disturbed about the office space question that I haven't been able to make much headway."[9]

Beyond the difficulties over places to live and work, the UN delegates and staff members confronted another daily challenge familiar to everyday New Yorkers—commuting. The delegations favored Manhattan as their base of operations, but the General Assembly met at Flushing Meadows in Queens, and the Secretariat had its offices in still more distant Lake Success, Long Island. Despite a fleet of chauffeured limousines, every day offered new opportunities for dissatisfaction about long distances and wasted time.[10]

For the U.S. State Department and its delegation to the UN, the circumstances demanded a response, but they would have to be careful about it. The Americans did not want the United Nations to flee back to Europe, but neither did they want to touch off another outbreak of world capital fever among U.S. cities and towns. Meanwhile, citizen organizations with interests in international affairs pressured the Truman administration to intervene. In a letter to President Truman on October 14, 1946, the American Association for the United Nations and other prominent groups pleaded for an end to the uncertainty, for the sake of the UN's future.[11]

The time had come for the United States to abandon neutrality and take part in the headquarters decision. Five days after the letter from the American Association for the United Nations, President Truman met with his new chief delegate to the UN, Warren Austin, and the State Department's Dean Acheson at the White House. The pragmatic Truman considered the suburban counties north of New York City to be too expensive and problematic. In Austin's recollection, Truman did not specify an alternative but advised that "he would like a site on government property or one 'without cost or at a reasonable cost.'" This advice became a guiding criterion for the U.S. delegation and eventually for the next phase of the UN's search for a permanent home. Meeting at the Hotel Pennsylvania in Manhattan during the last two weeks of October, the American delegation formulated a new strategy. With all of the work that the UN had devoted to the New York suburbs, the sites in Westchester would have to remain on the table. But obviously, other less troublesome and less expensive choices were available and should be pursued.[12]

On November 1, 1946, on behalf of the United States, Warren Austin proposed that the United Nations reopen its search to include additional sites "available without cost or at reasonable cost" in the area of New York City, Westchester County, and one other long-time contender, San Francisco. Because the diplomats' reservations about a West Coast location were well known, this proposal offered the greatest new advantage to New York City. Significantly, but behind the scenes, UN secretary general Trygve Lie attended a meeting on November 5 at the home of Robert Moses, where he also conferred with Nelson Rockefeller and other members of the New York City booster committee. Afterward, New York City mayor William O'Dwyer received word that Lie believed it was likely that the UN would end up at Flushing Meadows Park.[13]

In the United Nations, decisions about real estate could not be separated from international politics, and veterans of earlier battles were poised to spring at their next opportunity. Despite the momentum for New York, champions of other headquarters sites leapt quickly to once again propose their favored locations and argue against others. Debates of the past came back to life. The Soviets proclaimed they would block any attempt to move to San Francisco and suggested returning to Europe instead. A sign of the Soviets' serious intent occurred in a procedural committee, where Ukraine tried to add Europe to the headquarters options. The British also had not given up on influencing the site choice. Philip Noel-Baker, the British diplomat who had battled the year before to keep the UN in Europe, regarded Flushing Meadows as unbearably depressing. Trying to broaden the field of contenders, the British argued that Boston and Philadelphia also should be considered. Then on November 9, 1946, they seized an opportunity and taught the Americans a lesson about politics (and attendance) in the United Nations General Assembly.[14]

Taking a little time off for a college football game on a Saturday afternoon must have seemed harmless enough to Warren Austin, Arthur Vandenberg, and other leading American delegates. But while they watched the gridiron battle between Army and Notre Dame, the British opened a new offensive on the site question. Reaching far beyond the Americans' attempt to steer the UN toward New York, the British proposed reopening the headquarters to any location in the United States—which would again reduce Flushing Meadows to just one of many competitors. The only American delegate present that afternoon, New York congressman Sol Bloom, disliked Flushing Meadows himself and offered little resistance. By the time the other Americans returned from the game, the British had succeeded in winning approval from the General Assembly for a wide-open search. And then, as if on cue, Americans from as many as sixty cities and towns across the United States unleashed a fresh bombardment of suggestions and invitations to their worthy communities. Some came from longtime world capital hopefuls, but these were joined by appeals from new contenders such as Martha's Vineyard; Muskegon, Michigan; and Bald Head Island, North Carolina. From resistant Westchester County came a new idea to place the United Nations in public, unpopulated Mohansic State Park.[15]

It appeared that United Nations site inspectors would once again be hitting the road to find a suitable home. The United States, having fumbled its first attempt to limit the new contenders to New York and San Francisco, tried again to assert control over the scope of the search. By November 14, a compromise emerged that included the sites most favored by the British without flinging open the search entirely. This time, a new Headquarters Site Subcommittee would inspect sites in four locations: New York and Boston, as before, but now San Francisco and long-hopeful Philadelphia also would be considered. The search would be especially cost conscious, guided by Truman's language about sites "which may be available without cost or at reasonable cost." The new Site Subcommittee included some of the same individuals from the UN's earlier misadventures, including Stoyan Gavrilovic from the first site tour in January. But this time, notably, they had no instructions to stay away from cities. In fact, for many, their recent experiences had been an excruciating lesson in the realities of the American suburbs. First, your neighbors might not like anyone moving in who could upset the status quo. And second, commuting could be a nightmare.[16]

FINALLY, PHILADELPHIA

After a year of missteps and resistance, the United States seemed once again to offer plentiful free land and unqualified interest in creating a permanent home for the UN. For ten days in November 1946, now with greater guidance from the State Department, a United Nations team embarked on a tour of the most determined, generous, and feasible of the world capital contenders. Eventually the new site inspectors would return to New York City and Westchester County, but their itinerary called for visiting San Francisco, Boston, and—for the first time—Philadelphia, where civic leaders had beckoned for attention from the organization's earliest days.

Philadelphia's campaign had evolved from its beginnings as a newspaper editor's crusade and sentimental civic cause into a case of professionally guided city planning. The *Philadelphia Record* remained an enthusiastic promoter, and the civic boosters who had trailed the UN to San Francisco, London, and New York remained very much involved. But now the chairman of the city's recently formed Planning Commission, Edward Hopkinson Jr., took the lead in organizing Philadelphia's appeal. Hopkinson was a descendant of a signer of the Declaration of Independence, but this phase of the city's campaign depended more on maps and statistics, the tools for recruiting businesses and conventions, than tourism-oriented photographs of Independence Hall or the Liberty Bell. For two and a half days in November, the Philadelphians had their chance to prove that their city could be everything that the United Nations wanted. The diplomats would see that Philadelphia had transportation, communication, cultural institutions, education facilities, and office space. Most especially, the Philadelphians could offer land for free, and they intended to extend such a gracious welcome that the delegates would not fear resistance.[17]

When the delegates arrived at the North Philadelphia railroad station on Monday, November 18, they found twelve black limousines waiting to take them into the city by way of the scenic East River Drive along the Schuylkill River in Fairmount Park—a route that bypassed densely populated factory neighborhoods. Immediately, they commented on the welcome change from the traffic tie-ups in New York. The motorcade traveled with a police escort, but the visitors heard no sirens to call unwanted attention to their presence. Their hosts provided just enough flourishes to demonstrate Philadelphia's cultural assets: a concert by the Philadelphia Orchestra at the ornate Academy of Music, two nights at the Barclay Hotel on fashionable Rittenhouse Square, and lunch amid the masterpieces of the Philadelphia Museum of Art. Business meetings took place on the top floor of the building that provided the best indication that Philadelphia might be pulling away from its red-brick past, the 1932 European modernist skyscraper that served as headquarters for the Philadelphia Savings Fund Society. The Philadelphians met with UN engineers and focused on practicalities as they guided the diplomats to a two-square-mile headquarters site on Belmont Plateau in Fairmount Park, situated within the city limits but nonetheless a scenic, pastoral setting west of the central business district. The site was, to a large extent, a brighter alternative to the Flushing Meadows situation in New York—still a park, but prettier and with a much easier commute. The UN visitors discovered that Philadelphia offered an eight-minute drive from the nearest railroad station to the proposed headquarters location. Their hosts promised that delegates would be able to telephone home before dinner and make it back to their apartments on Rittenhouse Square before the steaks were done. The Philadelphians also offered acreage in the Roxborough and Chestnut Hill districts of Northwest Philadelphia for housing the UN's staff. With the support of state and city government, the United Nations could have it all without charge.[18]

Most astonishingly, the diplomats found themselves ushered into the home of Mr. and Mrs. Kenneth Day, who lived in the proposed residential area for United Nations personnel. Kenneth Day had designed and built the house, but over Madeira and sherry, the couple vowed that they would be quite willing to give it over to the United Nations. "Really," said Mrs. Day, "somebody must break down to welcome the United Nations, and the delegates have to settle somewhere." An accompanying reporter observed that "the delegates could not believe their eyes and ears." Any resistance that might be brewing among other residents of the affected neighborhoods was dismissed as "panicky" by Philadelphia's UN boosters, who offered public assurance that homeowners who wanted to remain in the neighborhoods would be allowed to stay.[19]

Although careful to reserve judgment, the Site Subcommittee left Philadelphia on November 20, 1946, with the sense that the UN had an alternative to New York. Less than a year before, Philadelphia had been excluded because diplomats sitting in London had considered it too close to Washington, D.C. Now, the UN's representatives concluded that Philadelphia would meet their requirements, most of all their desire to escape commuting problems in and around New York. The earlier preference for a distinct, suburban location for the United Nations clearly was diminishing. "The Philadelphia sites are accessible, well located, [and] have fine transportation," the UN visitors stated before departing. And it had been refreshing to be welcomed, for a change. "The friendliness of Philadelphia has been coupled with an unmistakable sincerity which has made a deep impression upon us."[20]

Privately, however, the delegates wondered about Philadelphia's ability to reinvent itself as the Capital of the World. They could not shake their perceptions of Philadelphia as an industrial city with a well-known history of municipal corruption. Would the impressive Planning Commission make up for the machine politics that gripped City Hall? Would the smokiness that permeated the city clear up when the railroads converted from coal to diesel fuel? On the whole, could they reconcile themselves to living in Philadelphia when the other choices were New York, Boston, and San Francisco? The dissonance between Philadelphia's image and its aspirations remained, captured clearly in an editorial cartoon that appeared in the *Philadelphia Bulletin* at the end of the site visit. Against the backdrop of the city skyline, the cartoon showed UN delegates dressed in business suits and boarding an airplane labeled "to San Francisco." They shook hands with a figure representing Philadelphia—a portly William Penn, dressed in colonial-era stockings, breeches, and knee-length coat. "Au Revoir!" the headline over the cartoon proclaimed.[21]

Still, Philadelphia's location alone gave it an advantage over the diplomats' next destination, San Francisco. Traveling across the country required a sixteen-hour flight, which renewed memories of the time-consuming trips to reach the West Coast for the UN's first conference. The journey also required refueling along the way—this time, in Oklahoma. If the diplomats needed further prodding to end the world capital competition once and for all, they received it as they stepped off the plane in Tulsa. There, waiting to greet them—at 2:30 a.m.—were boosters from

Claremore, Oklahoma, the hometown of Will Rogers situated thirty miles east of Tulsa. Seizing their unusual opportunity to plead their case directly, they came to the airport with brochures offering Claremore as the future Capital of the World.[22]

San Francisco's boosters, who had been in New York courting the delegates since August, hustled back to the West Coast ahead of the diplomats. They had gone to great lengths to find the same range of suburban sites that the UN sought in Westchester County, and their attention to detail extended to the UN-style blue place cards for the conference room where they would present their new options. Mayor Lapham even paid a personal call on William Randolph Hearst to secure a pledge that the isolationist Hearst newspapers would not interfere with the city's chances.[23]

But as the San Franciscans discovered, by the time the UN Site Subcommittee reached the West Coast, the diplomats' priorities had turned resolutely from suburbs to city. Instead of the world-capital site in the countryside that the boosters had located near Crystal Springs, forty-five minutes away, the delegates showed greatest interest in the Presidio—the long-standing military installation within the city limits, overlooking the Golden Gate Bridge. The Presidio had the advantage of being close to downtown, and its walled perimeter and existing buildings suggested an easy transition. But it was federal property, which the San Francisco officials had no authority to offer, and views of the Golden Gate could not erase the memory of the sixteen-hour flight to the West Coast. The cosmopolitan character of the city, which San Francisco's boosters had long promoted, also prompted questions about the potential for racial conflict. The Chinese delegate in the UN group asked pointed questions about the Chinese Exclusion Act of 1882, which had banned immigrants from China in response to a backlash from native Californians. Perhaps mindful of Great Britain's control of Hong Kong, the British delegate speculated about conflicts that might occur between the children of British diplomats and the city's many Chinese American youngsters. San Francisco's chances remained alive but did not seem high as diplomats left on November 24 on a cross-country flight to Boston.[24]

With short notice, Boston's promoters once again offered the United Nations three locations that had been considered before: the Princemere estate on the North Shore; the Blue Hills region to the south; and an area of state-owned land west of the city near Framingham and Sudbury. The previous January, the UN site-inspection team had judged the Blue Hills area to be an acceptable alternative to the New York suburbs. Just outside

Boston on state property and with cooperative local neighbors, the Blue Hills site suited the UN's current desires for convenient commuting as well. But the Boston boosters found that the ground had shifted in other ways, along the deepening fault lines of the Cold War. The Soviet delegate on this trip, Nikolai D. Bassov, clearly recalled the incident in January when a Boston judge had denounced the Soviet Union at an event attended by other public officials, who did not object. In January, the Soviets' concerns had been granted only a published dissent at the end of the site-inspection group's recommendations. Now, in November, Soviet objections to Boston gained greater prominence. Boston's boosters were unfailingly gracious hosts and assured the diplomats that Massachusetts would embrace the opportunity to become the world's capital. But Bassov called for a referendum to measure whether Bostonians would welcome the UN. His proposal prompted a wave of call-in support to radio stations and public officials, but it also signaled potential conflict with the Soviets if the United Nations opted for a Boston site. The publicity also reawakened resistance in the area of Sudbury, a town that had battled the UN's interest from the beginning.[25]

By the end of the ten-day whirlwind, the traveling diplomats even found a beacon of hope in Westchester County, New York. On November 29, the day after Thanksgiving, they visited a newly offered tract of public land in Mohansic Park, situated near one of the five locations identified by the UN's own planning commission during the summer. In contrast to the vocal opposition by the United Westchester Citizens Committee to Save Our Homes, a coalition of twenty-seven homeowners near the park proclaimed their support for a Westchester world capital. One of them, lawyer Otto Koegel, guided the diplomats around his 1,000-acre farm and denounced the UN's opponents in the county as "completely professional, partly political, and partly sinister." Taken by surprise by Koegel's hospitality, the delegates saw a renewed chance for Westchester, although they were wary of the commuting distance from New York City as well as the vigorous opposition of the Save Our Homes committee.[26]

At the end of November, the United Nations once again seemed to have attractive options, including new choices in cities or within easy commuting distance. The most recent site inspections also ignited still more boosterism from world-capital hopefuls around the United States; Warren Austin took phone calls from promoters in Rhode Island, Vermont, Minnesota, Colorado, South Dakota, and Oregon, plus Los Angeles, California, and Niagara Falls, New York.[27]

Then, on the last day of November, the prospects for Flushing Meadows Park collapsed. The site where the boosters of New York City had devoted all of their energies was the last stop for the Site Subcommittee. When the diplomats gathered there on November 30, 1946, Mayor O'Dwyer reminded them of the more than $2 million the city had already invested in creating the General Assembly auditorium and grounds, and the magnificent plans for expanding this development into a permanent headquarters. Despite the New Yorkers' enticements, however, few delegates liked the site. An American on the Site Subcommittee reported to Warren Austin that his colleagues found Flushing Meadows "totally lacking in scenic beauty," not to mention that "it takes about 40 minutes to reach it from Midtown." Now, consulting engineers hired by the UN reported their conclusion that the "filled-in swamp land" of Flushing Meadows would require excessively expensive foundations to support large permanent buildings. Although Robert Moses and the engineers who had overseen development of the world's fair and subsequent park vigorously denied this, it nevertheless doomed New York's elaborate strategy. The Site Subcommittee voted to reject Flushing Meadows Park. The decision came on the basis of cost, rather than as a rejection of the city, but this seemed to doom any chance that the UN would stay in New York because Flushing Meadows was the city's only offer.[28]

Two days later, the United Nations Headquarters Site Subcommittee issued its final report (as if anything in the headquarters process could be considered final). Based on the most recent inspections, the subcommittee recommended two places as equally suitable for the United Nations' future home: the Presidio in San Francisco and the Belmont Plateau/Roxborough site in Philadelphia. Beyond these, the next best choice was in Westchester County. Once again guided by concerns about commuting as well as the need to keep costs down, the diplomats rejected the large sites in the northern reaches of the county, where they had found a friendly reception, and opted instead for one of the smaller sites near Harrison, New York, the closest possible location to Manhattan. As for Boston, the subcommittee ruled out the most favorable site in that region, in the Blue Hills, because the uneven terrain would not be suitable for building a large headquarters complex.[29]

The Headquarters Site Subcommittee had done its duty and advanced the site selection process. But the report also represented another giant step backward into earlier disputes. Once again, the United Nations had arrived at a choice between the East and West Coast, a battle that had been waged and settled—or so it seemed—a year before in London. Time had not erased the fact that Europeans tended to favor New York, while San Francisco beckoned to nations of the Pacific Rim. This time, furthermore, the East-West conflict also pitted members of the UN Security Council against each other and threatened to split the United Nations into factions aligned with the emerging Cold War. The Soviet Union responded to the new site recommendations by insisting that Flushing Meadows—rejected by the subcommittee—was the UN's best option. A choice between the East and West coasts also created a link between the headquarters decision and the contentious question of whether a Jewish state should be created in Palestine. Members of the Arab League opposed a permanent UN head-quarters in New York, fearing the influence that might be exerted by the presence of more than two million Jewish residents. American Jewish organizations already had played active roles in shaping UN policies on human rights and refugees. Placing the UN in New York would give these organizations convenient access to any future deliberations about Palestine, a question that surely lay ahead as postwar migrations of European Jews increased tensions between Zionists and the Arab League.[30]

Confusion erupted as the United States tried to uphold its pledge to aid the United Nations in its search, but without taking sides among the competitors. At issue was the Presidio, the military installation overlooking San Francisco Bay. On December 2, the same day that the Site Subcommittee released its report, the United States confirmed that this federal property could indeed be made available to the UN, subject to approval by Congress. To news reporters as well as diplomats, this seemed to signal that the United States favored the West Coast—a position squarely in opposition to the Soviet Union, which opposed San Francisco because of the travel distance. In fact, President Truman had no preference between the two sites, and on December 4, the State Department advised the U.S. delegation to support whichever site seemed to be favored most within the UN. But as the site report reached the full Headquarters Committee for hearings, the Soviets charged that the Americans were working behind the scenes for the Presidio. Hastily, the Americans worked to defuse the tension they had unwittingly ignited; in the process, they created still more confusion. Despite the U.S. government's assurances about the Presidio, just four days later Warren Austin announced that the United States actually preferred a UN headquarters in the East—finally breaking the Americans' silence on the matter, but seeming to contradict their earlier stance. Distancing the U.S. further from the Presidio option, Austin asked the

UN secretary general to calculate the additional expense that would be involved if the UN opted for the West Coast.[31]

If the United States and the Soviet Union both favored the East Coast, and the Site Subcommittee's favored site on the East Coast was Philadelphia . . . could it be that the United Nations was destined for the City of Brotherly Love? Philadelphia now seemed to meet all of the United Nations' specifications—if only the diplomats could be persuaded to live there. While the Headquarters Committee continued its hearings, the secretary general of the United Nations, Trygve Lie, quietly journeyed south from New York City to take a look around. He traveled by train with J. Stauffer Oliver, one of city's original boosters, and on the way back it seemed to Oliver that the secretary general had been persuaded. As Oliver later recounted it, during the ride back to New York, Lie said, "Until twelve o'clock today I was against Philadelphia, but that was solely because I did not know what a magnificent site Philadelphia has to offer. Now that I have seen it, I am fully convinced it is the place which should be selected." But at that moment, it seemed that New York City had fallen out of contention. And New York was where the secretary general most wanted the United Nations to be.[32]

THE ROCKEFELLER TWIST

Resolving the UN's dilemma required real estate, money, and the power of a prominent family. On December 6, the same day that the United States declared its preference for the East Coast, a New York real estate developer read in the newspaper that Philadelphia was emerging as the compromise site for the United Nations. The developer, forty-year-old William Zeckendorf of the firm Webb & Knapp, had been working with partners to assemble property along the East River in midtown Manhattan for a Rockefeller Center–style "city within a city." As portrayed in *Life* magazine in October 1946, Zeckendorf's development—labeled "X-City"—would replace a smelly district of slaughterhouses with an enormous elevated platform supporting office buildings, apartments, a convention hall, opera house, hotel, and heliport, with parking below. The magazine described Zeckendorf's real estate ambitions as "Napoleonic" in scale, and to help envision them he had commissioned the architect Wallace K. Harrison—one of the designers of Rockefeller Center, a Rockefeller relation by marriage, a confidant of Nelson Rockefeller, and a member of the booster committee that had been working to bring the UN to New York. The plans were grand, but for Zeckendorf, they also carried a risk. For the largest tract of land, he had paid $1 million for an option to buy for an additional $5.5 million. Time was running out because his option would expire at the end of the year.[33]

Day by day, dominos began to fall:

FRIDAY, DECEMBER 6, 1946. As Zeckendorf recalled it later, he put down the *New York Times,* turned to his wife, Marion, and declared, "I'm going to put those bastards on the platform!"

"Which bastards on what platform?" she asked.

"The UN—I'm going to put them on the platform over the slaughterhouses."[34]

Zeckendorf consulted with his partners. They thought he was crazy, but consented to Zeckendorf placing a telephone call to the mayor of New York. On the phone, the developer told William O'Dwyer that he had the perfect site for the United Nations. The call was timely, because later in the day the mayor also received a call from Secretary General Lie, who warned that unless New York came up with a new and better proposal, the United Nations would be on its way to Philadelphia. The secretary general, the mayor, and Robert Moses discussed the East River site that Zeckendorf had proposed—a "wildly remote prospect," Lie thought. The developer had said he would offer the East River site to the United Nations "for any price they wished to pay," but none of the officials interpreted this to mean that the site would be inexpensive. Surely it would not meet the UN's goal of a site that would be "without cost or at reasonable cost." Lie offered the mayor some advice, based on his close interactions with the New York City booster committee in recent months: get in touch with Nelson Rockefeller.[35]

O'Dwyer acted immediately. Rockefeller had been traveling in Latin America to launch a new venture, the International Basic Economy Corporation (IBEC), and to attend the inauguration of Mexican president Miguel Alemán. By the first week of December, he was taking some vacation time near Brownsville, Texas. But once O'Dwyer alerted him that New York had little time to lose and a new but potentially expensive option, Rockefeller boarded a flight to New York to try to salvage the city's chances.[36]

SATURDAY, DECEMBER 7. With Rockefeller en route, O'Dwyer directed Moses to create a map showing alternatives that could be offered to keep the United Nations in New York City. The map should show the East River site, along with others: an expanded area around Flushing Meadows Park; Governors Island; and another site in Manhattan south of Washington Square. Moses added an additional tract north of Tompkins

Square that had been set aside for a housing development, but that might be used instead for UN staff residences. The parks commissioner, stung by the UN's recent rejection of his favored site, told the mayor that "Flushing Meadow is still the best site unless it has been kicked around too much by uninformed critics. Governors Island is the best of the various alternatives." Asked by the mayor to think of alternatives in Westchester County that would not affect the city's water supply—a concern that had developed about some of the other sites there—Moses said he could think of only one: the property owned by the Rockefeller family at Pocantico Hills.[37]

SUNDAY, DECEMBER 8. Wallace Harrison met Nelson Rockefeller at the airport, and they proceeded directly to Flushing Meadows. It was past 6:00 p.m. as they huddled in the secretary general's office with Lie, Moses, Mayor O'Dwyer, the UN Headquarters Committee chairman Zuleta, and Warren Austin. The presence of the U.S. chief delegate at this meeting showed Austin becoming intimately involved with the New Yorkers' efforts to retain the UN, a charge later leveled by disappointed Philadelphians. The Vermont senator, who had worked previously with Nelson Rockefeller on Latin American affairs, assured Rockefeller that Flushing Meadows had no chance. Meanwhile, "other offers"—presumably the East River site—did not conform to President Truman's specification of "without cost or at reasonable cost." Zuleta's presence also was key. He was known to favor the United States, but he strongly disliked New York. The group talked about the land owned by the Rockefellers in Westchester County along the Hudson River, but acknowledged that the diplomats' resistance to commuting would be a barrier there, just as it was at Flushing Meadows and Lake Success. As they weighed the merits of the East River site and the Rockefeller property, the New Yorkers were reviving yet another dilemma that the UN previously had struggled to resolve—the merits of city versus suburb.[38]

MONDAY, DECEMBER 9. Knowing of the new discussions underway among the New Yorkers, and knowing that the UN Headquarters Committee might imminently vote on the report favoring Philadelphia or San Francisco, Warren Austin tried to buy time. If pushed to act now, he had instructions from the State Department to vote for Philadelphia; however, the United States hoped to postpone the vote to allow for consideration of additional sites in New York as well as in Boston (which the British continued to favor). On December 9, after consulting with the other members of the UN Security Council, Austin proposed delaying a decision on the headquarters until the 1947 session of the General Assembly. Adding to confusion over the United States' position, he at first included a recommendation for an East Coast location in his motion, but later in the day revised it so that San Francisco would remain in consideration. Austin's odd and unexpected maneuvers raised suspicions among the Philadelphians, who thought they had the prize within reach, and among San Franciscans who had not yet given up. A member of Philadelphia's booster committee stationed himself in the delegates' lounge at Flushing Meadows. San Francisco's mayor, also back in New York, wrote individual notes to each delegate as reminders that his city remained in the running.[39]

TUESDAY, DECEMBER 10, 1946, was the day that ended the search for the Capital of the World.

While New York City officials gathered data about new sites in and around Manhattan, Nelson Rockefeller and his brother Laurance sought out their father, John D. Rockefeller Jr., at Rockefeller Center. The brothers proposed to develop a new option for the UN by offering the family's Westchester County land along the Hudson River consisting of the Rockwood Hall estate of their late great-uncle William, a property that the county officials also had previously proposed. Their father advised caution. This gift, if accepted, would be only the beginning. Undoubtedly, the United Nations would require much more land, including the family's various homes in the area, even the family seat at Pocantico Hills. The sons were prepared: they had agreed they would yield their own homes, and they had secured promises from their other brothers, John and David, to either give up their homes or provide money to buy other property in the neighborhood for the UN. Still, their father warned of the consequences. Not unlike other residents of suburban areas who had resisted the United Nations, he predicted that "should the thousands of people connected with the United Nations organization take up residence in the general area, the whole character of the countryside would be changed." He wondered whether the Rockefeller land would be any more suitable than the site the UN had been considering near the county seat at White Plains. The meeting ended with new assignments for Nelson Rockefeller to find out all he could about the site near White Plains and to contact a real estate broker to see about additional land that might be available along the Hudson River near Rockwood Hall. Meanwhile, Wallace Harrison arrived and worked with Nelson Rockefeller to create a map of Rockefeller properties. Harrison also had in his possession a map of the East River site for William Zeckendorf's X-City, the project he had been working on long before it became part of the UN discussion.[40]

While the map making and telephoning continued in Nelson Rockefeller's office, John D. Rockefeller Jr. began to draft a letter that was never delivered—an offer to give Rockefeller property in Westchester County to the United Nations.[41]

At 7:30 p.m., Nelson Rockefeller telephoned his father's Park Avenue apartment to report on the day's activities. He had found that the UN's possible site near White Plains would cost $9 million, which seemed to put it out of the question. From real estate brokers, he had learned of additional Hudson River properties that might be combined with Rockefeller land to create a suitable site for the United Nations.[42]

It was then that John D. Rockefeller Jr. asked his son the pivotal question: What was the ideal site for the United Nations, regardless of whether Rockefeller homes were involved?

Nelson Rockefeller had worked all day to put together an offer of the Rockefeller properties, but he also had been told by Warren Austin that the commuting-weary diplomats were unlikely to agree to a site so distant from Manhattan. If that were the case, one expedient option remained: William Zeckendorf's X-City site, where the United Nations could have a "city within a city" much like Rockefeller Center. Wallace Harrison knew the site well, and Zeckendorf wanted to make the deal.[43]

As the father recalled it, Nelson Rockefeller replied quickly, "The East River site from 42nd Street to 48th Street is without any question the ideal site." Although it seemed to John D. Rockefeller Jr. that such a site would cost upwards of $25 million, Harrison had sounded out the developers and had come to believe that it could be acquired for a mere $8.5 million. Hearing this information from his son, John D. Rockefeller Jr. said, "Why should we not acquire and give this site?" On the other end of the line, the people in Nelson Rockefeller's office heard him say, "Why, Pa! That's most generous!" John D. Rockefeller Jr. authorized his son to make the deal.[44]

Now it was up to Wally Harrison. With his map of the East River site, he set out into the night to track down Zeckendorf. He found him around 9:30 p.m. at the nightclub Monte Carlo, known to be the developer's frequent haunt, in the midst of hosting a party celebrating his anniversary and the birthday of a business partner. It had been four days since Zeckendorf had first called the mayor of New York City to suggest the X-City site. Now, he and Harrison moved to a table together to look over the map. Zeckendorf conferred with his partners and then, with a fountain pen, he outlined the portion of the property between First Avenue and Franklin

D. Roosevelt Drive, running from Forty-Second to Forty-Eighth streets, that he would make available for sale. In the margins of the map he wrote an amount that would more than cover his investment and the impending sum due on his option: "8,500,000 to U.N. Dec. 10 for 30 days."

William Zeckendorf signed his name, giving the United Nations a thirty-day option to buy the land.[45]

Deal in hand, Harrison stopped at the St. Regis Hotel to telephone Nelson Rockefeller's office, where a champagne celebration began but the work continued. Rockefeller, Harrison, and other staff members at the office drafted letters to offer John D. Rockefeller Jr.'s gift of $8.5 million to buy the East River site for the United Nations. They began to work on satisfying two conditions that Rockefeller had stipulated. They obtained assurance from Robert Moses that the city would agree to close streets to create an unobstructed waterfront site. They tried to reach Warren Austin to ask about Rockefeller's other condition—that this gift be free from federal taxes, which he had been obliged to pay on his previous gift of a library for the League of Nations. Beyond this, they put lawyers to work to ascertain whether Zeckendorf had authority to issue this option, and concluded that he did. At 11:30 p.m., Nelson Rockefeller called his father to report that they had secured the option, and he read the letters over the telephone. The letters were dated December 10, but editing and revisions continued until 12:45 a.m. on December 11. At 1:30 a.m., the Rockefeller team finally reached Warren Austin, who had been at a dinner with Secretary of State Byrnes.[46]

Wednesday, December 11. Unaware of this scramble of events, on the morning of December 11, the *New York Times* carried the following headline: "U.N. Body to Renew Site Debate Today," with the subheading, "Philadelphia Is Seen as Choice If a Location Is Voted, but Further Stalemate Looms."[47]

The Rockefeller team rushed to beat any further action by the UN Headquarters Committee. At 7:30 a.m. on December 11, Nelson Rockefeller arrived at his father's Park Avenue apartment with the documents to be signed. By 8:15 a.m., he was at the Hotel Pennsylvania to deliver them personally to Warren Austin, who immediately called Secretary of State Byrnes to gain his approval. Austin called together the American delegates, who also approved. And then Nelson Rockefeller, surely the most prominent messenger in Manhattan on this December day, carried the paperwork to Presbyterian Hospital, where for health reasons the Headquarters Committee chairman Zuleta rested as a patient at night even as he

After months of pursuing a suburban location, an offer of $8.5 million from John D. Rock-
efeller Jr. turned the UN's attentions toward this intensely urban site on the East River,

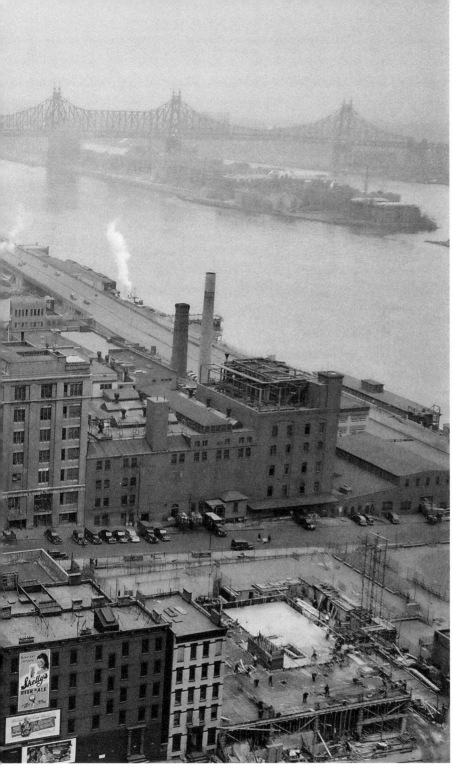

where developer William Zeckendorf had planned to build a Rockefeller Center–style "city within a city." (United Nations Photo Library)

continued his diplomatic duties by day. By 10:30 a.m., Zuleta was back at work, convening a new meeting of the Headquarters Committee.[48]

Only the day before, Warren Austin had asked the committee to delay action on a headquarters decision until the following year. Now, adding to perceptions of the United States' erratic actions on the site question, he withdrew that motion. He proposed instead that a subcommittee be formed immediately to inspect the East River site that was now available, thanks to John D. Rockefeller Jr.'s generous gift. By 3:00 p.m., the subcommittee members were on the site, where they somehow managed to look past the slaughterhouses and envision a skyscraper headquarters. "They were not seeing the sides of beef, the broken sidewalks or the smokestacks," reported a journalist who came along. "They were definitely entranced by the idea of a skyscraper capital, thinking of it in terms of Rockefeller Center, to them the epitome of western architecture." Their imaginings of a high-rise home for the UN may have been helped by their next stop—an office in Rockefeller Center, where they went to work writing their report. In it, not surprisingly, they recommended that the United Nations accept the Rockefeller gift, which itself seemed to have fallen from the sky.[49]

Over the next two days, the choice of location for the UN was sealed as the Headquarters Committee and then the General Assembly voted to accept $8.5 million from John D. Rockefeller Jr. for the purpose of purchasing the site along the East River in midtown Manhattan. In the Headquarters Committee, Egypt upheld the Arab League's distaste for New York by pushing for a postponement, but the motion fell to defeat. In the General Assembly the five powers of the Security Council embraced the windfall. Most of the resistance to New York—other than the Arab states and the long-time champion for San Francisco, Australia—collapsed in the delegates' relief over such an expedient solution and the prospect that international diplomacy would not require venturing beyond the cultured confines of Manhattan. An international dilemma had been resolved by local action, driven by individuals who identified a clear objective, adapted to changing circumstances, and controlled the wealth and power necessary to achieve the results they desired.[50]

EPILOGUE

THE DREAM OF CREATING a world capital city, which had sprung so readily to life at the end of the Second World War, came to an end. Instead, in the tradition of earlier self-proclaimed world capitals from Rome to London and Paris, the largesse of the Rockefeller family bestowed the "world capital" honor on an existing city—New York. This pleased the secretary general of the United Nations, who later reflected with satisfaction that "the United Nations would be at the turbulent center of twentieth century life, where, jostled by all the problems and all the challenges of struggling, swarming humanity, its work for peace would have a reality and substance unattainable in the relative tranquility that so many had seemed to desire." Among the general public, some protested that $8.5 million would be better spent on feeding the poor, helping veterans, or solving the postwar housing shortage. But many more praised John D. Rockefeller Jr. for his generosity, which they saw as a necessary act to secure the future of the United Nations and peace for the world.[1]

Around the United States, in cities as sizeable as Chicago and Denver, and in towns as small as Claremore, Oklahoma, civic boosters set aside their visions for transforming their own hometowns into the Capital of the World—some more graciously than others. San Francisco's boosters, diplomatically, wished the United Nations well. After Roger Lapham completed his term as mayor, he maintained a role in international affairs as head of the U.S. government's Economic Cooperation missions to China (1948–49) and Greece (1950–51). In Boston, the *Globe* decried the "steam roller tactics" that secured the UN for New York, and former mayor and governor Maurice Tobin moved on to federal government service as labor secretary in the Truman administration. Many of the lesser contenders congratulated themselves on the publicity they had generated, if nothing else, but others did not easily yield the fight. In Sault Ste. Marie, Michigan, Stellanova Osborn persisted with renewed invitations to place the United Nations headquarters on Sugar Island. In the Black Hills, Paul

Bellamy regretted that the UN had not seen how perfect a site near Rapid City would be, and during 1947 he corresponded with Philadelphia boosters who viewed the Rockefeller deal as nothing short of treachery. Bellamy remained involved with Black Hills booster efforts for the rest of his life; Philadelphia entered an era of reform that included sweeping changes to the urban core. Among these were expanded state and national parks around Independence Hall, which was later designated as a World Heritage Site by the United Nations Educational, Scientific, and Cultural Organization (UNESCO).[2]

The United Nations headquarters complex now standing in New York City, completed in 1953, is a place created from bold intentions and cold realities. When the international team of architects appointed by the UN for the project began its work in 1947, some of the designers still spoke of creating a "world capital" on the East River site in Manhattan. Rockefeller family confidant Wallace K. Harrison, whom the UN appointed as planning director for the project, spoke of creating a "garden city of the world" and imagined the day when "the people of the city, long used to dark, high-walled streets, will be surprised to discover this midtown zone of open, beautiful space where you can walk through and around the buildings." His descriptions reflected the ongoing interest in creating a place that would offer both urban conveniences and a pastoral setting, but without resorting to the suburbs.[3]

Some ideas offered for the UN complex sustained the notion that a world capital should consist of more than a few city blocks. One of the architects on the design team, Sven Markelius of Sweden, proposed extending a bridge across the river to Roosevelt Island, where a residential development would keep alive the idea that the United Nations capital would be a community as well as an office complex. William Zeckendorf, the developer who had assembled the properties where the UN headquarters stands, pushed for a grand concourse that would culminate in a symbolic communications tower directly north of the UN. However, by the late summer and early fall of 1947, the limitations of the UN's budget as well as the size of the site precluded the most far-reaching of the architectural dreams, and the city of New York would not agree to Zeckendorf's concourse plan. Harrison, who had been instrumental in creating the memorable symbols of the Trylon and Perisphere for the New York World's Fair of 1939, guided the UN designers toward plans that would achieve "efficiency, economy, and simplicity" rather than monumentality. He reimagined the headquarters as a "workshop for peace"—not a Capital of the World but a place for diplomatic business more akin to his earlier major project, Rockefeller Center. Although the architects worked to create a General Assembly hall as the "heart" of the complex, the site is dominated by the tall slab for the Secretariat, the organization's office machinery. Intended to be international, the General Assembly building is topped by a dome reminiscent of the U.S. Capitol building, a feature intended to appeal to members of Congress, whose votes were needed for the loan for construction. The dome marks the UN as a "capitol"—a building—rather than a capital city. The United Nations occupies a distinctive complex of buildings, but they are far less than the Capital of the World that captured public imagination at the end of the Second World War.[4]

In their exuberance and attention to detail, the world capital campaigns of 1944–46 offer insight into a period that lies midway between the booster strategies of the nineteenth century, such as the development of the American West, and the more intense place marketing and branding efforts of cities around the world in the late twentieth and early twenty-first centuries. The world capital campaigns drew upon earlier practices of industrial and tourist promotion to emphasize centrality, accommodations, and unique cultural assets such as history and scenery. They deployed their campaigns through printed materials such as brochures, press releases, and favorable publicity in cooperative newspapers. In addition to print media, they spread their messages with personal ambassadors and, occasionally, press agents. Increasing globalization later in the twentieth century added intensity to the competition among cities, including escalating rivalries for honors such as hosting the Olympic Games, but this is best understood as a continuation of earlier trends rather than as a wholly new development of the 1980s and 1990s.

Viewed in retrospect, the misadventures of the United Nations in 1945–46 also provide an object lesson in the art and science of site selection—or, more precisely, how not to go about it. With more world-altering issues to confront, the UN understandably did not have real estate uppermost on its agenda, but its actions exposed the weaknesses of the new organization. First, a vacuum of information allowed promoters of sites to rush in with their own expectations for what and where the United Nations headquarters should be. The UN's criteria, when drafted, were so broad that any of the unwanted suitors could claim to meet them. The range of choices was narrowed without thorough knowledge of local circumstances, and the search for a site proceeded without first determining exactly what the new organization wanted to build. When resistance developed, the negotiating

Developer William Zeckendorf proposed a grand concourse adjacent to the UN buildings, but did not win approval from city officials. (Rockefeller Archive Center)

EARL PURDY del.

Aerial view of United Nations headquarters complex, a "workshop for peace." (United Nations Photo Library)

skills of the world's most experienced diplomats could not compensate for the scarcity of facts about the UN's needs. While the diplomats tried to emphasize the best of intentions, homeowners imagined the worst of possibilities. In the end, individual determination, from the protests in the suburbs to Nelson Rockefeller's declaration to his father that the UN belonged in Manhattan, mattered more than tangible factors such as infrastructure—the sort of variable typically stressed in textbooks about site selection.[5]

On a broader scale, the search for the Capital of the World illustrates the dynamics of the world as it became a more interconnected place in the twentieth century. The UN headquarters saga demonstrates the complex tangle of interactions that operate among individuals, families, communities, regions, and nations. Scholarly interest in globalization has focused predominantly on the period since 1980, but the world capital competition illuminates the ways in which local and global factors were becoming enmeshed earlier in the twentieth century. As scholars of globalization have noted, the world has become simultaneously more homogenized and more divided, a duality that seems well illustrated by the world capital competition. In striving to meet the stated needs of a new international organization, U.S. cities and towns became nearly indistinguishable to the diplomats; at the same time, they competed vigorously with each other to prove their unique qualifications. Even in the realm of international affairs, local factors could be decisive. At this transitional moment at the end of the Second World War, local people, cities, and towns mobilized to define and defend their place in a changing world. Individuals and communities reached outward from deeply felt attachments to local places, people, and histories. But as resistance to the UN's plans also showed, becoming global could also be perceived as a danger to these same valued characteristics. At the end of World War II the tension proved greatest in the middle ground of the American suburb, especially in small towns within the commuting orbits of major cities, where community traditions already seemed at risk.

Today, "Capital of the World" survives as a slogan for New York City rather than a place of dreams. As reporters noted while trailing UN diplomats through darkness in Connecticut, the search for the Capital of the World could have been a movie. Or perhaps it should have inspired a Broadway show, with tap-dancing civic boosters, diplomats step-kicking in circles, and choruses of "Anything You Can Do, I Can Do Better," "I Left My Heart in San Francisco," and "Oklahoma!" For the grand finale, diplomats and boosters could dedicate the United Nations headquarters in New

York with a rousing rendition of "Accentuate the Positive," from the 1944 film *Here Come the Waves*. Looking back, if it all seems a little bit crazy, then we have lost touch with the atmosphere of determination, hope, and anxiety that characterized American society at the end of the Second World War. We have forgotten the time when people in cities and towns across the United States imagined themselves on the world stage—and not just on the stage, but at its center as the stars of the show.

ABBREVIATIONS IN APPENDIX AND NOTES

CAC Carl Albert Center Congressional Archives, University of Oklahoma, Norman, Okla.

CHS California Historical Society, San Francisco, Calif.

CSA California State Archives, Sacramento, Calif.

CSL Connecticut State Library, Hartford, Conn.

CU Avery Architectural and Fine Arts Library, Columbia University, New York, N.Y.

DPL Denver Public Library, Denver, Colo.

DWU Dakota Wesleyan University, Mitchell, S.D.

FDR Franklin D. Roosevelt Presidential Library, Hyde Park, N.Y.

FSU Claude Pepper Library, Florida State University, Tallahassee, Fla.

HSP Historical Society of Pennsylvania, Philadelphia, Pa.

HST Harry S. Truman Presidential Library and Museum, Independence, Mo.

INHP Independence National Historical Park Archives, Philadelphia, Pa.

ISL Indiana State Library, Indianapolis, Ind.

LOC Library of Congress, Washington, D.C.

MSA Michigan State Archives, Lansing, Mich.

NJSA New Jersey State Archives, Trenton, N.J.

NYMA New York Municipal Archives, New York, N.Y.

NYPL New York Public Library, New York, N.Y.

NYT *New York Times*

PR *Philadelphia Record*

PSA Pennsylvania State Archives, Harrisburg, Pa.

RAC Rockefeller Archive Center, Sleepy Hollow, N.Y.

SDSA South Dakota State Archives, Pierre, S.D.

SFC *San Francisco Chronicle*

SFCB *San Francisco Call Bulletin*

SFE *San Francisco Examiner*

SFN *San Francisco News*

SFPL San Francisco Public Library, San Francisco, Calif.

UA Urban Archives, Temple University, Philadelphia, Pa.

UCB University of Colorado at Boulder Libraries, Boulder, Colo.

UM Bentley Historical Library, University of Michigan, Ann Arbor, Mich.

UN United Nations

UNA United Nations Archives, New York, N.Y.

UNO Special Collections, University of New Orleans, New Orleans, La.

UR University of Rochester Library, Rochester, N.Y.

USD Richardson Manuscript Collections, I. D. Weeks Library, University of South Dakota, Vermillion, S.D.

UV University of Vermont, Burlington, Vt.

UVA Albert and Shirley Small Special Collections Library, University of Virginia, Charlottesville, Va.

APPENDIX: CAPITALS OF THE WORLD

THIS STUDY HAS IDENTIFIED 248 localities involved in the world capital competition to varying degrees, 202 as a result of actions by residents or officials with jurisdiction over the nominated communities. The scope of proposals indicates the previously unexplored public fascination with the prospect of creating a Capital of the World, evolving perceptions of the postwar world, and wide-ranging interaction between localities and world affairs.

The world capital proposals in this list are coded as follows:

(C) Campaigns—Sustained efforts characterized by activities such as repeated contact with the UN, formation of committees, and creation of publicity materials.

(I) Invitations—Proposals from individuals or groups in authority, such as public officials or chambers of commerce.

(S) Suggestions—Other proposals from individuals without authority.

Abbreviations in parentheses indicate locations of sources. More extensive descriptions and documentation are available on the web site [capital-of-the-world.com].

ALASKA

1 Anchorage (S). The *Anchorage Daily Times* suggested that Anchorage could meet all of the UN's needs as well as offer federal land and favorable business conditions. (*SFC*)

ARIZONA

2 Douglas (S). James L. Kennedy, private citizen, suggested Douglas as a central location on the "dividing line between the Spanish Republics and the English-speaking countries of the Western hemisphere" and "midway between the capital of China on the West, and the capital of U.S.S.R. on the East." He also pointed out the climate, water supply, and access to rail transportation. (UNA)

3 Grand Canyon (S). Lee F. Jones of Pasadena, California, suggested a head-quarters "within the depths of the Grand Canyon," a site also favored by New Mexico governor John Dempsey. (HST, Associated Press)

ARKANSAS

4 Intersection of Arkansas, Missouri, and Oklahoma (S). An Oklahoma City man, Henry T. Miller, suggested creating "Roosevelt, I.D." (International District) at this location. (HST)

CALIFORNIA

5 Berkeley (I). Berkeley City Council argued that because of "close proximity to San Francisco, the birthplace of the United Nations charter, it would be exceedingly appropriate to have the [world] Capital situated in this City." (UNA)

6 Catalina Island (S). Suggested by Los Angeles resident Maria Wolters. (CSA)

7 Crystal Springs (C). See chapter 9.

8 Los Angeles (S). Although the Los Angeles County Board of Supervisors and Chamber of Commerce endorsed San Francisco, locations in Los Angeles appeared among suggestions submitted to the UN and to Governor Earl Warren. (UNA, CSA)

9 Marin County—San Pablo Bay (S). Suggested by a real estate agent in Berkeley, Calif., E. E. Webster. (CSA)

10 Monterey Peninsula (S). S. F. B. Morse, president of Del Monte Properties Company, suggested Monterey for its climate, beauty, resort hotels, and central location one hundred miles from San Francisco. He also called attention to its historic role as a capital during Spanish and Mexican rule. UN site inspectors discussed the Monterey Peninsula but rejected it as too distant from San Francisco. (UNA, *SFN*)

11 Moraga Valley/Contra Costa County (C). A campaign endorsed by the Contra Costa Supervisors called attention to large expanses of land in the valley as well as accessibility by highway from San Francisco, but site inspectors eliminated this East Bay site in favor of possibilities closer to San Francisco. (CHS, *SFN*)

12 Palm Springs (I). The Palm Springs Chamber of Commerce delivered an early invitation to President Roosevelt in March 1945. Additional interest emerged in connection with a plan to create a peace memorial called the "Tower of Civilization and World Unity." (CSA)

13 Palo Alto (S). Andrew Swanson, a resident of San Francisco, suggested a location close to Stanford University. (CSA)

14 Pleasanton (S). The "old Hearst ranch" in Pleasanton, east of San Francisco, was suggested by the ranch manager, John A. Marshall. (CSA)

15 "Redwood Empire" (I). The California Legislature proposed a headquarters in the "Redwood grove in the West's Redwood Empire." (CSA)

16 San Francisco (C). See chapters 1, 2, 3, 5, and 9.

17 San Simeon (S). San Francisco resident Jerome Landfield suggested the Hearst Estate at San Simeon because of its magnificent buildings and available land. (CSA)

18 Santa Barbara (S). Suggested by a private citizen, Mary M. Simpson. "Where is there a more cultural, educational atmosphere, wonderful climate, winter sports, beaches, etc., etc., than in Santa Barbara?" she asked in a letter to Governor Warren. (CSA)

19 Santa Clara County (I). Board of Supervisors chairman C. P. Cooley invited consideration on the basis of climate and available sites. (UNA)

20 Santa Rosa (S). A private citizen, Leo B. F. Jenkins, urged consideration because "God has seen fit to create the fairest and most beautiful valley in all the world." (CSA)

21 Treasure Island and Yerba Buena Island (S). Harold French, a resident of Oakland, suggested these "world known" islands between San Francisco and Oakland. (CSA)

COLORADO

22 Colorado Springs (S). Robert Barnstone of the Colorado Sterling Silver Company advocated Colorado Springs as "a quiet restful town with America's most healthful climate," with "the charm and peace of Geneva plus the best of American living." (The Colorado Springs Chamber of Commerce endorsed Denver's bid.) (UNA, HST, DPL)

23 Denver (C). See chapters 5 and 6.

24 Dolores (S). On the letterhead of "New Age Gardens," private citizen Parker C. Kendall wrote to President Truman and to his "fellow world citizens" to suggest this location in the San Juan Basin, offering also "our Light of Reason on any debatable question." (UNA, HST)

25 Una (S). The idea to transform this small community into a new city for the UN came from Anna C. Hoyt, an employee of the Museum of Fine Arts in Boston, who thought that the new world capital should be called "Una," for "United Nations Association." She discovered that Una already existed in Colorado between the De Beque and Grand valleys. (*Denver Post*)

CONNECTICUT

The governor of Connecticut, Raymond E. Baldwin, invited the UN to the state, in addition to these local bids:

26 Hartford (I). Mayor Cornelius A. Moylan called attention to Hartford's location midway between Boston and New York and invited consideration of the city or nearby towns. Along with climate, transportation, and educational institutions, Hartford was one of the few world capital hopefuls to mention its "high class industries." (UNA)

27 New Haven (I). Charles A. Williams, president of the New Haven Chamber of Commerce, called attention to New Haven's rail connections to major U.S. cities, its "equable climate," available sites, and experts at Yale University. (CSL)

28 New London/Waterford (I). Mayor James A. May and other city officials promoted the "Greater New London area" as a location between New York and Boston with railroad connections and "no labor troubles." (UNA)

29 New Milford (S). Suggested by George Harvey, a local resident and former borough president of Queens County, New York. (*Providence Journal*)

30 Ridgefield (I). See chapters 5 and 7.

31 Stamford (I). See chapter 5.

FLORIDA

32 Jacksonville (I). Pointing out that Florida had an international heritage including France, Spain, England, and the United States, the Jacksonville Chamber of Commerce invited the UN to place the world capital on St. John's Bluff, where "Admiral Jean Ribault of the French Navy established a settlement in 1562." The invitation called attention to Jacksonville's location "on the main line of world aviation" as well as its railroads and steamship lines. (UNA)

33 Miami (C). In Miami, a World War II military hub, the campaign to attract the UN originated with a navy officer, Rear Admiral C. D. Leffler Jr. In addition to offering a favorable climate, the Miami Chamber of Commerce argued that the resort city would spare the UN entanglements with industrial labor conflicts. The boosters suggested a headquarters in Villa Vizcaya, a Biscayne Bay estate. (UNA, *Miami Herald*)

GEORGIA

34 Warm Springs (S). An Atlanta lawyer, Piromis Bell, wrote of his idea for creating a world capital at Warm Springs as a memorial to Franklin Roosevelt

in correspondence in with his friend Chase S. Osborn, the former governor of Michigan. (UM)

HAWAII

35 Honolulu County (C). Governor Ingram M. Stainback initiated a campaign to attract the UN to Hawaii. In contrast to other contenders who stressed proximity to world capitals, the Hawaiians stressed the advantages of being "far enough removed from any of the potentially explosive situations of the world." (UNA, HST, *Honolulu Advertiser*)

IDAHO

36 Farragut (S). Clark Collins of the Spirit Lake Chamber of Commerce and E. G. Younger of the Coeur d'Alene Chamber of Commerce recommended the U.S. Naval Training Station on Lake Pend Oreille in northern Idaho. (HST)

ILLINOIS

37 Champaign County (I). Champaign County appeared on a list of the UN's received invitations in December 1945. (UNA)

38 Chicago (C). See chapters 3, 5, and 6.

39 Morris (S). Suggested by Jo Ann Chally, a local resident. (HST)

40 Springfield (I). Following a suggestion in the *Illinois State Journal,* Mayor John W. Kapp invited the UN to Springfield because of its inspirational heritage as the home and burial place of Abraham Lincoln and its "liberty-loving people." (Associated Press)

INDIANA

While many world capital hopefuls stressed their superiority, Governor Ralph F. Gates promoted Indiana as "the typical state of the United States containing the center of population." Offering a variety of locations, primarily in state parks, he called attention to the state's transportation facilities and its residents' sacrifices for the war effort.

41 Dunes State Park (C). If the UN desired a site near a city, Indiana officials offered Dunes State Park, located on Lake Michigan only fourteen miles from downtown Chicago. *(Indianapolis Star)*

42 French Lick Springs (S). In addition to state parks, Governor Gates also suggested the possibility of this "internationally famous spa." (UNA, NYPL)

43 Indianapolis (S). A newspaper editorial suggested that Indiana's capital city should be promoted to the UN because its facilities could match anything

being offered by Chicago, Philadelphia, and San Francisco. *(Indianapolis News)*

44 Lincoln State Park (C). Indiana's governor described this park northeast of Evansville as a location with "both a practical and symbolic appeal" because of its scenic beauty and its association with Abraham Lincoln "and the tremendous blow which he struck for human freedom." (UNA)

45 Madison (S). Overlooking the Ohio River, Madison's bluffs should be offered to the UN as the "Riviera of America," a resident of Indianapolis, John Coulter, suggested to Governor Gates. Other sites mentioned as possibilities included Clifty Falls State Park and the government-owned Jefferson Proving Ground. *(Indianapolis Star)*

46 Michigan City/International Friendship Gardens (C). At the instigation of its public relations director, F. I. Lackens, International Friendship Gardens became featured in the Indiana governor's campaign, and nearby Michigan City considered itself a contender as a result. Governor Gates described the gardens as "100 acres of land dedicated to the various nations of the world" just one hour from Chicago by train or highway and noted the project's origins at the Century of Progress Exposition in Chicago in 1933. (UNA, *Michigan City News-Dispatch*)

47 Pokagon State Park (C). Governor Gates promoted this state park on the basis of its available acreage and the recreational opportunities of Lake James. He noted the land was "once ruled by the powerful Potawatomi Indian tribes." (UNA)

48 South Bend (I). The executive secretary of the South Bend Association of Commerce, E. L. Bach, invited the UN to consider his "typically American" city's location on cross-country transportation routes and its cultural, educational, and medical facilities. (UNA)

49 Straw Town (S). Clara J. Nuzum, the manager of the Auto License Branch in Elwood, Indiana, wrote to Governor Gates that Straw Town, northeast of Indianapolis, would be ideal for the UN: "It is almost the geographical center of the state; it lacked only one vote when the site of the state capital was chosen; transportation facilities are available; there is all the room wanted for great airports; White River at that spot offers opportunity for scenic effects, natural and artificial; it does not encroach upon existing cities in carrying out the plan of making the peace city an entirely new one." (ISL)

IOWA

50 Princeton (I). The Princeton Boosters Club offered a twenty-acre site overlooking the Mississippi River and sent its president to New York to personally lobby the UN. (Associated Press)

KANSAS

51 Lebanon (S). Forest R. Rees, president of the American Explorers organization, nominated Lebanon, the U.S. "geographical center." (HST)

52 Newton (S). A real estate salesman, Jacob J. Regler, suggested his town as a
location for an underground headquarters to protect the UN from atomic
bombs. (FDR)

53 Olathe (I). Blanche Worrell Nicholson of Clearfield, Utah, offered her 42-
acre site at Olathe, which she identified as the "exact geographical center"
of the United States. (HST)

54 Topeka (S). Suggested by U.S. senator Arthur Capper. (*Edwardsville [IL]
Intelligencer*)

LOUISIANA

55 New Orleans (C). The New Orleans Association of Commerce promoted its city as "the most centrally located city in this country with
reference to all the Americas," especially Latin America. The boosters
called attention to the city's French and Spanish heritage and plans
for other international projects such as a Pan-American exposition
or Olympic Games. Two possible sites were proposed: on the south
shore of Lake Ponchartrain within the city limits, or on the north
shore of the lake including parts of the parishes (counties) of St.
Tammany, Washington, and Tangipahoa. (UNA, UNO, *New Orleans
Times-Picayune*)

MAINE

56 Bar Harbor (I). Although Governor Horace Hildreth stated publicly that
Maine did not have the educational or housing facilities needed by the UN,
he nevertheless relayed an invitation from Bar Harbor stressing its qualities
as a summer resort and accessibility "via great circle route [from Europe]
only thirteen hours by air." (UNA, *Boston Post*)

57 Lucerne (S). Responding to reports that the British desired "a small town
in the East," the *Bangor Daily News* suggested Lucerne, a town nine miles
from Bangor with "a touch of the old world in the new with scenery beyond compare" and an airport enabling travel from London within twelve
hours. (UNA, *Bangor Daily News*)

58 Presque Isle (I). The chamber of commerce invited the UN to consider the
accessibility of the Presque Isle Army Air Field. (UNA)

59 Sanford (S). A private citizen suggested Sanford. "We do not have the
worldliness of our great cities to offer you," she wrote to the UN. "We have

only one air port, the best on the east coast. Yet God has given us the most wonderful gifts of nature." (UNA)

60   York (I). The selectmen promoted their town's advantages from an unspecified "historical, cultural, geographic, and practical standpoint." (UNA)

MARYLAND

61   Baltimore (I). Mayor Theodore R. Keldin extended an invitation, and the city council followed with a resolution promoting the city's proximity to the national capital and other major metropolitan areas, its location on Chesapeake Bay, and its "world renowned Johns Hopkins Hospital, Medical School, and University." (UNA)

62   Kent Island (S). A resident of Kent Island suggested a property south of his farm as more affordable than the Greenwich, Connecticut, site recommended by the UN site inspectors. (LOC)

MASSACHUSETTS

Efforts to bring the UN to Massachusetts originally focused on Boston, but in late December 1945 and early January 1946, the UN's interest in a Boston-area location triggered interest in numerous cities and towns.

63   Andover (I). With UN site inspectors en route to Boston, the Andover town selectmen notified Governor Maurice Tobin of their desire to offer a site. (*Boston Globe*)

64   Auburn (I). Frank H. Allan, chairman, Board of Selectmen, promised access to an airport, railroad center, four colleges, and golf courses. (UNA)

65   Belmont (I). A committee of civic leaders chaired by Harvard history professor Donald C. McKay identified 315 acres of Belmont that might be connected with additional property in Lexington, Waltham, and Concord to provide a sufficient site. (*Boston Globe*)

66   Barnstable (I). Unattributed invitation. (*Boston Globe*)

67   Beverly (C). See chapters 7 and 9.

68   Boston (C). See chapters 4 through 9.

69   Boylston (S). See Worcester.

70   Bridgewater (I). An offer from Bridgewater arrived during the UN's narrowing of site choices at the end of December 1945. (UNA)

71   Cambridge (I). The city manager of Cambridge, John B. Atkinson, commissioned plans for a headquarters facing the Charles River or on the shore of Fresh Pond. Atkinson argued that "Cambridge, the original laboratory in democracy, is, as a result of the war, one of the world's greatest scientific

research centers, an important matter for the UNO to consider." *(Boston Globe, Boston Herald)*

72 Canton (joined area campaign). See Quincy.

73 Cape Cod (I). The chamber of commerce and Barnstable County Commissioners offered a free site with the advantages of historical significance, good transportation, and an ideal climate. (UNA)

74 Concord/Lexington (S). See chapter 7.

75 Dedham (joined area campaign). See Quincy.

76 Greenfield (I). Unattributed invitation. *(Springfield Union)*

77 Hamilton (I). As the home of the late General Patton, Hamilton invited the UN's consideration. The town selectmen also endorsed nearby Beverly's campaign. *(Quincy Patriot-Ledger)*

78 Hingham (I). This invitation would have placed the UN on the peninsula known as "World's End," a site with a fine view of Boston, but an inauspicious name for a peace-keeping organization in the atomic age. *(Boston Globe)*

79 Holden (S). See Sterling.

80 Lenox (I). J. Joseph McCabe, chairman of the Board of Selectmen, described Lenox as unique and modern as well as rooted in the tradition of New England towns. (UNA)

81 Malden (joined area campaign). See Medford.

82 Manchester (I). Unattributed invitation. *(Boston Globe)*

83 Martha's Vineyard (I). Martha's Vineyard residents promised a suitable environment for "harmonious living and exchange of opinion." *(NYT)*

84 Medford/Middlesex Fells (C). In the Middlesex Fells woodlands north of Boston, a site including parts of Medford and Stoneham first drew attention in October 1945 when mentioned by Governor Tobin as a possible location for the World Court. As interest broadened to creating a UN headquarters in or near Boston, Congressman Angier Goodwin again suggested a site in the Middlesex Fells, and local officials in Medford organized a campaign. By January 1946, the Medford-centered campaign grew to involve other nearby towns north of Boston—Malden, Melrose, Reading, Stoneham, Wakefield, Winchester, and Woburn. *(Medford Daily Evening Mercury)*

85 Melrose (joined area campaign). See Medford.

86 Milton (joined area campaign). See Quincy.

87 Needham (joined area campaign). See Quincy.

88 Northampton (S). Attorney Luke F. Ryan suggested "the beautiful and un-spoiled small city" of Northampton. Placing the UN in a large city "could be only tragic for world government," he wrote. (UNA)

89 Norwood (joined area campaign). See Quincy.

90 Orange (I). Edward F. Haley, chairman of the Board of Selectmen, pointed out that Orange had "the finest civilian airport in the east with three runways ... able to withstand the largest planes." He suggested property between the airport and the Quabbin Reservoir. In addition to transportation facilities and the scenic White Mountains, Orange and surrounding communities offered "populations that are congenial, educated, and free of racial prejudice and discrimination." (UNA)

91 Pittsfield (I). Unattributed invitation. *(Springfield Union)*

92 Plymouth (I). County commissioners described Plymouth as the site where "a great nation had its beginning." (UNA)

93 Princeton (S). See Sterling.

94 Quincy/Blue Hills (C). After the UN selected the Boston area for consideration in December 1945, telephone calls from interested readers prompted the *Quincy Patriot-Ledger* to publish a front-page editorial promoting the Blue Hills state reservation lands as ideal because of their proximity to Boston, scenic beauty, and large mansions in the town of Milton. Based in Quincy, the campaign expanded into a coordinated effort with other nearby towns—Canton, Needham, Dedham, Norwood, Randolph, Milton, and Braintree. *(Quincy Patriot-Ledger)*

95 Randolph (joined area campaign). See Quincy.

96 Reading (joined area campaign). See Medford.

97 Rockland (I). The chairman of the Rockland Chamber of Commerce, Joseph Lelyveld, invited the UN to this ideal "conservative New England town." (UNA)

98 Shrewsbury (S). See Worcester.

99 South Weymouth (I). The chairman of selectmen, Harry Christensen, pointed out the suitability of the South Weymouth naval air base as a UN "city self-sufficient in itself." *(Quincy Patriot-Ledger)*

100 Springfield (I). Congressman Charles R. Clason relayed a constituent's suggestion that the UN consider placing its headquarters on the site of the Springfield Armory. Mayor J. Alvin Anderson Jr. promoted the advantages of Springfield's transportation facilities, cultural institutions, nearby colleges and universities, and skilled labor supply. (UNA)

101 Sterling (I). As UN site inspectors toured areas near Boston, a group of civic leaders in Sterling sought to expand the itinerary to include Mount Wachusett, a site embracing part of Sterling as well as Princeton, Holden, and Westminster. *(Worcester Evening Gazette)*

102 Stoneham (joined area campaign). See Medford.

103 Taunton (I). Unattributed invitation. *(Boston Globe)*

104 Wakefield (joined area campaign). See Medford.

105 Westminster (S). See Sterling.

106 West Newbury (I). Unattributed invitation. *(Boston Globe)*

107 Winchester (joined area campaign). See Medford.

108 Woburn (joined area campaign). See Medford.

109. Worcester (I). Chamber of commerce president Chandler Bullock, backed by the city council, described his city to the UN as "located almost exactly at population center [of the] New England states." Along with historical, educational, and cultural organizations, the UN would find good transportation, hotels, climate, and scenery. As it became clear that the UN preferred a location outside a city, officials suggested a site including the nearby town of Boylston, together with part of Shrewsbury. (UNA, *Worcester Evening Gazette)*

MICHIGAN

110 Battle Creek-Kalamazoo (S). A site between these two communities was suggested by Mary Frederiksen, a resident of Los Angeles, Calif. (HST)

111 Detroit (C). See chapter 1.

112 Muskegon (S). Dr. R. A. Vanderlinde of Los Angeles suggested a site "near the town of Muskegon, which is my birthplace" as well as Elysian Park in Los Angeles. (CSA)

113 Sault Ste. Marie (C). See chapter 3.

114 Three Rivers (S). Local resident Chet Shafer suggested his town because of its distinction as "the International Headquarters of the Guild of Former Pipe Organ Pumpers." (HST)

MINNESOTA

Three proposals from Minnesota responded to concerns at the UN about finding a U.S. location free of racial discrimination.

115 Brainerd (I). Clyde R. Gorham, president of the Brainerd Civic Association, called attention to the "capitol of Paul Bunyan's playground" with beautiful scenery and pleasant climate. The location was "removed from large centers

of population yet only three hours by air from Chicago," and the Brainerd boosters promised, "Race problem unheard of here." (UNA)

116 Duluth (I). Responding to news reports that the UN might desire a cool climate, the Duluth Chamber of Commerce extended an invitation. Like Brainerd, Duluth pointed out its location three hours by air from Chicago and declared, "Racial discrimination unknown." (UNA)

117 Minneapolis (I). Mayor Hubert H. Humphrey and the Minnesota United Nations Committee, a citizens group promoting support for the UN, described Minneapolis as an ideal location halfway between the Atlantic and the Pacific. They stressed transportation facilities and their city's internationalism and multicultural population. "Here is a city without racial intolerance," they boasted, "a community where both negro and white, along with Protestant, Jew and Catholic work together and live in the spirit of cooperation." (UNA)

MISSOURI

118 Jefferson City (S). Missouri governor Phil M. Donnelly urged consideration of Jefferson City in a telephone call to the office of UN delegate Stoyan Gavrilovic in London. (UNA)

119 Kansas City/Jackson County (S). The president of the University of Kansas City, Clarence R. Decker, proposed bringing the UN to Kansas City during a ceremony awarding an honorary degree to native son Harry S. Truman on June 28, 1945. He proposed the university campus or Swope Park as locations, and later in the year the Jackson County Plan Commission identified eight other potential sites. (HST, *Kansas City Star*)

120 Lake of the Ozarks (S). Suggested by C. H. Spink of Fort Worth. (HST)

121 St. Louis/Weldon Spring (C). See chapters 4 and 5.
Also see Arkansas, Site 4.

MONTANA

122 Glacier National Park (S). The junior chamber of commerce of Cut Bank, Montana, advocated Glacier National Park as a scenic, inspirational place "far removed from the foggy and soggy locales of the eastern seaboard or the congested industrial stress of the western coastal country." The Jaycees also called attention to the presence of the Blackfeet Indians and their service in two world wars. (*Congressional Record*)

NEBRASKA

123 Lincoln (I). Mayor Lloyd J. Mart and other city officials described Lincoln's residents as "cosmopolitan and tolerant" and the community as

"free from slums, racial dissention, and crime." Lincoln's location "slightly east of the Geographical Center of the United States" would offer equal accessibility from all directions, and the city's facilities included colleges and universities, business and government buildings, transportation services, a municipal park, and "a shopping center noted throughout the country." (UNA)

NEW HAMPSHIRE

124   Conway (I). World Fellowship Inc., a peace and social justice organization, encouraged the UN to choose its 274-acre site near Conway. (UNA)

NEW JERSEY

When the UN announced plans to consider sites in the vicinity of New York City, New Jersey cities and towns responded with a flood of invitations.

125   Asbury Park (I). Mayor George A. Smock II promoted Asbury Park as a wholesome community free of racial discrimination, with "a cosmopolitan understanding of the world's people, their customs, and habits based on 75 years of entertaining visitors from all sections of the globe in our resort city." (UNA)

126   Atlantic City (C). See chapters 5 and 7.

127   Atlantic Highlands (S). A private citizen, H. P. Brainard, recommended the Cliff Lodge scenic drive in Atlantic Highlands. (UNA)

128   Brigantine Island (I). Brigantine mayor Paul Burgess promised that the diplomats could occupy up to two square miles of undeveloped land without disturbing the island's five hundred residents. (UNA, *PR*)

129   Cape May (I). Grant Scott, Cape May commissioner of public safety, promoted "this historic seashore community" for its available land, scenic beauty, and reputation as a resort retreat for presidents and other government officials. (UNA)

130   Central Region (S). A consulting engineer, H. E. Kuntz, suggested an 11,000-acre site southeast of Princeton that he had surveyed in 1911 for a proposed "great capitol of aviation" and University of the Air. (NJSA)

131   Essex County (S). A local resident, Dr. Cornell Grossman, suggested a county park near Millburn. (UNA)

132   Flemington (S). Suggested by John H. Elder, a resident of the rural area north of Flemington. (UNA)

133   Fort Lee (I). The municipal clerk of Fort Lee, W. S. Corker, relayed his town's invitation. (UNA)

134 Hackensack (I). The city council passed a resolution inviting the UN to consider Hackensack. (UNA)

135 Hawthorne (S). W. E. Fairhurst, a resident of Hawthorne, created a sketch to show how a UN headquarters at this location "would be a beacon light to approaching ships at sea . . . as well as a guide to all planes, from all the world." (UNA)

136 Highlands (S). Suggested by Anna V. Drew, a local resident. (UNA)

137 Lakewood (I). The Ocean County Board of Freeholders offered UN property in Lakewood's Ocean County Park, formerly part of an estate owned by the late John D. Rockefeller. (HST, *Atlantic City Press*)

138 Monmouth County (S). Suggested by state senator Haydn Proctor.

139 Morristown (C). See chapter 7.

140 Northvale (S). Suggested by Raymond A. Hellstern of New York City.

141 Palisades State Park (S). Leo F. Caproni, an architect from New Haven, Conn., suggested this park as an alternative to controversial sites in Connecticut and New York. (UR)

142 Princeton (S). The president of Princeton University, Harold Dodds, suggested that Princeton seemed to match the British delegation's desire to locate the UN in a small town with accessibility to a large city. The UN's site inspection group visited two Princeton-area properties, one about six miles away in Hopewell Valley and another in the vicinity of Rocky Hill and Kingston, about four miles from the university. (UNA, *Princeton Packet*)

143 Ridgewood Borough (S). A New York real estate agent, E. Irving Huntington, offered to arrange an inspection of the Clarence Lewis estate in Ridgewood. (UNA)

144 Ventnor (S). H. Lee, a resident of New York City, called attention to the assets of seaside Ventnor: "fresh air, board walk, trains service, no factories, no smoke, plenty of help. Ocean, entertainments, piers, roller chairs, and other things too numerous to mention here." (UR)

145 West Orange (I). Mayor Bernard H. Dagnan invited consideration of West Orange because of its available sites and location sixteen miles from New York City. (UNA)

NEW YORK

Numerous New York cities and towns responded to the diplomats' interest in finding a suburban site in the East, and others came forward to offer alternatives when the UN's initial site selection in Connecticut met with local protests.

146 Bear Mountain/Berne (S). Suggested by Irma Fueslein of East Ninety-First Street in New York City. (UR)

147 Brookhaven, Long Island (I). Invitation issued by elected officials. *(New York Sun)*

148 Center Island, Long Island (S). Paul J. Bungart, an architect from Rockville Centre, N.Y., suggested this bird sanctuary on Long Island Sound. (UR)

149 Clayton (S). Suggested by Gus Charlebois, a local resident. (UNA)

150 Cooperstown (S). Suggested by Emil W. Spumy, a resident of Springfield Center, N.Y. (UR)

151 Croton-on-Hudson (I). Despite widespread resistance to the UN's plans for a headquarters in Westchester County, residents of Croton-on-Hudson voted to welcome the UN by a margin of 84–22 in a community meeting in August 1946. *(NYT)*

152 Glens Falls (I). Invitation submitted by Mayor John Bazinet. (UNA)

153 Governors Island (S). Ralph Albert Senesi of Youngstown, Ohio, suggested Governors Island as the place "where the U.S. government should spend $10 million to improve the grounds and to build there a permanent Temple of Peace to be known as the Franklin D. Roosevelt Memorial Hall." (UR)

154 Harmon-on-Hudson (S). E. E. Walker, the president of Wizard Granite Renovator in New York City, suggested this alternative to controversial sites in Westchester County. (UR)

155 Huntington Township, Long Island (I). A chamber of commerce committee invited consideration of Huntington Township's proximity to New York airports, a seaplane base, and parkways for driving to New York City. The boosters noted the area homes of "internationally known citizens" as well as the waterfront resorts and recreational opportunities of Long Island Sound. (UNA)

156 Hyde Park (C). See chapter 7.

157 Irvington-on-Hudson (S). A real estate agent, John P. Streb of Dobbs Ferry, N.Y., offered a 5.5-acre property with a sixteen-bedroom residence. (UNA)

158 Kingston (I). The Kingston Chamber of Commerce prepared an illustrated prospectus to demonstrate that a world capital in Kingston, facing the Hudson River, would fulfill the diplomats' desires for a nonurban location yet still allow them easy access to New York City. (LOC, *NYT*)

159 Lake Placid (I). This site of the 1932 Winter Olympic Games was suggested by local government officials who pointed out its hotels, arena, transportation services, and location relative to Boston and New York City. (UNA)

160 Lake Seneca (S). A federal employee in Washington, Clarkson J. Beall, suggested the Sampson Naval Training Station on Lake Seneca. "It seems a shame to dispossess other whole communities of people in Westchester County" with such an open site also available, he wrote. (UR)

161 Mohansic State Park (I). As an alternative to a site identified by the United Nations in Yorktown, where he lived, Daniel Rochford proposed this unpopulated park space. (UR)

162 Montauk Point, Long Island (S). Foster Bailey, a New York City resident, suggested "this beautiful garden spot." (UNA)

163 Monticello (I). Mayor Luis de Hoyos invited the UN to consider Monticello's "uniquely appropriate" climate and scenery. (*Associated Press*)

164 New York (C). See chapters 6 through 9.

165 Niagara Falls/Navy Island (C). Inspired by a suggestion from former congressman Robert H. Gittins, the *Niagara Falls Gazette* launched a campaign to create a world capital on an island between the United States and Canada. Business leaders and public officials from Niagara Falls, Ontario, joined their counterparts in New York in an extensive effort that included traveling to London to appeal to the UN. Originally aiming to place the UN on Canada-owned Navy Island, they changed their proposal to nearby Grand Island, in U.S. territory, after the UN opted for a United States location. (UNA, *Niagara Falls Gazette*)

166 Ogdensburg (I). Mayor-elect Homer M. Wallace promoted his city's U.S.-Canadian border location on the St. Lawrence River because of its "unlimited space for construction of suitable new structures," its accessibility by rail and sea, and its proximity to Ottawa, Boston, New York, and Washington. (UNA)

167 Plattsburgh (I). Edward B. Doherty, president of the Plattsburgh Chamber of Commerce, offered to submit a proposal for Plattsburgh. (UNA)

168 Port Jervis (S). Signing himself as "G.I. Joe," a resident of Ossining, N.Y., suggested Port Jervis. (UR)

169 Potsdam (I). Pointing out Potsdam's reputation as the "Switzerland of America," Harry Bullard, president of the Potsdam Chamber of Commerce, promised that Potsdam "has everything to offer," including colleges, hotels, churches, a modern hospital, and the Adirondack Mountains, all "easily accessible to every North American metropolis." (UNA)

170 Riverdale, the Bronx (C). See chapter 8.

171 Saratoga Springs (C). The chamber of commerce promoted Saratoga as the "Birthplace of Freedom" for its role in the American Revolution as well

as "the world's largest spa." The booster committee called attention to Saratoga's transportation facilities, healthful climate, and the availability of federally owned land. (UNA, UR)

172 Skaneateles (I). The president of the chamber of commerce, Charles T. Major, invited consideration of a site on Skaneateles Lake, pointing to its reputation as the "Luzerne of America." Selection of this small, peaceful community would put a stop to the competition among large cities, he argued. (UNA)

173 Southampton, Long Island (I). Invitation issued by Mayor Alex Cameron. (UNA)

174 Staten Island (I). The Staten Island Chamber of Commerce invited the UN to consider the borough, and private citizens also suggested Staten Island in letters to the UN, to the governors of New Jersey and New York, and to John D. Rockefeller Jr. (UNA, UR, NJSA, RAC)

175 Sterling Park (S). Seeking to steer the UN away from their own towns, an alliance of Westchester County homeowners produced an elaborate brochure promoting Sterling Park, in Orange County, as a superior location. (HST)

176 Syracuse (S). After reading an editorial published in the Syracuse *Post-Standard*, private citizen John Elton Whiteside wrote to the UN to call attention to the advantages of the Syracuse Army Air Base and the city's location between the capitals of the United States and Canada. He portrayed distance from a major metropolitan area as an advantage. (UNA)

177 Ticonderoga (S). State assemblyman A. Judson Moorhouse recommended Ticonderoga for its Revolutionary-era significance, congenial climate, and scenic beauty. (UNA)

178 Watertown (I). The president of the chamber of commerce, H. J. French, invited attention to his town because of its modern airport, railroad, improved streets, utilities, and available sites, including property held by the U.S. government. (UNA)

179 Westchester County (I). See chapters 7, 8, and 9.

180 Westhampton Beach, Long Island (I). Mayor Ernest H. Bishop described his town as an "ideal location" because of its commuting distance to New York, resort facilities, and the runways of the Suffolk County Army Air Base. (UNA)

181 Yorktown Heights (I). Lydia Locke offered her estate in Yorktown Heights, consisting of 250 acres, two lakes, two large houses (twenty-three and seventeen rooms), and other structures. (UR)

NORTH CAROLINA

182 Asheville (S). Walter B. Smith of St. Petersburg, Florida, suggested Asheville as "the ideal location." (HST)

183 Bald Head Island (S). U.S. senator Josiah Bailey suggested this island near Southport, N.C., at the mouth of the Cape Fear River. The island offered seventeen thousand undeveloped acres, enough "to give all the foundation for whatever the United Nations could desire." *(NYT)*

184 Pinehurst (I). A delegation of local residents met with Governor Joseph Broughton to promote Pinehurst as a UN location. (UNA)

NORTH DAKOTA

185 Border with Manitoba (S). Edwin E. Prong, describing himself as "an American youth" and "world citizen" living in Detroit, suggested the North Dakota border as a location where an international territory could be created by the United States and Canada. (UNA)

186 International Peace Garden (S). This location on the U.S.-Canadian border was suggested by Governor Fred Aandahl at the National Governors Conference in July 1945. U.S. senator Milton R. Young subsequently argued that the gardens, dedicated in 1932, should be seen as a precedent for the UN and therefore an "ideal setting for the organization upon which all humanity builds its hopes." (HST)

OHIO

187 Cincinnati (C). See chapters 5 and 6.

188 Cleveland (S). Responding to controversy over the UN's selected sites near New York, an editorial in the *Cleveland News* stated that Cleveland would be honored to have the UN. (UNA)

189 Greenville (I). Chamber of commerce officials called attention to peace established by the 1795 Treaty of Greenville between the United States government and Ohio Indian tribes. (UNA)

OKLAHOMA

190 Claremore (C). See chapter 4.

191 Stillwater (S). An editorial in the *Stillwater Daily News Press* argued that the UN "would be away from complexities of unreal things as found in coastal areas." (*Stillwater Daily News Press*)

192 Tuskahoma (C). See chapter 4.

Also see Arkansas, Site 4.

PENNSYLVANIA

193 Bethlehem (I). Mayor Robert A. Pfeiffle wrote to Pennsylvania governor Edward Martin, "We wonder if there is any more appropriate site name than Bethlehem for the home of an organization dedicated to putting into practice the teachings of the Prince of Peace." (UR, PSA)

194 Delaware and Chester Counties (C). Robert Gray Taylor, a resident of Media, Pa., in October 1945 launched an extensive personal campaign to interest the United Nations in the general area of Media and Paoli, eventually identifying two potential sites: 8,200 acres between the towns of Newtown Square, Wawa, Media, and Edgmont (priced at $6.3 million) and an additional 2,550 acres adjacent to Newtown Square including parts of Ithan, Bryn Mawr, Foxcroft, Springfield Township, and Swarthmore (price $5.1 million). Taylor also formed the Delaware Valley Association for United Nations Headquarters and extended his efforts to northeastern Pennsylvania communities. (PSA, UNA)

195 Easton (C). Seeking to capitalize on its proximity to New York, Easton promoted a site directly north of the city on the basis of its scenic environment near the Pocono Mountains, its railroads and highways, and the presence of eight colleges within twenty miles. The movement for Easton originated with local business leader Hugh Moore, chairman of the board of the Dixie Cup Company and an activist in international peace organizations. (PSA, UNA)

196 Falls Township/Bucks County (I). Charles Henry Moon, an advisory board member of the Pennsbury Memorial historic site, suggested the site of William Penn's reconstructed home on the Delaware River. (PSA)

197 Gettysburg (I). Offering historical inspiration as "America's greatest historic shrine" and the symbolism of "Lincoln's inspiring concept of peace and freedom for all mankind," the chamber of commerce also noted Gettysburg's location "well removed though accessible without difficulty from great centers of population." (UNA)

198 Lancaster (I). Mayor Dale E. Cary stressed Lancaster's eastern U.S. location, transportation services, and heritage. "Lancaster was founded in the eighteenth century by English immigrants and is rich in historical heritage and scenic beauty," he wrote. "Most of our people are descendants of original settlers making for a conservative and truly patriotic atmosphere." (UNA)

199 Philadelphia (C). See chapters 1, 2, 5, 6, and 8.

200 Phillipsburg (I). A local booster committee offered a site north of Phillipsburg in and around Forks Township. (PSA)

201 Pike County (I). The county commissioners invited inspection of several sites along the Delaware River between Matamoras and Bushkill or "any site selected within the limits of the county." The commissioners pointed out that their county fulfilled all of the UN's criteria, including locations within eighty miles of New York. (NJSA)

202 Poconos Region/Monroe County (S). Roy M. Houser, president of the Monroe County Chamber of Commerce in Stroudsburg, urged consideration of this "internationally famous resort area." The cities of Scranton, Wilkes-Barre, and Easton joined with Monroe County to promote the Tobyhanna Military Reservation as a site because "it would be a colossal blunder if the World Peace Shrine were to be located within the congested areas of any large city, where it would be just another suburb." (UNA, PSA)

203 Punxsutawney (I). M. R. Tibbey, secretary of the Punxsutawney Chamber of Commerce, invited the UN on the basis of the annual February ritual of watching to see if a groundhog would see its shadow. (HST)

204 Valley Forge (S). John Robbins Hart, rector of Washington Memorial Chapel and president of the Valley Forge Historical Society, suggested this historic site of the American Revolution. "Bostonians naturally prefer Boston, New Yorkers New York, etc., but all people have a special devotion to Valley Forge and would come to a harmonious agreement in its selection," he wrote. (UNA)

205 Williamsport (I). Two sites in Lycoming County near Williamsport were offered as part of a regional effort by the Delaware Valley Association for United Nations Headquarters. (See Delaware and Chester Counties.)

PHILIPPINES

206 Baguio (S). *The Philippines Mail,* published in Salinas, Calif., reprinted an editorial from the Philippines advocating this city. (UNA)

RHODE ISLAND

207 Bristol (I). The Town Council invited the UN to use "any facilities at the command of the town." *(Providence Journal)*

208 Cranston (S). See Providence.

209 Foster (S). See Providence.

210 Glocester (S). See Providence.

211 Johnston (I). The town council invited consideration of Neutaconkanut Hill, which also figured in a proposal by a coalition of civic leaders in Providence. *(Providence Journal)*

212 Newport (C). See chapter 4.

213 Portsmouth (I). Included in offer from Bristol.

214 Providence (I). Political and business leaders in Providence invited the UN site inspectors to consider land on Neutaconkanut Hill outside the city, incorporating eighty-five square miles of land in the towns of Johnston, Cranston, Scituate, Foster, and Glocester. *(Providence Journal)*

215 Scituate (S). See Providence.

216 Warwick (S). Local residents advocated sites in the Spring Green section or on the Warwick Neck peninsula. *(Providence Journal)*

217 Westerly (I). The town council and chamber of commerce emphasized the town's transportation connections to New York and Boston, its solid utility infrastructure, and its reputation as "a famous health resort." *(Providence Journal)*

SOUTH CAROLINA

218 Myrtle Beach (S). The Myrtle Beach American Legion Post suggested this as an accessible point midway between New York City and Miami. The veterans also listed Myrtle Beach's amenities as beautiful gardens, the army air field and bombing range, and "numerous antebellum plantations owned by distinguished men such as Bernard Baruch, George Vanderbilt, and Nicholas Roosevelt." (UNA)

SOUTH DAKOTA

219 Black Hills Region (C). See chapters 1, 2, 3, and 5.

TENNESSEE

220 Carthage (I). Congressman Albert Gore, Tennessee governor Jim McCord, Nashville mayor Thomas L. Nummings, and Carthage mayor Guy A. Drake invited the UN to consider Carthage as a tribute to the hometown of former secretary of state Cordell Hull. The officials described Carthage as "within three or four hours by plane to every part of the United States together with ideal climatic conditions and every other advantage which would make a pleasant location for the capital of the world." (UNA)

221 Great Smoky Mountains (I). A Great Smoky Mountain UNO Invitation Committee, headed by Tennessee attorney Hansel Proffitt, promoted the central location and accessibility of the region, along with its climate and recreational facilities. The committee pointed out that underground shelters from nuclear bombs could be constructed in the mountains. Knowing of the UN's growing concern about racial tensions in the South, the committee described the Great Smokies region as "having no racial problems

or distinctions such as can be found in the confusion of sociological conditions in Northern, Eastern, and Southern areas." (UNA)

TEXAS

222   Corpus Christi (I). Promoters described Corpus Christi as centrally located "in almost the exact geographical center of the world" and noted that the city's name "dedicated to the Prince of Peace and Lord of Lords" was "symbolic of the great purpose, 'World Peace,' to which the United Nations Organization is dedicated." Boosters emphasized the town's international character because of its Spanish-speaking population and proximity to Mexico, and suggested that Jewish people might establish a homeland in South Texas, where "there is enough land and wealth and happiness for each, and everyone is welcome to find here a new and happier home." (HST, UNA)

223   Eastland (I). The chamber of commerce wrote, "Ample space is available located in West Texas in an area of the United States which makes for clear calm thinking and away from an atmosphere of discord and animosity." (HST)

224   Galveston (I). The junior chamber of commerce invited interest in the island's "year-round climate, excellent facilities of fishing, hunting, swimming and other recreations which have been attracting thousands of visitors here annually in addition to hundreds of conventions." Galveston would be accessible by air and by sea, the boosters noted. (UNA)

225   Mason County (S). George L. Denman, a private citizen, sent Eleanor Roosevelt an article from the *Spokesman-Review* of Spokane, Washington, that described Mason County in central Texas as having 968 square miles of ample room for construction of "the world's greatest capital." (UNA)

226   San Antonio (I). Mayor Gus B. Mauermann and chamber of commerce president C. W. Miller invited the UN's consideration. (UNA)

UTAH

227   Salt Lake City (I). Mayor Earl J. Glade invited consideration of his city for its "comparative isolation which experience has shown is so much desired by governmental administrative bodies." Nevertheless, "it is easily accessible by air or surface transportation." He suggested a location at the base of Ensign Peak one mile from the city's business district. (UNA)

VERMONT

228   Burlington (I). Donald L. Anderson, executive director of the chamber of commerce, promoted Burlington's centrality and its nonurban character.

"A study of the great circles and azimuths from Eastern United States to all points on the earth's surfaces reveals that Burlington, Vermont, is the city in the United States which is nearest to many of the capitals and centers of the world," Anderson wrote. Burlington boosters also promoted their area's scenic reputation as the "Switzerland of America." (UNA)

229   Fort Ethan Allen/Essex (I). After an offer of interim facilities by Vermont governor Mortimer R. Proctor, UN staff members investigated the feasibility of Fort Ethan Allen.

VIRGINIA

Governor Colgate W. Darden Jr. and the president of the Virginia Chamber of Commerce, Wilfred A. Roper, promoted their state's history and accessibility.

230   Alexandria (I). Twenty-one acres of "beautiful unimproved land overlooking the Potomac River" in the Seminary Hill section of Alexandria were offered by Sarah Daingerfield Stirling. (HST)

231   Charlottesville (C). Residents of Charlottesville, including officers of the chamber of commerce, formed a Peace Headquarters Location Committee to call attention to the "peaceful countryside" of Virginia and their association with Thomas Jefferson and Monticello. They also promoted Charlottesville's proximity to other cities, its plans for an airport, its climate, and its cultural and educational institutions. (UNA, *Charlottesville Daily Progress*)

232   Fredericksburg (I). Promoting Fredericksburg as "America's most historic city located fifty miles from the capitol of the United States," chamber of commerce president Edward H. Cann called attention to the boyhood home of George Washington as well as the local climate, recreational opportunities, and proximity to Washington-based embassies. Fredericksburg would be "most suitable for a worldwide aviation terminal," he wrote. (UNA)

233   Northern Neck (S). Walter Johnson, a resident of Heathsville, Va., and one-time Republican candidate for Congress, suggested this region for its association with George Washington and because it was "one of the finest spots in all the world to live." (UNA, *Richmond Times-Dispatch*)

234   Portsmouth (I). Roy J. Dunn, managing director of the chamber of commerce, promoted Portsmouth as "the South's City of the Future." He called attention to the port of Hampton Roads' significance in the war effort, its business potential in times of peace, and the availability of undeveloped land and transportation services. (UNA)

235   Richmond (I). The president of the chamber of commerce, Lewis G. Chewning, invited consideration of his city as a cultural center with

proximity to Washington and a supply of housing, hotels, and offices. "Richmond is rich in New World history and tradition," he wrote. "Virginians nurtured and helped develop the ideals of our Republic. This historical background is a notable community asset, providing an atmosphere appreciated by representatives of older nations." (UNA)

236 Uno (S). A short news article by the Associated Press noted that the tiny town of Uno, population thirty, would be a "typographically perfect" choice for the United Nations Organization but "hasn't much to offer beyond its name." *(Norfolk Virginian-Pilot)*

237 Virginia Beach (I). The directing manager of the chamber of commerce invited consideration of this "ideal location from the standpoint of available space, climate, transportation, recreation, and all the conveniences which tend to make life attractive and pleasant." (UNA)

238 Williamsburg/Newport News (C). Encouraged by the publisher of the *Newport News Times-Herald* and Newport News City Council, a Virginia Peninsula Committee Sponsoring Williamsburg for United Nations Home organized a campaign to advocate a site at Camp Peary, a navy training camp on the York River. The campaign called attention to the historic resonance of nearby Colonial Williamsburg as well as to Camp Peary's modern facilities and room for future growth. (UNA, *Virginia Gazette*)

WASHINGTON

239 Grand Coulee (S). Local resident Edwin L. Rice wrote to President Truman to suggest the Grand Coulee Dam; he enclosed an American Airlines advertisement depicting Grand Coulee as the "Heart of the World." (HST)

240 Seattle (S). Interest in Seattle was reported without further elaboration by the *Philadelphia Record* in March 1945, but by the end of the year the Seattle Chamber of Commerce announced support for San Francisco. *(Philadelphia Record, San Francisco Examiner)*

WEST VIRGINIA

241 Berkeley Springs (S). U.S. senator Harley M. Kilgore suggested this site with ample land and no need to displace population. (HST)

242 Harper's Ferry (S). Quoting Thomas Jefferson, "who said the scene at Harper's Ferry is worth crossing the ocean to see," James M. Thomson of Gaylord, W. Va., pointed out the site's accessibility from Washington and Baltimore and judged the climate more suitable than the UN's favored sites in the Northeast. (HST)

243 White Sulphur Springs (S). Congressman E. H. Hedrick advocated White Sulphur Springs. Referring to the UN's decision to reject sites in the South,

Hedrick stated, "Though White Sulphur Springs is below the Mason Dixon line there is no discrimination." The site offered attractive scenery, housing, an airport, and railroad facilities, he pointed out. (HST, *Congressional Record*)

WISCONSIN

244 Apostle Islands (S). An editorial in the *Washburn (Wisc.) Times* suggested that these islands in Lake Superior offered an ideal location, climate, and scenery, and "with a history going back to the very dawn of time, the Apostle Islands offer an appropriate location for an organization that seeks to bring the dawn of a new era in the unhappy annals of mankind." *(Congressional Record)*

245 Beloit (I). The Beloit Chamber of Commerce promoted its location one hundred miles from Chicago; transportation connections; schools; churches; Beloit College; and scenery. (UNA, *Beloit Daily News*)

246 Kenosha (I). City Manager James G. Wallace proposed a site of 1,503 acres along the Lake Michigan shore south of Kenosha, "a beautiful city, a healthful city, an orderly city; a pleasant city in which to love, a delightful city in which to spend a summer vacation." The invitation stressed Kenosha's proximity to Chicago and Milwaukee and the availability of transportation and necessary utilities. (UNA)

247 Milwaukee (I). Mayor John L. Bohn promoted his city's advantages: "central world location, excellent railroad and air transportation facilities, great industries, fine hotels, excellent harbor, fine education institutions, ideal climatic conditions, excellent sites available, wholesome environment and a loyal and patriotic citizenry." (UNA)

248 South Milwaukee (S). A local resident, Frank S. Markarian, suggested South Milwaukee's Grant Park as an ideal site "about in the middle of North America—in the heart of the Middle West—wherein flourishes the cradle of American culture." (UNA)

NOTES

INTRODUCTION

1 Ezra Stoller, *The United Nations* (New York: Princeton Architectural Press, 1999), vii; *NYT*, Oct. 16, 21, and 25, 1949; UN Photographs 36603, 71039, and 71041, UN Department of Information Photo Library (http://www.unmulti-media.org/photo).

2 As Akira Iriye noted in *Global Community: The Role of International Organization in the Making of the Contemporary World* (Berkeley: University of California Press, 2002), scholarship on globalization has focused predominantly on the role of nation-states, leaving room for further exploration of the role of individuals and organizations. Civic boosterism has received greater attention for the nineteenth and early twentieth centuries in works such as Carl Abbott, *Boosters and Businessmen: Popular Economic Thought and Urban Growth in the Antebellum Middle West* (Westport, Conn.: Greenwood, 1981); William Cronon, *Nature's Metropolis* (Princeton, N.J.: Princeton University Press, 1991), 31–41; and David M. Wrobel, *Promised Lands: Promotion, Memory, and the Creation of the American West* (Lawrence: University Press of Kansas, 2002). Additional scholarship focuses on the phenomenon of place-marketing and postindustrial rebranding in the late twentieth and early twenty-first centuries, for example, William J. V. Neill, Diana S. Fitzsimons, and Brendan Murtagh, *Reimagining the Pariah City: Urban Development in Belfast and Detroit* (Brookfield, Vt.: Ashgate, 1995) and Miriam Greenberg, *Branding New York: How a City in Crisis Was Sold to the World* (New York: Routledge, 2005).

   Previous accounts of the UN headquarters site selection have been limited to brief narratives in books such as Evan Luard, *A History of the United Nations*. Vol. 1, *The Years of Western Domination, 1945–55* (New York: St. Martin's, 1982), 79–85, and in *Yearbook of the United Nations, 1946–47* (Lake Success, N.Y.: UN Department of Public Information, 1947), 41–42, 114–15, and 272–76. The topic is absent from other works about the early history of the UN: Townsend Hoopes and Douglas Brinkley, *FDR and the Creation of the U.N.* (New Haven, Conn.: Yale University Press, 1997); Stanley Meisler, *United Nations: The First Fifty Years* (New York: Atlantic Monthly Press, 1995); Gary B. Ostrower, *The United Nations and the United States* (New York: Twayne, 1998); and Stephen C. Schlesinger, *Act of Creation: The Founding of the United*

Nations (Boulder, Colo.: Westview, 2003). Accounts of the campaign to bring the UN to New York, with limited attention to other competitors, appear in Samuel Zipp, *Manhattan Projects: The Rise and Fall of Urban Renewal in Cold War New York* (New York: Oxford University Press, 2010), 33–38; Eugenie L. Birch, "New York City: Super Capital—Not by Government Alone," in David Gordon, ed., *Planning Twentieth-Century Capital Cities* (New York: Routledge, 2006); and in biographies such as Cary Reich, *The Life of Nelson A. Rockefeller: Worlds to Conquer, 1908–1958* (New York: Doubleday, 1996), 383–85, and Robert A. Caro, *The Power Broker: Robert Moses and the Fall of New York* (New York: Random House, 1974), 771–75.

3 Titus Livy, *The Early History of Rome*, Book I, Chapter 16, trans. Aubrey De Selincourt (1960; repr. New York: Penguin Classics, 2002), 49. Usage of "Capital of the World" derived from America's Historical Newspapers (www.newsbank.com) and the American Periodicals Series (www.proquest.com), including "The Immediate and the Future Results of the Conference," *Advocate of Peace* (Sept. 1899), 177; *Duluth (MN) News-Tribune*, Aug. 19, 1913; *Wilkes-Barre (PA) Times*, April 25, 1917; *Oregonian*, May 11, 1919; *Wyoming State Tribune*, May 18, 1919; *Kansas City (MO) Star*, March 21, 1920; *Columbia (SC) State*, March 7, 1919.

4 John R. Gold and Margaret M. Gold, eds., *Cities of Culture: Staging International Festivals and the Urban Agenda, 1851–2000* (Burlington, Vt.: Ashgate, 2005).

5 Wolfgang Sonne, *Representing the State: Capital City Planning in the Early Twentieth Century* (Munich: Prestel, 2003), 241–85; "Works Out World Centre Scheme," *American Architect,* Sept. 3, 1919, 313; Edgar Ansel Mowrer and Lilian T. Mowrer, *Umano and the Price of Lasting Peace* (New York: Philosophical Library, 1973), 93–104; Soterios Nicholson, *A World-City of Civilization* (Rome: Communication Office of Hendrik C. Andersen, 1913).

6 Quotation from *Boston Herald*, Nov. 18, 1945. The early-twentieth-century understanding of "world city" is explained by Peter Hall, *The World Cities* (Stockholm: Aldus/Bonnier, 1966), who traced the term to Patrick Geddes, *Cities in Evolution: An Introduction to the Town Planning Movement and the Study of Civics* (London: Ernest Benn, 1915). This usage precedes the later concept of "global cities" used by social scientists to describe the concentration of financial institutions and specialized service firms in "command centers" since 1980. On global cities theory, see especially J. Friedmann, "The World City Hypothesis," *Development and Change* 17.1 (1986): 69–84, and Saskia Sassen, *The Global City*, 2nd ed. (Princeton, N.J.: Princeton University Press, 2001). Other scholars have called attention to the international context of cities in earlier periods; see Janet Abu-Lughod, *New York, Chicago, Los Angeles: America's Global Cities* (Minneapolis: Minnesota University Press, 1999), and Carl Abbott, "The International City Hypothesis: An

Approach to the Recent History of U.S. Cities," *Journal of Urban History* 24 (Nov. 1997): 28–52.

7 This study has identified 248 localities involved in the world capital competition to varying degrees, 202 of them as a result of action by residents or officials with jurisdiction over the nominated communities. (See appendix.) Previously published case studies include Elton Atwater, "Philadelphia's Quest to Become the Permanent Headquarters of the United Nations," *Pennsylvania Magazine of History and Biography* 3 (April 1976): 243–57; Richard R. Chenoweth, "The Black Hills: United Nations Capital," *South Dakota History* 5 (Spring 1975): 151–64; and Leslie Perrin Wilson, "The United Nations in Concord? 'My How the Fur Flew,'" *Concord Journal*, Nov. 30, 2000, 6, republished in *Concord Magazine*, Autumn 2003, http://www.concordma.com/magazine/autumn03/unitednations.html. The campaigns of South Dakota and Philadelphia are compared in Edward A. Fierro, "Local Movements in Postwar America to Establish United Nations Headquarters: Case Studies of Publicity Techniques" (Master's thesis, University of South Dakota, 1973). Also see Charlene Mires, "The Lure of New England and the Search for the Capital of the World," *New England Quarterly* 79.1 (March 2006): 37–64, and Mires, "Sault Ste. Marie as the Capital of the World? Stellanova Osborn and the Pursuit of the United Nations, 1945," *Michigan Historical Review* 35.1 (Spring 2009): 61–82.

8 "The Story of the Permanent Headquarters," in U.N. Permanent Headquarters Corner-Stone Ceremony (program), box 247, Nelson Rockefeller—Personal Projects (RG II 4 L), RAC.

9 On the significance of the UN to Europeans, especially the British Empire, see Mark Mazower, *No Enchanted Palace: The End of Empire and the Ideological Origins of the United Nations* (Princeton, N.J.: Princeton University Press, 2009).

10 As early as 1942, a Gallup Poll found 64 percent of respondents agreeing that the U.S. government "should take steps now before the end of the war, to set up with our allies a world organization to maintain the future peace of the world." By 1945, 64 percent responded "yes" when asked if the United States should join a world organization, and far more—95 percent—agreed when the question was phrased to ask if the United States should join an organization to maintain peace. See H. Schuyler Foster, *Activism Replaces Isolationism: U.S. Public Attitudes, 1940–1975* (Washington: Foxhall, 1983), 20–22; William A. Scott and Stephen B. Withey, *The United States and the United Nations: The Public View, 1945–1955* (New York: Manhattan, 1958), 9–15.

11 On comparative U.S. and Canadian boosterism, see Steven V. Ward, *Selling Places: The Marketing and Promotion of Towns and Cities, 1850–2000* (New York: Routledge, 1998), 145; Joseph F. Bradley, *The Role of Trade Associations and Professional Business Societies in America* (University Park: Penn State University Press), 41–43; Scott M. Cutlip, *The Unseen Power: Public Relations,*

a History (Hillsdale, N.J.: Erlbaum, 1994); Roland Marchand, *Creating the Corporate Soul: The Rise of Public Relations and Corporate Imagery in American Big Business* (Berkeley: University of California Press, 1998).

12 As such, the world capital campaigns provide a concrete example of the "progressive sense of place" theorized by the British geographer Doreen Massey as "not self-enclosing and defensive, but outward-looking." Massey, "A Global Sense of Place," in T. Barnes and D. Gregory, eds., *Reading Human Geography* (London: Arnold, 1997), 315–23. On press boosterism in the United States, see Michael Schudson, "The U.S. Model of Journalism: Exception or Exemplar?" in Hugo de Burgh, ed., *Making Journalists: Diverse Models, Global Issues* (New York: Routledge, 2005), 94–106.

13 Scholarship on the history of tourism establishes the connection between leisure travel and place-marketing; see for example Ward, *Selling Places;* Christopher M. Law, *Urban Tourism: The Visitor Economy and the Growth of Large Cities,* 2nd ed. (New York: Continuum, 2002); and Salah Wahab and Chris Cooper, *Tourism in the Age of Globalisation* (New York: Routledge, 2001). On public relations practices, see Scott M. Cutlip, *Public Relations History: From the 17th to the 20th Century; The Antecedents* (Hillsdale, N.J.: Erlbaum, 1995). Westchester County resistance is detailed in James D. Hopkins, *Our Voices Were Heard: The Selection of the United Nations Headquarters* (Pleasantville, N.Y.: Edwin G. Michaelian Institute for Sub/Urban Governance, 1984).

14 On changing experiences of time and space, see Stephen Kern, *The Culture of Time and Space, 1880–1918,* rev. ed. (Cambridge, Mass.: Harvard University Press, 2003). The UN headquarters competition adds to Kern's work by carrying these issues into the later decades of the twentieth century. Discussion of the meshing of local and global appears in David Held et al., *Global Transformations: Politics, Economics, and Culture* (Stanford, Calif.: Stanford University Press, 1999), and Rob Wilson and Wimal Dissanayake, eds., *Global/Local: Cultural Production and the Transnational Imaginary* (Durham, N.C.: Duke University Press, 1996).

CHAPTER 1

1 Norman B. Lubinsky to Mr. and Mrs. Paul E. Bellamy, Oct. 10, 1944, box 54, Paul E. Bellamy Papers, USD (hereafter Bellamy Papers).

2 Paul E. Bellamy, "A Father's Tribute to His Son—Lt. Paul Herbert Bellamy," box 54, and correspondence during service in the Philippines, box 51, Bellamy Papers.

3 *Rapid City (SD) Daily Journal,* July 12, 1945.

4 Resolution, Nov. 3, 1944, box 55, Bellamy Papers; on booster strategies, see William Cronon, *Nature's Metropolis* (Princeton, N.J.: Princeton University Press, 1991), 31–41.

5 *Rapid City (SD) Daily Journal*, Nov. 3, 1944; *Sioux Falls (SD) Argus-Leader*, May 4, 1945.

6 Common Council Resolution, Sept. 12, 1944, in City of Detroit, *Journal of the Common Council from January 4, 1944, to December 26, 1944* (Detroit: Inland, 1945), 2289; Henry S. Sweeny, "Who Was the First to Suggest the USA for the UNO?" *Convention and Tourists' News Supplement* (Detroit: Detroit Convention and Tourist Bureau), undated tear sheet stamped "received Dec. 24, 1945," folder 15, box 83, Records of the Executive Office, Harry F. Kelly, Governor, 1943–46 (RG 42), MSA; E. A. Batchelor, "Personal and Confidential: J. Lee Barrett," *Detroit (MI) Saturday Night*, Feb. 2, 1929.

7 Common Council resolution, Sept. 12, 1944.

8 Dominic J. Capeci Jr. and Martha Wilkerson, *Layered Violence: The Detroit Rioters of 1943* (Jackson: University Press of Mississippi, 1991). The selective memory of Belle Isle's history remains apparent on a state historical marker, erected in 1979: "Belle Isle. This island, a jewel in the hearts of Detroiters, has provided shining memories for visitors of all ages. . . ." See Michigan State Historic Preservation Office, "Belle Isle," Historic Sites Online, www.mcgi. state.mi.us/hso/sites/15230.htm.

9 In his influential study of urban decline in Detroit, historian Thomas Sugrue noted that in the 1940s and 1950s "urban economic troubles were marginalized in a national debate that was framed by the discourses of growth, affluence, and consensus." In such circumstances, local officials failed to solve problems that continued to build into the urban crises of the 1960s. If they were not engaging with these problems, then what were they doing instead? For Detroit, and for other cities, the world capital campaigns that unfolded over the next two years suggest at least part of an answer to this question. Pursuing booster strategies that promoted the city's assets without acknowledging pressing realities, civic leaders could construct images of their cities that omitted urban decline and imagine a future that did not seem to require solving the problems that hastened decline in the postwar years. Thomas Sugrue, *The Origins of the Urban Crisis: Race and Inequality in Postwar Detroit* (1996; repr. Princeton, N.J.: Princeton University Press, 2005), 29–30, 155.

10 Edward R. Stettinius Jr., interview by Walter Johnson, Oct. 10, 1948, transcript, box 355, Edward R. Stettinius Jr. Papers, UVA (hereafter Stettinius Papers); Edward R. Stettinius Jr., *Roosevelt and the Russians: The Yalta Conference,* ed. Walter Johnson (1949; repr. Westport, Conn.: Greenwood, 1970), 204–5; Russell D. Buhite, *Decisions at Yalta: An Appraisal of Summit Diplomacy* (Wilmington, Del.: Scholarly Resources, 1986), 3–7; *NYT*, Feb. 8 and Feb.14, 1945.

11 Townsend Hoopes and Douglas Brinkley, *FDR and the Creation of the U.N.* (New Haven, Conn.: Yale University Press, 2000), 172–73; Buhite, *Decisions at Yalta*, 35, 54; U.S. Department of State, *The Conferences at Malta and Yalta* (Washington, D.C.: USGPO, 1955), 730–97.

12 In its early years, "United Nations Organization" was commonly used to distinguish the world security organization from the "United Nations" allies in the war. This book uses "United Nations" throughout except when "United Nations Organization" appears in quotations or is otherwise necessary for clarity.

13 Edward R. Stettinius Jr., *Report to the President on the Results of the San Francisco Conference* (Washington, D.C.: U.S. Department of State, 1945), 26–27; Stettinius, *Roosevelt and the Russians*, 17–19; Hoopes and Brinkley, *FDR and the Creation of the U.N.*, 174–76.

14 Quotation in Stettinius, *Roosevelt and the Russians*, 203–4. The State Department collected data on the following potential sites for the UN's first conference: Miami Beach, Palm Beach, and St. Petersburg, Fla.; Atlantic City, N.J.; New York City; Philadelphia; Cincinnati; St. Louis; San Francisco; and Los Angeles. Documented in Warren Kelchner, Department of State Division of International Conferences, Memorandum to Secretary of State, Jan. 5, 1945, box 322, Stettinius Papers. Roosevelt's interest in the Azores and Hawaii documented in Memorandum, Conversation Between the President, the Secretary of State and Undersecretary, Sept. 6, 1944, reel 34, Cordell Hull Papers, NYPL (hereafter Hull Papers); French Lick was discussed among State Department staff in September 1944, as noted in Memorandum of the Under Secretary of State, Sept. 2, 1944, reel 34, Hull Papers.

15 Edward R. Stettinius Jr., interview by Walter Johnson, Nov. 4, 1948, transcript, box 279, Stettinius Papers; Stettinius, *Roosevelt and the Russians*, 206–7; Roger W. Lotchin, *The Bad City in the Good War: San Francisco, Los Angeles, Oakland, and San Diego* (Bloomington: Indiana University Press, 2003), 15.

16 Quotations in Stettinius, *Roosevelt and the Russians*, 206–7.

17 Quoted in Helen Abbot Lapham, *Roving with Roger* (San Francisco: Cameron, 1971), 170; Roger Lapham, "An Interview on Shipping, Labor, San Francisco City Government and American Foreign Aid," interview by Corinne L. Gilb, Jan. 30-June 13, 1957, Regional Cultural History Project, University of California at Berkeley (transcript in SFPL), 184.

18 Lapham, interview by Gilb, 11–13, 42–49.

19 Lotchin, *The Bad City*, 41, 104–13, 161, 194; *Your Victory Vacation in San Francisco … after the War* (San Francisco: Californians, n.d.); Virtual Museum of the City of San Francisco, "Chronology of San Francisco War Events," www.sfmuseum.org.

20 William Issel, "Business Power and Political Culture in San Francisco," *Journal of Urban History* 16.1 (Nov. 1989): 52–77; J. Philip Gruen, "Everyday Attractions: Tourism and the Generation of Instant Heritage in Nineteenth-Century San Francisco," in Nezar AlSayyad, ed., *Consuming Tradition, Manufacturing Heritage: Global Norms and Urban Forms in the Age of Tourism* (New York: Routledge, 2001), 161–72.

21 Lapham, interview by Gilb, 101–3, 140–45; "Henry Francis Grady: A Yankee Trader," San Francisco Chamber of Commerce press release, December (n.d.), 1944, Henry F. Grady Biography File, SFPL.

22 *SFN*, Feb. 14, 1945; Gruen, "Everyday Attractions," 153.

23 San Francisco Chamber of Commerce Minutes, Volume 16, Board of Directors Meeting, Feb. 15 and March 8, 1945, San Francisco Chamber of Commerce (MS 871), CHS; "S.F. Proposed as World Capital," *SFCB*, March 9, 1945.

24 *SFCB*, March 9, 1945. On the same day, the *Philadelphia Record* carried the headline "Business, Labor Support City as World 'Capital.'"

25 J. David Stern to Franklin D. Roosevelt, March 3, 1945, box 188A, United Nations 1945–1946 Papers of Delegates to Meeting to Select Site for Capitol, HSP; *PR*, March 5, 1945. This account of the Philadelphia campaign is adapted in part from Charlene Mires, *Independence Hall in American Memory* (Philadelphia: University of Pennsylvania Press, 2002), 208–10.

26 J. David Stern, *Memoirs of a Maverick Publisher* (New York: Simon & Schuster, 1962), 52, 56, 60, 64, 100; Harry Altshuler, *PR*, May 14, 1945; "Golden Anniversary Stirs Stern Memories," *Editor & Publisher*, Nov. 8, 1958, 71; *Philadelphia Bulletin*, Sept. 22, 1932, and Oct. 11, 1971.

27 Stern, *Memoirs*, 193.

28 Franklin Delano Roosevelt, "Address to the Congress Reporting on the Yalta Conference," March 1, 1945, in *The Public Papers and Addresses of Franklin Roosevelt*, comp. Samuel I. Rosenman, vol. 3 (New York: Russell & Russell, 1950), 570–86. The strategy to promote the UN idea with references to the Constitution emerged in discussion within the State Department during January 1945. See Conversations with Latin American Ambassadors, Meeting Minutes, Jan. 26, 1945, container 2, Leo Pasvolsky Papers, LOC.

29 Stern, *Memoirs*, 70, 84.

30 Edwin O. Lewis, recorded interview by John Roberts for the Oral History Research Office, Columbia University, Jan. 2, 1969, transcript in INHP; *Philadelphia Bulletin*, June 17, 1918, July 1, 1942, and Oct. 18, 1942.

31 *PR*, March 5, 1945.

32 *PR*, March 6–13, 16–19, and 27, and April 4, 1945.

33 Philadelphia was famously labeled "the most corrupt and the most contented" by Lincoln Steffens in *The Shame of the Cities* (New York: McClure, Phillips, 1904); on cities in 1945, see Jon C. Teaford, *The Metropolitan Revolution: The Rise of Post-Urban America* (New York: Columbia University Press, 2006), 40–48.

34 *PR*, March 17, 1945.

35 *PR*, March 10 and 14, 1945.

36 *PR*, March 27, 1945; *NYT*, April 29, 1945.

37 *SFN*, March 28, 1945; *PR*, March 30, 1945.

38 Nelson A. Rockefeller to Francis Case, June 4 and July 10, 1945, box 246, Nelson Rockefeller—Personal Projects (RG III 4 L), RAC; Francis Case to Franklin Delano Roosevelt, March 15, 1945, and Franklin Delano Roosevelt to Francis Case, April 7, 1945, Black Hills Capital Site, General Project Files, Francis Case Papers, DWU.

39 Karl Mundt to Arthur H. Vandenberg and Sol Bloom, April 7, 1945, and Mundt to Edward R. Stettinius, May 5, 1945, box 55, Bellamy Papers; *Rapid City (SD) Daily Journal*, April 17, 19, 20, 26, and 28, and May 9 and 11, 1945; *Sioux Falls (SD) Argus-Leader*, April 26 and 28, and May 17, 1945; *PR*, April 22, 25, and 29, and May 4 and 6, 1945.

CHAPTER 2

1 *SFCB*, April 25, 1945.

2 J. Philip Gruen, "Everyday Attractions: Tourism and the Generation of Instant Heritage in Nineteenth-Century San Francisco," in Nezar AlSayyad, ed., *Consuming Tradition, Manufacturing Heritage: Global Norms and Urban Forms in the Age of Tourism* (New York: Routledge, 2001), 152–90; *SFN*, March 23, 1945.

3 F. P. Walters, *A History of the League of Nations* (London: Oxford University Press, 1952), 36–37; Memorandum, "Status of the Question, Permanent Seat of the Organization, Informal Suggestions," April 12, 1945, box 322, Edward R. Stettinius Jr. Papers, UVA (hereafter Stettinius Papers); Resolution, City Council of Quebec, March 16, 1945, file 7, box 7, Records of the Preparatory Commission of the United Nations (S-0539), UNA (hereafter Prep. Comm. Records); *SFE*, April 25, 1945.

4 "Memorandum on Conference Organization and Procedure for the United Nations Conference on International Organization," State Department Information Memorandum 1, March 23, 1945, folder 4, box 1, UNCIO Records (S-1006), UNA; *SFN*, March 26, and April 4 and 20, 1945; *SFC*, April 9, 1945; *SFCB*, April 18, 1945.

5 *NYT*, April 13, 1945; *Rapid City (SD) Daily Journal*, April 12 and 13, 1945; *PR*, April 16, 1945; *SFE*, April 13, 1945; *SFCB*, April 14, 1945; *SFC*, April 14, 1945.

6 *SFC*, April 13, 1945; *SFN*, April 20, 1945; *SFCB*, April 21, 1945; *SFE*, April 24, 1945.

7 *Denver Post*, April 22, 1945.

8 *St. Louis Post-Dispatch*, April 22, 1945; Charles F. Darlington, Memoirs of the San Francisco Conference (typescript), Chapter 12, p. 219, box 5, Charles F. Darlington Papers, HST; Stephen C. Schlesinger, *Act of Creation: The Founding of the United Nations* (Boulder, Colo.: Westview, 2003), 233.

9 *SFC*, May 7, 1945; *SFE*, May 18, 1945; quoted in Helen Abbot Lapham, *Roving with Roger* (San Francisco: Cameron, 1971), 179–80; "Memorandum on

Transportation from New York City and Washington to the Site of the United Nations Conference on International Organization," Department of State Information Memorandum Number 8, March 30, 1945, box 1, folder 4, UNCIO Records (S-1006), UNA.

10 *SFN*, April 21, 1945; *SFC*, April 21 and 23, 1945; *SFCB*, April 20, 1945.

11 Akira Iriye, *Global Community: The Role of International Organizations in the Making of the Contemporary World* (Berkeley: University of California Press, 2002), 9–36; Edward R. Stettinius, *Charter of the United Nations: Report to the President on the Results of the San Francisco Conference* (Washington, D.C.: U.S. Department of State, 1945), 262–66; Carol Anderson, *Eyes off the Prize: The United Nations and the African American Struggle for Human Rights, 1944–1955* (New York: Cambridge University Press, 2003), 39–57; *SFN*, April 30, 1945; *SFC*, May 1, 1945.

12 *SFN*, May 19, 1945; *SFCB*, April 25 and May 3, 1945; *SFC*, April 28, 1945; *NYT*, May 15, 1945.

13 Frank Mazzi, "Harbingers of the City: Men and Their Monuments in Nineteenth-Century San Francisco," *Southern California Quarterly* 55 (Summer 1973): 141–62; Gerald Booth, *Fairmont Hotel: A Pictorial History* (San Francisco: Fairmont Hotel Management Co. and Somerset Van Ness Corporation, 1986); Dan Siefkin, *Meet Me at the St. Francis: The First Seventy-Five Years of a Great San Francisco Hotel* (San Francisco: St. Francis Hotel Corp., 1979); Oscar Lewis and Carroll D. Hall, *Bonanza Inn: America's First Luxury Hotel* (1893; New York: Knopf, 1933); Robert Dallek, *An Unfinished Life: John F. Kennedy, 1917–1963* (Boston: Little, Brown, 2003), 114–15.

14 *The San Francisco Civic Center: A Study in Urban Form* (San Francisco: American Institute of Architects, San Francisco Chapter, 1987), 2; Joan Elaine Draper, "The San Francisco Civic Center: Architecture, Planning, and Politics" (Diss., Montana State University, 1979), 1, 5, 56–57, 235–39; *SFN*, April 5, 1945; "A Memorandum Concerning the San Francisco Civic Center, Headquarters of the United Nations Conference on International Organization," Department of State Memorandum 18, April 16, 1945, folder 1, box 1, UNCIO Records (Series S-1006), UNA; *War Memorial of San Francisco: Souvenir Edition* (n.p., n.d.), San Francisco Buildings File, War Memorial, SFPL.

15 *NYT*, April 26, 1945; *SFN*, April 26, 1945; Tom Brokaw, *The Greatest Generation* (New York: Random House, 1998).

16 Memorandum of Conversation, April 25, 1945, box 313, and Stettinius notes on Opening Session of UNCIO, April 25, 1945, box 355, Stettinius Papers.

17 Address of the President, April 25, 1945, folder OF-85B, Official Files box 524, HST; Crider, *NYT*, April 26, 1945; Richard Rhodes, *The Making of the Atomic Bomb* (New York: Simon & Schuster, 1986), 622–23.

18 *NYT*, April 26, 1945.

19 *NYT*, April 26, 1945; "San Francisco and the Bay Area," Department of State

Information Memorandum 10, n.d., box 1, folder 4, UNCIO Records (Series S-1006), UNA; Ramsey Oppenheim, *San Francisco, World City* (1941; repr. San Francisco: United Nations Conference Committee, 1945); *SFN*, April 23, 1945.

20 *PR*, April 25, 1945.

21 *Philadelphia: Cradle of Liberty* (n.d., n.p.), Free Library of Philadelphia Brochures Collection, UA; *PR*, May 6 and 13, 1945.

22 Schlesinger, *Act of Creation*, 11–12, 73–74, 82, 120, 135–38.

23 Schlesinger, *Act of Creation*, 159–74.

24 Stettinius notes, May 8, 1945, box 355, Stettinius Papers; *SFN*, May 8, 1945; *SFC*, May 8, 1945; *NYT*, May 9, 1945.

25 *PR*, May 18, 1945; "Johnson Elected Head of Temple," *Philadelphia Bulletin*, Sept. 17, 1941, and Jan. 19, 1966; Resume of L. Stauffer Oliver, March 1, 1937, typescript in George D. McDowell Philadelphia *Evening Bulletin* Collection, "Oliver, L. Stauffer—Judge Biography" envelope, UA; L. Stauffer Oliver, *The Bench Is a Hard Seat* (Philadelphia: Dorrance, 1965), 1, 106–8.

26 *PR*, May 18, 1945.

27 *PR*, May 18, 1945.

28 *PR*, May 19, 1945.

29 *Sioux Falls (SD) Argus-Leader*, May 27, 1945.

30 *Sioux Falls (SD) Argus-Leader*, May 28, June 1 and 2, 1945; Adlai Stevenson to Betty Morrison, June 5, 1945, box 322, Stettinius Papers; Leland Case to Francis Case, May 23, 1945, Francis Case Papers, DWU; Paul Bellamy to Alger Hiss, June 18, 1945, Paul E. Bellamy Papers, USD (hereafter Bellamy Papers).

31 *PR*, May 20 and 23, 1945.

32 *Foreign Relations of the United States, Diplomatic Papers, 1945*. Vol. 1, *General: The United Nations* (Washington, D.C.: USGPO, 1967), 813–37; Schlesinger, *Act of Creation*, 175–225.

33 Memoranda of Conversations, May 21, 1945, and May 28, 1945, box 313, Stettinius Papers; Stettinius, *United Nations, A Personal Record*, book IV, chapter 2, p. 2, box 304, Stettinius Papers.

34 *PR*, May 22, 1945.

35 *United Nations of the World* (n.d., n.p.), brochure, box 55, Bellamy Papers; Steven V. Ward, *Selling Places: The Marketing and Promotion of Towns and Cities, 1850–2000* (New York: Routledge, 1998), 9–28; *PR*, May 19 and 23, 1945.

36 Susan Schulten, *The Geographical Imagination in America, 1880–1950* (University of Chicago Press, 2001), 204–38; Schlesinger, *Act of Creation*, 113.

37 Stettinius, *Charter of the United Nations*, 27, 32–45.

38 Schlesinger, *Act of Creation*, 209–25; David L. Bosco, *Five to Rule Them All: The UN Security Council and the Making of the Modern World* (New York: Oxford University Press, 2009).

39 "Rules for League Contest," *NYT*, July 27, 1926.

40 Illustration of Twin Peaks capital designed by Vincent G. Raney published in *SFN*, April 24, 1945.

41 *SFN*, May 28, 1945; Marin County design by William Wilson Wurster, Theodore C. Bernardi, and Ernest Bern published in *SFN*, July 5, 1945.

42 Roger Lapham, "An Interview on Shipping, Labor, San Francisco City Government, and American Foreign Aid," interview by Corinne L. Gilb, Jan. 30-June 13, 1957, Regional Cultural History Project, University of California at Berkeley, transcript p. 185, SFPL; *SFN*, June 27, 1945; *SFC*, June 24, 1945.

43 Stettinius notes, June 25, 1945, box 355, Stettinius Papers; *SFN*, June 25, 1945; *SFC*, June 26, 1945; *SFE*, June 26, 1945.

44 Stettinius notes, June 25, 1945, box 355, Stettinius Papers; *SFN*, June 25, 1945; *SFC*, June 26, 1945.

45 Stettinius notes, June 25, 1945, box 354, Stettinius Papers.

46 Stettinius notes, June 26, 1945, box 355, Stettinius Papers; *SFC*, June 27, 1946.

47 Stettinius notes, June 26, 1945, box 355, Stettinius Papers.

48 Stettinius, *Charter of the United Nations*, 52–53, 66–80, 125–36, 190–202.

49 Draft Memorandum, "Position of United States on Location of the Permanent Seat of the United Nations," July 14, 1945, and Memorandum, "Considerations Governing the Choice of Location of the Permanent Seat of the United Nations," August 22, 1945, box 427, Stettinius Papers; Memorandum of Conversation, June 4, 1945, box 313, Stettinius Papers.

50 Draft Memorandum, "Position of United States on Location of the Permanent Seat of the United Nations," July 14, 1945, and Memorandum, "Considerations Governing the Choice of Location of the Permanent Seat of the United Nations," August 22, 1945, box 427, Stettinius Papers.

51 Draft Memorandum, "Position of United States on Location of the Permanent Seat of the United Nations," July 14, 1945, box 427, Stettinius Papers.

CHAPTER 3

1 George J. Joachim, *Iron Fleet: The Great Lakes in World War II* (Detroit, Mich.: Wayne State University Press, 1994), 52–53; K. Jack Bauer, "Inland Seas and Overseas: Shipbuilding on the Great Lakes during World War II," *Inland Seas* 38.2 (1982): 84–94.

2 Fred Christopherson to M. Q. Sharpe, June 5, 1945, box 125, Merrell Quentin Sharpe Papers (hereafter Sharpe Papers), USD; *Rapid City (SD) Daily Journal*, June 20, 1945; Merrell Quentin Sharpe Biography File, SDSA.

3 Fred K. Warren to Paul E. Bellamy, July 9, 1945, box 55, Paul E. Bellamy Papers, USD (hereafter Bellamy Papers); John J. Dempsey endorsement in "Philadelphia: Cradle of Liberty" promotional brochure (n.p.), Free Library of Philadelphia Brochures Collection, UA; James A. Hagerty, "Governors to Seek Firm Labor Policy," *NYT*, July 1, 1945.

4 *Proceedings of the Governors' Conference 1945* (Chicago: Governors' Conference, 1945); *Sioux Falls (SD) Argus-Leader*, July 7, 1945.

5 *Proceedings of the Governors' Conference*, 124.

6 *Proceedings of the Governors' Conference*, 88–96, 176; *NYT*, July 3 and 4, 1945.

7 *Sioux Falls (SD) Argus-Leader*, July 3, 1945.

8 *Sioux Falls (SD) Argus-Leader*, July 3, 1945; Edward Martin to Harry F. Kelly, April 13, 1945, M. Q. Sharpe to Harry F. Kelly, May 28, 1945, box 83, Records of the Executive Office, Harry F. Kelly (RG 42), MSA (hereafter Kelly Records). Colorado Governor John Vivian's papers in the Colorado State Archives contain no record of the fourteen communities he claimed as qualified.

9 John J. Bukowczyk et al., *Permeable Border: The Great Lakes Basin as Transnational Region, 1650–1990* (Pittsburgh: University of Pittsburgh Press, 2005), 3, 117–19; *Sioux Falls (SD) Argus-Leader*, July 2, 3, and 7, 1945.

10 *Proceedings of the Governors' Conference*, 181; *Sioux Falls (SD) Argus-Leader*, July 5, 1945.

11 *Sioux Falls (SD) Argus-Leader*, July 3 and 5, 1945.

12 *Sault Ste. Marie (MI) Evening News*, May 22, 1945.

13 *Sault Ste. Marie (MI) Evening News*, April 19, 1945.

14 Joachim, *Iron Fleet*, 52, 57, 63–64; Graeme S. Mount, John Abbott, and Michael J. Mulloy, *The Border at Sault Ste. Marie* (Toronto: Dundurn, 1995), 38.

15 *Sault Ste. Marie (MI) Evening News*, May 22 and 23, 1945; *Niagara Falls (NY) Gazette*, May 2 and Aug. 9, 1945.

16 *Sault Ste. Marie (MI) Evening News*, June 4, 8, and 16, and July 3, 1945; Memorandum of Correspondence, Maurice E. Hunt, June 19, 1945, box 522, OF 85-A, HST; *PR*, June 5, 1945.

17 Maurice E. Hunt and W. J. McMeeken to W. L. Mackenzie King and Edward R. Stettinius, undated letter reprinted in brochure, *Small Towns with Big Ambitions* (n.d., n.p.), box 55, Bellamy Papers; Joachim, *Iron Fleet*, 65–66.

18 Stellanova Osborn, *Eighty and On: The Unending Adventurings of Chase S. Osborn* (Sault Ste. Marie, Mich.: Sault News Printing, 1941); Robert M. Warner, "Introduction," in *Chase S. Osborn, the Iron Hunter* (Detroit, Mich.: Wayne State University Press, 2002), 7–12; Richard D. Shaul, "To a Different Drum," *Michigan History*, Sept./Oct. 2004, 32. For a more extensive discussion of the Osborn family role in the world capital campaign, see Charlene Mires, "Sault Ste. Marie as the Capital of the World? Stellanova Osborn and the Pursuit of the United Nations, 1945," *Michigan Historical Review* 35.1 (Spring 2009): 61–82.

19 Stellanova Osborn, unpublished autobiography (first draft 1972–73), 84–85, 125, and "Auto-Biography," typescript dated Dec.11, 1978, box 35, Stellanova Osborn Papers, UM (hereafter S. Osborn Papers).

20 Stella Lee Brunt to Chase Osborn, Sept. 27, 1921, box 36, S. Osborn Papers; Stellanova Osborn, unpublished autobiography, 143–60, 198, and U.S. Labor

Department Certificate of Citizenship, June 28, 1933, box 35, S. Osborn Papers; *NYT*, Nov. 21, 1923; *Detroit Free Press*, April 22, 1984.

21 Chase S. Osborn and Stellanova Osborn, *Schoolcraft, Longfellow, Hiawatha* (Lancaster, Pa.: Cattell, 1942); Chase S. Osborn and Stella Brunt Osborn, *The Conquest of a Continent* (Lancaster, Pa.: Science Press, 1939), 1, 82, 112, 115–16, 120, 125, 138.

22 UN campaign materials bearing Chase Osborn's name are found in boxes 91, 92, and 93, Chase S. Osborn Papers, UM (hereafter C. Osborn Papers); box 83, Kelly Records; and file 9, box 5, Records of the Preparatory Commission of the United Nations (S-0539), UNA (hereafter Prep. Comm. Records).

23 Stellanova Osborn recorded her role and Chase Osborn's disinterest in the UN campaign in correspondence with close friends and relatives, including her mother, after Sault Ste. Marie ended its efforts. See Stellanova Osborn to Mrs. Nelson Long, Dec. 28, 1945, and additional correspondence in boxes 91 and 92, C. Osborn Papers. On Warm Springs, Chase Osborn to Piromis Bell, May 16, 1945, box 92, C. Osborn Papers. Quotation from Chase S. Osborn, "A Message to the Joint Meeting of the Algonquin Club with the Detroit Marine Society," Oct. 20, 1945, file 9, box 5, Prep. Comm. Records.

24 Chase S. Osborn, "Message."

25 Niagara Falls plan in promotional brochure, *Proposed United Nations Headquarters: Navy Island, Niagara Falls* (n.p., 1945), LOC.

26 William Cronon, *Nature's Metropolis: Chicago and the Great West* (Princeton, N.J.: Princeton University Press, 1991); Robert Rydell, *World of Fairs: The Century of Progress Exhibitions* (Chicago: University of Chicago Press, 1993).

27 Lisa Krissoff Boehm, *Popular Culture and the Enduring Myth of Chicago, 1871–1968* (New York: Routledge, 2004), 105–26.

28 James C. Schneider, *Should America Go to War? The Debate over Foreign Policy in Chicago, 1939–1941* (Chapel Hill: University of North Carolina Press, 1989), 1–36; Patrick D. Kennedy, "Chicago's Irish Americans and the Candidacies of Franklin D. Roosevelt, 1933–1944," *Illinois Historical Journal* 88.4 (Winter 1995): 263–78; Robert D. Ubriaco Jr., "The Yalta Conference and Its Impact on the Chicago Congressional Elections of 1946," *Illinois Historical Journal* 86.4 (Winter 1993): 225–44.

29 Roger Biles, *Big City Boss in Depression and War: Mayor Edward J. Kelly of Chicago* (DeKalb: Northern Illinois University Press, 1984), 14–15; Roger Biles, "Edward J. Kelly: New Deal Machine Builder," in Paul M. Green and Melvin G. Holli, eds., *The Mayors: The Chicago Political Tradition*, rev. ed. (Carbondale: Southern Illinois University Press, 1995), 111–13; Dennis H. Cremin, "Chicago's Front Yard," *Chicago History*, Spring 1998, 22–43.

30 Perry Duis and Scott LaFrance, *We've Got a Job to Do: Chicagoans and World War II* (Chicago: Chicago Historical Society, 1992), 34–40, 71; Biles, *Big City Boss*, 82–85.

31 *Chicago Tribune,* June 30, 1945; Carl Smith, *Urban Disorder and the Shape of Belief: The Great Chicago Fire, the Haymarket Bomb, and the Model Town of Pullman* (Chicago: University of Chicago Press, 1994).

32 Biles, *Big City Boss,* 3, 85–87; *Chicago Tribune,* June 30, 1945.

33 *Journal of the Proceedings of the City Council of the City of Chicago for the Council Year 1945–46,* July 17, 1945, 3750–51, Chicago Public Library.

34 Chicago plan reprinted in *Chicago Herald-American,* Nov. 19, 1945; "Morgan, Charles Leonard," *Who's Who in Chicago and Illinois* (Chicago: Marquis, 1945), 632.

35 Claude Pepper Personal Diaries, July 2, 1945, box 2, FSU; *NYT,* July 3 and 8, 1945.

36 Pepper Personal Diaries, July 23–28, 1945, FSU; Stephen C. Schlesinger, *Act of Creation: The Founding of the United Nations* (Boulder, Colo.: Westview, 2003), 263–79; *NYT,* July 29, 1945.

37 Harry S. Truman, Remarks of the President in the Auditorium at Kansas City, Missouri, Upon Receiving the Honorary Degree Doctor of Laws, June 28, 1945, box 504, PPF-1403, HST; Memorandum of Conversation, Mr. George F. Green, Aug. 2, 1945, box 522, OF 85, HST; Bryce Smith to Harry Truman, Aug. 22, 1945, box 175, PPF-109, HST; *Kansas City (MO) Star,* June 28, 1945; Theodore R. Keldin, Mayor of Baltimore, to Secretary of State, July 25, 1945, box 9, Prep. Comm. Records; Baguio promoted in editorial of *The Philippines Mail,* August 1945, tear sheet in box 5, Prep. Comm. Records.

38 Harry S. Truman to Edward Stettinius, June 27, 1945, box 525, OF 85-B, HST; Roger Lapham to Edward Stettinius, July 17, 1945, box 699, Edward R. Stettinius Jr. Papers, UVA (hereafter Stettinius Papers).

39 Robert Jungk, *Brighter Than a Thousand Suns: A Personal History of the Atomic Scientists* (New York: Harcourt Brace Jovanovich, 1958), 196; Leslie R. Groves, *Now It Can Be Told: The Story of the Manhattan Project* (New York: Harper, 1962), 305–6; Robert James Maddox, *The United States and World War II* (Boulder, Colo.: Westview, 1992), 301–2.

40 Roger W. Lotchin, *The Bad City in the Good War: San Francisco, Los Angeles, Oakland, and San Diego* (Bloomington: Indiana University Press, 2003), 210–11; *SFCB,* Aug. 14, 15, and 16, 1945; Maddox, *The United States in World War II,* 335.

41 *Miami Herald,* Aug. 8, 1945; *New Orleans Times-Picayune,* Aug. 8, 1945; *Cincinnati Enquirer,* Aug. 8, 1945; *Beloit (WI) Daily News,* Aug. 6, 1945; *Niagara Falls (NY) Gazette,* Sept. 24, 1945.

42 Paul Boyer, *By the Bomb's Early Light: American Thought and Culture at the Dawn of the Atomic Age,* rev. ed. (Chapel Hill: University of North Carolina Press, 1994), 13–14; *Boston Globe,* Aug. 22, 1945.

43 *Rapid City (SD) Daily Journal,* July 12, 1945; Paul E. Bellamy, Man of the Year Acceptance Speech, typescript, box 54, Bellamy Papers.

CHAPTER 4

1 Preparatory Commission of the United Nations, *Handbook*, rev. ed. (London: Preparatory Commission of the United Nations, 1945), 8; Philip Ziegler, *London at War, 1939–1945* (New York: Knopf, 1995), 140, 337; A. N. Wilson, *London: A History* (New York: Modern Library, 2004), 137.

2 *NYT*, Aug. 25, 1945.

3 On continuities between the League of Nations and the UN for European powers, especially the British Empire, see Mark Mazower, *No Enchanted Palace: The End of Empire and the Ideological Origins of the United Nations* (Princeton, N.J.: Princeton University Press, 2009).

4 *NYT*, Aug. 25, 1945; Bryce Wood and Minerva Morales, "Latin America and the United Nations," *International Organization* 9.3 (Summer 1965): 714–27.

5 Edward R. Stettinius Jr., Memorandum, "Matters to be Reviewed with the President and Secretary Byrnes" (n.d.), and Calendar Notes, Aug. 23, 1945, box 247, Edward R. Stettinius Jr. Papers, UVA (hereafter Stettinius Papers); Daily Presidential Appointments File, Aug. 20 and Aug. 23, 1945, Matthew J. Connelly Files, HST; Charles P. Noyes, Memorandum, Aug. 24, 1945, in *Foreign Relations of the United States, Diplomatic Papers 1945*. Vol. I, *General: The United Nations* (Washington, D.C.: USGPO, 1967), 1439–40; Chan Gurney to M. Q. Sharpe, September 24, 1945, box 55, Paul E. Bellamy Papers, USD (hereafter Bellamy Papers).

6 F. P. Walters, *A History of the League of Nations* (London: Oxford University Press, 1952), 416–18; "The League of Nations' Palace," *World Affairs* 99.1 (March 1936): 16–17; Evan Luard, *A History of the United Nations*, vol. 1 (New York: St. Martin's, 1982), 69–82; Stanley Meisler, *United Nations: The First Fifty Years* (New York: Atlantic Monthly Press, 1995), 26–27.

7 This and subsequent quotations from Oct. 3, 1945, meeting in "Extract from the Verbatim Record of the Twenty-First Meeting of the Executive Committee, 3 October 1945," in Appendix, *Report by the Executive Committee to the Preparatory Commission of the United States*, UN Document PC/EX/133/Rev. 1, Nov. 12, 1945, UNA; Victor Hoo biography in *NYT*, April 11, 1946. Private conversations prior to the committee's debate documented in *Foreign Relations of the United States, Diplomatic Papers 1945*. Vol. I, *General: The United Nations* (Washington, D.C.: USGPO, 1967).

8 "Herbert Vere Evatt," *Encyclopedia of World Biography*, 2nd ed., in *Biography Resource Center* (Farmington Hill, Mich.: Thomson Gale, 2007), galenet.galegroup.com/servlet/BioRC.

9 *NYT*, Feb. 1, 1943.

10 Stettinius, Calendar Notes, Sept. 3 and 12, 1945, and Memorandum of Conversation, Sept. 13, 1945, box 247, Stettinius Papers; "Philip Noel-Baker," in *Les Prix Nobel en 1959* (Stockholm: Norstedt, 1960), 90–91.

11　*NYT*, Dec. 9, 1951. This characterization of the debate is influenced by the work of cultural geographers on the concepts of geographic planes and time-space convergence, usefully summarized in Phil Hubbard, Rob Kitchin, and Gill Valentine, *Key Thinkers on Space and Place* (London: Sage, 2004), 1–13.

12　United Nations, *Report by the Executive Committee to the Preparatory Commission of the United Nations* (PC/EX/113/Rev. 1), Nov. 12, 1945, 116–17, UNA.

13　Two votes were taken, with only Iran and Mexico changing positions by abstaining on the second vote. On the first, asking, "Should the permanent headquarters of the United Nations be situated in the United States of America?" those in favor (nine) were Australia, Brazil, Chile, China, Czechoslovakia, Iran, Mexico, USSR, and Yugoslavia; those against (three), France, Netherlands, United Kingdom; abstaining (two) Canada and the United States. On the second vote, asking, "Should the permanent headquarters of the United Nations be situated in Europe?" those in favor (three) France, Netherlands, United Kingdom; against (seven) Australia, Brazil, Chile, China, Czechoslovakia, USSR, Yugoslavia; abstaining (four) Canada, Iran, Mexico, United States.

14　*Presented to the United Nations Organization by the People of San Francisco, October 1945,* San Francisco History Center, SFPL.

15　Little has been written about booster activity at midcentury, but the practices employed by the world capital hopefuls resemble the strategies of civic boosterism in earlier decades, as well as the intensive place-marketing efforts of cities since the 1980s. See Steven V. Ward, *Selling Places: The Marketing and Promotion of Towns and Cities, 1850–2000* (New York: Routledge, 1998).

16　Edwin D. Mead, "The Meaning of Massachusetts," *New England Quarterly* 3 (January 1930): 25–54; Dona Brown, *Inventing New England: Regional Tourism in the Nineteenth Century* (Washington, D.C.: Smithsonian Institution Press, 1995); Joseph A. Conforti, *Imagining New England: Explorations of Regional Identity from the Pilgrims to the Mid-Twentieth Century* (Chapel Hill: University of North Carolina Press, 2001).

17　*Boston Globe*, Nov. 7, 1937, and *Boston Transcript*, Nov. 9, 1937, in Maurice J. Tobin Scrapbooks, Boston Public Library; William A. Leahy, "The Population: Gains and Losses," and George Caspar Homans, "The Harbor and Shipping of Boston, 1880–1930," in Elisabeth M. Herlihy, ed., *Fifty Years of Boston: A Memorial Volume Issued in Commemoration of the Tercentenary of 1930* (Boston: Subcommittee on Memorial History of the Boston Tercentenary Committee, 1932), 62, 279–89; Vincent A. Lapomarda, "Maurice Joseph Tobin: The Decline of Bossism in Boston," *New England Quarterly* 43.3 (Sept. 1970): 355–81; Cynthia Horan, "Organizing the 'New Boston': Growth Policy, Governing Coalitions, and Tax Reform," *Polity* 22.3 (Spring 1990): 494.

18　*Boston Traveler*, Sept. 9, 1938, and Nov. 9, 1938; *Boston Herald*, Sept. 29, 1939; *Boston Post*, June 2, 1945; Maurice J. Tobin, Inaugural Address, 1945, in Gerald

F. Coughlin, comp., *Addresses and Messages to the General Court, Proclamations, Official Addresses and Statements of His Excellency Governor Maurice J. Tobin* (Boston: Commonwealth of Massachusetts, 1946), 5–13; Lapomarda, "Decline of Bossism," 355–81.

19 Oliver Wendell Holmes, "The Autocrat of the Breakfast-Table," *Atlantic Monthly*, April 1858.

20 Promoting New England as "distinctively the summer playground of the eastern part of the United States," the chamber of commerce boasted in 1911 that "Boston, so often referred to as 'the Hub of the Solar System,' is literally the 'hub' of this vast volume of tourist and vacation travel." As a place reference, the term became so common that no explanation was necessary, as in *Around the Hub: A Boys' Book about Boston* (Boston: Roberts Brothers, 1881) and *A Ramble 'Round the Hub* (Boston: Hovey, Shepard, and Smith, 1905). On Boston promotion, also see George French, ed., *New England: What It Is and What It Is to Be* (Boston: Boston Chamber of Commerce, 1911), 282; *Boston Post*, Aug. 24, 1938.

21 *Boston Globe*, Nov. 9, 1945.

22 *Christian Science Monitor*, July 27, 1945; Memorandum of Correspondence, Maurice J. Tobin, Oct. 3, 1945, HST; Site Subcommittee of Committee 8 Verbatim Minutes of Meetings, Volume XIII, UNA. See also Boston Chamber of Commerce publications in the collections of the Massachusetts Historical Society: Geo. W. Engelhardt, *Boston, Massachusetts* (Boston: Engelhardt, 1897); George French, *New England: Boston, Massachusetts; A Great, Modern Manufacturing and Commercial Community Built on Historic Ground around America's National Shrines* (Boston: Convention Bureau, Boston Chamber of Commerce, 1931).

23 *Boston Globe*, April 19 and Nov. 20, 1940; *Boston Post*, June 15, 1940; *Boston Advertiser*, April 20, 1941; Everett B. Mero, comp., *Celebrating a 300th Anniversary: A Report of the Tercentenary of Massachusetts Bay Colony in New England, 1630–1930* (Boston: Tercentenary Conference of City and Town Committees, 1931); Frederick R. Black, *Charlestown Navy Yard, 1890–1973* (Boston: Boston National Historical Park, National Park Service, 1988), 505–65.

24 Site Subcommittee of Committee 8 Verbatim Minutes of Meetings, Vol. XIII, UNA; promotional brochure, *UNO: Boston Answers Seven Questions* (n.p.,1945), 12, Rotch Library, School of Architecture and Planning, Massachusetts Institute of Technology, Cambridge, Mass.

25 Barbara Miller Solomon, *Ancestors and Immigrants: A Changing New England Tradition* (Chicago: University of Chicago Press, 1956); Stephen H. Norwood, "Marauding Youth and the Christian Front: Antisemitic Violence in Boston and New York during World War II," *American Jewish History* 91.2 (2003): 233–67.

26 *Boston Globe*, Nov. 24, 1945; *UNO: Boston Answers Seven Questions*, 2–3.

27 John E. Fogarty to James F. Byrnes, Oct. 26, 1945, enclosed with *An Invitation to the United Nations Organization to Establish Permanent Headquarters in Historic Newport, Rhode Island*, box 7, Records of the Preparatory Commission of the United Nations (S-0539), UNA (hereafter Prep. Comm. Records).

28 *NYT*, Jan. 31, 1945, and Jan. 11, 1967; *Providence (RI) Journal*, Nov. 17, 1945; John W. Haley, "Newport and the UNO," radio program by the "Rhode Island Historian," WJAR–Providence, Jan. 2, 1946, John Nicholas Brown Papers, John Nicholas Brown Center, Brown University, Providence, R.I.

29 Daniel Snydacker, "The Great Depression in Newport," *Newport History* 58 (Spring 1985): 42–55; Barbara A. Schreier and Michele Majer, "The Resort of Pure Fashion: Newport, Rhode Island, 1890–1914," *Rhode Island History* 47.1 (1989): 22–34; *NYT*, Oct. 8, 1942, and April 5, 1949; *Providence (RI) Journal*, Nov. 18, 1945.

30 *Providence (RI) Journal*, April 3 and May 29, 1945.

31 *An Invitation to the United Nations Organization to Establish Permanent Headquarters in Historic Newport, Rhode Island*; *Providence (RI) Journal*, May 10, May 11, and Nov. 17, 1945; *NYT*, Oct. 26, 1941, March 21, 1947, and Feb. 7, 1966.

32 *An Invitation to the United Nations Organization to Establish Permanent Headquarters in Historic Newport, Rhode Island*; *NYT*, Feb. 24, 1921.

33 For elaboration, see Charlene Mires, "The Lure of New England and the Search for the Capital of the World," *New England Quarterly* 79 (March 2006): 37–64.

34 H. Wayne Morgan and Anne Hodges Morgan, *Oklahoma: A Bicentennial History* (New York: Norton, 1976); Arrell Morgan Gibson, *Oklahoma: A History of Five Centuries*, 2nd ed. (Norman: University of Oklahoma Press, 1981); "Choate, Ben," *The Oklahoman*, Jan. 24, 1992.

35 Gibson, *Oklahoma*, 232; Donald K. Tolman, "Through the Ether: The Birth of Radio in Central Oklahoma," *Chronicles of Oklahoma* 61 (2): 130–47; Keith Tolman, "Printing Ink and Flyingwires: Oklahoma Journalism and the Promotion of Aviation," *Chronicles of Oklahoma* 72 (1): 22–35; Duane K. Hale, "Uncle Sam's Warriors: American Indians in World War II," *Chronicles of Oklahoma* 69 (4): 408–9.

36 Ben P. Choate to Harry S. Truman, Oct. 6, 1945, box 7, Prep. Comm. Records, UNA; Ben P. Choate to John D. Rockefeller Jr., Oct. 25, 1945, folder 27, box 27, Office of Messrs. Rockefeller (RG III 2 Q), World Affairs, RAC; Ben P. Choate to William Stigler, Oct. 6, 1945, box 5, W. G. Stigler Collection, CAC (hereafter Stigler Collection); Ben P. Choate to Robert S. Kerr, Oct. 21, 1945, box 14, Robert S. Kerr Collection, CAC (hereafter Kerr Collection).

37 Ben P. Choate to Harry S. Truman, Oct. 6, 1945, box 7, Prep. Comm. Records; Ben P. Choate to William Stigler, Oct. 6, 1945, box 67, Stigler Collection; Ben P. Choate to John D. Rockefeller Jr., Oct. 25, 1945, folder 237, box 27, Office of Messrs. Rockefeller (RG III 2 Q), World Affairs, RAC.

38 *McAlester (OK) Democrat,* undated clipping (prior to Nov. 2, 1945), box 14, Kerr Collection.

39 Ben P. Choate to Robert S. Kerr, Oct. 21, 1945, and Don McBride to Robert S. Kerr, Nov. 28, 1945, box 14, Kerr Collection; Southeast Oklahoma Development Association, Oklahoma State Planning and Resources Board, and University of Oklahoma, *A Social and Economic Survey of Six Counties in Southeastern Oklahoma* (Norman: University of Oklahoma Press, 1946), 225–33; Marsha L. Weisiger, "The Reception of *The Grapes of Wrath* in Oklahoma: A Reappraisal," *Chronicles of Oklahoma* 70 (4): 394–415; *Tulsa Daily World,* Nov. 12, 1945.

40 Ben P. Choate to John D. Rockefeller Jr., Oct. 25, 1945; Bobby H. Johnson, "Singing Oklahoma's Praises: Boosterism in the Soonerland," *Great Plains Journal,* Fall 1971, 57–65; Ward, *Selling Places,* 9–28.

41 *Oklahoma Proposes the Tuskahoma Area* (n.d., n.p.), brochure, box 5, Stigler Collection; McAlester Chamber of Commerce, "Information Brief," Nov. 15, 1945, box 7, Prep. Comm. Records.

42 Ben Yagoda, *Will Rogers: A Biography* (Norman: University of Oklahoma Press, 1993); Peter B. Dedek, *Hip to the Trip: A Cultural History of Route 66* (Albuquerque: University of New Mexico Press, 2007), 28–62; Jim Ross, "'Proud of What It Means': Route 66, Oklahoma's Mother Road," *Chronicles of Oklahoma* 73 (3): 260–77.

43 Yagoda, *Will Rogers*; Lewis Nichols, "The Play," NYT, April 1, 1943; Richard Rodgers and Oscar Hammerstein 2nd, *Oklahoma!* (New York: Random House, 1943), 20, 37, 120, 130, 142; Timothy P. Donovan, "Oh, What a Beautiful Mornin': The Musical *Oklahoma!* and the Popular Mind of 1943," *Journal of Popular Culture* 8 (3): 477–88.

44 Elmer Tanner to United Nations Council, Dec. 1, 1945, and N. B. Johnson to United Nations Council, December (n.d.), 1945, box 7, Prep. Comm. Records.

45 Elmer Tanner to George B. Schwabe, Dec. 3, 1945; Frank B. Elrod to George B. Schwabe, Dec. 8, 1945; Maggie Fry to George B. Schwabe, Dec. 8, 1945; Evelyn Fun to George B. Schwabe, 1945, all in box 2, George B. Schwabe Collection, CAC; White House acknowledgments to Claremore appeals in box 524, Truman Official Files, HST; *Tulsa Daily World,* Dec. 2, 1945.

46 L. U. Reavis, *Saint Louis: The Future Great City of the World,* 2nd ed. (St. Louis: St. Louis County Court, 1870); Patrick E. McLear, "Logan U. Reavis: Nineteenth-Century Urban Promoter," *Missouri Historical Review* 66 (4): 567–88; John R. Gold and Margaret M. Gold, *Cities of Culture: Staging International Festivals and the Urban Agenda, 1851–2000* (Burlington, Vt.: Ashgate, 2005), 86, 154.

47 St. Louis Chamber of Commerce, *St. Louis Invites the United Nations,* promotional booklet (1945), Missouri Historical Society, St. Louis, Mo.

48 *Oklahoma Proposes the Tuskahoma Area,* promotional brochure, Stigler Collection.

49 *Rapid City (SD) Daily Journal,* Oct. 10, 1945.

CHAPTER 5

1 Janet R. Daly Bednarek, *America's Airports: Airfield Development, 1918–1947* (College Station: Texas A&M University Press), 158; *Philadelphia Bulletin,* July 5, 1945.

2 L. Stauffer Oliver, "Record of the Trip of the Philadelphia Delegation to London," Nov. 12–13, 1945, United Nations 1945–1946 Papers of Delegates to Meeting to Select Site for Capitol, HSP; Robert L. Johnson to Harry S. Truman, Oct. 25, 1945, box 524, Truman Official Files, HST.

3 Oliver, "Record," Nov. 13–14, 1945; Carl Solberg, *Conquest of the Skies: A History of Commercial Aviation in America* (Boston: Little, Brown, 1979), 259–309.

4 Paul E. Bellamy, "Statement of Paul Bellamy on Leaving for London," Nov. 12, 1945, box 4, Records of the Preparatory Commission of the United Nations (S-0539), UNA (hereafter Prep. Comm. Records); *Rapid City (SD) Daily Journal,* Nov. 21, 1945; *Chicago Daily Tribune,* Nov. 15, 1945; *Chicago Herald-American,* Nov. 15 and 20, 1945.

5 *Chicago Herald-American,* Nov. 20, 1945; Thomas E. Hachey, ed., "A Confidential Account of Mayor Kelly's Visit to London, November 1945," *Journal of the Illinois State Historical Society* 70 (November 1977): 276–82.

6 *SFE,* Nov. 22 and 24, 1945; *SFC,* Nov. 25, 1945; *Boston Herald,* Nov. 25, 1945; *Boston Globe,* Nov. 26, 1945.

7 Oliver, "Record," Nov. 15–21, 1945; *Chicago Herald-American,* Nov. 21 and 23, 1945.

8 Oliver, "Record," Nov. 15–21, 1945; Paul E. Bellamy to Karl Mundt, March 20, 1953, box 50, Paul E. Bellamy Papers, USD (hereafter Bellamy Papers).

9 Paul Bellamy, "Report on World Capital," Sept. 12, 1945, box 56, Bellamy Papers; Chase S. Osborn to Preston William Slosson, Dec. 4, 1945, box 83, Records of the Executive Office, Harry F. Kelly, Governor, MSA; *The Oklahoman,* Dec. 27, 1945.

10 Paul Bellamy, "Report on World Capital"; Chase S. Osborn to Preston William Slosson, Dec. 4, 1945; *The Oklahoman,* Dec. 27, 1945; Memorandum of Conversation, Oct. 13, 1945, box 247, Papers of Edward Stettinius Jr., UVA (hereafter Stettinius Papers); Committee 8 (General Questions) Verbatim Minutes, Nov. 28, 1945, box 4, Prep. Comm. Records; Radio program transcript, Nov. 27, 1945, box 55, Bellamy Papers.

11 *NYT,* Dec. 2, 1945; Robert L. Stearns and Gilbert J. Brown to Denver Chamber of Commerce, Nov. 27, 1945, box 141, Denver Chamber of Commerce Records (WH1216), DPL.

12 Verbatim Minutes, First Meeting of the Site Sub-Committee of Committee 8, Dec. 1, 1945, box 5, Prep. Comm. Records; on gifts, Verbatim Minutes, Committee 8, Dec. 11, 1945.

13 Report by the Executive Committee to the Preparatory Commission of the United Nations, Nov. 12, 1945 (UN Document PC/EX/113/Rev. 1), 116–18, UNA.

14 The campaign for Atlantic City originated with the *Atlantic City Press* in October and gathered statewide momentum, including support from Governor Walter E. Edge, an Atlantic City native. Resolution of the Board of Commissioners of Atlantic City, N.J., Oct. 25, 1945, and *To the United Nations Organization, an Invitation from the State of New Jersey and the City of Atlantic City*, box 6, Prep. Comm. Records; Verbatim Minutes, Site Sub-Committee, Dec. 1, 1945; *Atlantic City (NJ) Press*, Oct. 18, Nov. 1, and Nov. 20, 1945, and Dec. 19, 1985; Steven V. Ward, *Selling Places: The Marketing and Promotion of Towns and Cities, 1850–2000* (New York: Routledge, 1998), 55.

15 Verbatim Minutes, Site Sub-Committee, Dec. 1, 1945; subsequent testimony by Bellamy from this source. Black Hills campaign materials in box 4, Prep. Comm. Records.

16 Oliver, "Record," Dec. 1, 1945.

17 Bellamy, Memorandum for Committee of the Preparatory Commission, Dec. 5, 1945, enclosed with Bellamy to Eduardo Zuleta Angel, Dec. 5, 1945, box 4, Prep. Comm. Records.

18 Verbatim Minutes, Site Sub-Committee, Dec. 1, 1945.

19 Verbatim Minutes, Site Sub-Committee, Dec. 1, 1945.

20 Verbatim Minutes, Site-Subcommittee, Dec. 1, 1945; Chicago campaign materials in box 4, Prep. Comm. Records; *NYT*, Dec. 2, 1945; "In the U.S. Tradition," *Time*, Dec. 10, 1945, www.time.com/time/magazine/article/0,9171,852637,00.html.

21 Robert L. Stearns, "A Travel Guide for the Future," *University of Colorado Bulletin*, June 1943, 6; Stearns, "The Post-War Era and America's Responsibility for World Peace," speech transcript, n.d., Robert L. Stearns Collection, box 12, Archives, UCB (hereafter Stearns Collection); "Biographical Data concerning Robert L. Stearns," box 4, Stearns Collection; *Boulder Daily Camera*, undated news clipping, box 5, Stearns Collection.

22 Denver Chamber of Commerce, *Industrial Denver* (n.d.) and Denver Chamber of Commerce Collection, Minutes of Meetings, Nov. 2, 9, and 30, 1945, DPL; *Denver: The Queen City of the Plains* (Denver: Tammen Curio, 1905); *Denver Today: Descriptive—Statistical—Pictorial* (Denver: Denver Chamber of Commerce, 1912); *Denver! The City of Hospitality!* (Denver: Denver Convention and Tourist Bureau, n.d.); James A. Marsh to Harry S. Truman, Oct. 4, 1945, box 6, Prep. Comm. Records; Stephen J. Essex and Brian S. Chalkley, "The Winter Olympics: Driving Urban Change, 1924–2002," in John R. Gold

and Margaret M. Gold, *Olympic Cities: City Agendas, Planning, and the World's Games, 1896–2012* (New York: Routledge, 2007), 50.

23 Verbatim Minutes, Site Sub-Committee, Dec. 1, 1945.

24 Oliver, "Record," Dec. 1, 1945.

25 Oliver, "Record," Dec. 1, 1945; Verbatim Minutes, Site Sub-Committee, Dec. 1, 1945.

26 Oliver, "Record," Nov. 30-Dec. 1, 1945 (November 30 by John G. Herndon due to illness of Oliver); *Philadelphia: Cradle of Liberty* (Philadelphia: Citizens Committee to Make Philadelphia the Permanent Home of the United Nations, 1945); Christopher M. Law, *Urban Tourism: The Visitor Economy and the Growth of Large Cities*, 2nd ed. (New York: Continuum, 2002).

27 Oliver, "Record," Dec. 1, 1945; Verbatim Minutes, Site Sub-Committee, Dec. 1, 1945.

28 Telephone conversation summary, Oct. 22, 1945, box 247, Stettinius Papers; Verbatim Minutes, Site Sub-Committee, Dec. 1, 1945; San Francisco campaign materials in San Francisco Chamber of Commerce Minutes, 1945, CHS, and box 5, Prep. Comm. Records.

29 Verbatim Minutes, Site Sub-Committee, Dec. 1, 1945.

30 Oliver, "Record," Dec. 1–2, 1945; Bellamy, Memorandum for Committee of the Preparatory Commission.

31 Verbatim Minutes, Site Sub-Committee, Dec. 8 and 20, 1945.

32 Verbatim Minutes, Site Sub-Committee, Dec. 20, 1945; campaign materials for St. Louis and New Orleans in boxes 6 and 7, Prep. Comm. Records; J. Christopher Schnell, "Chicago versus St. Louis: A Reassessment of the Great Rivalry," *Missouri Historical Review*, April 1977, 245–65; New Orleans–San Francisco rivalry chronicled in *The Logical Point: An Illustrated Monthly for the Advancement of the World's Panama Exposition* (1910), Louisiana Collection, UNO, New Orleans, La.

33 Verbatim Minutes, Committee 8 (General Questions), Nov. 28-Dec. 15, 1945, UNA; *London Observer*, Dec. 16, 1945; *NYT*, Dec. 16, 1945.

Two votes were taken in Committee 8. In the first, delegates were asked whether the Executive Committee recommendation should be amended to place the United Nations in Europe. The amendment was defeated 23–25, with two abstentions. Nations voting in favor of Europe were Belgium, Canada, Colombia, Denmark, Ethiopia, France, Greece, India, Iran, Iraq, Lebanon, Liberia, Luxembourg, Netherlands, New Zealand, Norway, Poland, Saudi Arabia, Syria, Turkey, Union of South Africa, United Kingdom, and Uruguay. (The two Latin American nations voting in favor, Uruguay and Colombia, had entered and seconded the motion in order to force a vote; having done so, they were obligated to vote in favor.) Voting against were Argentina, Australia, Bolivia, Brazil, Byelo-Russia, Chile, China, Cuba, Czechoslovakia, Dominican Republic, Egypt, El Salvador, Guatemala, Haiti, Honduras,

Mexico, Nicaragua, Panama, Paraguay, Peru, Philippine Commonwealth, Soviet Union, Ukraine, Venezuela, and Yugoslavia; abstaining were Ecuador and
the United States.

The second vote, on accepting the Executive Committee report and therefore a location in the United States, passed by a wider margin, 30–14, with six
abstentions. (Some nations abstained to protest the procedure of taking an
additional committee vote on the Executive Committee's recommendation.)
Voting in favor were Argentina, Australia, Bolivia, Brazil, Byelo-Russia, Chile,
China, Cuba, Czechoslovakia, Dominican Republic, Egypt, El Salvador, Guatemala, Haiti, Honduras, India, Iran, Mexico, Nicaragua, Panama, Paraguay,
Peru, Philippine Commonwealth, Poland, Soviet Union, Turkey, Ukraine,
Uruguay, Venezuela, Yugoslavia; against, Belgium, Canada, Denmark, France,
Greece, Iraq, Lebanon, Liberia, Luxembourg, the Netherlands, Norway, Saudi
Arabia, Union of South Africa, United Kingdom; abstaining, Colombia, Ecua-
dor, Ethiopia, New Zealand, Syria, and the United States. After the balloting,
the result was made unanimous in favor of the United States as headquarters
location.

34 Verbatim Minutes, Committee 8, Dec. 13, 17, and 21, 1945; Text of Mayor F. H.
LaGuardia's Sunday Broadcast to the People of New York, Dec. 16, 1945, reel
248, Office of the Mayor Subject Files, NYMA.

35 *Beloit (Wisc.) Daily News*, Dec. 17, 1945; *New Orleans Item*, Dec. 18, 1945; *Miami Herald*, Dec. 28, 1945; *Rocky Mountain News*, Dec. 30, 1945.

36 This number includes proposals published in newspapers and submitted to
U.S. public officials as well as those communicated directly to the United Na-
tions; therefore, it exceeds the total in UN records and repeated in the press
and subsequent histories of the UN. Correspondence in boxes 4, 5, 6, and 7,
Prep. Comm. Records. *Washington Post*, Dec. 19, 1945; *Stillwater (OK) Daily
News Press*, Dec. 17 and 19, 1945.

37 Mabel Morris to the United Nations, Dec. 2, 1945, box 4, Prep. Comm.
Records.

CHAPTER 6

1 Committee 8 (General Questions), Verbatim Minutes, Dec. 20, 1945, and
Summary Record of Meetings, Dec. 20, 1945, box 4, Records of the Prepara-
tory Commission of the United Nations (S-0539), UNA (hereafter Prep.
Comm. Records); *SFC*, Dec. 4, 21, and 22, 1945; *SFCB*, Dec. 7, 1945; *SFN*,
Dec. 8 and 22, 1945.

2 *SFCB*, Dec. 22, 1945; *SFC*, Dec. 22, 1945; *SFN*, Dec. 22, 1945. The Preparatory
Commission's actions were a sharp departure from the methodical procedures
followed by other international governing bodies such as the Bureau International des Expositions (BIE) or the International Olympic Committee, which

screened proposals for hosting world's fairs or the Olympic Games. See John R. Gold and Margaret M. Gold, *Cities of Culture: Staging International Festivals and the Urban Agenda, 1851–2000* (Burlington, Vt.: Ashgate, 2005), 82, 149.

3 Verbatim Minutes, Committee 8 (General Questions), Dec. 15, 1945, UNA.

4 United Kingdom Delegation, "Some Further Considerations in Choosing the Site in the United States," Dec. 16, 1945, box 1, Prep. Comm. Records; on the British position, see Leo Pasvolsky, Memorandum of Conversation, Oct. 11, 1945, and Adlai Stevenson to Secretary of State, telegram, Nov. 28, 1945, in *Foreign Relations of the United States, Diplomatic Papers 1945*. Vol. 1, *General: The United Nations* (Washington, D.C.: USGPO, 1967), 1457, 1480–83.

5 United Kingdom Delegation, "Some Further Considerations."

6 United Kingdom Delegation, "Some Further Considerations"; Gunnar Myrdal, *An American Dilemma: The Negro Problem and Modern Democracy* (New York: Harper & Row, 1944); David W. Southern, *Gunnar Myrdal and Black-White Relations: The Use and Abuse of "An American Dilemma," 1944–1969* (Baton Rouge: Louisiana State University Press, 1987).

7 United Kingdom Delegation, "Some Further Considerations"; *NYT*, May 18 and Dec. 18, 1945; *Chicago Tribune*, Dec. 18, 1945; *Rocky Mountain News*, Dec. 20, 1945; *Times of London*, July 21, 1976; United Nations Charter, Chapter IX, Article 55.

8 Verbatim Minutes, Committee 8, Dec. 21, 1945; Charles Kingsley Webster diary, Dec. 26, 1945, reprinted in P. A. Reynolds and E. J. Hughes, *The Historian as Diplomat: Charles Kingsley Webster and the United Nations, 1939–1946* (London: Martin Robertson, 1976), 81.

9 Verbatim Minutes, Committee 8, Dec. 22, 1945.

10 Verbatim Minutes, Committee 8, Dec. 22, 1945. In the vote on the West, the nations voting against were Argentina, Belgium, Brazil, Byelo-Russia, Canada, China, Colombia, Czechoslovakia, Denmark, Ethiopia, France, India, Liberia, Netherlands, New Zealand, Norway, Poland, Soviet Union, Turkey, Ukraine, United Kingdom, and Yugoslavia. Abstaining were Bolivia, Cuba, Dominican Republic, Egypt, Haiti, Mexico, Nicaragua, Peru, Syria, the United States, Uruguay, and Venezuela.

In the vote on the East, votes in favor were cast by Argentina, Belgium, Brazil, Byelo-Russia, Canada, Colombia, Cuba, Czechoslovakia, Denmark, Ethiopia, India, Iran, Mexico, Netherlands, New Zealand, Norway, Peru, Poland, Soviet Union, Turkey, Ukraine, United Kingdom, Uruguay, Venezuela, and Yugoslavia. Voting against were Australia, China, Ecuador, France, and Liberia; abstaining were Bolivia, Chile, Dominican Republic, Egypt, Haiti, Honduras, Nicaragua, Saudi Arabia, Syria, and the United States.

11 Denver Chamber of Commerce Minutes, Board of Directors, April 11, 1946, box 141, Denver Chamber of Commerce Records (WH1216), DPL; *Sioux Falls*

(SD) Argus-Leader, Dec. 22, 1945; *SFN*, Dec. 26, 1945; *The Oklahoman*, Dec. 28, 1945.

12 *Indianapolis Star*, Dec. 23, 1945; *Michigan City (IN) News-Dispatch*, Dec. 22, 1945; *Niagara Falls (NY) Gazette*, Dec. 24, 1945; *PR*, Dec. 23, 1945.

13 Correspondence in boxes 4, 5, 6, and 7, Prep. Comm. Records; on the construction of New England identity prior to World War II, see Dona Brown, *Inventing New England: Regional Tourism in the Nineteenth Century* (Washington, D.C.: Smithsonian Institution Press, 1995); Joseph A. Conforti, *Imagining New England: Explorations of Regional Identity from the Pilgrims to the Mid-Twentieth Century* (Chapel Hill: University of North Carolina Press, 2001); Joseph S. Wood with Michael P. Steinitz, *The New England Village* (Baltimore, Md.: Johns Hopkins University Press, 1997).

14 Memorandum by the Australian Delegation, Dec. 27, 1945, Document PC/ICH/W6, box 2, Prep. Comm. Records.

15 Interim Committee on Headquarters, Qualifications and Standards, Dec. 28, 1945, Document PC/ICH/2, box 2, Prep. Comm. Records.

16 Memorandum by the Australian Delegation; Interim Committee on Headquarters, Qualifications and Standards, Dec. 28, 1945, UNA; Interim Committee on Headquarters, "Areas and Cities in the East of the U.S.A. From Which Offers Have Been Received Grouped on a Geographical Basis," Dec. 27, 1945, Document PC/ICH/W7, box 2, Prep. Comm. Records; Elizabeth Tandy Shermer, "Sunbelt Boosterism: Industrial Recruitment, Economic Development, and Growth Politics in the Developing Sunbelt," in Michelle Nickerson and Darren Dochuk, eds., *Sunbelt Rising: The Politics of Place, Space, and Region* (Philadelphia: University of Pennsylvania Press, 2011), 31–57.

17 Verbatim Minutes, Interim Committee on Headquarters, Dec. 27, 1945, box 5, Prep. Comm. Records; subsequent quotations and descriptions of Dec. 27 meeting from this source. William Ecenbarger, *Walkin' the Line: A Journey from Past to Present along the Mason-Dixon* (New York: Evans, 2000), 13–17; Thomas D. Cope, "Charles Mason and Jeremiah Dixon," *Scientific Monthly* 62 (June 1946): 541–54.

18 On the interaction between U.S. race relations and international affairs, see Thomas Borstelmann, *The Cold War and the Color Line: American Race Relations in the Global Arena* (Cambridge, Mass.: Harvard University Press, 2001), and Mary L. Dudziak, *Cold War Civil Rights: Race and the Image of American Democracy* (Princeton, N.J.: Princeton University Press, 2000).

19 Thomas J. Sugrue, *The Origins of the Urban Crisis: Race and Inequality in Postwar Detroit* (1996; repr. Princeton, N.J.: Princeton University Press, 2005), 17–31; Margaret B. Tinkcom, "Depression and War, 1929–1946," in Russell F. Weigley, ed., *Philadelphia: A 300-Year History* (New York: Norton, 1982), 642–44; Stephen H. Norwood, "Marauding Youth and the Christian Front:

Antisemitic Violence in Boston and New York during World War II," *American Jewish History* 91.2 (2003): 233–67; *NYT*, April 18 and July 12, 1945.

20 *Charlottesville (VA) Daily Progress*, Dec. 6 and 13, 1945; Thomas L. Farrar to Gladwyn Jebb, Oct. 19 and Dec. 5, 1945, box 5, Prep. Comm. Records; Virginia Peninsula Committee to Gladwyn Jebb, Dec. 13, 1945, and Gladwyn Jebb to Virginia Peninsula Committee, Dec. 15, 1945, box 7, Prep. Comm. Records (misfiled with Newport, Rhode Island); *Virginia Gazette*, Nov. 16, 1945, and Jan. 4, 1946.

21 Interim Committee on Headquarters, Rough Time-Table for Inspection Group, Document PC/ICH/W11, postdated to expected date of inspection tour, Jan. 2, 1945, box 2, Prep. Comm. Records; on isolationism and the *Chicago Tribune*, Jerome E. Edwards, *The Foreign Policy of Col. McCormick's Tribune* (Reno: University of Nevada Press, 1971); Joseph Gies, *The Colonel of Chicago* (New York: Dutton, 1979).

22 Stellanova Osborn to Mrs. Nelson Long, Dec. 28, 1945, box 92, Chase Osborn Papers, UM; *Indianapolis Star*, Dec. 28 and 30, 1945; *Chicago Herald-American*, Dec. 28, 1945; *St. Louis Post-Dispatch*, Dec. 29, 1945; Aloys P. Kaufmann and George C. Smith to Huntington Gilchrist, Dec. 28, 1945, box 6, Prep. Comm. Records.

23 M. Q. Sharpe, Dwight Griswold, and Lester C. Hunt to Gladwyn Jebb, Dec. 28, 1945, box 4, Prep. Comm. Records.

24 Verbatim Minutes, Interim Committee on Headquarters, Dec. 28, 1945, box 5, Prep. Comm. Records; subsequent quotations and description of Dec. 28 meeting from this source.

25 Adlai Stevenson to Gladwyn Jebb, Dec. 1, 1945, box 4, Prep. Comm. Records.

26 On diplomats and the North Shore, Joseph E. Garland, *Boston's Gold Coast: The North Shore, 1890–1929* (Boston: Little, Brown, 1981).

27 John Nicholas Brown to Sherman Stonor, Jan. 25, 1946, John Nicholas Brown Papers, John Nicholas Brown Center, Providence, R.I.

28 Mayor's Committee on Permanent Headquarters for United Nations Organization to UNO Preparatory Commission, Dec. 17, 1945, box 7, Prep. Comm. Records; Fiorello LaGuardia to William O'Dwyer, Dec. 5, 1945, reel 82, Office of the Mayor (William O'Dwyer), Subject Files, NYMA (hereafter O'Dwyer Subject Files); *NYT*, Dec. 3, 10, and 17, 1945; Miriam Greenberg, *Branding New York: How a City in Crisis Was Sold to the World* (New York: Routledge, 2005), 10.

29 James J. Lyons to Preparatory Commission Site Committee, Dec. 14, 1945, and Harold Dodds to Adlai Stevenson, Dec. (n.d.), 1945, box 4, Prep. Comm. Records; James J. Lyons to Eleanor Roosevelt, Dec. 27, 1945, copy in reel 82, O'Dwyer Subject Files; *NYT*, Dec. 16, 1945.

30 John Roberts Hart to Roberto MacEachen, Dec. 29, 1945, and Robert Gray

Taylor to Gladwyn Jebb, Oct. 22, 1945, and Dec. 27, 1945, box 4, Prep. Comm. Records.

31 L. Stauffer Oliver to Francis J. Myers, Jan. 4, 1946, United Nations 1945–1946 Papers of Delegates to Meeting to Select Site for Capitol, HSP; *PR*, Dec. 29, 1945.

CHAPTER 7

1 Stoyan Gavrilovic, interview by Clark Eichelberger, Columbia Broadcasting System, Jan. 26, 1946, transcript in box 62, Clark M. Eichelberger Papers, NYPL (hereafter Eichelberger Papers); *NYT*, Feb. 3, 1965.

2 Gavrilovic, interview by Eichelberger.

3 George A. Smock to Huntington Gilchrist, Jan. 4, 1946, and Clyde Potts to Stoyan Gavrilovic, Jan. 3, 1946, box 8, Records of the Preparatory Commission of the United Nations (S-0539), UNA (hereafter Prep. Comm. Records); William O'Dwyer to Stoyan Gavrilovic, Jan. 14, 1946, box 246, Nelson A. Rockefeller Papers—Personal Projects (RG 4), RAC; *Niagara Falls (NY) Gazette*, Jan. 5, 1946; *Sioux Falls (SD) Argus-Leader*, Jan. 4, 1946; *SFC*, Jan. 7, 1946.

4 Townsend Scudder, *Concord: American Town* (Boston: Little, Brown, 1947), 356–59; Federal Writers Project of the Works Progress Administration for the State of Massachusetts, *Massachusetts: A Guide to Its Places and People* (Boston: Houghton Mifflin, 1937), 213. Concord's population rose from 7,056 in 1925 to 7,972 in 1940 and 8,382 in 1945; federal, state, and town census figures compiled in Town of Concord, Massachusetts, "Population History" (October 2005), ConcordMA.virtualtownhall.net/Pages/ConcordMA_TownClerk/population.

5 *Boston Post*, Nov. 9, 1945; Adlai Stevenson to Gladwyn Jebb, Dec. 1, 1945, box 4, Prep. Comm. Records.

6 Residents' reactions appear in *Concord (MA) Journal*, Dec. 20 and 27, 1945, Jan. 3 and 10, 1946 (including letters with poetry), and Jan. 17, 1946 (including quotations of Emerson); *Concord (MA) Enterprise*, Jan. 3, 17, and 24, 1946. I thank Leslie Perrin Wilson, Curator of Special Collections, Concord Free Public Library, for sharing materials on the Concord dispute. See Wilson, "The United Nations in Concord? 'My How the Fur Flew,'" *Concord (MA) Journal*, Nov. 30, 2000. On world federalists, see Scudder, *Concord*, 387–90.

7 *Concord (MA) Journal*, Dec. 27, 1945, and Jan. 3, 1946; *Boston Globe*, Jan. 5, 1946.

8 *Greenwich (CT) Time*, Jan. 3, 1946.

9 Commissioners of Plymouth to Gladwyn Jebb, Dec. 24, 1945, and J. Joseph McCabe, Chairman, Board of Selectmen, to Gladwyn Jebb, Dec. 12, 1945, box 4, Prep. Comm. Records, UNA; *Presenting Orange, Massachusetts, as a*

Permanent Seat of United Nations Organization (undated, c. Dec. 1945-Jan. 1946). I thank David Glassberg for supplying me with a photocopy of the brochure from Orange, Mass. Booster appeals to the UN reflected the symbolism of the New England village described by Joseph S. Wood: "The village is the material symbol of a strongly held American tradition of New England covenanted community, cultural enlightenment, and democratic self government." Joseph S. Wood with Michael P. Steinitz, *The New England Village* (Baltimore, Md.: Johns Hopkins University Press, 1997), 136. As Wood has demonstrated, this ideal was a nineteenth-construction that differed from historical reality of the sixteenth through eighteenth centuries.

The number of Massachusetts hopefuls varies in press accounts; no comprehensive list was published, and the absence of archived public papers of Maurice J. Tobin prevents verification. See appendix for known competitors in Massachusetts.

10 Itinerary in *Report and Recommendations of the Inspection Group on Selecting the Permanent Site and Interim Facilities for the Headquarters of the United Nations* [c. Feb. 1946], box 1, Executive Assistant to the Secretary General (S-0186), United Nations Interim and Permanent Site Headquarters—Records, UNA.

11 "Interim Committee on Headquarters: Names of Members of the Inspection Group," Jan. 6, 1946, and Inspection Group, "Interim Committee of Headquarters of the United Nations Program at Regional Planning Association," Jan. 8, 1946, boxes 41 and 42, Papers of Huntington Gilchrist, LOC (hereafter Gilchrist Papers).

12 Robert Moses to H. V. Kaltenborn, Dec. 27, 1945; Moses to James A. Farley, Jan. 3, 1946; and Moses to Henry Gruere, Jan. 18, 1946, all in boxes 26 and 27, Robert Moses Papers, NYPL (hereafter Moses Papers); R. S. Childs to Huntington Gilchrist, Jan. 7, 1946, box 40, Gilchrist Papers.

13 William O'Dwyer to Stoyan Gavrilovic, Jan. 14, 1946, box 246, Nelson A. Rockefeller—Personal Projects (RG 4), RAC; Interim Committee on Headquarters, Inspection Group—Terms of Reference (Preparatory Commission of the United Nations Document PC/ICH/1/Rev. 1), Dec. 31, 1945, Gilchrist Papers, box 41; *NYT,* Jan. 9, 1946; *Boston Globe,* Jan. 11, 1946.

14 *Poughkeepsie (NY) New Yorker,* Aug. 27, 1945; Resolution by Poughkeepsie Kiwanis Club, Aug. 28, 1945, and Resolution by American Legion Post 427, Aug. 29, 1945, box 1, Frederick A. Smith Collection, FDR (hereafter Smith Collection).

15 *Providence (RI) Journal,* Jan. 6, 1946; *PM,* Jan. 9, 1946.

16 *NYT,* Jan. 8, 1946; *Proposed Site, United Nations, Hyde Park, New York,* promotional brochure, Prep. Comm. Records; Pierre Jay to Huntington Gilchrist, Jan. 25, 1946, box 40, Gilchrist Papers; Benjamin Hufbauer, *Presidential*

Temples: How Memorials and Libraries Shape Public Memory (Lawrence: University Press of Kansas, 2006), 23–41.

17 Memorandum of telephone conversation, Jan. 2, 1946, box 1, Smith Collection; Russell Van Nest Black, "The Hyde Park District, Dutchess, County, New York State: A Report upon Its Possibilities for Development as the United Nations Headquarters," typescript, Jan. 23, 1946, Prep. Comm. Records.

18 *Boston Globe*, Jan. 11, 1946; C. Earl Morrow, "Land Suitable for Urban Expansion in the New York Metropolitan Region," *Regional Plan Bulletin* 66 (New York: Regional Planning Association, 1945); Roger Panetta, "Westchester, the American Suburb: A New Narrative," in Roger Panetta, ed., *Westchester: The American Suburb* (New York: Fordham University Press, 2006), 22–53.

19 *Boston Globe*, Jan. 11, 1946; *Tarrytown (NY) Daily News*, Jan. 11, 1946; Herbert C. Gerlach to Gladwyn Jebb, Dec. 15, 1945, box 7, Prep. Comm. Records.

20 *Hartford (CT) Courant*, Jan. 12, 1946; *Boston Globe*, Jan. 11 and 12, 1946; Raymond Baldwin to George Barrett, Jan. 2, 1946, box 448, Office of the Governor, Raymond E. Baldwin (RG5), CSL (hereafter Baldwin Records).

21 *Stamford (CT) Advocate*, Feb. 15, 1946.

22 *Boston Globe*, Jan. 14, 1946.

23 *Princeton (NJ) Herald*, Jan. 11 and 18, 1946.

24 *Morristown (NJ) Daily Record*, Dec. 24, 1945, Jan. 12 and 13–15, 1946; Clyde Potts to Stoyan Gavrilovic, Jan. 3, 1946, Huntington Gilchrist to Stoyan Gavrilovic, Jan. 28, 1946, and Huntington Gilchrist to Clyde Potts, Jan. 30, 1946, box 8, Prep. Comm. Records; Headquarters Site Selection Committee Minutes, Jan. 29, 1946, box 41, Gilchrist Papers; Walter R. Sharp to Huntington Gilchrist, Jan. 23 and 24, 1946, box 40, Gilchrist Papers.

25 *Atlantic City (NJ) Press*, Jan. 12, 13, and 15, 1946; *To the United Nations Organization, an Invitation from the State of New Jersey and the City of Atlantic City*, promotional brochure, Nov. 1945, box 8, Prep. Comm. Records; Bryant Simon, *Boardwalk of Dreams: Atlantic City and the Fate of Urban America* (New York: Oxford University Press, 2004); Steven V. Ward, *Selling Places: The Marketing and Promotion of Towns and Cities, 1850–2000* (New York: Routledge, 1998), 41–55.

26 *Atlantic City (NJ) Press*, Jan. 13 and 15, 1946; *NYT*, Jan. 14, 1946.

27 *NYT*, Jan. 17, 1946; *Boston Globe*, Jan. 15, 16, and 17, 1946.

28 *Quincy (MA) Patriot-Ledger*, Jan. 10, 11, and 14, 1946.

29 *Boston Globe*, Jan. 16 and 18, 1946; *Quincy (MA) Patriot-Ledger*, Jan. 17 and 18, 1946; *Beverly, Massachusetts Welcomes United Nations Organization*, promotional brochure, Jan. 1946, box 40, Gilchrist Papers.

30 *Boston Globe*, Jan. 19, 1946; *Providence (RI) Journal*, Jan. 19, 1946; *Worcester (MA) Evening Gazette*, Jan. 19, 1946.

31 *NYT*, Jan. 20, 1946; *Worcester (MA) Evening Gazette*, Jan. 26, 1946; *Boston Globe*, Jan. 26, 1946.

32 *Boston Globe*, Jan. 20 and 21, 1946; *Providence (RI) Journal*, Jan. 21, 1946; *Quincy (MA) Patriot-Ledger*, Jan. 21, 1946

33 *NYT*, Feb. 5, 1946.

34 *Greenwich (CT) Time*, Jan. 11, 14, and 24, and Feb. 6, 1946; *The Yale Farms*, undated promotional brochure, box 41, Gilchrist Papers; "Instructions Given to Consultants," Jan. 13, 1946, box 40, Gilchrist Papers; Ernest P. Goodrich, "United Nations Organization Proposed Permanent Headquarters Site at North Greenwich–Stamford Connecticut and New York," undated typescript, box 43, Gilchrist Papers.

35 *NYT*, Feb. 8, 1946; Charles D. Musgrove, "Building a Dream: Constructing a National Capital in Nanjing, 1927–1937," in Joseph W. Esherick, ed., *Remaking the Chinese City: Modernity and National Identity, 1900–1950* (Honolulu: University of Hawai'i Press, 2000), 139–57; Institute of Transportation Engineers, "Ernest P. Goodrich," www.ite.org/aboutite/honorarymembers/GoodrichEP.asp.

36 Account of telephone call and subsequent actions in John L. Gray, interview by Penny Bott, June 20, 1975, transcript in Greenwich Public Library, Greenwich, Conn., 2–5.

37 *Greenwich (CT) Time*, Jan. 31, 1946.

38 *Greenwich (CT) Time*, Feb. 1, 1946.

39 Meeting agendas Jan. 25, 28, 29, 30 and 31, and Feb. 1, 1946, box 41, Gilchrist Papers. In addition to the North Greenwich–Stamford report, studies commissioned included Frederick J. Adams, untitled study of North Shore area near Boston, Jan. 27, 1946; Arthur C. Coney, "Report on Feasibility of the Sudbury-Marlborough Site in the Boston Region for the Headquarters of the United Nations," undated; Joseph D. Leland and Roland N. Greeley, "Report to the Interim Committee on Headquarters of the United Nations of the Blue Hills Area, State of Massachusetts, U.S.A., as a Possible Site for the United Nations Headquarters," Jan. 27, 1946; Regional Plan Association, "General Data, New York Metropolitan Region and Sites Under Consideration for United Nations Headquarters," Jan. 26, 1946; Harold M. Lewis, "Report on Ridgefield, Conn.–Poundridge, N.Y., District as a Site for the United Nations Headquarters," Jan. 23, 1946; and Harold M. Lewis, "Report on Westchester-Amawalk District as a Site for United Nations Headquarters," Jan. 23, 1946. Typescripts of reports in box 43, Gilchrist Papers.

40 *Report and Recommendations of the Inspection Group*, 22. On the permanent site recommendations, the French delegate François Brière dissented because he felt that the group had exceeded its instructions. On the interim headquarters, the vote for New York was five to two, with Brière dissenting on the basis of instructions and the delegate of Iraq, Awni el Kalidy, favoring Atlantic City.

41   The inspection group's report listed other sites given serious consideration for the interim headquarters as Saratoga Springs, Minnewaska, Poughkeepsie, and White Plains, New York, and Asbury Park and Lakewood, New Jersey. *Report and Recommendations of the Inspection Group*, 61–62; on Fort Ethan Allen, Walter Sharp to Huntington Gilchrist, Jan. 23, 1946, and telephone message Jan. 28, 1946, box 40, Gilchrist Papers; on the Sperry Plant, Walter Sharp to Huntington Gilchrist, Jan. 17 and Jan. 23, 1946, and Stoyan Gavrilovic to William O'Dwyer, Jan. 18, 1946, box 40, Gilchrist Papers; Meeting agendas, Jan. 8, 13, 15, 17, 18, 24, 25, 28, 29, 30, and 31, and Feb. 1, 1946, box 41, Gilchrist Papers.

42   *Report and Recommendations of the Inspection Group*, 10–18, 58–80.

43   *Sioux Falls (SD) Argus-Leader*, Feb. 6, 1946; *SFC*, Jan. 13, 1946; *Niagara Falls (NY) Gazette*, Feb. 12, 1946.

44   *Greenwich (CT) Time*, Feb. 5, 1946; Herbert Gerlach to Thomas E. Dewey, Feb. 1, 1946, and Herbert Gerlach to Stoyan Gavrilovic, Feb. 1, 1946, Thomas E. Dewey Papers, UR; *Stamford (CT) Advocate*, Feb. 15, 1946.

45   Telegrams and letters in box 476, Baldwin Records; also in this collection, see pamphlet, Henry N. Flynt, *Should Greenwich Be a Community of Homes or the Suburb of the World Capital?* (Feb. 25, 1946). Letters about suburban character appear in *Greenwich (CT) Time*, Feb. 5, 1946.

46   *Greenwich (CT) Time*, Feb. 6, 1946.

47   *Greenwich (CT) Time*, Feb. 6, 1946.

48   Greenwich Town Meeting, Minutes Book 9, 70–72, Greenwich Town Hall, Greenwich, Conn.

49   *New York Post*, Feb. 6, 1946; *Chicago Daily Tribune*, Feb. 10, 1946; *Greenwich (CT) Time*, Feb. 4, 1946.

CHAPTER 8

1   *NYT*, Jan. 11, 1946; *Times of London*, Jan. 11, 1946.

2   Quoted in *NYT*, Feb. 8, 1946; C. T. S. Keep to Inspection Committee, United Nations Organization, Feb. 5, 1946, box 40, Papers of Huntington Gilchrist, LOC (hereafter Gilchrist Papers); Arthur H. Vandenberg Jr., *The Private Papers of Senator Vandenberg* (Boston: Houghton Mifflin, 1952), 237–51; Harry S. Truman, *The United States and the United Nations* (Washington, D.C.: USGPO, 1947), 25–27.

3   James A. Gazell, "Arthur H. Vandenberg, Internationalism, and the United Nations," *Political Science Quarterly* 88.3 (Sept. 1973): 375–94; Garry Boulard, "Arthur H. Vandenberg and the Formation of the United Nations," *Michigan History* 71.4 (July/Aug. 1987): 38–45.

4   Quoted in *NYT*, Feb. 8, 1946; Arthur Vandenberg to George A. Osborn, Oct. 10, 1945, box 83, Records of the Executive Office, Harry F. Kelly, Governor, 1943–46, RG42, MSA (hereafter Kelly Records).

5　Report of the Permanent Headquarters Committee to the General Assembly, Feb. 14, 1946, in United Nations, *Official Records, Plenary Meetings of the General Assembly Verbatim Record, 10 January–14 February 1946* (London: United Nations Organization, 1946), 671–76; *NYT*, Feb. 10, 1946.

6　*NYT*, Feb. 10, 1946.

7　*NYT*, Feb. 10, 11, and 14, 1946; *SFN*, Jan. 2, 1946. On additional site suggestions: Leo F. Caproni to Thomas E. Dewey, Feb. 8, 1946; E. E. Walker to Thomas E. Dewey, Feb. 13, 1946; and Irma Fueslein to Thomas E. Dewey, Feb. 11, 1946, Thomas E. Dewey Papers, UR (hereafter Dewey Papers). "Cut Bank Jaycees Send Invitation to UNO," *Congressional Record*, Feb. 13, 1946; "Governors of South Dakota, Wyoming, and Nebraska File Brief With United Nations Organization on Subject of Locating the World Capital," *Congressional Record*, Feb. 8, 1946.

8　Report of the Permanent Headquarters Committee, 673; *NYT*, Feb. 12, 1946.

9　The committee approved its report, incorporating these compromises, by 22–17, with four abstentions and eight absentees (the vote was taken after 11:00 p.m.). Voting in favor: Argentina, Belgium, Brazil, Byelo-Russia, Canada, China, Czechoslovakia, Dominican Republic, Greece, India, the Netherlands, New Zealand, Norway, Poland, South Africa, Turkey, Ukraine, Soviet Union, Britain, Uruguay, Venezuela, and Yugoslavia. Against: Australia, Bolivia, Chile, Cuba, Denmark, Ecuador, El Salvador, France, Honduras, Lebanon, Luxembourg, Mexico, Nicaragua, Peru, the Philippines, Saudi Arabia, and Syria. Abstentions: Colombia, Iran, Egypt, the United States. Absentees: Costa Rica, Ethiopia, Guatemala, Haiti, Iraq, Liberia, Panama, and Paraguay. In the General Assembly, the chair declared the report adopted after only one delegate, Pedro Lopez of the Philippines, rose to speak; Lopez later requested to have his vote recorded in opposition.

10　Text of speech in Official Records, Plenary Meetings of the General Assembly Verbatim Record, 10 January–14 February 1946, 535–37; *NYT*, March 18, 1957.

11　Wilkie Bushby to Edward R. Stettinius Jr., Feb. 10, 1946, box 247, Papers of Edward Stettinius Jr., UVA (hereafter Stettinius Papers).

12　Federal Writers' Project, *The WPA Guide to New York City* (1939; repr. New York: Random House, 1992), 514–15; *NYT*, Jan. 8, 1966.

13　*NYT*, Jan. 8, 1966.

14　James J. Lyons to United Nations Preparatory Commission Site Committee, Dec. 14, 1945, box 5, Records of the Preparatory Commission of the United Nations (S-0539), UNA (hereafter Prep. Comm. Records); *NYT*, Dec. 16, 1945; *WPA Guide to New York City*, 527.

15　*NYT*, Feb. 24, 1946.

16　*NYT*, Feb. 26, 1946.

17　*NYT*, March 20 and 23–25, 1946; David L. Bosco, *Five to Rule Them All: The*

UN Security Council and the Making of the Modern World (New York: Oxford University Press, 2009), 43–44.

18 Report by the Secretary-General on the Interim Site, April 30, 1946, file 2, Executive Assistant to the Secretary General (1946–61: Cordier) (S-0186), United Nations and Permanent Site Headquarters Records, UNA (hereafter Cordier Site Records); Trygve Lie, *In the Cause of Peace: Seven Years with the United Nations* (New York: Macmillan, 1954), 65–66.

19 Edward R. Stettinius, Calendar Notes, March 24 and May 15, 1946, box 248, Stettinius Papers; *NYT*, March 24, 1946.

20 Robert A. Caro, *The Power Broker: Robert Moses and the Fall of New York* (New York: Knopf, 1974); Lyons to O'Dwyer, Dec. 29, 1945, reel 82, Office of the Mayor (William O'Dwyer), Subject Files, NYMA (hereafter O'Dwyer Subject Files); Minutes of Meeting, 11 a.m. March 27, 1946, Stettinius Office, Savoy Plaza Hotel, box 248, Stettinius Papers.

21 *Greenwich (CT) Time*, Feb. 6, 1946, and March 4, 1946. A total of 5,505 residents voted to protest, while 2,019 voted against protesting. However, the *Greenwich Time* reported that more than 12,000 eligible voters did not participate, due in part to the unusual wording of the ballot, on which a vote of "yes" meant support for a protest, not support for the UN's site selection. Confusion and objections to the referendum also described in Raymond E. Baldwin to Theodore Yudain, March 6, 1946, and Maris Macintyre Leavitt to Raymond E. Baldwin, Aug. 8, 1946, box 476, Office of the Governor (RG5), Raymond E. Baldwin, CSL (hereafter Baldwin Records). Other informal polling reported in James D. Hopkins, *Our Voices Were Heard: The Selection of the United Nations Headquarters* (Pleasantville, N.Y.: Edwin G. Michaelian Institute for Sub/Urban Governance, 1984), 9.

22 Caro, *The Power Broker*, 771.

23 Executive Committee Minutes, United Nations Committee of the City of New York, March 19, 1946, box 157, Nelson A. Rockefeller—Personal Activities (RG III 4A), RAC.

24 Report by the Secretary-General on the Interim Site, April 30, 1946; Lie, *In the Cause of Peace*, 72–73; notes on private meetings in the Secretary General's office, March 27–April 9, 1946, box 1, Records of Secretaries-General Trygve Lie and Dag Hammarskjold (S-0847), UNA; William O'Dwyer to Grover Whalen, March 20, 1946, and Robert Moses to Trygve Lie, March 23, 1946, roll 84, Office of the Mayor, NYMA.

25 Meeting Minutes, March 27, 1946, Stettinius Papers.

26 Lie, *In the Cause of Peace*, 59–60.

27 Report by the Secretary-General on the Interim Site, April 30, 1946; *NYT*, April 12, 1946.

28 Report by the Secretary-General on the Interim Site, April 30, 1946; Lie, *In*

the Cause of Peace, 65; Lie, *Report of the Secretary-General on the Work of the Organization* (New York: United Nations, 1946), 40–42.

29 *NYT,* April 12, 1946.

30 Trygve Lie to William O'Dwyer, April 11, 1946, reel 84, Office of the Mayor, NYMA; Edward Stettinius, Calendar Notes, April 10, 1946, and Dean Acheson to Edward Stettinius, May 14, 1946, box 248, Stettinius Papers. A referendum in Lake Success on April 20, 1946, approved of the UN's move by a vote of 118 to 70 (from among 325 registered voters); *NYT,* April 21, 1946.

31 Robert Moses, Confidential Memorandum to Design Consultants on Flushing Meadow Plan, April 29, 1946, and Nelson Rockefeller to Winthrop Aldrich, April 26, 1946, box 246, Nelson A. Rockefeller—Personal Projects (RG 4), RAC; James J. Lyons to Trygve Lie, April 4, 1946, file 6, box 1, Cordier Site Records; *NYT,* April 12 and 21, 1946.

32 Le Corbusier, "Report," June 19, 1946, 26, Cordier Site Records; Stanislaus von Moos, *Le Corbusier: Elements of a Synthesis* (Cambridge, Mass.: MIT Press, 1979), 239–43.

33 Le Corbusier, "Report," June 19, 1946, 1, 26; *NYT,* June 30, 1946; Minutes of Conference with United Nations Headquarters Commission, New Haven Lawn Club, June 13, 1946, and Conference of United Nations and Connecticut Committees on Contacts and Legal Questions, Hunter College, New York City, June 27, 1946, box 476, Baldwin Records.

34 Le Corbusier, "Report," 1.

35 Le Corbusier, "Report," 16–18, 22–35; Le Corbusier, *Looking at City Planning,* trans. Eleanor Levieux (1946; New York: Grossman, 1971), 13–23; Stephen Gardiner, *Le Corbusier* (New York: Viking, 1974), 36–37.

36 Lewis Mumford, "A World Centre for the United Nations," *Journal of the Royal Institute of British Architects* (August 1946): 427–32; Lawrence J. Vale, "Designing Global Harmony: Lewis Mumford and the United Nations Headquarters," in Thomas P. Hughes and Agatha C. Hughes., eds., *Lewis Mumford: Public Intellectual* (New York: Oxford University Press, 1990), 256–82.

37 *NYT,* July 30 and Aug. 1, 3, and 15, 1946. On diplomacy with local communities, see: Minutes of Conference of United Nations and Connecticut Committees on Sites and General Questions, Outpost Inn, Ridgefield, Conn., July 20, 1946, box 476, Baldwin Records; community meetings also documented by Verbatim Minutes of a Conference Between United Nations Headquarters Commission with Representatives of the Town of Bedford, Aug. 1, 1946, file 7, box 1, Cordier Site Papers; Westchester County negotiations and resistance described by Hopkins, *Our Voices Were Heard,* 11–14.

38 *NYT,* Aug. 15, 1946; Hopkins, *Our Voices Were Heard.*

39 *Peekskill (NY) Evening Star,* Aug. 24, 1946.

40 *NYT,* Sept. 8, 1946; on postwar domesticity, see Elaine Tyler May, *Homeward Bound: American Families in the Cold War Era* (New York: Basic Books, 1988).

41 James T. Patterson, *Grand Expectations: The United States, 1945–74* (New York: Oxford University Press, 1996), 113–14; Walter Haas to Clark Eichelberger, April 9, 1946, box 62, Clark M. Eichelberger Papers, NYPL (hereafter Eichelberger Papers).

42 E. B. White, "Talk of the Town," *New Yorker,* June 30, 1945, 11.

43 Edward R. Stettinius to Harry S. Truman, May 23, 1946, and Harry S. Truman to Warren R. Austin, Aug. 3, 1946, OF 85-A 1946, HST; *NYT*, June 3 and 6, 1946.

44 Robert Gray Taylor to Andrew Cordier, June 27, 1946, and July 16, 1946, box 1, Cordier Site Papers; Notes on Private Meeting in the Secretary General's Office, June 4, 1946, box 1, Records of Secretaries-General Trygve Lie and Dag Hammarskjold (S-0847), UNA; Walter R. Sharp to Huntington Gilchrist, Jan. 24 and 26, 1946, box 40, Gilchrist Papers. In addition, Taylor's activities are documented by extensive correspondence in Papers of Edward G. Martin, Pennsylvania State Archives, Harrisburg, Pa. Taylor resume and news clippings are in the Philadelphia Bulletin Clippings Collection, UA.

45 *PR*, Nov. 11, 1946.

46 San Francisco Chamber of Commerce, Minutes of Board of Directors Meetings, April 11, May 9, and Aug. 12, 1946, San Francisco Chamber of Commerce (MS 871), CHS; Helen R. MacGregor to Earl Warren, Memorandum of Telephone Conversation, Oct. 1, 1946, Earl Warren Papers, Federal Files—United Nations Conference, CSA; Roger D. Lapham to Sumner Welles, Aug. 20, 1946, box 62, Eichelberger Papers; "U.N. Headquarters Campaign Intensified by Chamber Group," *Bay Region Business*, Aug. 15, 1946; "Bay Area Campaign for U.N. Site Continuing," *Bay Region Business*, Aug. 29, 1946; *SFC*, Aug. 11 and 16, 1946.

47 Grover Whalen to Nelson A. Rockefeller, Oct. 2, 1946, box 246, Nelson A. Rockefeller—Personal Projects (RG 4), RAC; *SFC*, Aug. 13, 23, and 27, and Sept. 11, 1946.

48 *NYT*, Aug. 21, 1946.

CHAPTER 9

1 *NYT*, Oct. 27, 1946; perceptions of Westchester in Notes on Secretary General's Private Meetings with Under-Secretaries General, Sept. 10, 1946, United Nations Central Registry 1946–47 (S-0847), box 1, UNA.

2 Nelson A. Rockefeller to Francis Case, June 4 and July 10, 1945, box 246, Nelson A. Rockefeller—Personal Projects (RG 4), RAC (hereafter NAR Personal Projects).

3 Stoyan Gavrilovic to Nelson A. Rockefeller, Jan. 31, 1946, and Edward Stettinius to Nelson A. Rockefeller, Feb. 23, 1946, box 246, NAR Personal Projects; Nelson A. Rockefeller to Harold Stein, Oct. 24, 1946, box 248, NAR Personal

Projects; Mrs. Mark Elworthy to Nelson A. Rockefeller, June 19, 1945, box 21, Nelson A. Rockefeller Personal Files—Washington (RG III 4 O), RAC; Cary Reich, *The Life of Nelson A. Rockefeller: Worlds to Conquer, 1908–1958* (New York: Doubleday, 1996), 385.

4 Correspondence to John D. Rockefeller Jr., including overtures from West-chester County officials, in box 27, Office of the Messrs. Rockefeller—World Affairs (RG III 2 Q), RAC; donation recorded in this location in John D. Rockefeller Jr. to Winthrop Aldrich, June 2, 1946.

5 *NYT*, Sept. 24 and Nov. 20, 1946.

6 *NYT*, Oct. 24, 1946.

7 Minutes, Third Meeting of the Secretariat Committee for the General Assembly, Aug. 22, 1946, file 6, box 2, Executive Assistant to the Secretary General (1946–61: Cordier) (S-0186), United Nations and Permanent Site Headquarters Records, UNA (hereafter Cordier Site Records); Robert Moses to Winthrop W. Aldrich, Sept. 27, 1946, box 28, Robert Moses Papers, NYPL (hereafter Moses Papers); Robert Moses to Nelson A. Rockefeller, Sept. 27, 1946, box 246, NAR Personal Projects; *NYT*, Oct. 19, 1946.

8 *NYT*, Sept. 18, 1946; Byron F. Wood and Charls M. Fenck, Memorandum, Oct. 1, 1946, file 4, box 1, Cordier Site Records. On concern for New York's reputation, Minutes of Meeting of Design Consultants on Flushing Meadow Plan, April 26, 1946, reel 84, and William O'Dwyer to Sal B. Hoffman, Aug. 20, 1946, reel 82, Office of the Mayor (William O'Dwyer), Subject Files, NYMA (hereafter O'Dwyer Subject Files).

9 Nelson Rockefeller to Robert Moses, Oct. 9, 1946, reel 82, and William Reid to William O'Dwyer, Oct. 11, 1946, reel 84, O'Dwyer Subject Files; *NYT*, Sept. 18, 1946; Byron F. Wood to F. J. Sanders, Sept. 24, 1946, file 4, box 1, Cordier Site Records; William Reid to William O'Dwyer, Oct. 11, 1946, reel 84, O'Dwyer Subject Files.

10 *NYT*, Dec. 4, 1946.

11 Clark Eichelberger and others to Harry S. Truman, Oct. 14, 1946, box 63, Clark M. Eichelberger Papers, NYPL (hereafter Eichelberger Papers).

12 Minutes of the Third Meeting of the United States Delegation, Oct. 18, 1946, and Minutes of the Thirteenth Meeting of the United States Delegation, Nov. 1, 1946, in U.S. State Department, *Foreign Relations of the United States, 1946*. Vol. 1, *General: The United Nations* (Washington, D.C.: USGPO, 1946), 101–6; Warren F. Austin, "Memo of Recalled Events Related to Choice of Site for United Nations Headquarters," Dec. 21, 1946 (hereafter Austin chronology), Austin Papers, UV (hereafter Austin Papers).

13 William Reid to William O'Dwyer, Nov. 6, 1946, reel 84, O'Dwyer Subject Files; *NYT*, Nov. 1, 1946.

14 The UN General Committee, which had responsibility for determining the agenda for the General Assembly, advanced the American resolution for

postponement onto the Assembly agenda by a vote of eight to three, with one abstention, on Nov. 5, 1946; the same committee rejected an amendment proposed by Ukraine to consider placing the headquarters in Europe by a vote of seven to two, with three abstentions. United Nations Department of Public Information, *Yearbook of the United Nations, 1946–47* (Lake Success, N.Y.: United Nations, 1947), 272.

15 Austin chronology; on Noel-Baker's opinion of Flushing Meadows, see Trygve Lie to P. J. Noel-Baker, Sept. 3, 1946, box 1, Cordier Site Records; on Bloom's opinion of Flushing Meadows, see Memorandum for the President, Oct. 17, 1946, OF 85-A 1946, HST; *NYT*, Nov. 6, 15, 17, and 30, 1946. The British amendment to consider any site in the United States passed 28–15, with two abstentions, in the General Assembly on Nov. 9, 1946; the Assembly then voted to approve the American resolution for postponement, as amended by the British, by 33–2 with two abstentions. United Nations, *Yearbook*, 272–73.

16 Austin chronology; *NYT*, Nov. 15, 1946; *PR*, Nov. 15, 1946. On the shift in emphasis from suburbs to city, see President of the United States, *The United States and the United Nations*, Report Series 7 (Washington, D.C.: USGPO, 1947), 25. The specifications for the new search and appointment of the Site Subcommittee were approved by the UN Headquarters Committee on Nov. 14, 1946, by a vote of 39–2 (opposed only by Argentina and Bolivia); United Nations, *Yearbook*, 273.

17 *PR*, Nov. 17, 1946.

18 *PR*, Nov. 17, 18, 19, and 21, 1946. In adjacent Delaware County, the irrepressible Robert Gray Taylor also promised cooperation for more than ten thousand acres of property, but at the steep prices that were to be expected in the Main Line suburbs.

19 *NYT*, Nov. 20, 1946; *PR*, Nov. 21, 1946.

20 *NYT*, Nov. 20, 1946; *PR*, Nov. 21, 1946.

21 I. N. P. Stokes to Warren F. Austin, Confidential Memorandum US/A/Site/6, Nov. 29, 1946, box 45, Austin Papers, UV; *Philadelphia Bulletin*, Nov. 21, 1946.

22 *NYT*, Nov. 22, 1946. Based on a trip to San Francisco for a UN Charter Day celebration in July 1946, Secretary General Trygve Lie already had judged San Francisco too crowded, expensive, and "too far from political centers of the world for the useful functioning of the organization." See Notes on Secretary General's Private Meetings with Under-Secretaries General, July 2, 1946, box 1, United Nations Central Registry 1946–47 (S-0847), UNA.

23 *The San Francisco Bay Region as a Site for Headquarters of the United Nations*, promotional booklet, n.d. [1946], SFPL; Office of the Mayor of San Francisco, Memorandum, Nov. 19, 1946, Earl Warren Papers, Federal Files—United Nations Conference, CSA (hereafter Warren Papers); Helen Abbot Lapham, *Roving with Roger* (San Francisco: Cameron, 1971), 211–14; *NYT*, Nov. 23, 1946.

24 *NYT,* Nov. 24 and 25, 1946.

25 *NYT,* Nov. 25, 1946.

26 Otto Koegel documented the Westchester County campaigns and conflicts in a collection of newspaper clippings and other documents deposited at the Westchester County Archives, Elmsford, N.Y.; *NYT,* Nov. 29, 1946.

27 Austin chronology.

28 Austin chronology; Stokes to Austin, Nov. 29, 1946; United Nations Permanent Headquarters Committee: Sub-Committee 1, Report of the Sub-Committee, Dec. 2, 1946, Austin Papers; William O'Dwyer to James Byrnes, Dec. 2, 1946, Gilmore D. Clarke and others to William O'Dwyer, Dec. 3, 1946, and Lazarus White to Howard K. Menhinick, n.d., reel 83, O'Dwyer Subject Files; Robert Moses to William O'Dwyer, Aug. 30, 1946, box 28, Moses Papers; *NYT,* Dec. 1 and 3, 1946.

29 United Nations Permanent Headquarters Committee: Sub-Committee 1, Report of the Sub-Committee, Dec. 2, 1946.

30 UN Permanent Headquarters Committee: Sub-Committee 1, Report of the Sub-Committee, Dec. 2, 1946; United Nations, *Yearbook,* 273; *NYT,* Dec. 3 and 4, 1946; American Jewish Committee, *The American Jewish Year Book 5707 (1946–47),* vol. 48 (Philadelphia: Jewish Publication Society of America, 1946), 372–401, 424–47.

31 Austin chronology; United Nations, *Yearbook,* 273–74; *NYT,* Dec. 7, 1946.

32 J. Stauffer Oliver to Dewitt Wallace, May 8, 1947, Paul E. Bellamy Papers, USD (hereafter Bellamy Papers); Trygve Lie, *In the Cause of Peace: Seven Years with the United Nations* (New York: Macmillan, 1954), 59–60.

33 Robert Sellmer, "The Man Who Wants to Build New York Over," *Life,* Oct. 28, 1946, tearsheet in box 248, NAR Personal Projects; Robert Moses to Gilmore D. Clarke, Aug. 24, 1946, box 4, collection 2, Wallace K. Harrison Archives (hereafter Harrison Archives), CU; William Zeckendorf with Edward Mc-Creary, *Zeckendorf: The Autobiography of William Zeckendorf* (New York: Holt, Rinehart, and Winston, 1970), 64–65; Reich, *The Life of Nelson A. Rockefeller,* 386.

34 Zeckendorf, *Autobiography,* 68–69.

35 Zeckendorf, *Autobiography,* 69; Lie, *In the Cause of Peace,* 112–13; William Zeckendorf to Nelson A. Rockefeller, Nov. 19, 1965, and Nelson A. Rockefeller to William Zeckendorf, Dec. 10, 1965, box 247, NAR Personal Projects.

36 Reich, *The Life of Nelson A. Rockefeller,* 384; Nelson Rockefeller's itinerary in box 145, Nelson Rockefeller—Personal Activities—Trips, RAC.

37 Robert Moses to William O'Dwyer, Dec. 7, 1946, reel 84, O'Dwyer Subject Files; *NYT,* Dec. 8, 1946.

38 *NYT,* Dec. 9, 1946; Wallace K. Harrison, "Nelson A. Rockefeller," unpublished manuscript dated Dec. 1, 1975, box 2, collection 2, Harrison Archives; Nelson A. Rockefeller, Transcript of Remarks, United Nations Week

Climaxing Event, Oct. 26, 1946, box 62, Eichelberger Papers; on Zuleta, U.S. Delegation to the United Nations, Memorandum of Conversation, Oct. 22, 1946; Austin chronology; L. Stauffer Oliver, "Memo Re The Selection of the 18-Acre Tract on the East River in Manhattan as the Site for the Permanent Headquarters of the United Nations," Feb. 1, 1947, Bellamy Papers; John D. Rockefeller Jr., "Memorandum," n.d. [December 1946-January 1947], box 247, NAR Personal Projects. The memorandum by John D. Rockefeller Jr., completed by Jan. 17, 1947, provides an account of events written shortly after they occurred and was reviewed for accuracy by Nelson Rockefeller and others involved in the events. See John D. Rockefeller Jr. to Susan Cable, Jan. 17, 1947, Office of the Messrs. Rockefeller—World Affairs (RG III 2 Q), RAC.

39 Austin chronology; Oliver, "Memo"; Lie, *In the Cause of Peace*, 113; *NYT*, Dec. 10, 1947.

40 John D. Rockefeller Jr., "Memorandum."

41 Draft of letter in box 247, NAR Personal Projects.

42 John D. Rockefeller Jr., "Memorandum."

43 Samuel E. Bleeker, *The Politics of Architecture: A Perspective on Nelson A. Rockefeller* (New York: Routledge, 1981), 13–28, 75–79.

44 John D. Rockefeller Jr., "Memorandum"; Reich, *The Life of Nelson A. Rockefeller*, 386.

45 Raymond B. Fosdick, *John D. Rockefeller Jr.: A Portrait* (NY: Harper & Brothers, 1956), 398–401; Reich, *The Life of Nelson Rockefeller*, 386–87; John D. Rockefeller Jr., "Memorandum"; Harrison, "Nelson A. Rockefeller." Zoning map with agreement of sale and draft of letter offering Rockefeller estate in box 247, NAR Personal Projects.

46 John D. Rockefeller Jr., "Memorandum"; John D. Rockefeller Jr. to Eduardo Zuleta Angel, Dec. 10, 1946, box 246, NAR Personal Projects.

47 *NYT*, Dec. 11, 1946.

48 John D. Rockefeller Jr., "Memorandum"; Reich, *The Life of Nelson A. Rockefeller*, 387.

49 *NYT*, Dec. 12 and 13, 1946.

50 Lie, *In the Cause of Peace*, 114; Egypt's motion to postpone was rejected by 36–6, with five abstentions, in the Headquarters Committee on Dec. 12, 1946. The General Assembly approved the gift 46–7 on Dec. 14. United Nations, *Yearbook*, 274–75.

EPILOGUE

1 Trygve Lie, *In the Cause of Peace: Seven Years with the United Nations* (New York: Macmillan, 1954), 114; "Six Blocks in Area," *NYT*, Dec. 12, 1946; letters of approval and criticism in box 29, Office of the Messrs Rockefeller—World

Affairs (RG III), RAC; Evan Luard, *A History of the United Nations*. Vol. 1, *The Years of Western Domination, 1945–55* (New York: St. Martin's, 1982), 82–84.

2 L. Stauffer Oliver to John D. Rockefeller Jr., Dec. 14, 1946, box 29, Office of the Messrs Rockefeller—World Affairs (RG III), RAC; *NYT*, Dec. 13, 1946; L. Stauffer Oliver to Paul Bellamy, Jan. 29, Feb. 1, Feb. 6, and Feb. 20, 1947, and Bellamy to Oliver, March 6 and April 22, 1947, box 55, Paul E. Bellamy Papers, USD; Scott Gabriel Knowles, ed., *Imagining Philadelphia: Edmund Bacon and the Future of the City* (Philadelphia: University of Pennsylvania Press, 2009).

3 United Nations Press Release (HQC/60), Jan. 13, 1947, and Wallace K. Harrison, *Talk Before American Society of Landscape Architects*, June 9, 1947, in box 3, collection 2, Wallace K. Harrison Archives, CU.

4 Wallace K. Harrison remarks to Ad Hoc Committee on Headquarters, Sept. 1947, box 4, collection 2, Harrison Archives, CU; Victoria Newhouse, *Wallace K. Harrison, Architect* (New York: Rizzoli, 1989), 114–43; George A. Dudley, *A Workshop for Peace: Designing the United Nations Headquarters* (Cambridge, Mass.: MIT Press, 1994), 5–31.

5 For example, see Dean M. Hanink, *Principles and Applications of Economic Geography: Economy, Policy, Environment* (New York: Wiley, 1997); Danny MacKinnon and Andrew Cumbers, *An Introduction to Economic Geography: Globalization, Uneven Development, and Place* (Harlow, England: Pearson, 2007).

ACKNOWLEDGMENTS

TRACES OF THE Capital of the World competition are scattered widely, and so I owe thanks to many dedicated librarians and archivists who helped me follow the trail of civic boosters from their hometowns to the world stage. I came across my first hint of this story quite by accident in the archives of Independence National Historical Park while working on a previous book. This led to many productive days at the United Nations Archives in New York, the Library of Congress, various state and university archives, presidential libraries, historical societies, and local history rooms of public libraries across the country. For travel and research in key repositories, I received generous support from the Massachusetts Historical Society (Andrew W. Mellon Fellowship); the Rockefeller Archive Center; the Harry S. Truman Presidential Library Institute; and the Franklin and Eleanor Roosevelt Institute. Additional support came from the Penn Humanities Forum, Villanova University and the Villanova University History Department, and Rutgers University.

I had the pleasure of writing this book with the advice and encouragement of colleagues in the history departments of Villanova University and Rutgers University–Camden. I am grateful to these and many other scholars who have sustained and strengthened the work. For advice on formulating the project and assistance with preparing grant proposals and seeking a publisher, I thank Carl Abbott, Peter Baldwin, David Contosta, Richard Davies, Allen Davis, Marc Gallicchio, Howard Gillette, David Glassberg, Randall Miller, Gary Nash, Howard Spodek, Morris Vogel, and Allan Winkler. I benefited from insightful critiques and questions during presentations at the Urban History Association, the National Council on Public History, the Massachusetts Historical Society, and the Penn Humanities Forum, and from editors and reviewers of the work in progress. Most especially, I appreciate the close readings of every chapter by the "second book club," Paul Rosier and Judith Giesberg, whose advice improved every page. Other friends and family members helped by providing good cheer and places to stay during my research travels. Thanks to the Mires family of Lake Forest, Illinois, and Durham, North Carolina; the Abbott family of Newburgh, Indiana; Jane Dye; Virginia Orange; and Heather Ewing.

Some material in this book appeared previously in the *New England Quarterly* 79 (March 2006): 37–64 and the *Michigan Historical Review* 35 (Spring 2009): 61–82, and is reprinted with their permission. The University of Pennsylvania Press also granted permission to adapt a brief account of the Philadelphia campaign from my first book, *Independence Hall in American Memory* (2002).

At NYU Press, I was fortunate to meet Gabrielle Begue, whose enthusiasm for the manuscript led to its publication. Anonymous reviewers of the manuscript offered insightful guidance, and the editorial skills of Deborah Gershenowitz sharpened the prose. The manuscript was copyedited by Emily Wright, and Colleen Rafferty accomplished the difficult task of securing the illustrations.

Because I began my career as a journalist, and wrote this book as newspapers struggled with the realities of our digital age, I feel a keen appreciation for the "first draft of history" that made it possible for me to recover the search for the Capital of the World. I was able to write this history because so many news reporters covered the story of their own hometowns. Although they usually did not see the big picture, and they often crossed the line from objectivity to boosterism, they wrote with gusto and attention to detail. Because they put their stories in print, I could piece together a chronology, which then led me to the archives of so many participants in these events. So I close with a salute to the news reporters of 1945 and 1946 and my hope that whatever may change with technology, their dedication to documentation and good stories will survive.

INDEX

Aandahl, Fred, 55, 248
Acheson, Dean, 201
Adams, Orson, Jr., 114
Africa, 97
African Americans, 13, 33, 59, 68, 119, 126, 131
Alameda Naval Air Station (in Calif.), 29
Alaska, 231
Albuquerque, N. Mex., 31
Alcott, Louisa May, 147
Aldrich, Winthrop, 181, 196
Alemán, Miguel, 211
Alexandria, Va., 253
Allan, Frank H., 238
America First Committee, 33, 69
American Association for the United Nations, 201
American Dilemma, 126
American identity, role in local-global connections, 88–100
American Revolution, legacy of, 19–21, 90, 133, 147–48, 157. *See also* Declaration of Independence, Independence Hall, Liberty Bell
Anchorage, Alas., 231
Andersen, Hendrik C., 2
Anderson, Donald L., 252
Anderson, J. Alvin, Jr., 240
Andover, Mass., 238
Anti-Semitism, 92, 126, 131, 132
Apostle Islands, Wis., 255

Appomattox, Va., 131
Arab League, 209, 218
Architecture (world capital designs):
    Black Hills, 102–5; Chicago: 71–74;
    Great Lakes region, 63–68; New
    York City (Queens), 138, 198–99;
    New York City (the Bronx), 176–78;
    New York City (Manhattan),
    220–25; Oklahoma, 102–3; San
    Francisco, 46–47; sketches by Le
    Corbusier, 186–87; Westchester
    County, N.Y., 162
Argentina, 37, 48, 49
Arizona, 231–32
Arkansas, 232
"Arsenals of democracy," 12, 59, 70. *See also* Manufacturing
Asbury Park, N.J., 243
Asheville, N.C., 248
Asia, 85, 97
Astor, William, 110
Atkinson, John B., 238
Atlantic City, N.J., 15, 88; alternate as
    interim site, 165–66; boosters in
    London, 110–12; UN site visit, 157–58
Atlantic Highlands, N.J., 243
Atlantic Union Movement, 60
Atlee, Clement, 170
Atomic bomb, 5, 36, 75–77, 81, 111, 113
Auburn, Mass., 128, 238
Austin, Warren F., 191–92, 201–2, 207–8, 212–18

Australia: Canberra as model capital, 85, 129–31; leader of small nations, 45, 172; role in site selection, 50, 87, 111, 116, 127, 166, 172, 218

Austria, 161

Aviation: changing relationship between distance and time, 23, 52, 57–58, 86–87, 96–97, 106; dirigible, 160; new transportation hubs, 24, 54, 117–18; travel by air, 31, 107–9, 150, 205

Azores, the, 15

Bach, E. L., 236

Baguio, the Philippines, 75, 250

Bailey, Foster, 246

Bailey, Joseph, 248

Balance of power, Europe-U.S., 3, 23, 50, 83–87, 119, 124, 196, 202

Bald Head Island, N.C., 202, 248

Baldwin, Raymond E., 155–56, 168, 234

Baltimore, Md., 75, 238

Bar Harbor, Maine, 128, 135, 237

Barnstable, Mass., 238

Barnstone, Robert, 233

Baruch, Bernard, 251

Bassov, Nikolai D., 207

Battle Creek, Mich., 241

Bazinet, John, 245

Beall, Clarkson J., 246

Bear Mountain, N.Y., 172, 245

Bedford, Mass., 109, 160

Belgium, 84

Belgrade, Yugoslavia, 145

Bell, Piromis, 234

Bellamy, Lucy, 9

Bellamy, Paul E.: at Governors Conference, 52, 55–56; in London, 108, 110, 112–14, 118–19; in San Francisco, 40–41, 43, 51, 195; Man of the Year, 77; proposes Black Hills, 9–12,

13, 26; response to rejection, 128, 219–20. See also Black Hills region

Bellamy, Lt. Paul Herbert, 9, 110

Belle Isle (Detroit), 13

Beloit, Wis., 81, 88, 255

Belmont, Mass., 238

Berg, Luvine, 102–5

Berkeley, Calif., 232

Berkeley Springs, W. Va., 172, 254

Berlin, Germany, 37, 48, 85

Berlin, Irving, 18

Berne, N.Y., 245

Berne, Switzerland, 85

Bernardi, Theodore C., 46–47

Bethlehem, Pa., 249

Bethune, Mary McLeod, 33

Beverly, Mass., 128, 159

Bishop, Ernest H., 247

Black Hills region, S.D.: campaign initiated, 10–12, 29; excluded, 51; mocked, 113, 121; persistence, 77, 128, 134, 146, 172–74; promoted at Governors Conference, 52–56; promoted in London, 108, 110–14, 118–19; promoted in San Francisco, 30, 40–41, 43–44, 195; promoted in Washington, 26; response to rejection, 219–20; site design, 102–5. See also Bellamy, Paul E.; Rapid City, S.D.

Bloom, Sol, 202

Blue Hills, Mass., 92, 159, 165, 206–7, 240; rejected, 208

Blue Star Mothers, 24

Bohn, John L., 255

Boosterism: centrality arguments, 100–106; continuities, nineteenth and twentieth centuries, 2, 221; contrasted with diplomacy, 82, 86–87, 107, 124, 140, 146–47; inversions of, 98, 190; place marketing, 221; as profession, 4, 11; role of press,

4, 23–24, 26, 43, 91, 109, 156, 199,
221; scholarship on, 257n2, 259n11,
272n15; skepticism about, 24–25, 121,
152; techniques, 2, 43, 58–63, 69–70,
80–82, 88–91, 98, 150–61, 178, 205–7;
and UN, 107–22, 128–29, 166, 191–92,
219; in U.S. West, 10, 43, 221
Border, U.S.-Canadian, 11–12, 52, 55,
56–68, 119, 172, 248
Born, Ernest, 46–47
Boston, Mass.: boosters in London,
109–11, 114, 116; campaign initiated,
81, 90–93; considered as interim
site, 164–67, 180; controversy with
Soviets, 161, 166, 207; favored by
British, 96, 212; as "the Hub," 91;
region designated for inspection,
132–37, 212; rejected, 208, 219; towns
in region, 122, 147–50, 238–41; vis-
ited by UN site inspectors, 158–61,
202–3, 206–7. *See also* Massachu-
setts; Tobin, Maurice
Boult, Adrian, 158
Boustra, Vincent, 127
Boylston, Mass., 241
Brainard, H.P., 243
Brainerd, Minn., 241
Braintree, Mass., 240
Brazil, 87, 126
Bridgewater, Mass., 238
Brière, Francois, 133, 136, 150
Brigantine Island, N.J., 157, 243
Bristol, R.I., 160, 250
Bronx, the, 138, 175–84
Brookhaven, Long Island, N.Y., 245
Brooklyn, N.Y., 175
Broughton, Joseph, 248
Brown, Bedford, 192
Brown, John Nicholas, 95
Brownsville, Tex., 211
Brussels, Belgium, 84, 85
Bryn Mawr, Pa., 249

Bucks County, Pa., 249
Buffalo, N.Y., 137
Bullard, Harry, 246
Bullock, Chandler, 241
Bungart, Paul J., 245
Bunyan, Paul, 241
Burgess, Paul, 243
Burlington, Vt., 128, 149, 252–53
Burt, Struthers, 25
Bush, George Herbert Walker, 168
Bush, Prescott S., 168
Bushby, Wilkie, 163, 175
Bushfield, Harlan J., 74
Bushkill, Pa., 250
Byelorussia, 15, 37, 49
Byrnes, James F., 83, 93, 215

Cairo, Egypt, 145
California, 35, 53, 99, 128, 172, 232–33.
See also San Francisco; *names of
other localities*
Cann, Edward H., 253
Cambridge, Mass., 238–39
Cameron, Alex, 247
Camp Peary (in Va.), 133, 254
Cape May, N.J., 243
Cape Town, South Africa, 145
Canada, 3, 11, 30, 57, 59. *See also names of
provinces, localities*
Canberra, Australia, 85, 129
Canham, Erwin, 114
Canton, Mass., 159, 240
Cape Cod, Mass., 128, 239
Capital of the World: competition, 3,
5, 19, 25, 26–27, 38–44, 53, 55–75, 81,
88–122, 128–29, 149, 150–61, 166, 172–
84, 190–93, 202, 207; concept, 1–2,
19, 98, 112, 129, 145–46, 171, 185–86,
219–21, 226. *See also* Architecture;
United Nations Headquarters
Capone, Al, 69
Caproni, Leo F., 244

Carthage, Tenn., 251
Cary, Dale E., 249
Case, Francis, 26
Catalina Island, Calif., 232
Catholicism, 161
Caylor, Arthur, 19
Center Island, Long Island, N.Y., 245
Central America, 31
Centrality, 10, 43–44, 59, 70, 81, 83, 86, 98, 100–106, 127, 138, 221
Cermak, Anton, 69
Chally, Jo Ann, 235
Chambers of commerce, as world capital promoters, 10–12, 18–19, 39, 55, 77, 81, 88, 91, 99, 101, 113, 118, 121, 127, 152, 159, 192
Champaign County, Ill., 235
Charlebois, Gus, 245
Charlottesville, Va., 88, 253; excluded, 133
Chesapeake Bay, 238
Chester County, Pa., 249
Chestnut Hill (in Philadelphia), 204
Chewning, Lewis G., 253
Chicago, Ill.: boosters in London, 108–11, 114–16, 118; campaign initiated, 55, 68–73, 75; as crossroads, 54, 68–69, 99; excluded, 133–34; Northerly Isle, 70–73; rivalry with St. Louis, 102, 119; site plan, 72–73; during World War II, 52, 70
Children and youth, 36, 92, 132, 172–73
Chile, 87, 127
China: positions on site selection, 50–51, 83, 84–85, 87, 127; role in San Francisco conference, 38, 45; role in site inspections, 150, 206
Chinese Americans, 29, 206
Choate, Ben P., 96–98
Choctaw Nation, 96–99, 102–3
Chopmist Hill (in R.I.), 160
Christensen, Harry, 240

Christianity, 63, 74, 161
Christopherson, Fred, 40, 52, 55
Churchill, Winston, 14, 30, 81, 127, 146, 190
Cincinnati, Ohio, 76, 122, 133; boosters in London, 119
City Beautiful movement, 34
City planning, 34, 77, 162, 203. See also Architecture; United Nations Headquarters
Civic boosterism. See Boosterism
Civic centers, 18, 33
Civic identity: Boston, 90–91, 95; Chicago, 69, 114; Cincinnati, 119; Claremore, Okla., 99–100; Newport, R.I., 93–95; Philadelphia, 24, 117, 205; San Francisco, 18, 29–30
Civil rights, 33, 126
Civic rivalries, 102, 119
Claremore, Okla., 81, 99–100, 206, 219
Clason, Charles R., 240
Class, 95, 136
Clayton, N.Y., 245
Clearfield, Utah, 237
Cleveland, Ohio, 248
Clifty Falls State Park (in Ind.), 236
Cohen, Benjamin, 109, 111, 119
Cold War, 190–91, 196, 207, 209
Collins, Clark, 235
Colombia, 111
Colorado, 55, 207, 233. See also Denver; names of other localities
Colorado Springs, Colo., 233
Columbia University, 180
Committee to Defend American by Aiding the Allies, 69
Compton, Karl T., 114
Concord, Mass.: omitted from site recommendations, 165; proposed, 128, 136, 238;
resistance in, 147–50, 164; response compared with Stamford, Conn.,

and Atlantic City, N.J., 156–57; visited by site inspectors, 160
Connecticut, 234; selected for consideration, 134; resistance in, 161–64, 172, 181; visited by site inspectors, 155–56. *See also* Fairfield County; Greenwich; Ridgefield; Stamford; *and names of other localities*
Contra Costa County, Calif., 25, 232
Conway, N.H., 128, 243
Conventions, competition for, 88, 90, 94, 111, 116, 119, 157
Cooley, C. P., 233
Coolidge, Calvin, 10, 11, 43, 159
Cooperstown, N.Y., 245
Corker, W. S., 243
Corpus Christi, Tex., 252
Cortlandt Township, N.Y., 188
Cosmopolitanism, 19, 29, 36, 59, 95, 116, 119, 206
Coulter, John, 236
Crandall, Arthur I., 156
Cranston, R.I., 251
Crimean Conference. *See* Yalta
Croton-on-Hudson, N.Y., 188, 245
Crystal Springs, Calif., 206
Cuba, 111, 116
Cut Bank, Mont., 242
Cutten, Ruth, 119, 155
Czechoslovakia, 40, 87

Dagnan, Bernard H., 244
Darden, Colgate W., Jr., 253
Davis, John W., 181
Day, Kenneth, 204
Daytona Beach, Fla., 121
Dayton, Ohio, 31
De Beque Valley, Colo., 233
Decker, Clarence R., 242
Declaration of Independence, 21, 39, 117, 203
Dedham, Mass., 159, 240

Delaware, 134
Delaware County, Pa., 140, 249
Delaware Valley (Pa.) Association for United Nations Headquarters, 249, 250
Democratic Party, 69, 90
Dempsey, John, 53, 232
Denman, George L., 252
Denmark, 49
Denver, Colo., 31, 88, 128, 219; boosters in London, 111, 114, 116
Detroit, Mich., 12–13, 27, 52, 55, 132, 261n9
Dewey, George, 34
Dewey, Thomas E., 1, 55
Diplomacy: contrasted with boosterism, 82, 86–87, 107, 124, 140, 146–47; failure in New York suburbs, 185, 188–89, 191
Discrimination, 29, 49, 126, 129–32, 172, 200, 241–42
Distance. *See* Time and space, perceptions of
Dixon, Jeremiah, 131
Dobbs Ferry, 245
Dodds, Harold, 244
Doherty, Edward B., 246
Dolores, Colo., 233
Domesticity. *See* Home, defense of
Dominican Republic, 33
Donnelly, Phil M., 242
Douglas, Ariz., 231
Drake, Guy A., 251
Drew, Anna V., 244
Duck Island, Sault Ste. Marie, Mich., 59
Dulles, Allen, 157
Duluth, Minn., 242
Dumbarton Oaks, 10, 12, 13, 37, 45, 81, 83
Dunes State Park (in Ind.), 235
Dunn, Roy J., 253
Durant, Will, 97

Easton, Pa., 146, 249, 250
Eastland, Tex., 252
Economic development, 3, 13, 18, 24, 88, 90, 93, 98, 111
Ecuador, 127
Eden, Anthony, 15, 33
Edgmont, Pa., 249
Egypt, 111, 116, 218
Elder, John H., 243
Elwood, Ind., 236
Emerson, Ralph Waldo, 147
England, 32, 59, 63, 96, 108. *See also* Great Britain; London
Eshleman, Benjamin, 39, 107, 109
Essex County, N.J., 243
Essex, Vt., 253
Ethiopia, 111, 131
Europe: *See* balance of power, Europe-U.S.; *names of nations*
Evatt, Herbert V., 31, 85

Fairfield County, Conn., 154, 155–56, 174–75, 185–90; map of sites, 189. *See also* Greenwich; Stamford
Fairhurst, W. E., 244
Falls Township, Pa., 249
Farragut, Idaho, 235
Finland, 161
Fitzgerald, F. Scott, 151
Flemington, N.J., 243
Florida, 234; *See also* Jacksonville; Miami
Flushing Meadows Park, Queens, N.Y.: compared to Fairmount Park (Philadelphia), 204; favored by Soviet Union, 209; promoted by New York City, 151, 164, 181, 183–84, 192, 211–12; rejected, 138, 207; UN General Assembly in, 196–203. *See also* Moses, Robert; New York City
Fogarty, John F., 93
Ford, Henry, 160

Forks Township, Pa., 249
Fort Adams (in R.I.), 94
Fort Ethan Allen (in Vt.), 164, 253
Fort Lee, N.J., 243
Fort Worth, Tex., 242
Foster, R.I., 251
Four Freedoms, 35
Foxcroft, Pa., 249
Framingham, Mass., 206
France: in League of Nations, 84; possible international zone in, 42; role in site inspections, 150; role in site selection, 50, 87, 120, 127, 133, 136, 172, 185; on UN Security Council, 45, 127
Franklin, Benjamin, 23
Fredericksburg, Va., 253
Frederiksen, Mary, 241
Freitas-Valle, Cyro de, 126
French, Allen, 148
French, Harold, 233
French, H. J., 247
French Lick, Ind., 15, 235
Frost, Robert, 60, 90
Fueslein, Irma, 245

Gallienne, Wilfred Hansford, 109
Galveston, Tex., 252
Gates, Ralph F., 235–36
Gavrilovic, Ivan, 145
Gavrilovic, Stoyan: chairs booster hearings, 111; in New York, 145, 200; role in site inspections, 145–46, 150, 158–60, 202
Gavrilovic, Vera, 145
Gaylord, W. Va., 254
Generational experience, 5, 35, 57, 59, 74, 83, 90, 111, 168, 170, 171, 175–76. *See also* Globalization; World War I; World War II
Geneva, Switzerland. *See* League of Nations

Georgia, 59, 62, 81, 234–35
Gerlach, Herbert, 196
German Americans, 69
Germany, 14, 16, 37, 57, 81
Gettysburg, Pa., 249
Gilchrist, Huntington, 135, 138, 150, 159
Gittins, Robert H., 246
Glacier National Park (in Mont.), 172, 242
Glad, Earl J., 252
Glens Falls, N.Y., 245
Global cities, 258n6. *See also* world cities
Globalization, 5, 221, 226, 257n2. *See also* Local-global connections and interactions
Glocester, R.I., 251
Gloucester, Mass., 92
Goelet, Robert, 94
Goodrich, Ernest P., 162
Goodwin, Angier, 239
Gore, Albert, 251
Gorham, Clyde R., 241
Governors' Conference, 52–56, 58, 74
Governors Island, N.Y., 211–12, 245
Grady, Henry F., 18
Grand Canyon, 53, 232
Grand Coulee, Wash., 121, 254
Grand Island, Niagara Falls, N.Y., 137, 246
Grand River, Ontario, 33
Grand Valley, Colo., 233
Gray, John L., 162
Great Britain, 37, 85, 120, 127, 129, 159, 206; influence on site selection, 124–26, 131–33, 135–36, 202. *See also* England; United Kingdom
Great Depression, 4, 24, 68, 70, 90, 147, 159, 175
Great Falls, Mont., 31
Great Lakes region, 52–77, 118; Lake Huron, 52–53, 70; Lake Michigan,

52, 68, 70, 87, 235, 255; Lake Superior, 255
Great Smoky Mountains (in Tenn.), 251
Great War. *See* World War I
Greece, 219
Green, Dwight H., 54
Greenfield, Mass., 239
Greenville, Ohio, 122, 248
Greenwich, Conn.: recommended for permanent headquarters, 3, 164–65, 186; referendum, 181, 289n21; resistance, 149–50, 161–64, 166–69; responses to resistance, 171–72, 174–75, 182, 195. *See also* Fairfield County; Stamford
Grew, Joe, 17
Griswold, Dwight, 53
Grossman, Cornell, 243

Hackensack, N.J., 244
Hague, the, 2, 30
Haiti, 31, 131
Haley, Edward F., 240
Halifax, Nova Scotia, 32
Hamilton Army Air Field (in Calif.), 48
Hamilton, Mass., 239
Hamilton, Ontario, 80
Hampton Roads, Va., 253
Harmon-on-Hudson, N.Y., 172, 245
Harp, Charles, 112
Harper's Ferry, W. Va., 254
Harrison, N.Y., 188, 208
Harrison, Wallace K., 196, 210, 212–15, 220–21
Hartford, Conn., 128, 132, 234
Hart, John Robbins, 250
Harvard University, 114, 136, 238
Harvey, George, 234
Hasluck, Paul, 131
Haverford College, 39, 109, 125
Hawaii, 15, 56, 235

Hawthorne, Nathaniel, 147
Hawthorne, N.J., 146, 244
Hearst, William Randolph, 206, 233
Heathsville, Va., 253
Hedrick, E. H., 254–55
Hellstern, Raymond A., 244
Heritage, in booster appeals, 19–21, 59, 62–64, 88, 90, 92–95, 99, 117, 101–2, 132–33, 157, 159–60. *See also* American Revolution, legacy of; Memory
Herndon, John G., 39, 107
Hiawatha, 62–65
Highlands, N.J., 244
Hildreth, Horace, 237
Hingham, Mass., 239
Hiss, Alger, 35, 41, 74
Hoboken, N.J., 157
Hodes, Barton, 114
Hodgson, William R., 127
Holden, Mass., 241
Holmes, Oliver Wendell, 91
Home, defense of, 188–90, 226
Honduras, 127
Hong Kong, 206
Honolulu, Hawaii, 88, 235
Hoo, Victor, 84
Hope, Bob, 29
Hopewell Valley, N.J., 244
Hopkinson, Edward, Jr., 203
Hopper, Hedda, 33
Hot Springs, Va., 15, 150
Houser, Roy M., 250
Housing shortage, 180, 184, 200
Hoyos, Luis de, 246
Hoyt, Anna C., 233
Hsu, Shuhsi, 150
Hull, Cordell, 15, 251
Human rights, 131, 174
Humphrey, Hubert H., 242
Hunt, Lester, 53
Hunter College, 178–80, 182–84. *See also* Bronx, the

Huntington, E. Irving, 244
Huntington Township, Long Island, N.Y., 245
Hurn, England, 108
Hyde Park, N.Y.: alternative for permanent headquarters, 164–65; association with Franklin Roosevelt, 31; proposed for UN, 81, 88, 119, 134; selected for site inspection, 137–38; village, 152; visited by site inspectors, 151, 152–54, 156. *See also* Poughkeepsie, N.Y.; Roosevelt, Franklin Delano

Idaho, 235
Illinois, 54, 235
Immigrants, 5, 59, 68, 69, 70–71, 88, 90, 92, 93, 96
Imperialism, 29, 33, 81, 83, 96, 97, 159–60
Independence Hall, 21–23, 24, 31, 87, 88, 184, 203, 220. *See also* Philadelphia
Independence, Mo., 75
India, 129, 172
Indiana, 88, 119, 128, 134, 235–36. *See also* names of localities and parks
Indianapolis, Ind., 128, 235–36
Indian Territory, 96
International Friendship Gardens (in Ind.), 128, 236
International Peace Garden (in N.D.), 55, 172, 248
Internationalism, 58, 60–62, 68, 69, 88, 171; limits of, 4, 69
Iowa, 236
Iran, 83, 111, 127
Iraq, 150
Ireland, 108
Irish Americans, 69, 90, 92, 93, 118, 132
Irvington-on-Hudson, N.Y., 245
Isolationism, 15, 54, 69, 70, 120, 133, 171
Italian Americans, 92
Ithan, Pa., 249

Jackson County, Mo., 75, 242
Jacksonville, Fla., 88, 234
Jacobs, Sophia Yarnall, 39, 41, 43
Jamestown, Va., 133
Japan, 16, 33, 45, 51, 58, 75
Japanese Americans, 17–18, 29, 60
Jay, Pierre, 152
Jeanneret-Gris, Charles Édouard: see
    Le Corbusier
Jeanneret, Pierre, 185
Jebb, Gladwyn, 81, 106, 109, 111
Jefferson City, Mo., 242
Jefferson Proving Ground (in Ind.), 236
Jefferson, Thomas, 10, 30, 88, 133, 253,
    254
Jenkins, Leo B.F., 233
Jewish Agency for Palestine, 33
Jews, 172, 209
Johns Hopkins University, 238
Johnson, Holgar, 163
Johnson, N.B., 100
Johnson, Robert L., 37, 38–39, 42, 107,
    110
Johnson, Walter, 253
Johnston, R.I., 250
Jones, Lee F., 232
Joseph, Harold K., 152
Journalists. *See* Newspapers; Radio

Kalamazoo, Mich., 241
Kansas, 237
Kansas City, Kans., 99
Kansas City, Mo., 31, 75, 242
Kapp, John W., 235
Kaufmann, Aloys, 134
Keldin, Theodore R., 238
Kelly, Edward J., 69–71, 84, 90, 108–9,
    134
Kendall, Parker C., 233
Kennan, George F., 190
Kennedy, James L.
Kennedy, John F., 34

Kenosha, Wis., 255
Kent Island, Md., 238
Kerr, Robert S., 98, 128
Khalidy, Awni el, 150
Kilgore, Harley M., 172, 254
King, W. L. Mackenzie, 59
Kingston, N.J., 244
Kingston, N.Y., 164, 245
Kirby, Gustavus T., 155
Koegel, Otto, 207
Krieger, Ed, 63–65
Krimm, Ray, 37, 39, 43
Kuntz, H. E., 243

Lackens, F.I., 236
LaGuardia, Fiorello, 121, 138, 151
Lake James (Ind.), 236
Lake of the Ozarks, Mo., 242
Lake Placid, N.Y., 245
Lake Ponchartrain, New Orleans, La.,
    237
Lake Pond Oreille (Idaho), 235
Lake Seneca, N.Y., 246
Lake Success, Long Island, N.Y., 165,
    183–84, 190–93, 200
Lakewood, N.J., 244
Lancaster, Pa., 249
Landfield, Jerome, 233
Lapham, Roger: during UN Charter
    conference, 30, 35–36, 38–39, 48–49;
    in London, 90, 109, 118; mayor
    of San Francisco, 16–18; reacts to
    rejection, 123–24, 126–28; role in site
    selection, 74–75, 192–93, 206, 213,
    219. *See also* San Francisco
Latin America: importance to world
    capital competitors, 98, 116, 119, 132;
    interests of Nelson Rockefeller,
    194–96, 211, 212; positions on site
    selection: 50, 83–84, 87; at San
    Francisco conference, 41. *See also*
    Central America; South America

Le Corbusier, 185–86
League of Nations: architectural competition, 185; as Capital of the World, 2; gift from John D. Rockefeller Jr., 195, 215; as potential site for UN, 23–24, 42, 50, 84–86; selection of Geneva, 30; U.S. rejection of, 15, 22, 74, 171; veterans of, 39, 83, 91, 114, 123,
Lebanon, Kans., 237
Lee, H., 244
Leffler, C.D. Jr., 234
Lelyveld, Joseph, 240
Lenox, Mass., 122, 149, 239
Lewis, Clarence, 244
Lexington, Mass., 128, 136, 147, 238
Liberia, 131
Liberty Bell, 20, 81, 110, 117, 121, 203. See also Philadelphia
Lie, Trygve, opinion on Hunter College, 179–80, 182; preference for New York City, 183, 210, 219; role in site selection, 191–92, 211–12
Lincoln, Abraham, 71, 235, 236, 249
Lincoln, Neb., 242–43
Lincoln State Park (Ind.), 236
Literature, 90, 98, 99, 147–48, 151
Local-global connections and interactions: conflicts and limitations of, 146–50, 164, 170, 226–27; demonstrated by booster competition, 111–12; in Great Lakes region, 52–54; immigration and ethnicity, 5, 59, 68, 69, 70–71, 88, 90, 92, 93, 96; resulting from war, 9–10, 13, 57, 76–77; role of localities, 4, 10, 23, 26–27, 102, 124, 218, 226–27; role of national identity, 88–89, 95; in San Francisco, 17–19. See also Aviation; Globalization
Locke, Lydia, 247
London, England, as Capital of the World, 2, 219; UN General Assembly in, 145, 150, 169, 170–75; UN Preparatory Commission in, 50, 75, 81–90, 100, 107–41; during World War II, 82
Long Island, N.Y., 150, 164–65, 245–47. See also names of localities
Longfellow, Henry Wadsworth, 63
Lopez, Pedro, 174
Los Alamos, N.M., 76
Los Angeles, Calif., 25, 31, 90, 121, 207, 232, 241
Louisiana, 237
Lower Pontnewydd, Wales, 122
Luce, Clare Booth, 166
Lucerne, Maine, 121, 237
Lycoming County, Pa., 250
Lyons, James Joseph, 175–75, 184

MacEachen, Roberto, 131–32, 135, 138
Mackinac Island, 52–56, 58
Madison, Ind., 236
Maine, 128, 134, 237–38
Major, Charles T., 247
Malden, Mass., 239
Manchester, Mass., 239
Manhattan. See New York City
Manitoba, Canada, 248
Mansions, 93–95, 152–53, 155, 159
Manufacturing, 13, 52, 57, 70, 90
Maps, 43–44, 102–6, 114, 196–97, 211, 213
Marin County, Calif., 46, 232
Markarian, Frank S., 255
Markelius, Sven, 220
Marshall, John A., 233
Martha's Vineyard, Mass., 202, 239
Martin, Edward, 53, 249
Mart, Lloyd J., 242
Maryland, 131, 238
Mason, Charles, 131
Mason County, Tex., 252
Mason-Dixon Line, 131–32

Massachusetts, 90–93, 128, 134, 149, 158–61, 238–41; North Shore, 136–37, 150, 165, 207

South Shore, 150–51, 206–7. *See also* Boston; *names of other localities*

Massachusetts Institute of Technology, 46, 114

Massasoit, 159

Matamoras, Pa., 250

Mauermann, Gus B., 252

May, James A., 234

Mayflower Compact, 92

McAlester, Okla., 99

McCabe, J. Joseph, 239

McCord, Jim, 251

McDonald, William J., 114

McKay, Donald C., 238

Media, Pa., 88, 249

Medford, Mass., 159, 239

Melrose, Mass., 239

Memory, 3, 5, 31, 34, 48, 84–85, 90, 92, 184

Metropolitan regions, 90, 93, 130, 136–41, 147–50, 166–69, 170, 175–76, 181, 226

Mexico, 29, 41, 83, 87, 98, 116, 120, 211

Miami, Fla., 69, 76, 81, 88, 234; booster in London, 119; excluded, 132

Mianus River Gorge (in Conn.), 156, 161, 162

Michigan, 56–68, 241. *See also* Detroit; Sault Ste. Marie; *and names of other localities*

Michigan City, Ind., 128, 236

Middle East, 31, 172

Middlesex Fells, Mass., 92, 159, 160, 239

Midwest (U.S.) region, 52, 57, 100–106; excluded, 133–34

Millburn, N.J., 243

Miller, C. W., 252

Miller, Henry T., 232

Milton, Mass., 159, 240

Milwaukee, Wis., 77, 255

Minneapolis, Minn., 241

Minnesota, 54, 207, 241–42

Missouri, 232, 242

Mohansic State Park (in N.Y.), 202, 207, 246

Molotov, Vyacheslav, 15, 16, 33

Monmouth County, N.J., 244

Monroe County, Pa., 250

Montana, 242

Montauk Point, Long Island, N.Y., 246

Monterey Peninsula, Calif., 88, 232

Monticello (home of Thomas Jefferson), 81, 88, 253

Monticello, N.Y., 246

Moon, Charles Henry, 249

Moore, Hugh, 249

Moorhouse, A. Judson, 247

Moraga Valley, Calif., 88, 232

Morgan, Charles, 71

Morris, Ill., 235

Morris, Mabel, 122

Morristown, N.J., 146, 157

Morse, S. F. B., 232

Moscow, 14, 31, 190

Moses, Robert, strategy to attract UN, 138, 151, 180–84, 192, 196, 200–1, 208, 211–12, 215

Mount Rushmore, 10, 41, 55

Mount Wachusett (in Mass.), 241

Movies, 69, 33, 225; promotional, 110, 112, 114, 117

Moylan, Cornelius A., 234

Mudalier, Ramaswami, 126, 172

Mumford, Lewis, 186

Mundt, Karl, 12

Munich, Germany, 85

Murrow, Edward R., 110

Music, 4, 18, 31, 48, 99, 226–27

Muskegon, Mich., 202, 241

Myrdal, Gunnar, 126

Myrtle Beach, S.C., 251

NAACP, 33

Nanjing, China, 162

National Congress of American Indians of the United States and Alaska, 100

Native Americans, 33, 43, 62–63, 96–100, 159–60, 236, 242, 248

Navy Island, Niagara Falls, Ont. *See* Niagara Falls

Nebraska, 26, 43, 53, 134, 123–24. *See also* Black Hills region

Needham, Mass., 159, 240

Netherlands, the, 87, 111, 138, 140

Neutaconkanut Hill (in R.I.), 250–51

New Age Gardens (in Colo.), 233

Newark, N.J., 157

New England region, 88, 90–95, 128–29, 135–36, 147–50, 155–56, 158–69; symbolism of New England towns, 149–50; town meetings, 93, 147. *See also* Northeast (U.S.) region

Newfoundland, 108, 109

New Hampshire, 128, 134, 243

New Haven, Conn., 125, 234, 244

New Jersey, 60, 111, 134, 138–40, 156–58, 243–44. *See also* Atlantic City; Princeton; *and names of other localities*

New London, Conn., 128, 234

New Mexico, 53, 232

New Milford, Conn., 234

New Orleans, La., 76, 237; excluded, 132; rivalries with St. Louis and San Francisco, 119

Newport, R.I., 81, 93–95; booster in London, 111; exclusion, 137

Newport News, Va., 133, 254

Newspapers: and boosterism, 4, 23–24, 26, 43, 91, 109, 156, 199, 221; competition among, 5, 19; editorials and commentary, 19–24, 58, 98, 111, 113, 117, 121–22, 156, 157, 158, 163, 169, 179, 194, 219; speculation by, 30, 55, 56

Newton, Kans., 237

Newtown Square, Pa., 249

New York City: compared with Philadelphia, 204–5; consideration by State Department, 15, 50; exclusion (1945), 138; difficulties for delegations, 179–80, 182, 199–201; as interim site (1946), 164, 175–84, 196–203; origins of campaign, 88, 121; strategy to attract UN, 151, 164–65, 181–84, 193, 195, 196–99; 210–18; suburban radius of, 5, 119, 133, 137–41, 149, 156–57, 162; UN Headquarters, Manhattan, 1–3, 220–25; visited by site inspectors, 145–46, 150–51. *See also* Bronx, the; Fairfield County, Conn.; Flushing Meadows Park; Governors Island; Long Island; Staten Island; Westchester County, Conn.

New York State, 55, 134, 137–38, 150–56, 161, 244–47. *See also* Hyde Park; New York City; Westchester County; *and names of other localities*

Niagara Falls, N.Y., 55, 58, 77, 128, 137–38, 146, 166, 246; boosters in London, 119; exclusion, 137; site plan, 66–67

Niagara Falls, Ont., 3, 55, 58, 207

Nicholson, Blanche Worrell, 237

Nobscot Hill, Mass., 160

Noel-Baker, Philip, 83, 109, 120, 124–26, 129–30, 136, 140, 202

North Carolina, 248

North Castle, N.Y., 162, 163

North Dakota, 55, 248

Northampton, Mass., 128, 240

Northeast (U.S.) region, 125, 132–41. *See also* New England

Northern Neck, Va., 253

North Tarrytown, N.Y., 155

Northvale, N.J., 244
Norway, 32, 40, 179
Norwood, Mass., 159, 240
Novato, Calif., 48
Nummings, Thomas L. 251
Nuzum, Clara J., 236

Oakland, Calif., 233
Oak Ridge, Tenn., 76
O'Dwyer, William, 151, 178, 182, 201, 207, 211–12
Ogdensburg, N.Y., 246
Ohio, 248. *See also* Cincinnati
Okinawa, 48
Oklahoma, 95–100, 110, 205–6, 232, 248; in popular culture, 99–100
Oklahoma City, Okla., 232
Olathe, Kans., 237
Oliver, L. Stauffer, 39, 107, 117, 140, 210
Olympic games, 2, 26, 86, 102, 116, 124, 221, 245
Orange, Mass., 128, 149, 240
Oregon, 207
Ormandy, Eugene, 35–36
Osborn, Chase S., 59–63, 235
Osborn, Chase S. III, 57
Osborn, George A., 56–57
Osborn, Stella Lee Brunt (Stellanova), 60–63, 110, 134, 219
Ossining, N.Y., 246
Othman, Fred, 121

Pacific region, 84–85, 87, 209
Padilla Nervo, Luis, 87
Pagenhart, E. H., 19
Palais des Nations, 2, 84. *See also* League of Nations
Palestine, 33, 110, 172, 209
Palisades State Park (N.J.), 172, 244
Palm Springs, Calif., 232
Palo Alto, Calif., 233
Paoli, Pa., 249

Parent generation, 5, 9, 21, 74, 108, 110, 168. *See also* Generational experience
Paris, France, 85, 199; as Capital of the World, 2, 219
Paris Peace Conferences, 86, 193, 199
Pasadena, Calif., 232
Patton, George S., 239
Pelt, Adrian, 138
Penn, William, 23, 39, 117, 179, 191, 205, 249
Pennsylvania, 39, 53, 131, 134, 191–92, 249–50. *See also* Philadelphia; *names of other localities*
Perkins, G. Holmes, 114
Petitions, 160, 163
Pfeiffle, Robert A., 249
Philadelphia, Pa.: boosters in London, 107–8, 110–11, 114, 117–18; boosters in San Francisco, 29–30, 38–39, 42–43, 45; consideration by State Department, 15, 50; as "City of Brotherly Love," 21, 37; as "Cradle of Liberty," 20, 37; excluded (1945), 140, 157; Fairmount Park recommended (1946), 208, 210–11; opinion of Harry S. Truman, 84; response to rejection, 140, 220; origins of campaign, 19–26; strategy to attract UN, 53, 81, 146, 191–92, 213; suburban competitors, 88, 191–92; visited by site inspectors (1946), 203–5. *See also* Declaration of Independence; Independence Hall; Liberty Bell; U.S. Constitution
Philippines, the, 9, 33, 40, 132, 174, 250
Phillips, Adrian, 112
Phillipsburg, Pa., 249
Pike County, Pa., 250
Pilgrims, 159
Pinehurst, N.C., 15, 248
Pittsfield, Mass., 240

Place and space, experiences of, 5, 48, 260n12
Place marketing, 221. *See also* Boosterism
Plattsburgh, N.Y., 246
Pleasanton, Calif., 233
Plymouth, Mass., 128, 149, 159–60, 240
Pocantico Hills (in N.Y.), 194, 212, 213–14. *See also* Rockefeller, Nelson; Westchester County
Pocono Mountains (in Pa.), 146, 157, 249–50
Pokagon State Park (in Ind.), 236
Poland, 15, 16, 37, 69, 161
Politics, urban, 69–71, 90–91
Popular culture, 4, 33, 69, 90, 98, 99. *See also* Music; Movies; World's fairs
Portsmouth, R.I., 160, 251
Portsmouth, Va., 121, 253
Potsdam Conference, 81
Potsdam, N.Y., 246
Port Jervis, N.Y., 246
Poughkeepsie, N.Y., 137, 151–54. *See also* Hyde Park, N.Y.
Presidio, the, 206, 208–10
Presque Isle, Maine, 237
Prince, Frederick H., 159
Princemere estate (in Beverly, Mass.), 159, 206
Princeton, Iowa, 236
Princeton, Mass., 240
Princeton, N.J., 138–40, 157, 244
Princeton University, 140, 157, 244
Proctor, Haydn, 244
Proctor, Mortimer R., 253
Proffitt, Hansel, 251
Prong, Edwin E., 248
Property, 5, 150, 164. *See also* Home, defense of
Providence, R.I., 93, 137, 160, 251
Public opinion, 4, 33, 181, 188

Public relations, 4, 12, 27, 29, 43, 109, 182, 190, 193, 196
Pulaski Skyway (in N.J.), 156
Punxsutawney, Pa., 122, 250
Puritans, 93, 147

Quebec City, 30
Queens County, N.Y., 234
Queens, N.Y., 175. *See also* Flushing Meadows Park
Quincy, Mass., 159, 240. *See also* Blue Hills region

Race relations: factor in site selection, 50–51; 125–26, 129–32; in site invitations, 241–42, 251–52; in U.S., 13, 132, 181, 200, 206
Radio, 5, 18, 25, 31, 35, 36, 38, 39, 96, 110, 113, 145, 154, 207
Railroads, 31–32, 54, 68, 70, 96, 107, 119, 147, 148
Randolph, Mass., 159, 240
Raney, Vincent G., 46
Rapid City, S.D., 9–12, 56, 77, 112, 191, 220. *See also* Black Hills region
Reading, Mass., 239
Redwood Empire (in Calif.), 233
Rees, Forest R., 237
Regler, Jacob J., 237
Republican Party, 55
Resistance, to UN plans: in Connecticut, 161–64, 166–69, 172, 174–75, 182; in New York suburbs, 4–5, 174–75, 182, 188–90, 226; in Massachusetts, 147–50, 160, 207; in Philadelphia, 24, 204–5
Reston, James B., 179
Revere, Paul, 147
Rhode Island, 93–95, 128, 134, 160, 207, 250–51. *See also* Newport; *names of other localities*
Rice, Edwin L., 254

Richmond, Va., 253–54
Rideout, Gertrude H., 148
Ridgefield, Conn., 119, 138, 155–56, 156
Ridgewood Borough, N.J., 244
Riggs, Lynn, 99
Riots, 13, 76, 132
Riverdale, the Bronx, N.Y., 138, 176–78.
    See also Bronx, the
Robinson, Jackie, 132
Rochford, Daniel, 246
Rockefeller Center, 165, 183, 194, 195,
    196, 210, 213, 214, 218
Rockefeller, David, 213
Rockefeller, John D., 194, 244
Rockefeller, John D. III, 213
Rockefeller, John D. Jr., 97, 98, 213–18,
    226, 247; gift to League of Nations,
    195, 215; gift to UN for site in Man-
    hattan, 3, 214–18, 219
Rockefeller, Laurance, 213
Rockefeller, Nelson A.: as assistant
    secretary of state, 26, 31, 41; role
    in securing UN in New York, 151,
    181–82, 192, 194–96, 210–18, 226
Rockefeller, William, 155, 195, 213
Rockland, Mass., 128, 240
Rockville Centre, N.Y., 245
Rockwell, Norman, 147
Rockwood Hall (in Westchester
    County, N.Y.), 155, 195, 213
Rocky Hill, N.J., 244
Rogers, Edith Nourse, 136, 148
Rogers, Will, 99, 206
Rome, Italy, 161; as Capital of the
    World, 2, 219
Romulo, Carlos, 33
Roosevelt, Eleanor, 154, 252
Roosevelt, Franklin D.: and the Black
    Hills, 10–11, 26; and Chicago, 69–70;
    death and remembrance, 30–31, 35,
    62, 127, 146, 179, 232, 234, 245; and
    Philadelphia, 20–21; presidential

library and museum, 154; seeks
    Congressional support for UN,
    21–22; sites favored by, 15; at Yalta,
    13–17. *See also* Hyde Park, N.Y.
Roosevelt, Nicholas, 251
Roosevelt, Theodore, 179
Roper, Wilfred A., 253
Rotary International, 157
Roxborough (in Philadelphia), 204
Russia. *See* Soviet Union
Russian Revolution, 83, 85
Ryan, Luke F., 240

Saksin, George, 150
Salem, Mass., 159
Salinas, Calif., 250
Salt Lake City, Utah, 88, 252
Sampson Naval Training Station (in
    N.Y.), 246
Samuel, Bernard, 24–25
San Antonio, Tex., 252
San Juan Basin (Colo.), 233
Sanford, Maine, 237–38
San Francisco, Calif.: booster campaign
    begins, 18–19, 25, 53, 74–75; boosters
    in London, 88–89,109, 111, 118; com-
    petition with New York City, 180,
    192–93, 201, 206, 218; favored by Sec-
    retary of State, 13–14, 84; excluded
    (1945), 123–28; issues of distance, 32,
    86, 125–26, 205; Presidio as potential
    site, 208–9; response to rejection,
    123–24, 128, 146, 166, 219,171–73;
    site plans, 46–47; UN Conference
    on International Organization
    (UNCIO), 13–14, 16, 17–19, 26–27,
    28–51; "victory riot," 76; visited by
    site inspectors (1946), 202–3, 205–6;
    during World War II, 17–18, 76
San Simeon, Calif., 233
Santa Barbara, Calif., 233
Santa Clara County, Calif., 233

Santa Rosa, Calif., 233

Saratoga Springs, N.Y., 81, 88, 246–47

Saudi Arabia, 31, 39, 56, 127

Sault Ste. Marie, Mich.: booster campaign, 56, 56–68, 82, 110; response to rejection, 134, 219; site plan, 64–65

Sault Ste. Marie, Ont., 3, 56–68, 82

Scituate, R.I., 251

Scott, Grant, 243

Scranton, Pa., 250

Seattle, Wash., 25, 60, 254

Self-government. See Sovereignty

Senesi, Ralph Albert, 245

Shafer, Chet, 241

Sharpe, Merrell Quentin, 53, 56, 128, 128

Shrewsbury, Mass., 241

Sidney, Sylvia, 33

Simpson, Mary M., 233

Site plans. See Architecture

Skaneateles, N.Y., 247

Smith, Fredric A., 151–52

Smith, Gerald L. K., 33

Smith, Walter B., 248

Smock, George A., II, 243

Smuts, Jan Christiaan, 32

Social justice, 96–97, 174

Somers, N.Y., 155, 188

South Africa, 32, 126

South America, 31

Southampton, Long Island, N.Y., 247

South Bend, Ind., 236

South Carolina, 251

South Dakota. See Black Hills region

South Milwaukee, Wis., 255

Southport, N.C., 248

South (U.S.) region, 126; excluded, 131–32, 134

South Weymouth, Mass., 160, 240

Sovereignty, 5, 74, 146–50, 164

Soviet Union: and Cold War, 190, 209; criticized in Boston, 161, 166, 207; positions on site question, 50, 85, 87, 120, 127, 201–2, 209; in San Francisco, 31, 37, 45; on site inspection team, 150; on UN Preparatory Commission, 83; on UN Security Council, 45; at Yalta, 13–16

Spain, 29

Spanish-American War, 5, 9, 34

Sperry Gyroscope Plant, offices for UN, 165, 179, 183–84

Spink, C. H., 242

Spirit Lake, Idaho, 235

Spokane, Wash., 252

Springfield Center, N.Y., 245

Springfield, Ill., 235

Springfield, Mass., 122, 128, 135–36, 240

Springfield Township, Pa., 249

Spurny, Emil W., 245

Square Hill, Jimmy, 33

St. Louis, Mo., 3, 32, 81, 100–2, 121, 134; campaign to become capital of U.S., 101–2; excluded, 134; rivalries, 102, 119

St. Petersburg, Fla., 248

St. Tammany Parish, La., 237

Stainback, Ingram M., 56, 235

Stalin, Joseph, 14, 127, 146, 190

Stamford, Conn., 155–56, 161–64, 166, 171–72, 174–75. See also Greenwich

Stanford University, 233

Stassen, Harold E., 54

Staten Island, N.Y., 175, 247

Stearns, Robert L., 111, 116

Sterling, Mass., 241

Sterling Park, N.Y., 190, 247

Stern, J. David, 19–24, 110

Stettinius, Edward Reilly Jr.:considers alternatives to New York, 180, 182; proposes San Francisco, 13–16, 17; receives booster appeals, 26, 58, 75; resigns as U.S. delegate, 191–92; at

San Francisco conference, 31, 33, 35–36, 37, 41–42, 48–49; strategy of neutrality, 83–84

Stevenson, Adlai, 69

Stewart, James G., 119

Stigler, William, 97

Stillwater, Okla., 3, 248

Stirling, Sara Daingerfield, 253

Stoneham, Mass., 239

Straw Town, Ind., 236

Strawberry Point (in Marin County, Calif.), 46

Streb, John P., 245

Stroudsburg, Pa., 250

Stuart, Robert B., 114

Suburbs and suburbanization 5, 25, 90, 102, 129, 147–50, 154–56, 166–69, 170, 174–75, 184, 202, 213, 226. See also Metropolitan regions

Sudbury, Mass., 149, 150, 158, 160, 164, 165, 206–7. See also Concord

Suffolk County Army Air Base (in N.Y.), 247

Sugar Island, Sault Ste. Marie, Mich., 62–65, 219

Sun Yat-sen, 162

Swanson, Andrew, 233

Swarthmore, Pa., 249

Sweden, 220

Swift, John E., 161

Switzerland, 42, 85, 185. See also Geneva

Syracuse, N.Y., 247

Taft, William Howard, 159

Tangipahoa Parish, La., 237

Tanner, Elmer, 100

Tarrytown, N.Y., 194

Taunton, Mass., 92, 240

Taylor, Robert Gray, 191–92, 249

Temple University, 37, 39

Tennessee, 251–52

Texas, 252

Thomson, James M., 254

Thoreau, Henry David, 147, 148, 160

Three Rivers, Mich., 241

Tibbets, Paul, Jr., 76

Tibbey, M.R., 250

Ticonderoga, N.Y., 247

Time and space: perceptions of, 5, 23, 35, 54, 58, 59, 82, 86–87, 102, 108–9, 134, 140; scholarship on, 260n14. See also Aviation

Tinian, Mariana Islands, 75

Tobin, Maurice J., 90–93, 97, 114, 149, 158, 160, 161, 219, 238–39

Tobyhanna Military Reservation (in Pa.), 250

Tokyo, 48, 75

Tokyo Rose, 18

Topeka, Kans., 237

Tourism, 10, 18, 26, 29, 53, 59, 77, 88, 90, 99, 112, 113–14, 157, 200, 221

Town meetings, 90, 93, 147, 168. See also New England

Tradition, 5, 90, 147–50, 157. See also Heritage; Memory

Transportation, 5, 10, 26, 33, 59, 70, 91

Treasure Island (in San Francisco), 18, 233

Truman, Harry S.: becomes president, 30; delivers UN Charter to Senate, 74; at headquarters dedication, 1; inspires invitations from Missouri, 75; positions on site question, 83, 201–3, 209, 212; receives booster appeals, 53, 58, 91, 93, 97, 100, 108; during San Francisco conference, 35, 37, 38, 42, 45, 48–49; visited by UN site inspectors, 150–51,

Tufts University, 114

Tulane University, 76

Tulsa, Okla., 98, 205–6

Tunney, Gene, 166

Tuskahoma, Okla., 3, 88, 96–99, 102–3, 110; site plan, 103

Ukraine, 15, 37, 49, 202
Una, Colo., 233
United Kingdom, 33, 45, 87, 150. *See also* England; Great Britain
United Nations: decision making, 83, 84, 120, 123–41, 172–75, 196; difficulties in New York, 179–80, 182, 199–201; effectiveness, 3, 170, 191; public opinion regarding, 4, 181, 188, 259n10; press relations, 42
United Nations Charter, 3, 37, 45, 48–49, 54, 74, 107, 126, 130, 131, 171, 232
United Nations Conference on International Organization (UNCIO), 29–51, 126, 171, 195; choice of San Francisco for, 13–16; preparations for, 18; transportation to, 30–32
United Nations General Assembly: accepts Rockefeller gift, 218; composition of, 45; in London, 150, 154, 166, 169; in New York (Flushing Meadows), 183, 193, 195, 196–203, 212; response to selection of Greenwich, Conn., 170–75
United Nations Headquarters, Manhattan, 1, 3, 210–18, 220–25
United Nations Headquarters Planning Commission, 182, 185–90, 192
United Nations Preparatory Commission, 49, 81–90, 107–41; choice of U.S., 84–87, 120; choice of U.S. East, 123–27; hearings for world capital boosters, 111–19
United Nations Secretary General. *See* Lie, Trygve
United Nations Secretariat, 39, 42, 136, 179, 180, 183, 200, 221

United Nations Security Council, 15, 41–42, 45, 84, 127, 150, 209, 212, 218; meets at Hunter College, New York City, 178–80
United Nations Headquarters, site selection: cost considerations, 155, 170–71, 174, 184, 196, 201–4, 212, 220; criteria, 112–13, 129–30, 221–22; exclusion of U.S. Midwest, 133–34; exclusion of U.S. South, 131–32; Greenwich-Stamford, Conn., 164–65, 286n40; influence of Great Britain, 124–26, 131–33, 135–36, 202; inspections of sites, 145–69, 202–10; interim site recommendations, 164–66, 287n41; neutrality of U.S., 83–84, 87, 127, 180, 191, 201; New York City suburbs, 185–90, 288n9; Northeast U.S., 129–34; process, 221–22; resistance by localities, 147–50, 160, 161–64, 166–69, 172, 174–75, 181, 204–5, 207, 213, 226; role of Rockefeller family, 210–18; search reopened (1946), 201–10; U.S. East over West, 123–27, 208, 280n10; U.S. over Europe, 84–87, 120, 123–29, 272n13, 278n33; urban, suburban, or rural setting, 46, 68, 71, 125, 129, 136–41, 149, 178, 186, 196, 206, 212. *See also* Capital of the World
United States, 3–4, 29, 37–38, 40, 45, 86; neutrality on site question, 83–84, 87, 127, 180, 191, 201; position on U.S. East or West, 209–10; selected as headquarters location, 87, 120. *See also names of states, localities*
United Westchester Citizens Committee to Save Our Homes, 190, 207
University of Chicago, 114
University of Colorado, 111, 116
University of Kansas City, 75, 242
University of Michigan, 60

Uno, Va., 254
U.S. Congress, 22, 26, 53, 74, 97, 100, 152
U.S. Constitution, 21–22, 37, 39, 45, 74
U.S. State Department: role in public support for UN, 22, 74; role in San Francisco conference, 13–15, 17, 29–30, 34, 36; role in site selection, 50–51, 53, 83, 107, 108, 152, 157, 192, 200–1, 209, 262n14. *See also* Byrnes, James; Stettinius, Edward
Urban redevelopment, 23–24, 77
Uruguay, 111, 131
Utah, 252

Valley Forge, Pa., 81, 140, 250
Van Roijen, Jan, 87
Vancouver, British Columbia, 88
Vandenberg, Arthur H., 170–71, 178, 202
Vanderbilt, George, 251
Vanderlind, R. A., 241
Vassar College, 137
Ventnor, N.J., 244
Vermont, 134, 191, 207, 212, 252–53
Virginia, 133, 253–54
Virginia Beach, Va., 254
Vivian, John, 55

Wakefield, Mass., 239
Wales, 122
Wallace, Homer M., 246
Wallace, James G., 255
Walker, E. E., 245
Waltham, Mass., 238
Warm Springs, Ga., 30, 62, 234–35
Warren, Earl, 35, 41, 48, 53, 128, 193, 232–33
Warwick, R.I., 251
Washington, D.C., 2, 10, 25–26, 30, 31, 35, 68, 85, 96, 121, 145, 151, 162
Washington, George, 133, 157, 253
Washington Parish, La., 237

Washington State, 254
Washington University (in St. Louis), 76
Waterford, Conn., 234
Watertown, N.Y., 247
Watson, Thomas J., 181
Wawa, Pa., 249
Webster, Charles Kingsley, 126, 131–33, 135–36
Webster, Daniel, 49
Webster, E. E., 232
Weldon Spring, Mo., 101, 119. *See also* St. Louis
Westchester County, N.Y.: invitation, 138, 245–47; map of sites, 189; resistance in, 166, 185–90, 192; Rockefeller family in, 194–95, 212–14; selected for consideration, 138, 174–75, 201–2, 208; visited by site inspectors, 154–55, 162, 203, 207
Westerly, R.I., 251
Westhampton Beach, Long Island, N.Y., 247
Westminster Abbey, 82
Westminster, Mass., 241
West Newbury, Mass., 241
West Orange, N.J., 244
West (U.S.) region, 95–96, 221; excluded, 123–27, 134, 209
West Virginia, 172, 254–55
Whalen, Grover, 178, 182
Wheeler, Ruth, 148
White, E. B., 191
White House, 30–31, 83, 191
White Plains, N.Y., 155, 186, 188, 213–14
White Sulphur Springs, W. Va., 254–55
Whiteside, John Elton, 247
White, Walter, 33
Wilkes-Barre, Pa., 250
Williamsburg, Va., 23, 133, 254
Williams, Charles A., 234
Williamsport, Pa., 250

Williams, Roger, 93
Wilson, Woodrow, 179
Winchell, Walter, 33
Winchester, Mass., 239
Wisconsin, 77, 255
Woburn, Mass., 239
Wolters, Maria, 232
Wood, Edward F.L. (Lord Halifax),
    32, 41
Worcester, Mass., 128, 135, 160, 241
World center for communication, 2
World Centre of Peace, 2
World cities, 2, 19, 30, 36, 258n6
World citizens, 19, 25–26
World Court, 45, 239
World federalism movement, 148
World Fellowship Inc., 128, 243
World's End peninsula (Hingham,
    Mass.), 239
World's fairs, 2, 5, 26, 98, 102, 103–4,
    124; Centennial Exhibition, 117;
    Century of Progress Exposition, 68,
    70, 71, 236; Golden Gate Exposition,
    18; Panama Pacific International Ex-
    position, 18, 119; New York World's
    Fair (1939), 18, 46, 138, 151, 181, 184;
    World's Columbian Exposition,
    68–69
World War I (Great War), 4, 5, 35, 36,
    53, 57, 68, 83, 86, 95, 168
World War II: aftermath, 3, 179–80;
    atomic bomb, 75–77; Crimean
    Conference, 13–16; in Europe, 38,
    57, 183; in London, 82, 183; in the

Pacific, 15, 38, 48, 75–77, 174; ser-
    vicemen and women, 9, 21, 35, 48,
    57, 59, 76, 93, 132; U.S. homefront,
    5, 17–18, 52, 57, 70, 90, 92, 94, 96,
    147, 168; veterans, 24, 34, 77, 168,
    179
Wright, Frank Lloyd, 10, 71
Wright, Richard Robert Sr., 33
Wurster, William, 46–47
Wyoming, 26, 43, 53, 134. See also
    Black Hills region

X-City, 210, 214–17

Yale Farms, 161–62
Yale University, 125, 161, 180, 234
Yalta, 13–16, 17, 19, 42, 83
Yerba Buena Island, Calif., 233
York, Maine, 238
Yorktown Heights, N.Y., 247
Yorktown, N.Y., 155, 188, 246
Yorktown, Va., 133
Younger, E.G., 235
Younger, Kenneth G., 150, 159
Young, Milton R., 248
Youngstown, Ohio, 245
Yugoslavia, 48, 85, 87, 111, 116, 145,
    161

Zeckendorf, Marion, 211
Zeckendorf, William, 210–11, 213–17,
    220, 222–23
Zionists, 209
Zuleta Angel, Eduardo, 200, 212, 215, 218

ABOUT THE AUTHOR

CHARLENE MIRES, a historian at Rutgers University–Camden, is also the author of *Independence Hall in American Memory* and a corecipient of a Pulitzer Prize in journalism. After traveling the country to research this book, she has returned home to Philadelphia, one of the many contenders in the race to become the Capital of the World.